Lecture Notes in Computer Scie

T0230235

Commenced Publication in 1973
Founding and Former Series Editors:
Gerhard Goos, Juris Hartmanis, and Jan van Leeuwen

Frank Eliassen   Alberto Montresor (Eds.)

Distributed Applications and Interoperable Systems

6th IFIP WG 6.1 International Conference, DAIS 2006
Bologna, Italy, June 14-16, 2006
Proceedings

 Springer

Volume Editors

Frank Eliassen
University of Oslo
Department of Informatics
P.O. Box, 1080 Blindern, Oslo, Norway
E-mail: frank@ifi.uio.no

Alberto Montresor
University of Trento
Department of Information and Communication Technology
via Sommarive 14, 38050 Povo (TN), Italy
E-mail: alberto.montresor@dit.unitn.it

Library of Congress Control Number: 2006926954

CR Subject Classification (1998): D.2, C.2.4, I.2.11, D.4, H.4

LNCS Sublibrary: SL 3 – Information Systems and Application, incl. Internet/Web
and HCI

ISSN   0302-9743
ISBN-10   3-540-35126-4 Springer Berlin Heidelberg New York
ISBN-13   978-3-540-35126-9 Springer Berlin Heidelberg New York

Springer is a part of Springer Science+Business Media

springer.com

© Springer-Verlag Berlin Heidelberg 2006
Printed in Germany

Typesetting: Camera-ready by author, data conversion by Scientific Publishing Services, Chennai, India
Printed on acid-free paper   SPIN: 11773887   06/3142   5 4 3 2 1 0

Preface

This volume contains the proceedings of the IFIP WG 6.1 International Working Conference on Distributed Applications and Interoperable Systems VI held in Bologna, Italy, on June 14-16, 2006.

The conference program presents the state of the art in research on distributed and interoperable systems. In recent years, distributed applications have indeed gained a practical and widely-known footing in everyday computing. Use of new communication technologies have brought up divergent application areas, including mobile computing, inter-enterprise collaborations, and ubiquitous services, just to name a few. New challenges include the need for service-oriented architectures, autonomous and self-managing systems, peer-to-peer systems, grid computing, sensor networks, semantic enhancements, and adaptivity and dynamism of distribution constellations.

Following the evolution of the field, DAIS 2006 focuses on architectures, models, technologies and platforms for interoperable, scalable and adaptable systems that are related to the latest trends towards service orientation and self-* properties. The papers presented at DAIS 2006 cover methodological aspects, tools and language of building adaptable distributed and interoperable services, fault tolerance and dependability, peer-to-peer systems, mobility issues, web services applications and performance issues and composition, semantic web and semantic integration, and context- and location-aware applications. Also included in these proceedings is an invited paper by Jan Bosch and colleagues (Nokia Research Center, Finland) addressing the apparent conflict between usability and the architectural drivers that drive success or failure of mobile services.

This year, the technical program of DAIS drew from 99 submitted papers, among which 10 were explicitly submitted as work-in-progress papers. From these 21 regular and 5 work-in-progress papers were selected for inclusion in the proceedings. As a rule, each paper was reviewed by three reviewers. The DAIS 2006 conference was sponsored by IFIP (International Federation for Information Processing), and it was the sixth conference in the DAIS series of events organized by the IFIP Working Group 6.1. The previous conferences in this series took place in Cottbus, Germany (1997), Helsinki, Finland (1999), Krakow, Poland (2001), Paris, France (2003), and Athens, Greece (2005). Since Paris, DAIS has been organized in conjunction with the FMOODS conference (Formal Methods and Open Object-Based Distributed Systems). This time the COORDINATION conference (Conference on Coordination Models and Languages) joined the federated event of DAIS and FMOODS.

Finally, we would like to take this opportunity to thank the numerous people whose work made this conference possible. We wish to express our deepest gratitude to the authors of submitted papers, to all program committee members for their active participation in the paper review process, to all external reviewers for their help in evaluating submissions, to the University of Bologna for hosting the event, and to Gianluigi Zavattaro for acting as a general chair of the joint event, who also provided the Conference Management System and support. Ketil Lund took care of the publicity for the event. The Steering Committee with Lea Kutvonen, Hartmut König, Kurt Geihs, and Elie Najm extended their helping hand for making DAIS 2006 a successful conference.

June 2006   Frank Eliassen and Alberto Montresor

Conference Committees and Organization

Chairs

Steering Committee: Lea Kutvonen, University of Helsinki, Finland
Elie Njm, ENST, Paris, France
Hartmut König, BTU Cottbus, Germany
Kurt Geihs, University of Kassel, Germany

General Chair   Gianluigi Zavattaro, University of Bologna, Italy

Program Co-chairs   Frank Eliassen, University of Oslo, Norway
Alberto Montresor, University of Trento, Italy

Publicity Chair   Ketil Lund, Simula Research Laboratory, Norway

Sponsoring Institutions

University of Bologna, Italy
IFIP WG 6.1

Program Committee

N. Alonistioti	University of Athens, Greece
D. Bakken	Washington State University, USA
A. Bartoli	University of Trieste, Italy
Y. Berbers	Katholieke Universiteit Leuven, Belgium
A. Beugnard	ENST-Bretagne, France
G. Blair	Lancaster University, UK
A. Corsaro	Alenia Marconi System, Italy
I. Demeure	ENST, France
P. Felber	Université de Neuchâtel, Switzerland
K. Geihs	University of Kassel, Germany
K.M. Goschka	Technical University of Vienna, Austria
S. Graupner	HP Labs, USA
R. Grønmo	SINTEF ICT, Norway
D. Hagimont	INP Toulouse, France
S. Hallsteinsen	SINTEF ICT, Norway
J. Indulska	University of Queensland, Australia
A. Keller	IBM Thomas J. Watson Research Center, USA
H. König	BTU Cottbus, Germany
R. Kröger	University of Applied Sciences Wiesbaden, Germany
H. Krumm	University of Dortmund, Germany
L. Kutvonen	University of Helsinki, Finland

W. Lamersdorf   University of Hamburg, Germany
C. Linnhof-Popien   University of Munich, Germany
K. Lund   Simula Research Laboratory, Norway
R. Meier   Trinity College Dublin, Ireland
E. Najm   ENST, France
R. Oliveira   Universidade do Minho, Portugal
K. Raymond   University of Queensland, Australia
R. Schantz   BBN Technologies, USA
A. Romanovsky   University of Newcastle upon Tyne, UK
W. Schreiner   Johannes Kepler University Linz, Austria
T. Senivongse   Chulalongkorn University, Thailand
K. Sere   Abo Akademi University, Finland
J.B. Stefani   INRIA, France
N. Wang   Tech-X Corporation, USA

Table of Contents

Mobile Service Oriented Architectures (MOSOA)
Jilles van Gurp, Anssi Karhinen, Jan Bosch 1

A Spatial Programming Model for Real Global Smart Space Applications
René Meier, Anthony Harrington, Thomas Termin, Vinny Cahill ... 16

Mobile Process Description and Execution
Christian P. Kunze, Sonja Zaplata, Winfried Lamersdorf 32

An Application Framework for Nomadic, Collaborative Applications
James O'Brien, Marc Shapiro 48

Interfering Effects of Adaptation: Implications on Self-adapting
Systems Architecture
Jacqueline Floch, Erlend Stav, Svein Hallsteinsen 64

Discovery of Stable Peers in a Self-organising Peer-to-Peer Gradient
Topology
Jan Sacha, Jim Dowling, Raymond Cunningham, René Meier 70

On the Value of Random Opinions in Decentralized Recommendation
Elth Ogston, Arno Bakker, Maarten van Steen 84

Information Agents That Learn to Understand Each Other Via
Semantic Negotiation
Salvatore Garruzzo, Domenico Rosaci 99

Discovering Semantic Web Services with Process Specifications
Piya Suwannopas, Twittie Senivongse 113

Towards Building a Semantic Grid for E-Learning
Wenya Tian, Huajun Chen 128

A Code Migration Framework for AJAX Applications
Arno Puder 138

High Performance SOAP Processing Driven by Data Mapping Template
Jun Wei, Lei Hua, Chunlei Niu, Haoran Zheng 152

An Approach for Fine-Grained Web Service Performance Monitoring
  Jan Schaefer 169

WSInterConnect: Dynamic Composition of Web Services Through Web
Services
  Josef Spillner, Iris Braun, Alexander Schill 181

Bounding Recovery Time in Rollback-Recovery Protocol for Mobile
Systems Preserving Session Guarantees
  Jerzy Brzeziński, Anna Kobusińska, Jacek Kobusiński 187

Intelligent Dependability Services for Overlay Networks
  Barry Porter, Geoff Coulson, Daniel Hughes 199

Model-Driven Development of Context-Aware Services
  João Paulo A. Almeida, Maria-Eugenia Iacob, Henk Jonkers,
  Dick Quartel 213

Utilising Alternative Application Configurations in Context- and
QoS-Aware Mobile Middleware
  Sten A. Lundesgaard, Ketil Lund, Frank Eliassen 228

Timing Driven Architectural Adaptation
  Andrew Wils, Yolande Berbers, Tom Holvoet, Karel De Vlaminck ... 242

Fault-Tolerant Replication Based on Fragmented Objects
  Hans P. Reiser, Rüdiger Kapitza, Jörg Domaschka,
  Franz J. Hauck 256

Towards Context-Aware Transaction Services
  Romain Rouvoy, Patricia Serrano-Alvarado, Philippe Merle 272

A Local Self-stabilizing Enumeration Algorithm
  Brahim Hamid, Mohamed Mosbah 289

Adding Fault-Tolerance to a Hierarchical DRE System
  Paul Rubel, Joseph Loyall, Richard Schantz, Matthew Gillen 303

Using Speculative Push for Unnecessary Checkpoint Creation Avoidance
  Arkadiusz Danilecki, Michał Szychowiak 309

A Versatile Kernel for Distributed AOP
  Éric Tanter, Rodolfo Toledo 316

Transformation of Centralized Software Components into Distributed
Ones by Code Refactoring
Abdelhak Seriai, Gautier Bastide, Mourad Oussalah   332

PAGE: A Distributed Infrastructure for Fostering RDF-Based
Interoperability
Emanuele Della Valle, Andrea Turati, Alessandro Ghioni   347

Author Index   355

Mobile Service Oriented Architectures (MOSOA)

Jilles van Gurp, Anssi Karhinen, and Jan Bosch

Software and Application Technologies Laboratory
Nokia Research Center
P.O. Box 407, FI-00045 NOKIA GROUP, Finland
{jilles.vangurp, anssi.karhinen, jan.bosch}@nokia.com

Abstract. Mobile services hold a promise of utilizing the phone also for other purposes than purely communication. However, repeated attempts at realizing mobile services in the market place have been met with limited success. This article (1) defines the architectural drivers that drive success or failure of mobile services, (2) analyzes three different architectural styles of realizing such a mobile service using the example of a movie ticket selling service and (3) presents the results of this analysis. The main result of the analysis is that a serious conflict exists between usability and essentially all the other architectural drivers included in our analysis, i.e. portability, deployability and scalability. This is due to the fact that, because of the restricted state of the art technology, only native client applications offer satisfactory usability, but these do not satisfy the other drivers.

1 Introduction

Mobile services hold a promise of utilizing the phone also for other purposes than voice and SMS communication. Turning the promise into reality has proven to be more complex than what was anticipated in the dawn of digital mobile communication. Offering highly usable, value adding services to consumers and enterprise users has challenged the technology developers, business developers and the mobile service concept developers. The mobile services field became divided into content services and added value functional services early on. The main function of content services is to deliver media content such as ringing tones, greeting cards and background pictures into the mobile phone. Such services were originally built on top of mobile messaging technology such as SMS and have achieved continuously growing success in consumer segment. A more challenging area has turned out to be the services that aim to provide end users with added value functionality such as, for example, route planning, e-commerce and mobile payment. Some of these services were originally built on top of mobile messaging technology and then later on a browser based approach using WAP technology. However, consumer acceptance and business model continued to be a challenge.

An example of technology that aims to deliver ready-to use services for consumers out-of-the-box is SIM-ATK (Application ToolKit). SIM-ATK works in GSM networks. It allows the operators to include pre-installed service menus in the SIM

F. Eliassen and A. Montresor (Eds.): DAIS 2006, LNCS 4025, pp. 1 – 15, 2006.

card delivered with the subscription. The service menus are automatically integrated with the native menus of the phone for seamless access by the end-user. These services use the short message protocol (SMS) to implement access to server functions. This sets some limitations for the implementation of the user experience as the interaction between the user and the server is not synchronous. Success of mobile service technology seems to have depended much on the level of integration into the native phone user interface and the ease with which end users can access the additional functionality offered by the services. An important landmark has been the iMode technology originally launched by NTT-DoCoMo in Japan around the turn of the millennium. iMode offers end-users seamless integration of basic services such as email, weather forecasts, sports results, various content services, online banking, stock trading, online gaming and ticketing services. An important factor for the success of iMode has been the "always on" aspect of the services, which is based on mobile packet data technology.

As the processing capability of the terminal devices has kept growing and faster data protocols have been deployed in the mobile networks it has become feasible to closely emulate the user experience of a PC with fast Internet access. Some of the recent devices include HTML browsers that are capable of displaying dynamic HTML pages with interactive scripts thus bringing the idea of "Internet in a pocket" closer to reality.

Browser based services are evolving rapidly as the capability of the terminals is growing. Traditional problems that plagued the early WAP/WML based solutions where the appearance of a service had to be tightly optimized for mobile device through custom design are slowly vanishing. To publish an existing WWW/HTML service for WAP access typically requires either a separate implementation of the user interface of the service or heavy automatic adaptation by a gateway which in many cases leads results in usability problems for mobile users of the service.

Another approach to offer highly usable mobile services and applications is to open the phone software platform for user installable native applications. This approach is available for example on phones using Symbian platform. A user installable application has access to all phone resources and can integrate with the native phone UI with no restrictions. This enables the creation of mobile services through a client-server pattern that are similar to the native functions available on a phone. A challenge in this approach is to ensure the compatibility of the phone software platform and installed applications. Additionally, the application installation process itself can be more complex than in a pre-installed services or browser based paradigms described earlier. The contribution of this paper is that it provides a comprehensive overview of the architectural alternatives that are available for the implementation of mobile services and analyses the different trade-offs of them.

The remainder of the paper is organized as follows. The next section presents the problem statement, followed by a section outlining the design drivers. Subsequently, three mobile service-oriented architectural styles are presented and analyzed. Related work and a summary section conclude the paper.

2 Problem Statement

Different brands, run-time platforms, screen sizes, networks and many other factors all contribute to the fact that there is a large variety of mobile devices on the market. To provide the best user experience, software developers of mobile applications must specialize their software for specific devices in order to take advantage of device specific features or device specific implementations of common features. A number of problems with device specific software exist:

- The number of devices that can be supported by specialized software is much smaller than the total number of devices. Specializing software for device specific features in any way causes the potential target market to shrink.
- Devices are sold on the market only for brief periods of time and are generally replaced by new devices months or at most a year after their introduction on the market.
- Developing software for a group of similar devices with a common set of specific features requires testing the software on all those devices.
- Device specific software may be hard to port to other devices that do not support the device specifics.

The goal of mobile services is to allow users to access these services through a mobile device. That means that a mobile service consists of a *client-side* component and a *server-side* component. The server-side component offers the feature, the client-side component makes it available to the user.

Necessarily, features, and usability of those features, in the client-side component depend strongly on the capabilities of the client device. Unfortunately, as outlined above making the client component usable by introducing device specific feature dependencies limits the potential market for the server.

As discussed in the introduction, the conflict between usability on one hand and market share on the other hand underlies the limited success in the market of mobile services so far. Solutions in the market so far have either suffered from poor usability (e.g. WAP [16]) or had the problem that the potential group of users able to adopt the solution was only a (small) subset of the entire group of mobile device owners.

Mobile service oriented architectures need to address the following goals:

- **Number of devices.** The service must be provided on a wide variety of mobile devices. The more devices it supports, the larger the market is.
- **Native features.** The service must make full use of native features. Native features add value to the phone and therefore to the services provided on that phone. Native features include both software (e.g. text input methods) and hardware features (softkeys, camera's, display resolution). Native features relevant to the service should preferably be used.
- **Time to market.** The service must have a quick time to market. It is important to reach the market before the competition.
- **Window of opportunity.** The service must not miss its window of opportunity. It is important to be able to target the devices the service is developed for as soon as these devices become available on the market. The devices are on the market for a relatively short period of time and the potential revenue of a service is constrained by this period of time.

- **Forward compatibility.** The service must be forward compatible with the successors of the devices it is targeting. Users of the service will want to continue using the service when they purchase a new phone (assuming the service is useful to them).

Any successful architecture solution for mobile services will need to address these goals explicitly to the extent that is technically feasible. We have the following reasons to believe that it is now possible to define such an architecture:

- **Device performance.** Moore's law [13] has gradually improved device speed, bandwidth and capabilities. These abilities may be exploited to provide an acceptable end user experience while meeting most of the goals outlined above.
- **Consolidation.** There is a growing set of common features supported across a wide variety of devices that may be of use when implementing mobile services. This common feature set is good enough for a wide range of applications so an increasing number of mobile services can be implemented for a (relatively) broad set of devices.
- **Market size.** Adoption of mobile devices in the market has grown exponentially. A large part of the world population now has access to mobile technology.

The problem in mobile service oriented architectures so far has been that existing architectures fail to reach all aforementioned goals due to the fact that they are conflicting given the current state of the art. In this article we evaluate three architectural alternatives against the goals outlined in this section. In the next section we translate these goals into architectural drivers.

3   Architectural Drivers

In this section we look at the architectural drivers that influence the design, development, deployment and ultimately the success of mobile services. In the next section we will compare three architectures and analyse how they are affected by the architectural drivers.

3.1   Usability

In order to be adopted by users, mobile services need to be usable. By usable we mean that:

- It must be easy for the user to find and access the service.
- It must be easy for the user to make use of the service (learnability, ease of use).
- It must be convenient for the user to make use of the service (performance, usefulness).

In practical terms this means that the service needs to be integrated with the mobile user interface because this provides users with the fastest route to the service and the best performance possible on the device. Access points to the service may be embedded in menus, associated with soft keys, etc.

Experience with mobile user interfaces has shown that it is important to minimize the number of navigation steps to particular features [12]. For example, access to the contact list or message overview is rarely more than two button presses away on most mobile phones. Less important features may be located deeper in the menu structure.

The second requirement benefits from integration with the mobile user interface for several reasons:

- User input is typically best facilitated using the 'native' capabilities of the device. For example, many phones include smart text input features that aim to minimize the amount of button presses.
- The user presumably already understands the native user interface so using the service through that interface is easier than through a different interface.

3.2 Portability

The potential market for mobile services is huge. World wide there are now billions of mobile devices in use. A large and growing percentage of these devices is internet enabled (i.e. equipped with a TCP/IP network stack, connected to a TCP network and equipped with software components such as browsers that make use of this capability). To capture enough market share, mobile services need to be available to as large a subset of these users as possible.

This is technically hard because differences between devices tend to be difficult to bridge. For example, screen size, number of supported colours as well as the number of keys tend to vary across devices. Furthermore, there are differences in device capabilities such as supported networks (GPRS, EDGE, UMTS, CDMA), add-ons (e.g. GPS), camera and connectivity (infra red, Bluetooth, USB, WLAN). Dependencies on such features need to be carefully considered because of portability.

3.3 Deployability

A potential obstacle for users of the service is the issue of client side deployment of software components. Installing software of any kind is something few users know how to do. Therefore, (additional) client side components of a mobile service, if needed, should be provisioned over the network. Any kind of installation impacts the size of the potential user population negatively. Similarly, software updates should be totally transparent to the user.

3.4 Scalability

If successful, the mobile service may be used often by a large number of users. The maximum for this is the amount of users that own a device that can run the client side component of the mobile service. The architecture needs to be able to scale to this amount of users. There are at least these factors to consider:

- **Business scalability.** The business model should not include human intervention (e.g. a person answering the phone) or any other activities that are resource intensive unless this cost can be accounted for in the total price of the mobile service for the user.
- **System scalability.** The system architecture needs to be able to scale to the number of transactions successful adoption of the mobile service in the market will cause.

If millions of users use a service several times per day, that means that the server side component of the service will be processing tens of millions of transactions.
- **Client scalability.** The client side architecture needs to scale well from low-end devices to high-end devices. Any scalability issues with the client side architecture will affect the potential amount of users for the service negatively.

4   Three Mobile Services Oriented Architectures

To highlight the properties of different architectural approaches we use an example mobile service realized using three alternative architectural styles. The example service is a movie ticket purchase that enables the user to purchase tickets for him- or her-self and a group of friends. The service also automatically generates notifications of the time of the show and the title of the movie for each. The usage scenario with totally seamless experience would be as follows: 1) User activates "ticket purchase" service through the phone. 2) User selects "movie tickets". 3) User selects the title. 4) User selects the time of the show. 5) User selects the friends he wants to include in the purchase from the phonebook of his/her phone. 6) User performs the purchasing transaction and is automatically authenticated and payment information is directed to the user's already existing billing connection (e.g. credit card, phone bill, etc.). 7) Friends receive a notification and an entry in their phone calendars.

4.1   MOSOA 1: Client-Server with Native Client

Using a native client application provides the greatest flexibility for implementing the user interface and integration with the phone features. Figure 1 presents a high level design of the sample service using the client server pattern and a native client based on, for example, Symbian.

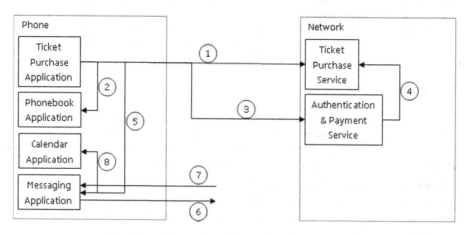

Fig. 1. A mobile service with a native client application

The user is presented with a native ticket purchasing application that must have been installed into the phone in advance. The ticket purchase application in the phone knows the server part and the payment service. Steps one to four of our use case are performed by the ticket purchase application in the phone and the corresponding server part denoted by interaction "1" in the diagram. Ticket purchase service manages the catalogue of available movie titles. Next step of the use case involves interaction between different applications inside the phone. User can select the group of friends using the native phonebook application. This is denoted by "2" in the diagram. Authentication and payment information is managed by a service in the network as shown by interaction "3". Information of the completed payment transaction is communicated to the ticket purchase service to complete the transaction, transaction "4". The client ticket purchase application then uses the messaging application in the phone to convey the notification and a calendar entry to the friends who were included in the purchase ("5" and "6"). Friends will receive a notification message with a calendar entry that the phone can automatically insert into the calendar ("7" and "8" respectively).

- **Usability.** Usability of a native client can be high since it provides the user with a native look and feel thus lowering the learning curve of the service. Typically, the native applications can be also tuned to effectively utilize the computing resources of the phone thus giving shorter start-up times and faster response times in the user interface. Integration with other native applications on the phone can also boost usability and the value of the service as we can see in our example. For example, it is simple for the end-user to keep one register of contacts and friends in the phonebook and use that asset for all communication and group transactions. Other good characteristics of native client applications include the possibility to support off-line functionality and special attached devices and special communication hardware like Bluetooth, IRDA and USB. Also the native client application can integrate directly to the power management system of the phone.
- **Portability.** Portability is a serious problem for native client applications. Only a small percentage of mobile phones support the installation of native applications. For the ones that support it, there exist different software platforms such as Symbian, PocketPC and Brew that are not compatible with each other. Also the native client application can depend on other native components that have to be present in the phone. This can create compatibility problems even inside one platform as the user must ensure that his or her phone includes all required components for the application to work.
- **Deployability.** Native client applications need to be installed using the native application management functions of the phone. Most platforms support different mechanisms to do this over the air (OTA), through USB connection or using a memory card. Application installation typically requires some technical ability from the end user and can thus be a major hurdle in the deployment of a new mobile service.
- **Scalability.** The native client server model scales well in performance as the resources of each client device are used partly in performing the service transactions. Requirements for the server side components are easy to isolate as the server transactions remain simple. Business scalability can be challenging as the deployability of native clients is rather complex. Communication costs from the

native clients to the network services and other users, like the notification function in our example, can prove to be a difficult issue also.

4.2 MOSOA 2: Client-Server with Mobile Java Client

The mobile Java client technology tries to avoid the portability and maintainability issues by providing a standard execution environment and deployment model for the client applications in a phone. The following diagram presents a high level design of our sample service using the client server pattern and a Java client application.

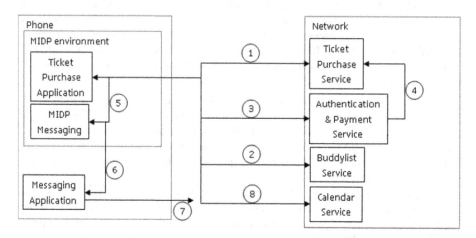

Fig. 2. A mobile service with a Java client application

The MIDP environment for mobile devices is not actually one standard configuration. MIDP standard has two variants: the earlier MIDP 1.0 that is supported by most Java-capable phones and the recent MIDP 2.0 that is supported by latest models. Inside these main variants are different capabilities like messaging, full screen UI and encrypted communication which are only supported by certain phone models. These issues diminish some of the benefits that MIDP and Java were supposed to bring to the developers of mobile services.

In our example we assume that MIDP messaging functions are available to the Java client application. Steps one to four in the example service take place between the Java client and the ticket purchase server ("1"). Next step in the use case involves selecting the friends from a buddy list service that is hosted in the network in our case ("2"). The actual purchase transaction with authentication and payment happens in similar fashion as with the native client. Ticket purchase client communicates with the authentication and payment service which verifies the payment to the ticket purchase service ("3" and "4").

The Java client uses MIDP messaging to send SMS notifications to the friends involved in the transaction ("5", "6" and "7"). For setting a calendar reservation we assume a network hosted calendar service which is used by all users involved in our example case ("8").

- **Usability.** A Java client application can try to support native look and feel through the use of standard MIDP widgets but in most cases developers want to have more control over the UI and define their own UI elements. This can make the individual application quite usable but will make for steeper learning curve as the user has to adapt to application specific UI paradigms. Hosting a complete virtual execution environment in a phone will inevitably cause some overhead in application start delays and response times of the user interface. There are many recommended practices to optimize Java for mobile platforms, which can yield good results. Mobile Java makes it possible to integrate with some phone resources and native applications but not all. This can degrade usability as the user has to maintain contact information of his or her friends and calendar in many places like in our example.
- **Portability.** Portability for mobile Java clients is better than for native applications but is still a complex issue to tackle. Typically the developer has to balance usability and portability tradeoffs to come up with a solution that is supported with large enough device base and offers still well enough usability. The availability of several different standards for mobile Java including MIDP 1.0, MIDP 2.0 and CLDC 1.1 is a problem for portability. Many individual API standards for phone specific resources like messaging, call functions, phone lights and vibration are another problem area. Mobile Java offers ways to detect if a given feature is supported by the device thus making it possible to write client applications that can dynamically adapt to phones with different capabilities.
- **Deployability.** Mobile Java offers rather simple model for over the air provisioning of client applications. The installation process can be made easy enough for average end user to perform. Online updates can be initiated by the client applications themselves if needed.
- **Scalability.** Much of the functionality in Java client model is typically in the server side. The overall scalability of a service design thus heavily depends on the scalability of the server side. Business scalability can be good as it is possible to distribute and sell the client applications through WWW, mobile browsers and SMS rapidly covering wide user base for example through TV commercials with URLs or SMS instructions to install the service. Communication cost from the Java clients to the network services can be an issue depending on the underlying data communication business model.

4.3 MOSOA 3: Client-Server with Mobile Thin Client

The browser based approach has been very successful in the Internet and PC world. Initially the usability of services offered with browser UIs was poor and different browsers had serious compatibility problems but the emergence of "de facto" browser functionality and technologies like browser side scripting have improved the user acceptance of these services greatly.

Developing browser based services for mobile clients today is in many ways facing similar problems as developing browser based services for the PC in the nineties: Technology just hasn't converged yet. However, we can observe rapid advances in

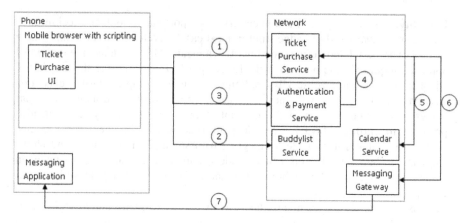

Fig. 3. A mobile service with a browser based client

mobile browsers and it appears that we might actually leap a few generations compared to corresponding PC technology. Despite this, it is not possible to simply apply the user interface patterns from the pc world to the mobile world. The screen size requires different approaches to efficiently present information and allow the user to work with the on screen information effectively [12].

The following diagram illustrates a browser based design of our example service. Majority of the functionality of the service now resides in the network. Some native phone applications, like the messaging in our example, can still be utilized for services but they are integrated to the service through the network instead of locally.

A browser based implementation of the example service must rely on the network side to provide the required service components. Integration to local phone resources from the mobile browser is currently very limited. The overhead to start using a browser based service is very low; it just requires the user to point the browser to the correct link to connect to the service. This can be facilitated through e.g. operator portal pages, SMS messages, TV commercials, etc.

For the first four steps of our use case the user interacts with the ticketing service through the browser ("1"). Selecting the friends to be included can be done from a buddy list service ("2") and possibly with some elementary data management within the browser, such as copy-paste through a clipboard (if that is supported in the device).

The actual purchasing transaction would follow the same general pattern as the earlier architectures ("3" and "4"). However, the next step has to be radically different from the client-server architectures. The ticket purchase service must be able to generate notifications and calendar entries to the list of friends ("5", "6" and "7"). All of the service components and data resources must reside in the network in contrast to the client-server models of previous examples. The user can still receive notifications using the native messaging application of the phone but it is not integrated to the user interface of ticket purchasing application thus degrading the user experience.

- **Usability.** Usability of an individual browser based service can be reasonably good for suitable applications. Typically, applications where the interaction between the user and the application is based on a forms paradigm fit well to the browser client architecture. Highly graphical user interfaces using direct manipulation paradigms are difficult to implement within a browser but emerging technologies like the AJAX will offer some level of support for it in the future. The main problem with browser based mobile service architecture is that it cannot use or integrate with the native applications and resources on the phone device. In practice the service components and resources used by an application must reside in the network. They can sometimes be integrated in the browser but the majority of the integration task must take place in the network. Another drawback of reliance on server-side components is that off-line operation is impossible: in order for the user to use the service the server resources must be accessible by the browser.
- **Portability.** Good portability is one of the strong points of a browser based architecture. Even so, the architect of a browser based mobile service is forced to select between many alternative technology stacks that are largely incompatible with each other. WAP/WML is the pioneer technology of mobile browser based services. In practice, it is currently being phased out due to the emerging of HTTP/HTML capable device generations. The actual capabilities of mobile browsers still vary considerably, however, and there is not yet a consensus on the basic capabilities similar to that in the PC world. New technologies like browser side scripting; AJAX (Asynchronous JavaScript And XML); XForms and HTML 5.0 are promising more interactive browser applications in the future but are rarely supported (even on PC based browsers) so far.
- **Deployability.** In principle the deployability of a browser based mobile service is as simple as it gets. It includes the normal deployment and configuration of the server side components and communicating the link (URL) of the service to the user population. Any user with a phone equipped with a browser that is compatible with the service can start using the service immediately. Any registration and authentication functions can be taken care of inside the browser session. Deployment can get more complex if a particular browser technology, like XForms, that is not pre-installed in the user's phone, is used. In this case the deployment phase is similar to client-server architectures.
- **Scalability.** The scalability in capacity of browser based architectures can be controlled by the traditional design solutions of the server side. This involves two main areas: the scalability of access to the service and the scalability of the communication between the service components in the network. The phone generally does not have much impact on the scalability of a browser based architecture except in special cases like when the amount of data sent to the browser exceeds its capacity (it does however restrict the amount of information that can be presented in a usable way [12]). The business scalability of a browser based architecture is very good. One can start with a low capacity server solution and increase the capacity gradually as the service becomes more popular.

5 Related Work

The notion of software architecture was popularized during the nineties. Perry & Wolf [15] in their article first identified the relevant concepts. Standardization efforts by the IEEE resulted in a recommended practice which has been widely adopted in the software industry [6]. Since the mid nineties, the notion of web service architectures has been popularized. The architectural style that underlies most web services, i.e. representational state transfer (REST), is a crucial ingredient of the hypertext transfer protocol which is also the transport of choice (though not the only one) for service oriented protocols such as SOAP or XMLRPC. In his doctoral thesis on REST [3], Fielding outlines the architectural principles that underlie the HTTP specification (of which he is a co-author) [7] and how these principles are crucial to providing scalability.

The World Wide Web consortium maintains a somewhat more narrow definition of what comprises a web definition. Their WS-Arch document [1], defines a web service as "a software system designed to support interoperable machine-to-machine interaction over a network". The definition is further constrained by specifying that the interfaces should be specified in a machine readable format (i.e. WSDL) and that other systems interact with the web service using SOAP messages.

For mobile services, this definition may very well be too narrow since handling SOAP on mobile devices is impractical due to the limited memory and processing capacity. However, REST principles as outlined by Fielding still apply to mobile service architectures. Scalability in the mobile world is of even more importance than scalability in the internet world because, especially in third world countries, there are vastly more people owning a mobile phone than there are people with access to PCs. The notion of local state is arguably of even more importance due to the inherently more unreliable network conditions (roaming between networks, areas not covered by any network).

A key difference between web service architectures and mobile service architectures is the client side. For web services, client side capabilities have a much higher degree of commonalities than is the case in mobile devices. The issues we outline in our problem statement mostly relate to the client side.

Some earlier work on mobile service architectures includes Hodes et al. [5], who propose an architecture for discovering and working, with local services. However, their work predates most of the internet services that have since emerged and consequently does not take these into account. Another article from this era by Jones et al. [10] analyzes WAP services from a usability angle. These articles are illustrative of the thinking on mobile web services in the late nineties. As described in our introduction, the approaches from this time (especially WAP) mostly failed in the market.

More recent work tends to focus on agents or semantic networks (e.g. [2]). However, such techniques are as experimental in the mobile internet as they are in the regular internet. While promising, we don't believe these approaches make explicit the requirements and challenges of mobile service architectures as we do in this article since they do not address all of the goals we outline in our problem statement section.

Some work has been done on evaluating conventional web service technology in mobile devices. For example, in [11], the authors evaluate the performance of SOAP over various protocols. This work suggests that the overhead of XML parsing is a major obstacle as is network speed. Additionally, some research has been done into using asynchronous messaging in mobile service architectures (e.g. [14]). Interestingly, recent developments in conventional web services also push towards an asynchronous style of working.

Additionally there has been a lot of effort evaluating usability of mobile user interfaces. For example in [16] the usability failure of WAP technology is analyzed. Our Nokia colleagues have written a comprehensive overview of usability issues in mobile user interfaces [12].

6 Summary and Conclusions

Table 1 summarizes the discussion from the previous section. The only quality attribute the native client scores best on is usability. This is probably the main reason why services with a native client (e.g. the ones discussed in the introduction) have more or less failed in the market. These services provided good usability on the devices where the client actually worked but at the cost of the other quality attributes in this table. Consequently lack of market share and the associated high cost of fixing that problem prevented the widespread adoption of such services.

As the table suggests, non-native clients are the solution to the problem. Unfortunately, this comes at the expense of usability. However, we also observe that this is increasingly less a problem as for example more Java MIDP APIs are standardized and deployed. Both the Java virtual machine and the browser are implemented as native application. In theory this means that they can provide the same level of usability as a native client. Features such as power management, user interface, input methods can all be put to use in the implementation of a browser.

Unfortunately, the above requires standardization of the way such features are exposed to the service application developers. Currently, there exist many standardized MIDP APIs for a wide range of mobile phone specific features. A continuing problem is that most of these APIs are optional so depending on such APIs is almost as bad as depending on native features directly.

Based on our experience with mobile device technology, we are convinced that a consensus on mobile device features is emerging and that consequently it will become easier to abstract from such features using e.g. MIDP APIs. The same has happened on the PC desktop where applications tend to be much more portable across different desktop platforms than is common on mobile platforms.

We have identified a clear trend that what we call a browser in this article will in the future evolve towards a standards based application container. In principle, given that proper standards emerge, this means that applications inside such a container can rely on features similar to those exposed in high end MIDP containers today. There are multiple ways of realizing such integration. An obvious way to this is through plug-ins. Additionally, features may be exposed through custom URL schemes like for example the tel://<phonenumber> [8] or the sms:// <phonenumber> [9] type schemes.

Table 1. Summary of architectural alternatives

	Native client	Java client	Browser
Usability	+	+/-	-
Portability	-	+/-	+
Deployability	-	+/-	+
Business Scalability	-	+/-	+
TCO	-	+/-	+

A second trend we have identified is that in future service application containers like outlined above, the notion of local device access will be of less importance than it is today. Resources will become themselves services. For example, there is no technical reason to have features such as contacts and SMS messages client side other than optimizing access to these resources and ensuring that these resources are available when the phone is offline.

Ultimately, there will be this convergence of applications and services where the particular client used to access the service depends on the user context. For example the same list of contacts may be manipulated from an office environment on a laptop and from a contact list service application on a phone.

Technically, the service components would be hosted on a heterogeneous grid-like environment where resource allocation and provisioning of client components is automatically managed without user intervention.

References

[1] David Booth, Hugo Haas, Francis McCabe, Eric Newcomer, Michael Champion, Chris Ferris, David Orchard. "Web Services Architecture", Web Services Architecture Working Group, http://www.w3.org/TR/ws-arch/, February 2004.

[2] P. Buhler and J. M. Vidal, "Semantic Web Services as Agent Behaviors," in Agentcities: Challenges in Open Agent Environments, LNCS/LNAI, B. Burg, J. Dale, et al., Eds. Berlin: Springer-Verlag, 2003.

[3] R. T. Fielding, " Architectural Styles and the Design of Network-based Software Architectures", Ph. D. thesis, University of California, Irvine, 2000.

[4] M. Baker. "Ian Foster on Recent Changes in the Grid Community", IEEE Distributed Systems Online, 5(2), February 2004.

[5] T. D. Hodes, R. H. Katz, E. Servan-Schreiber, L. Rowe, "Composable Ad-hoc Mobile Services for Universal Interaction", Proceedings of the 3rd ACM International Conference on Mobile Computing and Networking, pp. 1-12, 1997.

[6] IEEE Std 1471-2000 IEEE Recommended Practice for Architectural Description of Software-Intensive Systems, http://standards.ieee.org/reading/ieee/std_public/description/se/1471-2000_desc.html

[7] IETF RFC 2616, "Hypertext Transfer Protocol -- HTTP/1.1", http://www.ietf.org/rfc/rfc2616.txt

[8] IETF RFC 2806, "URLs for Telephone Calls", http://www.ietf.org/rfc/rfc2806.txt.

[9] IETF draft RFC, "SMS URI Scheme", http://www.ietf.org/internet-drafts/draft-wilde-sms-uri-11.txt.

[10] M. Jones, G. Buchanan, G. Marsden, M. Pazzani, Improving Mobile Internet Usability. Proceedings WWW'10, Hong Kong. 2001.

[11] J. Kangasharju, Sasu Tarkoma, Kimmo Raatikainen, " Comparing SOAP Performance for Various Encodings, Protocols, and Connections", LNCS Lecture Notes in Computer Science, Volume 2775 / 2003, pp. 397 - 406, 2003.

[12] Christian Lindholm, Turkka Keinonen, "Mobile Usability: How Nokia Changed the Face of the Mobile Phone", McGraw-Hill Professional, 2003.

[13] G. E. Moore, Cramming more components onto integrated circuits, Electronics Magazine, 38(8), pp. 114-117, April 1965.

[14] M. Musolesi, C. Mascolo, S. Hailes. Adapting asynchronous messaging middleware to ad hoc networking. In Proceedings of the 2nd Workshop on Middleware For Pervasive and Ad-Hoc Computing, pp. 121-126, ACM Press, New York, NY, 2004.

[15] D. E. Perry, A. L. Wolf, Foundations for the study of software architecture, ACM SIGSOFT Software Engineering Notes 17(4), pp. 40-52, October 1992.

[16] M. Ramsey and J. Nielsen. The WAP Usability Report. Neilsen Norman Group, 2000.

A Spatial Programming Model for Real Global Smart Space Applications

René Meier, Anthony Harrington, Thomas Termin, and Vinny Cahill

Distributed Systems Group, Department of Computer Science
Trinity College Dublin, Ireland
{rene.meier, anthony.harrington, thomas.termin,
vinny.cahill}@cs.tcd.ie

Abstract. Global smart spaces are intended to provide their inhabitants with context-aware access to pervasive services and information relevant to large geographical areas. Transportation is one obvious domain for such global smart spaces since applications can be built to exploit the variety of sensor-rich systems that have been deployed to support urban traffic control and highway management as well as within individual vehicles. This paper presents a spatial programming model designed to provide a standardised way to build context-aware global smart space applications using information that is distributed across *independent* (legacy, sensor-enabled, and embedded) systems by exploiting the overlapping spatial and temporal attributes of the information maintained by these systems. The spatial programming model is based on a *topographical approach* to modelling space that enables systems to independently define and use potentially overlapping spatial context in a consistent manner and in contrast to topological approaches, in which geogra-phical relation-nships between objects are described explicitly. Moreover, this approach facilitates the *incremental* construction of global smart spaces since the underlying systems to be incorporated are largely decoupled. The programming model has been evaluated by building a context-aware service for multi-modal urban journey planning, as part of the development of an overall architecture for intelligent transportation systems in Dublin.

1 Introduction

Global smart spaces extend the vision of pervasive computing, in which everyday objects communicate and collaborate to provide information and services to users, to large geographical areas [1]. They extend the notion of objects cooperating in a home or an office to the level of towns, cities, and even countries by integrating a variety of sensor-based and other systems to provide truly pervasive context-aware services. Such global smart environments will be heterogeneous as they likely will comprise a multitude of sensors, networks, and ultimately systems. They will provide access to information and services ranging from pervasive access to personal and professional information, to city-wide information systems [2, 3], to context-aware traveller assistance [4, 5], to optimised urban traffic control [6]. Users moving in such sensor-augmented spaces may use handheld devices, such as mobile phones and Personal Digital Assistants (PDAs), or integrated devices, such as (vehicular) on-board

F. Eliassen and A. Montresor (Eds.): DAIS 2006, LNCS 4025, pp. 16–31, 2006.

computers, to interact with these spaces and to use the services that they provide. Embedded control systems may likewise exploit these spaces to offer context-aware urban traffic control, such as public service vehicle priority.

Global smart spaces are on the verge of becoming a reality in the transportation domain where very many heterogeneous sensor-rich systems have already been deployed in towns and cities and along national road networks. Such a global smart space might enable users to access information ranging from information on places of interest, to prevailing road and weather conditions, to expected journey times, to up-to-date public transport information. It might also enable suitably privileged users to interact with the infrastructure, for example, to request a change to a traffic light or to reserve a parking space.

Programming Global Smart Space Applications. The basis for the provision of context-aware services and information to users will be the integration of the individual systems associated with global smart spaces into comprehensive platforms. This paper presents a programming model designed to provide a standardised way for global smart space applications to access context information that is provided by *independent* systems and related services. The spatial programming model supports a *topographical* location model and provides access to distributed context information based on (overlapping) temporal and spatial aspects. This enables applications to exploit and act upon information from a variety of deployed (and novel) systems and services as well as to share information between them. The spatial programming model hides the complexity and diversity of the underlying systems and their data sources and provides applications with a common view on the available information and its context. For example, a service might use the spatial programming model to retrieve public transport information, which might be provided by some underlying system, and then access relevant weather information provided by another system using the temporal and spatial context of this information.

The spatial programming model is part of the iTransIT framework for integrating individual transportation systems and related services. The iTransIT framework has been motivated by the needs of Dublin City and its multi-layered distributed architecture has been designed to enable information integration and sharing across independent Intelligent Transportation Systems (ITS) and pervasive context-aware user services. It enables *incremental* integration of independent systems and services over time while minimising the impact of such expansion as changes are local to the new system. This software architecture for global smart spaces proposes a layered data model to facilitate data exchange between systems and services with diverse data sets, quality of service requirements, and functional organizations. Data layers are defined within a common context model along the dimensions of space and time and may be distributed across multiple systems. Individual systems maintain one or more layers of the overall data model. This distribution of layers across a series of systems effectively allows applications to access elements of a certain part of the model with a specific quality of service. For example, a data layer might provide video streams from traffic cameras while another layer might maintain city-wide parking information provided by a car parking system. Applications may use the spatial programming model to access either or both of these layers with the quality of service of the respective information. This scenario also illustrates that systems may be integrated gradually and with minimal impact on other systems. Each of these layers might be integrated at a different time and the integration of one layer does not affect the data captured in the other layer. An application using the spatial programming model to access information from the video layer might eventually be updated to access the car parking layer as well. The iTransIT framework has been developed in cooperation with the Traffic Office of Dublin City Council (DCC) in the Republic of Ireland. Detailed framework (and spatial programming model) requirements were informed by a comprehensive audit of existing and planned future intelligent transportation systems in the Dublin City area.

Realising Global Smart Space Applications. The proposed spatial programming model has been implemented as part of a proof-of-concept architecture and data model that captures a variety of real transportation information derived from systems currently deployed in Dublin City. This programming model implementation has been evaluated by building a pervasive service for multi-modal urban journey planning. Such a smart traveller information service can be considered a canonical global smart spaces application since it exploits information generated by a variety of underlying heterogeneous systems in a context-aware manner. The evaluation is based on transportation information relevant to and derived from a real urban environment and demonstrates how our programming model enables application and eventually user access to such pervasive context information. In general, it is expected that the increased availability of re-usable information from a variety of independent systems will enable higher-level policies to be translated more easily into real world actions and will facilitate the emergence of novel transportation applications and truly pervasive context-aware user services.

Organisation of This Paper. The remainder of this paper is structured as follows: Section 2 surveys related work. Section 3 presents the spatial programming model and section 4 describes how this programming model has been realised as part of a framework for integrating independent transportation systems. Section 5 presents our evaluation of this work outlining how the spatial programming model provides global access to the context information required by a multi-modal traveller information system. Finally, section 6 concludes this paper by summarising our work.

2   Related Work

Temporal, spatial and quality of service attributes represent types of meta-data that may be integrated into a context model to provide more intelligent and focused use of data [7]. This approach has been applied in the Nexus framework [8] which provides a common context model infused with spatial information to build world models that are distributed across spaces possessing rich context data sources, known as Augmented Areas. The context model is presented as a global object-based ontology for developing interoperable world models. This interoperability is ensured through the use of a common but large data schema, the Standard Class Schema, to define various world models. The authors have defined a simple spatial query language that can be used to interact with objects representing an Augmented Area. An interface known as an Augmented World model provides a federated global view on all compliant local models. The focus of our work has been to develop a more constrained yet expressive set of abstractions which are used to both facilitate data modelling and to provide the basis for our spatial application programming interface. Using such a constrained set of abstractions simplifies management and maintenance in light of continuously evolving global smart spaces as novel systems are expected to use combinations of existing abstractions.

Gaia [9] is a canonical example of a middleware infrastructure to enable active or smart spaces in ubiquitous computing habitats that emphasises the notion of space programmability. Gaia extends the notion of traditional operating systems to ubiquitous computing environments by providing components such as the Context File System and an event manager to track active space state information. Gaia focuses on managing resources contained in physical spaces. User data and applications are abstracted into a user virtual space and can be mapped dynamically to the resources located in the current environment. Applications developed for a Gaia active space use a comprehensive set of services at runtime. The iTransIT framework adopts a different approach in that it uses a set of context abstractions exposed through the spatial programming model to provide an interface to a global smart space populated by heterogeneous systems. Aside from calls to the spatial application programming interface, systems may operate independently of the iTransIT framework.

Smart Messages [10] is a lightweight architecture similar to mobile agents that aims to make Space a first-order programming construct and describes a space-aware programming model for outdoor distributed embedded systems called Spatial Programming. In this model, content or services provided by nodes are accessed using spatial references. These are defined as {space:tag} pairs that are mapped to systems embedded in the physical space. These spatial references are used by various applications to transparently access network resources in a similar fashion to physical memory access using variable names in conventional systems. Our approach to accessing information in a global smart space is more generic compared to this {space:tag}-based naming scheme in that information can be located using multiple context dimensions including space and time as well as any functional aspect of the information. Information can be shared and integrated by exploiting combinations of these aspects and by exploiting overlapping context.

3   The Spatial Application Programming Model

The spatial programming model provides a standardised way for global smart space applications to access and use information and context that is distributed across independent systems and related services. The spatial programming model provides common access to such distributed information based on overlapping context thereby enabling applications to exploit and act upon information from a variety of systems and services as well as to share information between them.

3.1   Abstracting Information and Context

The spatial programming model uses a small set of predefined types for composing information and context, in which context is any information that can be used to characterise the situation of an information element [11], to ensure interoperability between data sets captured across distributed systems. These types are used to model data sets and their context according to the different roles data sets can assume in a global smart space as *spatial objects*. Spatial objects represent information as a series of parameters and context as attributes. Such types are central to providing applications with a common view on the wide range of information and the associated context that might be available in a global smart space. They hide the complexity and diversity of the independent systems and data sources comprising global spaces and represent the hooks for information integration through overlapping context such as space and time.

Developing such types is non trivial for any programming model for significant systems and is especially complex for global smart spaces due to the scale and multitude of inter-relationships that exist between sensors, systems, services, users, and their data sets. Lehman et al. [8] suggest an exhaustive ontology for defining how context information can be shared between applications in augmented areas. However, based on our experience with a real global smart space in the transportation domain, we have found that a relatively small number of types suffices to decompose a global smart space domain model. Using a small set of (coarse-grain) types rather than attempting to model the entire world in detail simplifies management and maintenance in light of continuously evolving spaces. Novel systems or services are expected to be modelled using combinations of existing types whereas an exhaustive model might have to be expanded to capture the specific characteristics of novel systems.

The types for modelling information and context as spatial objects currently supported by the spatial programming model are summarized in **Fig. 1**. They have been designed as a series of abstract object types and include three main types for modelling global information, which are *real world, system and data object*, as well as types for modelling context.

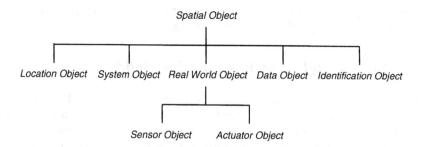

Fig. 1. Information and context abstractions

The three information types model the different roles that objects can assume within the spatial programming model. System objects represent general information describing software components, including systems and services, while real world objects represent physical entities. In a transportation smart space for example, system objects might capture operational status from a car parking system or from a journey time estimation service whereas real world objects might model roads and junctions.

Sensor and actuator objects are specialisations of real world objects and are used for modelling explicit infrastructural entities for example, detector loops and variable message signs of a car parking system. Data objects model any static or dynamic information from systems or services and might be used to model car parking opening times and rates charged. Based on an audit of deployed (and planned) transportation systems and services in the Dublin City area [12], we found that these categories of information types are sufficient to cover possible data sets in such a global smart space. Novel information can be integrated using spatial objects composing sets of parameters that model such data sets.

The main context type of the spatial programming model is the *location object*. Location objects are based on a topographical location model that uses geometry to model the space occupied or covered by an infrastructural element, a system or a service. The spatial programming model also supports temporal context. Temporal context is modelled implicitly, i.e., incorporated in other information types, rather than explicitly as a specific object. This enables information objects to include date and time attributes for representing their temporal context such as creation time and temporal validity. And finally, *identification objects* provide a type for logical identity, for example, to identify the name of a system or a service.

3.2 Modelling Space

The spatial programming model supports a topographical approach to modelling space. The relevant spatial context of sensors, systems, services and even users is modelled as a geometric shape. Individual shapes are defined by a sequence of coordinates based on a chosen, well-known coordinate system. These shapes explicitly represent spatial context derived form the real world. They may reflect the physical appearances of spatial objects modelling occupied space or may describe areas of interest that specify the regions covered by services. For example, a city-wide car parking system might use the spatial model to define the physical locations occupied by its car parks whereas a road weather service might use the spatial model to outline the locations occupied by weather stations as well as the areas to which reports from individual stations apply.

Using a topographical approach to modelling space enables systems, services, and applications to independently define and use potentially overlapping spatial context in a consistent manner. Unlike topological approaches [13], in which geographical relationships between spatial objects are described explicitly, topographical models define relationships between spatial objects implicitly and without explicit interactions between objects. The relations between spatial objects (and ultimately systems and users) are defined by the position of their respective shape within the common coordinate system. This is particularly significant in global smart spaces where multitudes of independent systems are distributed over large geographical areas and direct communication across systems may be limited or expensive. Applications using the spatial model can exploit these implicit relations to link diverse information together for a user specific purpose. They may access spatially related information for example, by means of exploiting the distance between shapes or by exploiting containment and intersection relations. This might for example enable a vehicle-based information system to retrieve the exact locations of car parking facilities within a certain distance from its current location.

The spatial programming model supports the model for defining geometric shapes defined by the OpenGIS standard [14]. Spatial objects can be represented by geometry types ranging from a point, to a line, to a polygon, to combinations of polygons. Points might be used to define the location of a specific traffic signal or an individual user. Individual polygons might represent the spatial context of a car park or an area of interest whereas a series of (overlapping) polygons might be used to compose a spatial model of a transportation network comprising roads, lanes, and intersections.

As mentioned above, these geometric shapes are specified using a common coordinate system. The selection of such a system depends on the domain of the global smart space for which the spatial programming model is being realised. Coordinates derived from third party location sensors, such as Global Positioning System (GPS) receivers, are mapped onto the chosen reference system if they are based on another system. For example, GPS coordinates may need be converted into a regional reference system chosen for a specific space. The Irish national grid reference system, a system of geographic grid references commonly used in Ireland, has been chosen as the coordinate system in our prototype.

3.3 Modelling Data

The spatial programming model defines a set of types for modelling the different roles spatial objects (and the context information they represent) can assume within a global smart space. Systems and services model their data using these types and a particular system may use and combine several types to accurately capture the roles of individual data sets. The example shown in **Fig. 2**, illustrates how a road weather system might use a system object to model general system data and a set of sensor objects to model individual weather stations. Each weather station comprises a location and an identification object and includes a data object that captures the actual measurements.

Spatial objects must specialise at least one of our types for modelling information and context. However, depending on their role, they may derive from several types. **Table 1** summarises how these types can be combined outlining the semantics for composing information and context into spatial objects. As outlined in the real world object row, **Table 1** shows that a real world object must comprise a location and an identification object and that it may include a set of data objects and a set of other real world objects. The compulsory containment of a location object is a reflection of the fact that real world objects are expected to model the physical space they occupy.

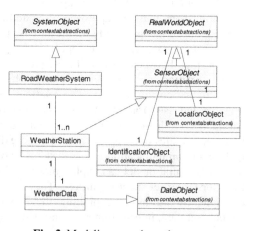

Fig. 2. Modeling a road weather system

In contrast, system and data objects may or may not comprise a location object and such a location object is probably modelling the space to which a system's or data object's information applies. Note that sensor and actuator objects are specialisations of real world objects that share the same composition semantics.

Table 1. The semantics for composing information and context types

	System Object	Real World (Sensor, Actuator) Object	Data Object	Location Object	Identification Object
System Object	0..n	0..n	0..n	0..1	0..1
Real World (Sensor, Actuator) Object	0	0..n	0..n	1	1
Data Object	0	0	0..n	0..1	0..1

3.4 Modelling Temporal Context

In addition to supporting spatial context, the spatial programming model also supports context along the dimension of time. The temporal relations between spatial objects are defined by a set of attributes. This set of attributes has been derived from our study of the transportation infrastructure in Dublin City [12] and are summarised in **Table 2**. The data object type includes these attributes and spatial objects model their temporal context by deriving from this type. Data objects also include a *ConfidenceLevel* attribute for modelling the accuracy of the captured data.

Table 2. Temporal context attributes of data object types

Attribute Name	Description
CreationDate	Time of data object creation
LastModificationDate	Time the data object was last updated
RetrievalLatency	Expected latency for retrieving the captured data
ExpectedLifetime	Expected duration to the next data object update
ConfidenceLevel	Level of confidence in the accuracy of the captured data

Applications may exploit temporal relations between spatial objects in the same way as they exploit spatial relations to link diverse information together for a user-specific purpose. They may access temporally related information, for example, by means of correlating modification time. Significantly, applications may exploit context along a combination of the spatial and temporal dimension. This might enable a road-user information system to use the location and time of an accident to retrieve the prevailing weather conditions at the accident site and subsequently to advice drivers of similarly dangerous road conditions.

3.5 Using the Spatial Model

Systems use spatial objects to model their contextual information and implement the spatial application programming interface to provide pervasive access to these objects. Each system models the subset of the spatial objects that is relevant to its respective purpose and context-aware applications exploit the spatial application programming interface to integrate and share information in a common way regardless of the specifics of the system implementing a particular part of the spatial model.

As shown below, the operations of the spatial application programming interface provide a means for applications to manage, locate and access spatial objects. A set of operations is available for locating spatial objects using geometric queries or queries based on parameters of objects. Geometric queries are based on a geometry class that defines OpenGIS shapes including points and polygons. Parameter-based queries use the container class outlined below to describe the parameter and attribute values of spatial objects. The parameter class includes native data values and may include the relevant temporal attributes of data objects. This class can be used in connections with queries but may also be used to access the typed parameter and attribute values of spatial objects. The spatial application programming interface enables applications to locate spatial objects using a variety of queries ranging from selection based on a parameter value, to selection based on temporal context, to selection based on spatial context, to combinations of these. For example, a weather station may be selected using the value of a measurement, the temporal occurrence of a measurement or the location of the station. Such queries may identify zero, one or more objects. For example, selecting the bus stops of a certain bus route in a particular area might identify multiple suitable stops. Spatial objects are uniquely identified within a given system by a type and identifier pair. These pairs are typically the result of some selection operation and may be used to either retrieve or update the parameters of spatial objects. An application might use bus stop and identifier pairs to retrieve the addresses and timetables of previously located stops.

Significantly, the spatial programming model enables a federation of independent systems to model their respective information and context *locally* as spatial objects. Each of these systems implements the spatial application programming interface to provide access to its respective set of spatial objects. This enables applications to use, share, locate and correlate these distributed objects using a common set of context operations irrespective of the complexities of the systems accommodating the objects and without the need for an overall close integration of the systems. This mapping of the spatial model and its programming interface onto individual systems therefore provides for truly pervasive context-aware applications and services in global and heterogeneous environments.

```
interface S_API {
    void insert(String elementType, OrderedParameterValues parValues);
    void remove(String elementType, int id);
    int[] select(String elementType, Geometry loc);
    int[] select(String elementType, String parName, Parameter parValue);
    int[] select(String elementType, Geometry loc, String parName,
            Parameter parValue);
    int[] select(String elementType);
    ElementTypeAndId[] select(Geometry loc);
    Geometry select(String elementType, int id);
    void update(String elementType, int id, String parName[],
            Parameter parValues[]);
    Parameter[] retrieve(String elementType, int id, String parName[]);
}
```

```
class Parameter{
  Calendar creationDate;
  Calendar modificationDate;
  Long retrievalLatency;
  Long expectedLifetime;
  Double confidenceLevel;
  String parameterValue;

  Integer getIntegerParameterValue();
  Double getDoubleParameterValue();
  String getStringParameterValue();
  Calendar getDateParameterValue();
  ...
}
```

4 The iTransIT Framework

The spatial programming model has been realised as part of a framework and a data model for integrating independent intelligent transportation systems. As illustrated in **Fig. 3**, the iTransIT architecture structures legacy systems, iTransIT systems, and context-aware end-user applications into three tiers. These tiers define the relationships between systems and applications and provide a scalable approach for integrating systems and their context information as individual components can be added to a specific tier without direct consequences to the components in the remaining tiers. The relationships between systems and applications can be characterized according to the interaction paradigms that describe the possible information flows between legacy and iTransIT systems.

4.1 Architecture Tiers

The legacy tier provides for the integration of legacy systems and describes existing as well as future transportation systems that have not been developed to conform to the iTransIT system architecture and layered data model. Such legacy systems often feature a form of persistent data storage and might include systems for traffic and motorway management that have commonly been deployed in many urban environments.

The purpose of the iTransIT tier is to integrate transportation systems that model spatial objects and implement the spatial applica-tion programming interface. This tier therefore comprises a federation of transportation systems that implement the spatial data model. The data model is distributed across these iTransIT systems, with each system implementing the subset of the overall model that is relevant

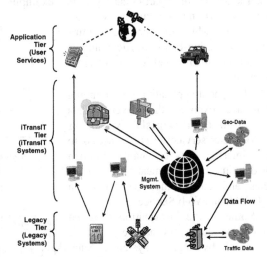

Fig. 3. iTransIT ITS architecture framework overview

to its operation. iTransIT systems maintain their individual information, which is often gathered by sensors or provided to actuators, by populating the relevant part of the spatial data model. However, some of the information maintained in an iTransIT system specific part of the data model may actually be provided by underlying legacy systems. Most significantly, traffic information captured in this tier is maintained with its temporal and spatial context; persistently stored data is geo-coded typically by systems exploiting a database with spatial extension.

The systems that may exist in the iTransIT tier can be classified according to the paradigms they exploit when interacting with other legacy or iTransIT systems. Such iTransIT systems may be purpose built and therefore optimized to accommodate application or user-specific requirements or may be general purpose. As shown in **Fig. 3**, the framework may incorporate a general-purpose iTransIT Management system. The iTransIT Management system is the canonical application of this domain and is expected to implement a major part of the spatial data model. It typically serves as a main repository for geo-coded data generated and used by connected legacy and iTransIT systems.

The application tier includes value added services that provide context-aware user access to and interaction with traffic information. These services use the distributed data model and the associated context to access information potentially provided by multiple systems and might include a wide range of interactive (Internet-based) and embedded control services ranging from monitoring of live and historical traffic information to the display of road network maps.

4.2 Common Spatial Data Model

The spatial data model, common to all iTransIT systems, is comprised of a set of potentially distributed layers and represents the central component of these systems. As shown in **Fig. 4**, individual iTransIT systems implement one or more of these layers (or parts of layers) and maintain the static, dynamic, live, or historical traffic data available in a particular layer. For example, a system might implement a data layer describing the current weather conditions while another layer capturing intersection-based traffic volumes might be maintained by a different system.

The spatial application programming interface exposes this layered data model to other iTransIT systems or indeed user services. Remote access to this interface may be enabled through widely used communication technologies and query languages based on CORBA and Web Services.

Some of the information captured in data model layers may be generated or used by legacy systems. Such information is mapped to a legacy

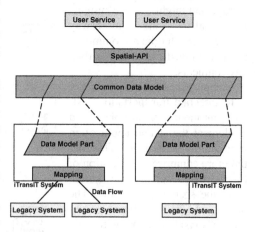

Fig. 4. iTransIT system architecture and common data model

system through data flows. These flows can be described using a set of flow classes, including event, stream, request/response, configuration and alarm flows, based on the characteristics and requirements of communication links provided by the KAREN framework architecture [15]. Using these descriptions, individual iTransIT systems implement interfaces that map specific legacy data to their data layers. This approach enables the use of communication technologies that can address the requirements of particular systems and their respective data flows. The objective of an iTransIT system might be to handle a certain data subset efficiently and to provide specific guarantees for the delivery of the data. For example, an iTransIT system may employ real-time communication technology to connect to a legacy system that is capable of supporting strong delivery guarantees.

5 Assessment

This section evaluates the spatial programming model for global smart space applications proposed in this paper. The main objective of the experiments has been to assess the feasibility of our programming model providing access to information generated by a variety of heterogeneous systems in a context-aware manner. The assessed transportation application scenario demonstrates that our programming model enables application and eventually user access to pervasive context information derived from a real urban environment through correlation of overlapping spatial context. This evaluation therefore demonstrates that using a spatial programming model enables the integration of individual systems associated with a global smart space into a comprehensive platform for the provision of context-aware services and information to users.

The application scenario has been derived from the requirements of a smart traveller information service enabling travellers to plan journeys involving multiple forms of transportation including walking, public transport, cycling, and private vehicles thereby bridging the coordination gap between these modes of transportation by suggesting journey routes according to traveller preference and availability of transportation means. Such a service can be considered a canonical global smart spaces application since it exploits context information generated by a variety of independent systems. The scenario has been assessed using a prototypical implementation of an iTransIT Management system as a platform for pervasive services. This Management system implements the spatial application programming inte-rface and uses spatial objects to model information concerning

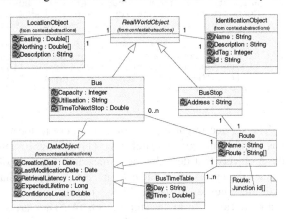

Fig. 5. Spatial objects modeling public transport information

a range of transportation systems currently deployed in Dublin City. The system includes global context layers modelling the road network comprising intersections, roads, lanes, traffic counts, traffic volumes, and congestions levels as well as the public transport network consisting of bus routes, stops, lanes, timetables and bus locations. It also includes system context layers modelling parking information and road weather data. These layers integrate data provided by a range of real legacy systems including the main traffic management system, a public transport information service, a congestion level application, a road weather service and a car parking information system. **Fig. 5** shows a small set of the spatial objects modelling these layers that have been implemented as relational tables in a MySQL database with spatial extension. The information from these spatial objects has been provided by the traffic management system, the public transport information service and by a journey time monitoring system.

5.1 The Evaluation Scenario

The evaluation scenario includes a tourist using the context-aware traveller information service to locate public transport stations within walking distance of her current location. The tourist has just visited The Book of Kells museum at Trinity College Dublin and is about to leave campus through the Nassau Street gate. She remembers that she used the number 15 bus to travel from her hotel to the city centre and would therefore like to locate nearby bus stops of this route.

She uses a handheld device with wireless service access to enter her query into the traveller information service, providing bus route number 15 and 5 minutes walking distance from her current location as parameters. The service uses coordinates derived from its GPS receiver (converted into Irish national grid coordinates) and an average pedestrian pace of 1.36m/s [16] to define the geometric shape of the search area. The service then uses the spatial application programming interface as outlined below to access the relevant context information.

```
1 int[] busStopId = sapi.select("BusStop", searchArea);
  for (int i = 0; i < busStopId.length; i++) {
2   Parameter busStopName=sapi.retrieve("BusStop", busStopId[i],"Name");
3   Geometry busStopLocation = sapi.select("BusStop", busStopId[i]);
4   Parameter linkToRoute = sapi.retrieve("BusStop", busStopId[i],
                                          "route_autoId");
    int routeId = linkToRoute.getIntegerValue();
5   Parameter routeName = sapi.retrieve("Route", routeId, "Name");
6   if (routeName.getStringValue().equals("15-outbound")) ||
       (routeName.getStringValue().equals("15-inbound")) {
7     //use results
    }
  }
```

The service might use a geometric query to locate all spatial objects representing bus stops in the given search area (1) and retrieve the parameters and attributes of these objects that describe the names and locations of specific bus stops (2, 3). The service then proceeds to identify the spatial objects that describe the routes associated with these bus stops. These "links" to route objects are modelled as parameters that can be retrieved from bus stop objects (4). They are subsequently used to retrieve the names of the bus stop routes (5) and information related to the previously indicated bus route (6) can then be used to advise the user (7). The results of such a scenario for locating bus stops within walking distance can be found in **Table 3**. Bus stops for both city centre-bound and suburb-bound stops have been retrieved since the user did not specify her preferences. Naturally, a traveller information service would display this information as an overlay to a map of Dublin City rather than in table form. Such an overlay might include the bus stop names and the headings of buses. This might further assist the user in locating and eventually walking to a convenient bus stop.

Table 3. Locating public transport stations within walking distance

Bus Stop Name	Route Name	Bus Stop Location (Irish national grid coordinates)
Kildare Street	15-outbound	(316230.8575, 233593.6385)
Dawson Street Upper	15-inbound	(316063.4310, 233792.1260)
Dawson Street Lower	15-inbound	(316036.3947, 233612.0083)
Suffolk Street	15-inbound	(315924.9190, 233981.6965)
Nassau Street	15-outbound	(316202.2930, 233883.7390)
College Green	15-outbound	(316038.3422, 234186.3123)

This application scenario demonstrates how a context-aware user service might use the spatial programming model to locate real-world entities in a given area of interest and how it might exploit explicit associations between spatial objects. Similar queries can be used by a range of related scenarios. For example, after selecting a bus stop, the user might wish to see the relevant timetable for the next hour or might wish to use the address of her hotel to locate a convenient stop near her destination and to display the route the bus will take. Other related scenarios might include retrieving the congestion levels along the route in order to get an indication of whether the bus is likely to be on time. Such a scenario might also be of interest to someone travelling by car to the airport or to work. These related scenarios have been implemented but due to space limitations are not describe in further detail.

This assessment is based on scenarios that access information integrated in the spatial model through a single spatial application programming interface. However, a context-aware user service may concurrently use multiple spatial application programming interfaces to access spatial objects in a similar way. The overlapping context of such distributed spatial objects may be used similarly to correlate objects. For example, the location of a bus stop available from one spatial application programming interface might be used to locate nearby train stations through another interface.

6   Summary and Conclusions

This paper presented a programming model for global smart space applications to access context information provided by independent systems and related services. The spatial programming model uses a small set of predefined types to model distributed context information as spatial objects. This provides a common view on such information and enables applications to exploit, act upon and share information based on overlapping temporal and spatial aspects. The spatial programming model supports a topographical location model in which spatial context derived form the real world is explicitly represented by shapes that reflect occupied space or describe areas of interest. This enables systems distributed over large geographical areas to independently define and use spatial context in a consistent manner.

The spatial programming model is part of the iTransIT framework for global smart spaces in the transportation domain that has been motivated by the needs of Dublin City. The multi-layered distributed iTransIT architecture enables incremental integration of independent systems and services over time while minimising the impact of such expansion as changes are local to the new system. The distributed data model, in which individual systems maintain one or more layers of the overall data model, facilitates data exchange between systems and services with diverse contextual data sets and functional organizations.

The evaluation of the spatial programming model is based on a prototypical implementation of an iTransIT management system that uses spatial objects to model real information relevant to and derived from a range of transportation systems currently deployed in Dublin City. The assessed scenario demonstrated that our programming model enables application and eventually user access to pervasive context information concerning a real urban environment through correlation of overlapping spatial context. This evaluation therefore demonstrates that using a spatial programming model enables the integration of individual systems associated with a global smart space into a comprehensive platform for the provision of truly pervasive context-aware services and information to users.

Acknowledgements. The work described in this paper was supported by the Dublin City Council in Ireland.

References

[1] A. Dearle, G. Kirby, R. Morrison, A. McCarthy, K. Mullen, Y. Yang, R. Connor, P. Welen, and A. Wilson, "Architectural Support for Global Smart Spaces," in *Proceedings of the 4th International Conference on Mobile Data Management (MDM 2003), LNCS 2574*. Melbourne, Australia: Springer-Verlag, 2003, pp. 153-164.

[2] K. Cheverst, N. Davies, K. Mitchell, A. Friday, and C. Efstratiou, "Experiences of Developing and Deploying a Context-aware Tourist Guide: The GUIDE Project," in *Proceedings of the Sixth Annual International Conference on Mobile Computing and Networking (MobiCom 2000)*. Boston, Massachusetts, USA: ACM Press, 2000, pp. 20-31.

[3] G. D. Abowd, C. G. Atkeson, J. Hong, S. Long, R. Kooper, and M. Pinkerton, "Cyberguide: A Mobile Context-Aware Tour Guide," *ACM Wireless Networks*, vol. 3, pp. 421-433, 1997.

[4] T. Sivaharan, G. Blair, A. Friday, M. Wu, H. Duran-Limon, P. Okanda, and C.-F. Sørensen, "Cooperating Sentient Vehicles for Next Generation Automobiles," presented at The First ACM International Workshop on Applications of Mobile Embedded Systems (WAMES'04), Boston, Massachusetts, USA, 2004.

[5] J. Kjeldskov, S. Howard, J. Murphy, J. Carroll, F. Vetere, and C. Graham, "Designing TramMateña Context-Aware Mobile System Supporting Use of Public Transportation," in *Proceedings of the 2003 Conference on Designing for User Experiences*. San Francisco, California, USA: ACM Press, 2003, pp. 1-4.

[6] J. Dowling, R. Cunningham, A. Harrington, E. Curran, and V. Cahill, "Emergent Consensus in Decentralised Systems using Collaborative Reinforcement Learning," in *Post-Proceedings of SELF-STAR: International Workshop on Self-* Properties in Complex Information Systems*, LNCS 3460: Springer-Verlag, 2005, pp. 63-80.

[7] N. Honle, U. Kappeler, D. Nicklaus, T. Schwarz, and M. Grossmann, "Benefits of Integrating Meta Data into a Context Model," in *Proceedings of the Third IEEE International Conference on Pervasive Computing and Communications Workshops*. Pisa, Italy, 2004, pp. 25-29.

[8] O. Lehmann, M. Bauer, C. Becker, and D. Nicklas, "From Home to World - Supporting Context-aware Applications through World Models," in *Proceedings of Second IEEE International Conference on Pervasive Computing and Communications (Percom'04)*. Orlando, Florida: IEEE Computer Society, 2004, pp. 297-308.

[9] M. Roman, C. Hess, R. Cerqueira, A. Ranganathan, R. Campbell, and K. Nahrstedt, "Gaia: A Middleware Infrastructure to Enable Active Spaces," *IEEE Pervasive Computing*, vol. 1, pp. 74-83, 2002.

[10] C. Borcea, C. Intanagonwiwat, P. Kang, U. Kramer, and L. Iftode, " Spatial Programming using Smart Messages: Design and Implementation," in *Proceedings of the Twenty-Fourth IEEE International Conference on Distributed Computing Systems (ICDCS'04)*. Tokyo, Japan, 2004, pp. 690-699.

[11] A. Dey and G. Abowd, "Towards a Better Understanding of Context and Context-Awareness," in *Workshop on The What, Who, Where, When, and How of Context-Awareness, as part of the 2000 Conference on Human Factors in Computing Systems (CHI 2000)*. The Hague, The Netherlands, 2000.

[12] R. Meier, A. Harrington, and V. Cahill, "Audit of ITS Applications and Services in Dublin City," Trinity College, Dublin, Ireland, Dublin City Council iTransIT Deliverable, August 2004.

[13] M. Bauer, C. Becker, and K. Rothermel, "Location Models from the Perspective of Context-Aware Applications and Mobile Ad Hoc Networks," *Personal and Ubiquitous Computing*, vol. 6, pp. 322-328, 2002.

[14] Open GIS Consortium Inc, "OpenGIS Simple Features Specification for SQL, Revision 1.1," OpenGIS Project Document 99-049, 1999.

[15] R. A. P. Bossom, "European ITS Framework Architecture - Communication Architecture, Annex 1: Supporting Information for Communications Analysis," vol. D3.3: European Communities, 2000.

[16] T. F. Fugger, B. C. Randles, A. C. Stein, W. C. Whiting, and B. Gallagher, "Analysis of Pedestrian Gait and Perception–Reaction at Signal-Controlled Crosswalk Intersections," National Research Council, Washington, D.C, USA, Transportation Research Record 1705 TRB 00-1439, 2000.

Mobile Process Description and Execution

Christian P. Kunze, Sonja Zaplata, and Winfried Lamersdorf

Distributed Systems and Information Systems
Computer Science Department, University of Hamburg
Vogt-Kölln-Str. 30, 22527 Hamburg, Germany
{kunze, zaplata, lamersdorf}@informatik.uni-hamburg.de

Abstract. Mobile devices are increasingly aware of their respective locations and vicinity and tend to communicate rather loosely with each other; therefore *asynchronous* communication paradigms are used predominately so far for corresponding mobile applications. However, while such communication mechanisms are suitable for simple activities, they may become insufficient for more complex tasks which consist of longer sequences of related activities tied together in *application-oriented processes*. This is of particular importance if the resulting operating sequence spans several mobile devices in frequently changing vicinities.

Therefore, the work presented here provides a concept for integrating explicit support for such mobile processes into mobile system infrastructures and for distributing their execution over different nodes in the network. For this purpose, a corresponding middleware platform (extension) for context-aware mobile applications is proposed. It supports such migrating processes and helps to execute them under the restrictions typically imposed by realistic mobile applications. In particular, this paper proposes a corresponding *process description language* and an *execution model* for mobile and distributed (business) processes in the context of the project DEMAC (Distributed Environment for Mobility-Aware Computing).

1 Introduction

Due to the constraints of mobile computing environments, mobile systems, in general, cannot provide the same degree of distribution transparency as systems in statically wired environments [4]. Just in contrast to those, the *restrictions of resources* in comparison to static devices, the *increased variability in performance and reliability* of wireless connections, the *finite energy sources* to rely on, and the *hazard of mobility* itself [13] lead to the perception that mobile environments should be aware of the changing vicinity and also should react and adapt to it accordingly.

However, in current systems this so-called context *awareness* and *adaptability* is, in most cases, still restricted to support more or less monolithic and ad-hoc static applications in fulfilling their momentary tasks. In general, that means that most existing middleware systems are rather application centric and thus restricted to offer assistance for basic but rather simple tasks. But, in order to

F. Eliassen and A. Montresor (Eds.): DAIS 2006, LNCS 4025, pp. 32–47, 2006.

approach the vision of pervasive computing [16, 17] more closely, also much more complex and eventually even unknown tasks and thus more generality must be supported by new mobile middleware systems.

Such complex application tasks can be regarded as sequences of related simple tasks tied together in a (business) process which is managed by a mobile client on behalf of a user. This means that a mobile client is required to reach and invoke all the services needed to execute such a process. It must also be capable of handling all intermediate results – regardless of their size and relevance to the expected final output. As a consequence, it may become a single point of failure and also a bottleneck during execution time. Altogether, this means that the capabilities of a mobile client limit the quantity of possible processes to be executed.

But since the user is, in most cases, just interested in some specific effects of a process (and not in its execution or intermediate results), this effect could be eased by transferring the control flow – and with it the whole process – to other devices, if possible. In combination with the possibilities of mobile computing middleware systems to utilise context information and to cooperate, such long-time mobile processes and their distributed execution provide additional efficiency to application process execution in mobile computing. Accordingly, this paper presents an outline of the system platform *Distributed Environment for Mobility-Aware Computing* (DEMAC) – which realises such an extension – with a special focus on a new description language and execution model for such *mobile processes*.

The following subsections of the paper introduce the definition of mobile processes, section 2 addresses related work, and section 3 provides a closer look at the coarse system architecture, the process definition language, and the execution engine. Finally, section 4 concludes the paper with a summary and an outline of future work.

1.1   Integrating Processes into Mobile Computing Systems

The work presented aims to extend the capabilities of mobile devices through cooperation with other devices in their vicinity and thus increase of their potential. This is achieved by integrating distributed (business) processes into an adequate mobile system infrastructure. Such an approach is different to most existing ones of integrating processes with mobile computing devices which just extend their traditional process infrastructure by including mobile device as process participants (cp. e. g. [12]). Accordingly, in our context, the term mobile process is defined and used as followed:

> *A mobile process is a sequence of (remote) services which may last over a longer period of time and span several devices during its execution. The results of the process are the effects the initiator expects from it.*

In traditional mobile middleware, a process executes the application logic by explicitly assigning local or remote services to the processs activities and by invoking them directly. In contrast to that, in our view, such application processes may (partly) diffuse into the mobile middleware: They just form a stub which collects information from the user to assemble the process and its general conditions and to pass the mobile process to the middleware.

In addition, as activities of mobile processes can last very long (like hours, days, or weeks) the changes of the device environment can be dramatic between the executions of adjacent activities. Therefore, a *late binding strategy* to assign services is – certainly – essential but not always sufficient. Consequently, the mobile processes as proposed here are executed based on an *opportunistic strategy*: As long as the process engine of a device is able to bind local or remote services to it's currently activity, it is responsible for the mobile process. However, in cases of failures or lack of respective service instances the engine is able to try to find other devices which are able to execute the mobile process and then transfers the remaining process and its execution to one of them.

Such a process distribution is especially advantageous in (realistic) heterogeneous and frequently changing mobile environments where device capabilities may highly differ. Thus, such process transfer opens up additional services which were not accessible according to the traditional execution approach. This also means that likelihood of a mobile process to be executed successfully increases substantially.

1.2   Requirements for Descriptions of Mobile Processes

In order to describe processes in ways which allow for execution strategies as described above, an abstract process description language has to be designed: In such a view, mobile processes have rather similar requirements for their description as traditional (business) processes, these are among others: the need for the ability to express the *business logic* with its data and control flow, the *participating parties* (as roles or individuals), and routines to recover from *failures* [9].

But they also have some specific requirements based on the nature of mobile environments and the opportunistic and distributed execution strategy (cp. section 1.1): E.g. mobile process descriptions must be lean and simple to process in order to save memory, CPU power, and energy resources, it must also include mechanisms to handle communication failures and the distribution of the process itself. This means especially that the state of the process and the user's non-functional conditions for the execution of the process must be expressible. The (late) binding mechanism to assign service instances to process activities as late as possible must be integrated into the description language by using a preferably very abstract notation of the desired services [13, 7].

Based on these "related work" is briefly reviewed in section 2 and for mobile process description languages in section 3.2.

2   Related Work

Since this paper concentrates specifically on the description and execution of mobile processes, some specific aspects of our approach are pointed out first - before, after that, related work in the area of mobile process descriptions is reviewed more extensively.

System Infrastructure. Since mobile process execution always relies on contextual information, the context modelling and context data acquisition are crucial for the respective developed concept and system infrastructure. The abstract and generic definition of context and its data as used in the *Context Toolkit* [5] by Dey is mainly suited for the mostly a priori unknown demands of mobile processes. Whereas the understanding provided by Schilit [14] or Schmidt [15] turned out to be too narrow to support the wide range of possible processes as required in our approach. The idea of the *NEXUS* project [6] to ensemble the context of an entity by federating local context clippings of entities within particular vicinity is used in the system infrastructure to construct a global context representation efficiently.

The mobile process infrastructure as addressed here also relates to recent research in the area of *mobile agents* [3]. However, in relation to that it differs in some important aspects: In contrast to an agent a mobile process does not contain executable code. In fact, mobile processes only provide meta-data about the structure of the described application and, thus, the estimated effects but not the way how this behaviour is achieved. In addition, they do not have a *social behaviour* either, nor could they act *autonomously* or *proactively*. Nevertheless, some parts, e.g. security and privacy concerns or the need to determine the execution state, have, in principal, similar requirements and, thus, solutions.

Process Description. A process description language for mobile processes has to consider aspects of distribution as well as support for high level flexibility and fault tolerance. An analysis of most prominent existing process description languages, such as *XPDL, BPEL4WS, WSCI, JPDL*, and *ebBPSS*, shows that the concepts and constructs provided by these languages are not in total adequate to describe highly dynamic processes on mobile distributed computing systems [18].

Closest to the required concepts as mentioned above is the meta-model language *XPDL* [10], which was developed as an abstract interchange format for different workflow engines. It provides a very general view on processes, is open for extensions and ready for all kind of automated and manual services. On the other hand, due to its high level of abstraction, it does not provide sufficient concepts to perform distributed process execution and handle errors as well as transactions.

In contrast, *BPEL4WS* [1] as a language for the orchestration of activities defined as web services, offers very specific and powerful elements to link tasks and to deal with unexpected circumstances as well. Processes defined with *BPEL4WS* are ready to be executed but limit cooperations between business partners using the Web Service protocol stack. Furthermore, process descriptions tend to become rather complex due to possible combinations of sequential blocks with graph-structured elements in order to express parallel behaviour. Again, the definition language is developed for running on a central workflow engine and does not provide concepts for distributed process execution.

The *Web Service Choreography Interface* (WSCI) [2] is an add-on of WSDL and concentrates on the choreography of web services by describing a task from the individual perspective of its participating services. Therefore, the description itself is lean because each one is intended for only one single participant. The disadvantage of *WSCI*, however, is that all possible participants have to be determined in advance so the processes' information can be distributed and a fixed compatible interface can be implemented within the *WSDL description* of each participant. Also dynamic processes or ad-hoc workflows as well as often changing vicinities of mobile devices cannot be handled with *WSCI*.

A very lean description language is provided by JPDL [8], which is an integral part of the *Java Business Process Management (JBPM)*. *JPDL* supports manual tasks, but the description of automated function logic is matched to the Java programming language and the composition of web services is not provided at all. For error handling, *JPDL* also relies on the JAVA platform and, therefore, cannot be considered to be totally platform-independent.

EbBPSS is the *Business Process Specification Scheme* of the *EbXML* framework [11]. In particular, it is designed to describe business transactions and therefore it focuses on the aspect of binary collaboration between several companies. Although *EbBPSS* has the ability to describe quality and security issues as fixed requirements for the scheduled cooperation, it depends highly on the ebXML framework which is in itself too complex for most of today's mobile computing systems. Standing alone, it does not support the description of required control flow constructs, such as error handling mechanisms or the possibility to integrate users and different kind of services.

So, in summary, none of the considered approaches supports transfers of process descriptions and allows a completely distributed administration of mobile processes. Late binding of participants is often possible, but there are no adequate concepts to choose participants by their respective quality or by other non-functional criteria. In most cases, the description of activities and their dependencies within the process is very extensive or requires a lot of computing power to work on it. This, however, is not suitable for relatively weak mobile devices. Finally, concepts for handling faults are insufficient for the error-prone mobile computing systems and the handling of connection resets and security issues has not been considered at all since these process description languages have been developed basically for reliable central workflow engines.

3   A Mobile Process Integration Service

These deficiencies of already established approaches for describing mobile processes (cp. section 2) adequately motivate the development of an enhanced description language which fulfils all of the specified requirements. Accordingly, this section presents relevant features such an approach based on (*a*) a process description language for distributed processes and (*b*) a corresponding mobile process execution engine. But as such an engine cannot be realised without an underlying system infrastructure, subsection 3.1 first provides an outline of the middleware architecture as developed for that purpose in the DEMAC project.

3.1   A Middleware Architecture for Supporting Distributed and Mobile Processes

The decision to design a tailored system infrastructure for supporting a seamless integration of mobile processes into a mobile computing middleware evolved from an analysis of the processes' requirements and the respective features as offered by existing middleware approaches. Especially the close cooperation between the mobile processes and the context model to distribute and execute the processes lead to the need of a specifically adjusted model and service architecture.

The resulting system architecture is based on four basic service components (see figure 1) which are briefly described overview before section 3 introduces the integration of mobile processes in more detail.

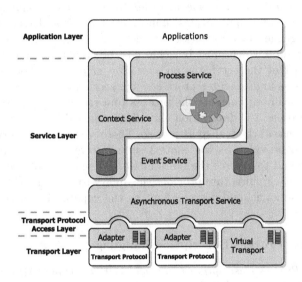

Fig. 1. The DEMAC Abstract Architecture

The Communication Basis. The *asynchronous transport service* and the *event service* form the communication platform of the architecture and provide communication with both push and pull semantics. This service abstracts from concrete transport protocols – like TCP/IP, Bluetooth or IrDA. To be independent from the underpinning protocols, the transport service uses its own addressing schema. These addresses are bound to a device and translated into concrete protocol specific addresses by the transport service. If the device is reachable by different protocols, non-functional aspects, like e.g. quality of service attributes, can be used to make an optimal choice.

The Context Service. The *context service* collects and maintains all information about the context of the device. It acquires its knowledge either by events from the event service or by direct message exchange using the transport service.

Towards the entities which use the service, it filters and partitions the information and provides only the amount of data they need. These are next to quality of service parameters also information about reachable devices and their services, location parameters and data about other users and their identity. To acquire the context information, a *federated approach* is chosen. Every device provides only local context information. To get the overall context, the information of the devices in the environment is merged. To find and resolve devices and services in the vicinity, the context service contains a *distributed registry* which uses peer-to-peer mechanisms to obtain its knowledge.

The Process Service. The *process service* realises the integration of process management into the DEMAC architecture. It is comprised of two parts: The first one is a *definition language* in order to describe the mobile process as well as the users' and applications' non-functional demands (cp. section 3.2). Using this language, an application is able to define a sequence of activities, intermediary results which must be achieved, and constraints for the execution. The second part of the service is an *execution engine* for process definitions. This unit resolves and executes processes (cp. section 3.3). It can either invoke the activities locally or delegate the process to a remote process service. When delegating a process, the description and all necessary data is transferred to the remote unit by use of the transport service. Thereby the process service relies on the information provided by the context service to find a device providing the needed service and to enforce the non-functional demands and constraints. The execution engine's architecture provides the ability to extend a compact core by plugging in functional modules to adapt to the capabilities of the underlying device.

3.2   DEMAC Process Description Language

The *DEMAC Process Description Language*[1] (DPDL) is an XML-based description language to integrate distributed long-time processes into mobile computing systems. *DPDL* follows the meta-description language *XPDL* [10] and inherits the structure and those constructs of XPDL which turned out to be suitable for describing mobile processes.

The basic idea of *DPDL* is to allow a distributed handling of the process over heterogeneous systems. An entire process may be passed on to another device to continue work on the process's tasks. So devices which are not capable of executing a particular task of the process can mark its latest execution state and search for other devices able to carry on at the position established so far. So, by sharing the potential of several mobile devices, this approach increases the likelihood of successful process execution - even under the (generally unstable) conditionals which are typical for mobile devices and applications.

Meta-model and Structure. As shown in figure 2, the basic container for the DPDL process description and all its data is a *Package*. A *Package* contains at

---

[1] http://vsis-www.informatik.uni-hamburg.de/projects/demac/dpdl1.0.xsd

least a single *WorkflowProcess*, which holds all tasks to be worked on (*Activities*) and the control flow as a fixed sequence to execute these tasks. *Activities* can be atomic or can be grouped to simple reusable blocks (*Activity Sets*), to a sequence of activities to be executed as a *Transaction* or to a set of repeatable actions within a *Loop*. Furthermore, an activity can represent an entire *Subprocess*.

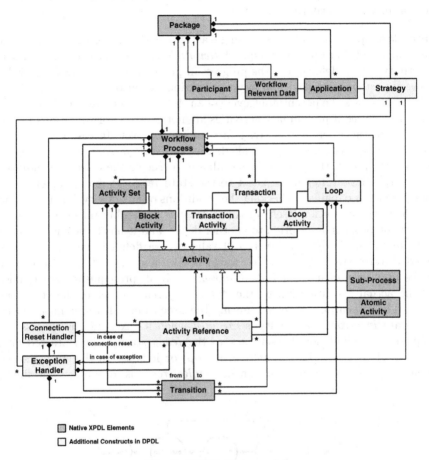

Fig. 2. DPDL Meta-model

To integrate non-functional criteria, the *Package* can also contain definitions of requirements for service qualities or for quality aspects of devices or networks. These requirements are modelled as *Strategies* and can be bound to activities or to the entire process.

To deal with likely occurrences of errors and connection resets DPDL introduces *Exception Handlers* and *Connection Reset Handlers*. These elements refer to another set of activities which should be executed in cases where the normal execution fails.

The introduction of *ActivityReferences* allows reusing the description of activities within the process, for example as a part of several error handling descriptions. *ActivityReferences* are linked by *Transitions* to describe the processes' control flow. *ActivityReferences* are unique within the process. They contain all information which is relevant for the execution of the activity in dependence of its position in the control flow, such as references to participants, error handling and non-functional criteria.

State Concept. The state of each single activity within the process is modelled as a property of its respective unique *ActivityReference*, so the execution state of an activity is well-defined and the progress in processing the activities is visible for every participating device at any time during execution.

Figure 3 shows the potential lifecycle of an *ActivityReference*. An *ActivityReference* is *inactive* if preliminary activities are not executed or conditions for the execution of the referenced activity are not checked yet. In case one or more of these conditions can not be fulfilled, the *ActivityReference* is set to the error state *skipped*. If these conditions evaluate to true or there are no conditions defined, the *ActivityReference* is set to the state *ready*. It may happen that a mobile device is capable of checking the conditions of an activity, but is not able to perform the execution itself. In this case, it will possibly take some time to transfer the process description to another device and it has to be checked close to the execution if the activity is still valid or if a defined expiration date is exceeded (error state *expired*). The states *skipped* and *expired* are also relevant for the appliance of a *Dead Path Elimination*. If all prerequisites are fulfilled and the actual execution starts, the *ActivityReference* is set to the state *executing*. The appearance of errors during the execution will result in a general error state *in error*. An activity is *executed* when its execution is successfully completed. It might now be set back to the *ready* state to be restarted later (for example if the activity is part of a loop) or it is set to the state *finished* which indicates the execution of the *ActivityReference* is terminated and finally closed.

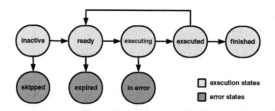

Fig. 3. Possible States of Activities in DPDL

Furthermore, a particular *ActivityReference* can be referenced as a start activity to mark the next task to be executed. This relieves other participating devices of dealing with tasks which have already been finished.

Description of Activities and External Data. Transfer and execution of processes on mobile computing systems also require rather efficient use of the available amount of system memory. This means, one of the most important requirements of mobile processes is to make process descriptions as lean as possible. DPDL allows describing activities as a short but significant identifier and supports to store data external to the actual process. For example, huge documents may be kept completely out of the description until their processing time has arrived. This is particularly suitable if the data is needed only once or is used in very few activities within the process. On the other hand the provision of flexibility is essential in this case because the availability of devices and their connectivity may appear as a bottleneck to the dynamic integration of external features. So, it depends on the kind of application to decide whether or not obtaining data from a remote location.

Listing 1. Description of Data and Activities

```
<DataFields>
    <DataField Id="PaintingName">
        <DataType>
            <BasicType Type="String"/>
        </DataType>
        <InitialValue>Mona Lisa</InitialValue>
    </DataField>
    <DataField Id="NewPainting">
        <DataType>
            <DeclaredType Type="Image"/>
        </DataType>
        <ExternalReference Location="http://www.xyz.com/Very_Large_Image.bmp"/>
    </DataField>
</DataFields>

<Applications>
    <Application Id="Printer">
        <UUID>123456789012345678901234567890012</UUID>
        <FormalParameters>
            <FormalParameter Id="SomeName" Index="1" Mode="IN">
                <DataType>
                    <BasicType Type="String"/>
                </DataType>
            </FormalParameter>
            <FormalParameter Id="SomePicture" Index="2" Mode="IN">
                <DataType>
                    <DeclaredType Id="Image"/>
                </DataType>
            </FormalParameter>
        </FormalParameters>
    </Application>
</Applications>

...

<Activity Id="Print">
    <Implementation>
        <Tool ApplicationId="Printer">
            <ActualParameters>
                <ActualParameter>PaintingName</ActualParameter>
                <ActualParameter>NewPainting</ActualParameter>
            </ActualParameters>
        </Tool>
    </Implementation>
</Activity>
```

Listing 1 shows the declaration of two variables by the use of the *DataField* construct and the definition of the corresponding data. While the content for the variable "PaintingName" can easily be hold within the process description for immediate access, the data item of the type "Image" is represented by an *ExternalReference* in order to save memory and network costs. Furthermore, the generic *Application* "Printer" is abstracted in the example listing by a *universal unique identifier (UUID)* which represents the category of adequate services to execute the respective activity, e.g. printing an image. The data involved in the task, in this case the painting's name and the image data itself, is finally called and mapped to the *Formal Parameters* of the generic *Application*.

Users and Devices. Mobile processes are highly related to tasks which require interaction with mobile participants such as users or devices or a combination of both. Therefore, special constructs are needed to describe which individuals are involved in which task and by what kind of communication channels these persons might be addressed or accessed. In *DPDL*, a participant is either totally specified or described in a generic way, e.g. by the declaration of a certain role. Descriptive properties of users (for example a digital identity) and devices (for example unique identifiers) can be combined to characterize a participant and help finding the required instance to execute the upcoming task (see listing 2).

Listing 2. Participants

```
<Participant Id="Smith" Name="John Smith">
      <Devices>
              <Device Id="111" Name="Personal Computer">
                      <UUID>123456789012345678901234567890 12</UUID>
              </Device>
              <Device Id="222" Name="Mobile Phone">
                      <Devicetype Type="Cellphone"/>
              </Device>
      </Devices>
</Participant>
...
<ActivityRef Id="1" ActivityId="Activity1" ParticipantId="Smith" ... />
```

Handling Errors and Connection Resets. Due to the high incidence of faults appearing in mobile computing systems, DPDL provides constructs to handle errors and unexpected connection resets. The description of *Exception Handlers* provides a definition of alternative control flow constructs to be executed when an error occurs. In case of a connection reset, the communication may be either restarted, the service partner may be changed, or the activity may

Listing 3. Connection Reset Handler

```
<ConnectionResetHandler Id="1">
      <ExceptionId>someException</ExceptionId>
      <Retries>2</Retries>
      <NewSearch>true</NewSearch>
</ConnectionResetHandler>
...
<ActivityRef Id="1" ActivityId="Activity1" ConnectionResetHandlerId="1" ... />
```

be skipped. The actual behaviour depends on the involved applications and the specific use-case and can also be modelled as a combination of activities (see listing 3).

Parallel Execution. In case there is no relevant data dependency within the control flow, parallel paths of the process can be executed by different mobile computing systems. To share a process description, the responsible mobile device decides to execute an arbitrary parallel path and thereby sets its first *ActivityReference* to the state *executing*. While in this state, it produces a snapshot of the process description as a copy of its own process and forwards this copy to exactly one other device. Because the path chosen by the first device is already in the state *executing*, the second device can only select one of the remaining parallel paths.

In order to synchronize parallel paths, there has to be a defined meeting point, for example a stationary device. The participating devices can pass their copies of the process description to the given address. The service at the meeting point collects all incoming parallel paths belonging to the shared identifier and merges the copies to a single process description. If required, this one can be forwarded again to continue execution.

Modification of Activities. In order to provide a maximum of flexibility, the description considers the possibility that activities may be modified throughout the execution of the process. For example, the single activity "Send a new text by e-mail" may be substituted by a more detailed *Activity Set* containing the two activities "Write text" and "Send e-mail". If no suitable service for executing the entire task can be found, other services may cooperate to compensate this lack of capability by executing intermediate steps. However, to control the amount of modification the initiator of the process can protect activities against unintentional changes by using suitable values for the Activity's *Editable* attribute. For example, the activity may be declared not editable at all, or the modifications might be further restricted by the definition of non-functional criteria, such that no semantically dependent activity can be substituted without compromising the overall correctness of the process.

The responsibility for exchanging or modifying activities resides with the context service which decides whether or not the upcoming task can be executed locally. The necessary knowledge about semantic equivalence of services and their exchangeability or possible reconfiguration is kept by the distributed registry as part of the federated context services of all vicinal devices (cp. section 3.1).

Integration of Non-functional Criteria. To narrow the selection of potentially participating devices and services according to the user's interests and intentions, the process description may contain a set of non-functional criteria. The user who initiated a process can define a *Strategy* to assert a certain level of quality throughout the execution of the process. This way, *Strategies* help to ensure the user's goals as they were intended originally. Each *Strategy* contains a set of requirements which each hold a key-value-pair consisting of an identification argument and a target value. Listing 4 shows, exemplarily, how to define a limitation of the factor "cost" for the execution of a certain activity.

Listing 4. Description of non functional Criteria

```
<Strategy Id="123" Name="ActivityStrategy">
    <StrategyProperty Id="1" Name="Cost">
        <Requirements>
            <Requirement Name="MaxNetworkCost" Value="10"/>
            <Requirement Name="MaxServiceCost" Value="0"/>
        </Requirements>
    </StrategyProperty>
</Strategy>
...
<ActivityRef Id="1" ActivityId="TestActivity1" StrategyId="123"/>
```

Before executing an activity with specific requirements, the context service has to collect the relevant quality information, so the process service can ensure that only those services and devices are involved in the activity's execution which meets the specified requirements.

3.3   Mobile Process Execution

Depending on their intended purpose, mobile devices can have many different properties and a wide range of capabilities. To integrate most mobile devices and to benefit from the collaboration of heterogeneous systems, the mobile process execution engine must support different levels of performance.

Therefore, the execution engine is characterized by a modular design (cp. figure 4). A *Core Module* provides basic functionality such as receiving, storing, and forwarding process descriptions. It can be run independently on less powerful devices, like PDAs or cellphones, which do not provide enough memory or computing power to execute complex tasks but are useful to transport the process descriptions to other (different) environments. The core module also provides the interface for applications to initiate processes by passing the *DPDL* process description to the execution engine.

A more powerful *Base Module* is responsible for executing the described tasks of the process. It uses the core component to communicate with other devices and can be enhanced by further task-specific Extension Modules. *Extension Modules* are strongly dependent on the characteristics of the device, for example, an additional component supporting user interaction can only be realised if the respective device has a proper user interface.

The complete set of all installed components together with the DPDL description of mobile processes realises the *DEMAC process service*, which can have different combinations of execution modules, as shown in figure 4.

Finally, the mobile process execution engine cooperates closely with the *DEMAC context service* in order to get information about the device's vicinity, such as available services, environmental data or its own identity. If a new process description is received by the core module, the process data is made

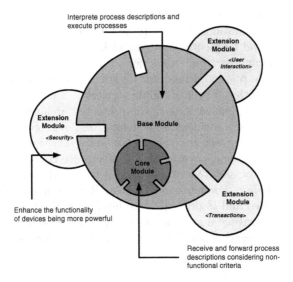

Fig. 4. Modular Execution Engine for Mobile Processes

persistent and the process's *Strategies* are extracted from the *Package*. In case there is no base module attached or the proper component to execute the process locally is missing, the *context service* is requested to find a device suitable to the specified constraints to continue the execution. Otherwise, the execution engine within the responsible mobile device starts working on the process itself. It picks the upcoming *Start Activity*, examines it and requests the context service to find suitable services to process the task, depending on the defined *Participants*, *Strategies* and/or *Conditions* of this activity. If an adequate service for executing the upcoming activity cannot be found, the local execution engines marks the latest execution state, stops working on the process and again requests to find an alternative device to continue. This way, sharing the different properties and potentials of context aware mobile computing systems even complex and long-time processes can be executed in a step-by-step-manner.

4   Conclusion

This paper describes an approach to make mobile computing middleware platforms capable of supporting abstract descriptions as well as new execution models of *mobile distributed long-term business processes*. Due to (*a*) distributed and cooperative nature of such processes and (*b*) restrictions and specific characteristic of mobile computing environments, already existing description languages and execution models for centrally coordinated processes do not suffice. Therefore, an extended, technology independent *description language* is proposed and a corresponding *execution platform* and its realisation are described in this paper.

Thus, the paper presents the *DEMAC Process Description Language* which extends the XPDL meta-model by concepts for distributing and executing processes in mobile and frequently changing vicinities. It also describes the prototype realisation of an *execution engine* for such mobile processes. Thereby the paper argues that the presented modular design is able to support most of the heterogeneous capabilities of typical mobile devices.

As a prototypical implementation of the presented architecture has been realised already, future work includes implementation – on top of this platform – some of the project's use cases and sample scenarios. These include, e.g., a prototype of a *claim manager application* for an insurance company which creates customised mobile processes out of a template base and executes them using the DEMAC middleware. Furthermore, the overall performance of the system is continuously evaluated and improved. More fundamental questions arise in the fields of integrating privacy and security mechanisms as well as developing an adequate transaction concept for distributed and mobile processes.

References

1. Andrews, Tony and Curbera, Francisco and Dholakia, Hitesh and Goland, Yaron and Klein, Johannes and Leymann, Frank and Liu, Kevin and Roller, Dieter and Smith, Doug and Thatte, Satish and Trickovic, Ivana and Weerawarana, Sanjiva. Business Process Execution Language for Web Services Version 1.1. Specification, IBM, BEA Systems, Microsoft, SAP AG, Siebel Systems, 2003.
2. Arkin, Assaf and Askary, Sid and Fordin, Scott and Jekeli, Scott and Kawaguchi, Scott and Orchard, David and Pogliani, Stefano and Riemer, Karsten and Struble, Susan and Takacsi-Nagy, Pal and Trickovic, Ivana and Zimek, Sinisa. Web Service Choreography Interface (WSCI) 1.0. Specification NOTE-wsci-20020808, World Wide Web Consortium, 2002.
3. Braun, Peter and Rossak, Wilhelm. *Mobile Agents - Basic Concepts, Mobility Models, and the Tracy Toolkit.* Elsevier and Morgan Kaufmann and dpunkt.verlag, 2005.
4. Capra, Licia and Emmerich, Wolfgang and Mascolo, Cecilia. Middleware for Mobile Computing: Awareness vs. Transparency. In *In Proceedings of the 8th Workshop on Hot Topics in Operating Systems*, 2001. extended version.
5. Dey, Anind K. Understanding and Using Context. *Personal and Ubiquitous Computing Journal*, 5(1):4–7, 2001.
6. Dürr, Frank and Hönle, Nicola and Nicklas, Daniela and Becker, Christian and Rothermel, Kurt. Nexus–A Platform for Context-Aware Applications. In Roth, Jörg, editor, *1. Fachgespräch Ortsbezogene Anwendungen und Dienste der GI-Fachgruppe KuVS*, 2004.
7. Forman, Georg H. and Zahorjan, John. The Challenges of Mobile Computing. Technical Report TR-93-11-03, University of Woshington, 3 1994.
8. JBoss Company. JBoss jBPM 3.0 - Workflow and BPM made practical. Documentation, JBoss Company, 2005.
9. Leymann, Frank and Roller, Dieter. *Production Workflow - Concepts and Techniques*. PTR Prentice Hall, 2000.
10. Norin, Roberta and Marin, Mike. Workflow Process Definition Interface – XML Process Definition Language. Specification WFMC-TC-1025, Workflow Management Coalition, 2002.

11. Riemer, K. EbBPSS Business Process Specification Schema, Version 1.01. Specification, Oasis ebXML Business Process Project Team, 2001.
12. SAP AG. SAP Mobile Infrastructure: An Open Platform for Enterprise Mobility. Technical report, SAP AG, 2003.
13. Satyanarayanan, Mahadev. Fundamental Challenges in Mobile Computing. In *Proceedings of the Fifteenth ACM Symposium on Principles of Distributed Computing,* 1996.
14. Schilit, Bill N. and Adams, Norman and Want, Roy . Context-Aware Computing Applications. In *Proceedings of the 1st International Workshop on Mobile Computing Systems and Applications*, pages 85–90, 1994.
15. Schmidt, Albrecht and Beigl, Michael and Gellersen, Hans-W. There is more to Context than Location. In *Proceedings of the International Workshop on Interactive Applications of Mobile Computing*, 1998.
16. Weiser, Mark. The Computer for the Twenty-First Century. *Scientific American,* 256(3):94–104, 1991.
17. Weiser, Mark. Ubiquitous Computing. *IEEE Computer Hot Topics*, 1993.
18. Zaplata, Sonja. Prozessintegration in Middleware für mobile Systeme. Master's thesis, University of Hamburg, 2005.

An Application Framework for Nomadic, Collaborative Applications

James O'Brien and Marc Shapiro

INRIA Rocquencourt, France and LIP6, Paris, France
james@jaimz.org, marc.shapiro@acm.org
www.jaimz.org

Abstract. To maintain availability and responsiveness, mobile applications sharing data often work on their own copy and transmit local changes to other participants. Existing systems for recording, transmitting and reconciling concurrent changes are usually ad-hoc and specific to particular applications. In contrast, we present Joyce; a general application programming framework for creating highly dynamic mobile, collaborative applications. The framework abstracts application semantics using an action-constraint formal model and provides communication and consistency services based on this model. The framework exposes an interface that allows application programmers to concentrate on core functionality without worrying about these issues. Applications made with the framework can run seamlessly across changing combination of devices, users and synchrony. We discuss the principles behind the framework, its implementation and evaluate its utility by creating a complex, shared application.

1 Introduction

Today's computing environment is increasingly nomadic; applications run on laptops and devices that are not geographically fixed, and it is increasingly collaborative; applications are often used concurrently by more than one person or device. Such an environment is characterized by a high degree of change in the number of participants, change in connectivity between those participants, and change in the synchrony of collaboration. Programmers need tools to create good collaborative, nomadic applications: applications that adapt to mobility, adopt a collaborative posture and retain the richness and control of desktop applications.

The major difficulty with such applications is maintaining the consistency of shared data. Commonly used application architectures, for example Model-View-Controller [Krasner 88], implicitly assume that data is modified by one user using one device. Many applications fail to benefit from collaboration and mobility due to the prohibitive cost of re-architecting to take account of concurrency control issues.

Certain classes of application, for example *personal information managers*, are designed specifically to be shared between mobile devices. The techniques used however, are specific to the domain of the application and intrusive to the application logic. Moreover, most of these applications use some form of lock-step synchronisation which requires the user's intervention. Finally, the concurrency control wheel tends to be reinvented with each application, extending development

F. Eliassen and A. Montresor (Eds.): DAIS 2006, LNCS 4025, pp. 48–63, 2006.

time and resulting in segregated, incompatible systems. This is not an approach that scales well to general application construction and the increasing popularity of pervasive, mobile computing is likely to underscore its shortcomings.

Functionality time-consuming to implement and common between different applications is usually encapsulated in an *application framework*. An application framework is designed to handle the logic common to all applications sharing a particular aspect: for example Apple's Cocoa framework [Cocoa] handles interaction with the windowing system for graphical desktop applications. Frameworks differ from libraries in that applications using them exhibit an *inversion of control* [Schmidt 00]; it is the framework logic, rather than the application logic that controls the execution of the application process.

In this paper we describe an application framework called *Joyce* that introduces a new programming pattern for highly dynamic, collaborative applications and provides an implementation of that pattern. Joyce enables applications to run across changing combinations of devices, changing combinations of users, and changing combinations of synchrony. We describe what we believe are the current and future requirements of collaborative, nomadic applications and why current techniques do not meet these requirements, we then go on to explain the principles behind our system and describe a realistic application, "Babble", created to evaluate the system.

2 Requirements

Applications created with our framework must meet the following expectations:

- *We expect to be mobile and only occasionally connected*: the applications will be used concurrently by a mixture of users on a mixture of devices. Devices may transition between on-line and off-line at any time so we cannot assume constant connectivity or a complete knowledge of the collaborative group membership. We also cannot assume any particular physical device configuration (e.g. local storage).
- *We expect nomadic, collaborative applications to be as rich as current single-user, single-device applications*: the applications must be at least as responsive and featureful as current desktop applications and will preferably exhibit improvements in usability.
- *We expect to be fully aware of group activity but we do not expect to be bound to a distracting WYSIWIS environment*: these environments (**W**hat **Y**ou **S**ee **I**s **W**hat **I** **S**ee) attempt to keep the application display of each participant precisely in sync. Where such a scheme is necessary (conferencing applications for example) we expect the framework to allow us to build it. However, in applications where real-time collaboration is not the objective, WYSIWYS produces a display that constantly distracts the user from his local task. This leads to a feeling of loss of control which in turn leads to application usability lower than the single-user equivalent; as we have already stated, this is unacceptable. We expect to be continuously *aware* of group activity but also in *control* of how and when the activity is applied.
- *We expect to be aware of the group history of the application state and we expect a manipulatable history that works well in collaborative environments*: projects such as FlatLand [Edwards et al. 00] and GINA [Berlage et al. 93] have demonstrated the benefits of manipulatable history but current implementations of undo/redo in a collaborative environment are complex and application specific. [Sun 02].

To meet these expectations and remain generic the framework needs to be adaptable across two major criteria. Firstly, the framework must be able to cope with different degrees of *coupling* between the participants [Berlage et. al. 93]. Coupling is the degree of co-ordination between participants. For example, when syncing mobile devices all the devices involved are connected and they all receive each other's updates at the same time. In contrast, collaborative systems can fall anywhere between same place/same time systems where collaborators work "shoulder-to-shoulder", to different place/different time systems where collaborators may be dispersed across time zones. We should be able to use the framework to build applications anywhere within this spectrum.

Secondly, any concurrency control system is closely linked to the semantics of the object being shared [Munson et al. 96]. In traditional database systems this semantic is one of read/write operations to some storage. This was found to be too restrictive and techniques were developed to expose a richer set of semantics based on the programmatic interface of the shared data structures [Munson et. al. 96][Schwarz et. al. 84]. This allows more concurrent activity by more narrowly defining what constitutes a conflict. From a user's perspective however, a modification has more semantics than can be expressed solely in data structure interfaces; our framework must be able to express higher-level application semantics and user intentions.

From these general requirements we developed a more concrete list of problems to be moved from the domain of the application to the domain of our framework:

1. **Modeling activity:** Joyce should provide an application-agnostic way of representing concurrency semantics that is rich enough to articulate object, application and user-level semantics.
2. **Communicating activity:** The framework should ensure that, even with partial connectivity, modifications from one participant will propagate to all the others.
3. **Consistency:** Joyce must provide an application-agnostic mechanism for bringing diverging, replicated states to consistency, concurrent with the user modifying that state.

In satisfying these problems it is vital that Joyce not degrade the performance and responsiveness of the application.

2.1 Previous Work

An early approach to concurrency control was simply to acquire a lock on a piece of data before modifying it, the data being stored at some central location. If the lock could not be acquired then the application either blocked until the lock was available or failed. Many early research systems were based around a locking mechanism called floor-control [Sarin et al. 85] in which one participant modified the shared object while the others observed, waiting their turn. This approach has the advantage of simplicity and is still used in web-based collaborative systems such as Wiki [Wiki] and JotSpot [JotSpot]. However, locking has proven problematic for mobile applications since it requires a constant connection to the central data store, and even if a connection is present an application may spend a great deal of time blocked until a lock becomes available.

The DistView [Prakash et al. 94] framework used replicated lock tables to prevent blocking becoming too great a hindrance and the GroupKit [Roseman et al. 96] system allowed operations on shared data whilst a lock was pending; if the lock request was refused the operations were undone. The concept of *tickle locks* [Greif et al. 86] was developed to minimise the amount of time waiting on a lock - essentially the requester would 'tickle' the participant holding the lock and, if there was no response, the lock would be transferred.

Even with these improvements, locking proved restrictive and lead to awkward interaction as applications either blocked or backed-out failed changes. Instead, mobile applications often adopt an *optimistic replication* scheme [Saito et al. 05] in which each participant takes a local replica of the shared state and modifies that replica without regard to concurrent changes from other applications. At some later point all the replicas are synchronised to produce a common state. The technique is termed optimistic since the applications 'optimistically' assume that their local changes will not conflict with concurrent changes at other replicas. This is the approach used in our framework since local states require no locking and the applications can remain responsive.

The dOPT algorithm of Ellis and Gibbs [Ellis et al. 89] introduced *operational transform* (OT) in which remote operations are 're-written' so that their effect locally is the same as their effect where they were issued, regardless of any local operations that have happened in the mean time. OT has proven particularly popular in real-time collaborative text editing systems such as ShrEdit [McGuffin et al 92], Grove [Ellis et al 88] and SubEtherEdit [SubEtherEdit].

The use of OT leads to very responsive applications but the technique is more a mechanism to maintain consistency despite out-of-order messaging than a synchronisation mechanism. Moreover, although the technique itself is generic, OT implementations are usually application specific and very complex. The semantics of an operation is obfuscated by the transform and often lost entirely if an incoming operation has to be transformed against many prior operations. If a history mechanism (such as undo/redo) is required this leads to further application-specific complexity [Sun 02]. There are also known scenarios where current OT techniques may lead to an inconsistent state [Li 04]. Finally, OT is intended primarily for real-time, synchronous editing systems rather than multi-synchronous, occasionally-connected systems.

Bayou [Edwards 97] introduced several mechanisms that support multi-synchronous distributed applications. Bayou is a log-based optimistic replication system that models operations using a read/write semantic augmented with application-defined conflict detection and resolution mechanisms. Operations are communicated using an epidemic propagation scheme that guarantees updates from one participant will reach all the others given sufficient connectivity [Demers 87]. Bayou has good solutions for maintaining communication in the face of occasional connectivity but forces applications to adhere to the limited read/write semantic.

Although concurrency control has been studied extensively and many techniques have been developed we find none of the principles and algorithms suitable to be integrated into the general application development cycle. Either the techniques are too application specific (as with OT), do not work in a multi-synchronous environment (as with floor-control) or do not wholly express application and user semantics (as with Bayou).

3   The Multi-log

Joyce is a programming framework built around an operation-based replication and collaboration system designed specifically for applications operating in the kind of dynamic environment described in section 1. Joyce connects participants working on replicated copies of shared data and distributes the modifications made by one participant to all the others. It allows participants to disconnect and reconnect without loss of information or responsiveness; an application can continue to run while disconnected and modifications will be propagated to it on reconnection.

The core data-structure used by Joyce is a distributively maintained, shared, semantic data-store: the *multi-log*. The multi-log is designed to provide a fine-grained model of activity within a collaborative group, based on a reified model of application semantics. It is a graph structure in which vertices represent data modifications made by applications and edges represent the semantics of those modifications in terms of invariant relations that must hold between them. The framework is responsible for synchronising both the multi-log and the replicated states.

3.1   Basic Definitions

We define a *data object* as the distinguishable unit of data that is being shared, this may be anything from a calendar to a document to a database. Each data object has an associated *group* which is the set of all nodes working on replicated copies of that data object; a node being some application process that is modifying the data. It is possible that the members of the group may change from one moment to the next as may the connectivity between members. We cannot require that any member have a complete knowledge of all the others but we do provide a mechanism that any one node can use to discover a peer group – the subset of the group that can be contacted. The framework ascertains the peer group either by broadcasting an announcement and listening for replies or by joining an application-level multicast tree [Castro et al. 02] corresponding to the shared object.

3.2   Modeling Application Activity

Joyce defines an action/constraint formalism that allows applications to define a fine grained model of their concurrency semantics, at both the object and user level.

Following the command pattern [Gamma et. al. 95], Joyce applications are architected primarily as a set of commands that modify a particular kind of data object. Command invocations are recorded in an application log as a series of *actions*. Joyce also records a set of *constraints* that describe the semantics of the modification that the command invocation was part of. These constraints are guaranteed to be preserved by the framework.

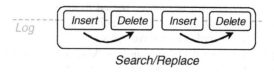

Search/Replace

Fig. 1. Joyce logs modifications with their semantics. A text editor may model search and replace as insert and delete actions that are ordered and atomic.

A requirement outlined in 2.1 is that the framework be able to represent both object and application-level semantics; this is achieved by defining *object* and *log constraints*. Object constraints represent semantic invariants between *classes* of commands, and by extension the data object that those commands are designed to modify, whereas log constraints express invariants between actions that share a log. Log constraints are used to express user intent and application semantics and stand in contrast with previous systems where only the chronological order of operations is recorded [Petersen et al. 1997]. The set of object and log constraints have been derived from those constraints that have proven expressive in our previous work on reconciliation. Readers interested in the motivation behind these constraints are advised to consult [Kermarrec 01] and [Preguiça et al. 03].

3.3 Modeling Group Activity

The multi-log is a semantic graph formed by processing individual application logs. Vertices in the multi-log are actions and edges represent the constraints between them. Edges are placed between actions from differing source logs to indicate that a modification from one peer is dependant on or mutually exclusive with a modification from another. In this way we create a picture of the activity within a group that is independent of the chronology of the actions. Instead of trying to use timestamps to derive dependency information we use the invariants expressed in the multi-log semantic graph.

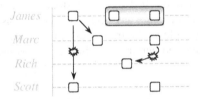

Fig. 2. This multi-log describes a semantic graph containing an ordering constraint, two conflicts and a parcel

It is a vital task of the framework to keep the multi-log on each node as representative of group activity as possible. To achieve this, the multi-log is distributively maintained using an epidemic propagation scheme [Demers 87]. Epidemic propagation is well known to exhibit good behaviour in the face of varying connectivity since a node's updates may still propagate through intermediaries even if that node is no longer connected [Demers 87].

3.4 State Consistency

Problem 3 in section 2.1 requires Joyce to have a method of bringing divergent states to consistency. To achieve this, we provide a reconciliation engine, based on our previous IceCube engine, that can calculate a consistent subset of actions from the multilog. A consistent subset of actions is one in which no actions conflict and all the constraints in the subset are satisfied. IceCube treats this as an optimisation problem: each action has an associated weight indicating how important the action is; the

IceCube algorithm heuristically determines the subset of actions from the multi-log such that the total value of the actions not in the set is minimised.

The consistent subset produced by the reconciliation engine forms a *schedule* a sequenced ordering of actions that may be selected for *commitment*. Commitment is the act of irrevocably selecting a reconciliation schedule for execution at every member in order to make their replicated states consistent. The schedules that have been committed are recorded in a special multi-log entry called the *commit log* which consists of commit and abort meta-actions that reference actions in the multi-log.

A node that generates commit-log updates is called a *primary* and there is usually only one per Joyce group. By default, Joyce assigns the creator of a data object to be the primary for that object, but other mechanisms, for example consensus mechanisms [Lamport 98] may be used. Epidemic propagation ensures commit log updates arrive at all nodes in the right order and eventual consistency is reached.

3.5 Multi-log Persistence

The traditional file system storage model is cumbersome when applied to nomadic, collaborative applications. Nomadic devices may not have local storage and continuous connection to a file server is not feasible. Joyce provides an automatic persistence service wherein one or more *storage nodes* join a collaborative group and persist the multi-log to backing store.

Joyce applications take snapshots of their data at specific times. A snapshot is most often taken when a state has reached some milestone in the editing process or when the framework detects that the state has been brought to consistency. Taking a snapshot of the consistent state allows the framework to truncate the multi-log by removing the committed and aborted actions - all future actions can be issued against the consistent snapshot.

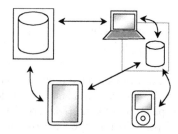

Fig. 3. A Joyce group containing two storage nodes: a 'server' node and a laptop running its own node

If a group member disconnects or crashes the act of re-joining the group, and re-contacting the storage node, restores the application state with a minimum of data loss.

4 Application Model

Joyce provides a skeleton architecture designed to foster applications that meet the expectations outlined in section 2. The key principle of the architecture is that the user interacts with a *local view* of the global activity which is as responsive as a corresponding single-user application would be. The user should feel in full control of this local view and not overwhelmed by group activity.

The multi-log is the history of the global activity within a collaborative group. The local view is a *projection* of a subset of this global history. The framework maintains a consistent subset of actions from the multi-log, the *active subset*, that is run against some base application state to generate the local view.

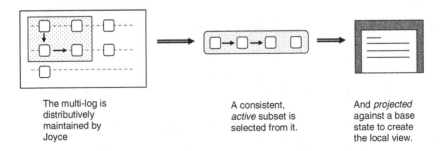

The multi-log is distributively maintained by Joyce

A consistent, *active* subset is selected from it.

And *projected* against a base state to create the local view.

Fig. 4. The local application is a projection of the global history

The active subset contains two kinds of action: actions that have been committed by the primary and a consistent subset of *tentative actions* - actions generated locally or remotely that have not yet been committed or aborted. It is by manipulating which actions are included in this tentative set that the user and application controls what appears in the local view.

The framework is designed to keep the local view responsive by adding locally generated actions to the active subset immediately, implementing undo/redo as local operations and filtering incoming updates to determine which should appear in the active subset.

4.1   The Tentative Interaction Cycle

To reflect local modifications quickly, the architecture populates the active subset using an interaction cycle derived from the Model-View-Controller pattern [Krasner 88]. An interaction cycle is the programmatic path between a user triggering a local modification and the result of that modification being reflected in the application output. MVC introduced a cycle in which input from the user is evaluated by a controller into a set of modification messages for the model; the model applies the modifications and sends a set of update messages to the view which reflects the modification back to the user.

This pattern simplifies the construction of GUI applications but assumes that modifications always come from a local (i.e. in-process) controller; and inversely that modifications from the controller are always for the local model. The pattern also has the more subtle assumption that the local controller is the authoritative source of the modifications - it has no notion of a global state that might be defined elsewhere.

We expand MVC by introducing a *coordinator* component, whose job is to maintain the active subset and apply it to the model. During our interaction cycle (figure 5)

user input is evaluated into a set of actions and constraints; these are sent to the coordinator, which logs them in the multi-log and immediately includes them in the active subset - causing them to be applied to the model and reflected in the view. We call this the *tentative interaction cycle* since the actions applied to the state are local, tentative actions.

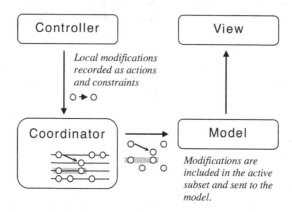

Fig. 5. The tentative interaction cycle in Joyce. The controller generates modifications and sends them to the coordinator for execution and logging.

When an update to the multi-log arrives, the coordinator interrupts this cycle to recalculate the active set. It uses the reconciler to create a consistent schedule from the updated pool of tentative actions in the multi-log, which becomes the new active subset. Note that this reconciliation has no effect on the globally consistent state as defined by the commit log - it is local to the receiving node.

If the multi-log update includes a commit log update, the aborted actions and their dependants are removed from the tentative action pool and the active subset is prepopulated with the committed actions before the local reconciliation occurs.

The actions in the active subset are recorded relative to a base state, usually a snapshot of a previous stable state. To apply a new active subset, Joyce restores the base state, then runs the new active subset against it. The schedule produced by the reconciler is guaranteed to respect ordering constraints and so can be executed sequentially.

4.2 Filtering, Undo and Redo

A user can define which applications are included in his active subset by defining *filters* over the set of tentative actions in the multi-log. A filter is simply a predicate that pre-excludes matching tentative actions from a reconciled schedule. This prevents the coordinator including the filtered action and its dependants in the active subset.

The simplest example of filtering is masking out specific collaborators. Here, the filter matches every action from a particular source. Actions from the source will not be accepted into the active subset and thus will not contribute to the local state. It is important to note that filtering does not remove actions from the multi-log, just from the tentative action set. All information about group activity is retained, an important expectation (section 2). Later, the filter may be removed, allowing the previously masked work to be reintegrated into the view.

Undo is implemented as a filter that masks out a specific action. To undo a modification the user selects the action and creates the filter; when the active subset is recalculated it will be equal to the previous active subset less the undone action and its dependants (those actions that are parceled with or strong ordered after it). If subsequent remote actions arrive that are dependant on the undone action the process ensures those actions will not appear in the active subset.

Since constraint information is used to calculate the dependants, undo in Joyce is selective. The undo operation is confined only to those operations directly effected [O'Brien 04] and the corresponding redo can be done at any time if no intermediate arrivals conflict with the undone action. This contrasts with the stack-like, linear model used in most applications.

5 An Example Application: Babble

To refine Joyce for real-world development we created a free-flow collaborative editor called *Babble*. A text editor is complex enough to exercise the whole framework but familiar enough that the contributions of Joyce are well highlighted; particularly fluid collaboration, selective undo/redo and passive storage.

When 'opening' a file in Babble, Joyce discovers and joins the collaborative group for the document, restores the most recent snapshot it can find and brings the local multi-log up to date. Babble is then notified of the reconstructed state and the local interaction cycle can begin.

Edits from collaborators can be "tagged": on mouse-over we can display context information about the edit taken directly from the multi-log.

Fig. 6. Babble will synchronise to the current group state on start-up

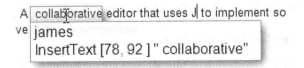

Fig. 7. A tagged edit

If concurrent edits conflict, Joyce will choose an edit for Babble to apply and instruct Babble to highlight the effected content with a red shading. In keeping with the local view principle, Joyce will chose local edits over remote ones unless specifically instructed otherwise.

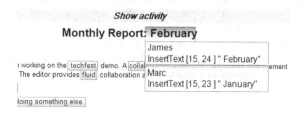

Fig. 8. Viewing a conflict

Active subset manipulation (that is, selective undo, redo and filtering) is triggered through a *history editor*. Actions are arranged in the editor according to character position and dependencies. In the figure below, the action in the second column has a dependency on the action in the first. Selecting the first column action also highlights the second-column action and the modifications that both actions made are highlighted in the content display. In this way the user can visualize the extent of a prospective undo.

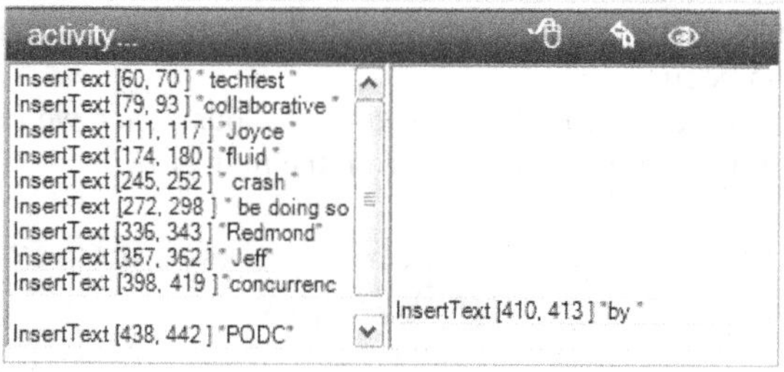

Fig. 9. The history editor

Since this representation can be confusing in a large document the history editor may be set to display only the *local history* – the history at the current carat position.

The history editor may also display higher-level operations such as a search-and-replace, which is implemented as a parcel of inserts and deletes. Selection of the constraint representation also selects its constituent actions. When an undo is triggered a filter is placed on the selected actions, the active set is recalculated, and the results displayed. The effect on the content is that the highlighted content modifications have been undone but the modifications of non-dependant actions remain in place.

5.1 Representing Text Editing in Joyce

Applications built with Joyce are architected as a collection of *actions* that implement the application commands and *constraints* that represent the concurrency semantics of those commands. To implement Babble we needed a set of actions and constraints that encapsulated text editing.

Text editors are usually built around a linear character buffer addressed using character coordinates from 0 (before the first character) to N (after the last character). Two operations modify this buffer: *insert(p, c)*, that inserts character *c* at position *p*, and *delete(p, n)* that removes a range of *n* characters starting at position *p*. Most shared text editors are built around the same structure but use *operational transforms* to rewrite remote inserts and deletes such that their local effect is the same as their effect at their source. Essentially, the edit points of inserts and the edit points and spans of deletes are shifted in order to compensate for operations that have been applied to the local state. This gives good performance in distributed, real-time editing but is complex to implement, especially if multi-synchrony and undo-redo are required, intrinsic qualities of Joyce applications.

Babble borrows the idea of translating edit points from OT but uses a more systematic approach that meets the requirements of the Joyce framework. Our representation of a text buffer is more complex than a simple character array but captures the dependencies between edits and allows us to show, hide, re-combine and re-order editing operations as directed by Joyce.

The representation is in three parts:

1. **The content:** a linear text buffer similar to that used by non-concurrent and OT editors. However, with the exception of snap-shots and undo/redo, characters are only ever inserted into the buffer, not removed.
2. **The mask:** a collection of character position intervals that indicates deleted text. Masked text is not displayed and therefore cannot be edited.
3. **The history:** a hierarchical collection of character position intervals that record the operations that have been applied to the content.

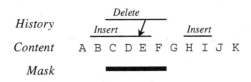

Fig. 10. Babble represents a text buffer in three layers. This buffer is displayed as ABGHIJK.

The actions defined by Babble are:

1. **Insert (p, s):** insert the string s into the content at position p.
2. **Delete (p, a):** insert a mask of length a into the mask structure at position p.

To define constraints, we say that one Insert must follow another if the edit point of the second intersects the span of the first. A Delete must follow another Delete *or* Insert if the spans of the two actions intersect. This is recorded in the history and communicated to Joyce using *ordering* log constraints. In the buffer depicted below there have been two inserts and two deletes and the appropriate constraints have been set.

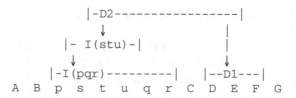

Fig. 11. Ordering constraints are set in the history and multi-log according to the intersections of operation spans

Note that ordering constraints are transitive in Joyce so there is no need to set a constraint from D2 to I(pqr).

5.2 Replaying Out-of-Order Changes

Babble is required to be able to replay local and remote operations in any order, since they may be recombined in any consistent order by the Joyce reconciler when the active subset is calculated.

When replaying an action, Babble uses the history to detect whether the action being replayed needs to be transformed. The replay mechanism uses the history structure to keep track of the mutations to the content: i.e. where content has been inserted. When an action is replayed out of order, its edit point is shifted according to the mutations that have happened to the content since that action was first issued. For example, if an action at site A inserts text of length 3 at position 2 then receives an action b from a remote site that inserts text at position 4, then the edit point of b is shifted to take account of the local action. The mask data structure allows us to apply the same mechanism to deletes since no content is actually removed.

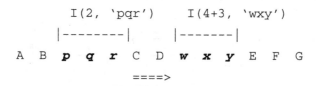

Fig. 12. Remote action I(4, 'wxy') is shifted due to a prior mutation in the content

When comparing local and remote edits, Babble will raise a conflict if the edit points of two insertions are identical or the span of a delete intersects with another delete or the edit point of another insert. The conflict is expressed to Joyce with a *mutual exclusivity* constraint and highlighted in the user interface as above.

6 Summary and Future Work

Joyce is a programming framework that provides three main contributions: a clearly defined idea of what collaborative, nomadic applications should be, a systematic model for creating such applications and an implementation of the principles and mechanisms described in the model.

Babble demonstrates that the creation of a complex, shared application is possible with the framework. One developer was able to take the application from design to functionality in little over two months since the framework abstracted away both maintenance of occasionally-connected groups and concurrency control mechanics. The result is a full-featured, shared text editor with demonstrable advantages over similar applications: improvements in the undo/redo and storage user experience compared to contemporary single-user editors, and greater control over the local state than contemporary collaborative editors.

The creation of Babble was greatly simplified by Joyce but was still not as simple as we would have liked. Re-casting an application into Joyce's action/constraint model is difficult and requires an approach unfamiliar to most application developers. How to extensively unit test such applications remains unclear. Future work should investigate whether constraints can be automatically derived from a data type.

With regard to the programming model, strict adherence to the MVC cycle is preferable but can lead to unacceptable performance. Pure MVC implies an asynchronous model in which programs depend only on events to be notified of model changes. In reality, most MVC applications shortcut from the controller to the view to provide more immediate feedback.

In Babble there is a similar, probably typical, compromise in that local actions are constructed synchronously in the history structure and appended to the multi-log on completion. If a multi-log update arrives, special code exists to detect whether the action being constructed is *going* to conflict. If MVC is any guide, this will be a typical compromise in Joyce applications; we should anticipate it and provide a lower-level API to the reconciler so that applications can detect possible conflicts themselves.

The toolkit and application described in this paper was implemented at Microsoft Research Cambridge using .NET. Our immediate focus is producing and releasing a streamlined Java version of the toolkit along with a more advanced, styled-text version of Babble and a presentation tool.

We expect further developments of the kind of application described in this paper to raise interesting and difficult questions in the areas of user-interface, application construction and security. Using Joyce, we can cope with dynamic reconfigurations of devices, users and synchrony but we can't reconfigure an *application instance* to adapt to the device it is running on or the scenario it is being used in. An interesting approach may be to completely de-couple actions from applications. Joyce applications lessen the requirement on the user to switch mental 'modes' since his focus is always on the artefact being created. Decreasing modality increases usability. Future implementations may go further and disintegrate actions from applications completely to further lessen modality across the whole system. Actions may be associated with particular data types and always triggered in the same way. If we create a set of actions and constraints for editing XML we may be able to declaratively *generate* applications by using an XML file to weave together actions that have registered against XML schema types in a central system pool.

References

[Berlage et. al. 93]   T. Berlage and A. Genau. "A Framework for Shared Applications with a Replicated Architecture". *Proc. ACM Symposium on User Interface Software and Technology*. 1993

[Cocoa]   http://developer.apple.com/cocoa

[Cooper 03]   A. Cooper, R. Reimann, R.M. Reimann, H. Dubberly. "About Face 2.0: The Essentials of Interaction Design". *John Wiley & Sons, Inc.* 2003

[Castro et al. 02]   M. Castro, P. Druschel, A. M. Kermarrec, A. Rowstron. "SCRIBE: A large-scale and decentralized application-level multicast infrastructure". *IEEE Journal on Selected Areas in communications* (JSAC), 2002

[Demers 87]   A. Demers, D. Greene, C. Hauser, W. Irish, J. Larson, S. Shenker. HH. Sturgis, D. Swinehart, and D. Terry. "Epidemic Algorithms for Replicated Database Management". *Proc. Sixth Symposium on Principles of Distributed Computing*, Vancouver, B. C., Canada, 1987

[Edwards 97]   W.K. Edwards, E. D. Mynatt, K. Petersen, M. J. Spreitzer, D. B. Terry, and M. M. Theimer. "Designing and Implementing Asynchronous Collaborative Applications with Bayou". *Proc. User Interface Systems and Technology*, Banff, Canada, 1997

[Edwards et. al. 00]   W.K. Edwards, T. Igarashi, A. LaMarca, E.D. Mynatt. "A Temporal Model for Multi-Level Undo and Redo". *Proc. User Interface Systems and Technology*, San Diego, CA, 2000

[Ellis et al 88]   Ellis, C., Gibbs, S.J. and Rein, G., "Design and Use of a Group Editor", *MCC Technical Report Number STP-263-88*, Sept. 1988

[Ellis et al 89]   C.A. Elllis and S.J. Gibbs. "Concurrency Control in Groupware Systems". *Proc. SIGCHI Conference on Human Factors in Computing Systems*, Portland, OR, 93

[Gamma et. al. 95]   E. Gamma, R. Helm, R. Johnson, J. Vlissides. "Design Patterns, Elements of Reusable Object-Oriented Software". *Addison-Wesley*, 1995

[Greif et al. 86]   I. Greif, R. Seliger, and W. Weihl (1986). "Atomic Data Abstractions in a Distributed Collaborative Editing System". Proc. of the Thirteenth Annual Symposium on Principles of Programming Languages St. Petersburg, Florida. 1986

[JotSpot]   http://www.jotspot.com

[Kermarrec 01]   A.M. Kermarrec, A. Rowstron, M. Shapiro, and P. Druschel. The IceCube approach to the reconciliation of divergent replicas. In Proc. of Twentieth ACM Symposium on Principles of Distributed Computing PODC, Newport, RI USA, August 2001

[Krasner 88]   G.E. Krasner and S.T. Pope, "A Description of the Model-View-Controller User Interface Paradigm in the Smalltalk-80 system." *Journal of Object Oriented Programming*, 1988

[Li et al. 04]   D. Li and R. Li. "Ensuring Content and Intention Consistency in Real-Time Group Editors", *24th IEEE International Conference on Distributed Computing Systems* (ICDCS'04), 2004

[McGuffin et al 92]   L. McGuffin, and G. Olson, "ShrEdit: A Shared Electronic Workspace", *CSMIL Technical Report, Cognitive Science and Machine Intelligence Laboratory*, University of Michigan, 1992

[Munson et al. 96]   J. Munson and P. Dewan. "A Concurrency Control Framework for Collaborative Systems". *Proc. ACM Conference on Computer Supported Cooperative Work.* 1996

[Lamport 98]   L. Lamport. "The Part-time Parliament". *ACM Transactions on Computer Systems.* May 1998

[O'Brien 04]   J. O'Brien and M. Shapiro, "Undo for Anyone, Anywhere, Anytime". *Proc. SIGOPS European Workshop,* 2004

[Peterson et. Al 97] K. Petersen, M.J. Spreitzer, D.B. Terry, M.M. Theimer, A.J. Demers. "Flexible Update Propagation for Weakly Consistent Replication". *Proc. Sixteenth ACM Symposium on Operating System Principles* (SOSP), Saint-Malo, Franco, 1997

[Prakash et al. 94]   Prakash, A. and Shim, H. S. 1994. "DistView: support for building efficient collaborative applications using replicated objects". *Proc. ACM Conference on Computer Supported Cooperative Work* (CSCW '94), Chapel Hill, North Carolina, 1994).

[Preguiça et al. 03] N. Preguiça, M. Shapiro, C. Matheson: Semantics-based reconciliation for collaborative and mobile environments. In *Proc. Tenth Int. Conf. on Coop. Info. Sys. (CoopIS),* 2003

[Roseman et al. 96]   M. Roseman, S. Greenberg. "Building real-time groupware with GroupKit, a groupware toolkit". *ACM Trans. Comput.-Hum. Interact.* Mar. 1996

[Saito et al. 05]   Y. Saito and M. Shapiro. "Optimistic replication". *ACM Comput. Surv. 37, 1,* 2005

[Sarin et. al. 85]   S. Sarin and I. Greif. "Computer based real-time conferencing systems". *Computer 18,* 10 October 1985

[Schmidt et. al. 00] D. Schmidt, M. Stal, H. Rohnert, F. Buschmann. "Pattern-Oriented Software Architecture Volume 2, Patterns for Concurrent and Networked Objects", *Wiley,* 2000

[Schwarz et. al. 84] P.M. Schwarz and A.Z. Spector. Synchronizing shared abstract types. *ACM Transactions on Computer Systems* 2, 3, 1984

[SubEtherEdit]   http://www.codingmonkeys.de/subethaedit/

[Sun 02]   C. Sun, "Undo as concurrent inverse in group editors", *ACM Transactions on Computer-Human Interaction* (TOCHI), 2002

[Wiki]   http://c2.com/cgi/wiki?WikiWikiWeb

Interfering Effects of Adaptation: Implications on Self-adapting Systems Architecture

Jacqueline Floch, Erlend Stav, and Svein Hallsteinsen

SINTEF ICT NO-7465 Trondheim, Norway
{jacqueline.floch, erlend.stav, svein.hallsteinsen}@sintef.no

Abstract. When people are moving around using handheld networked devices, the environment for the provided services vary influencing service quality properties and user needs. In order to maintain usability and usefulness for mobile users, dynamic service adaptation is needed. Several forms of adaptation may be applied. For example, the application structure may adapt from thin client to self-reliant client, or network handover may be performed. The selection of an adaptation type is however far from obvious. Adaptation usually has impact on system resources or service quality. Also, one adaptation may require other adaptations that again have impact on resources and quality. This paper illustrates the complexity of selecting an adequate adaptation form. We argue that adaptation selection requires advanced reasoning and identify implications on the architecture of self-adapting systems.

1   Introduction

When people are moving around using handheld networked devices, the operating environment for the provided services vary influencing service quality properties and user needs. To retain usability, usefulness, and reliability under such circumstances, systems should adapt to the changing environments. Service adaptation is about finding the application configuration that best fits the context, where context includes both system context such as battery level and network resources, and user context such as position, noise and user needs. Adaptation may be performed at several levels and in different ways. Adaptation may be applied on the applications, or on the resources and devices required by the applications. It may require modifications to the application structure, to the selection of application components, or to their deployment. A close analysis of the problem of adaptation shows that the selection of the "best configuration" is complex and requires reasoning on dependent context elements and adaptation forms. This paper presents a mobile service scenario that illustrates this complexity and draws out a set of requirements on the architecture of self-adapting systems. The MADAM project is currently developing solutions based on the requirements derived from the scenario analysis [1]. Current approaches to self-adaptation usually describe abstract motivations. The research literature lacks presentations of scenarios that would provide a common base for understanding business problems, extracting valuable business requirements, and justifying the research problem relevance.

F. Eliassen and A. Montresor (Eds.): DAIS 2006, LNCS 4025, pp. 64–69, 2006.

2   Scenario Example

The application domain for our scenario is inspection and maintenance support for janitors. Janitors use handheld networked devices during their work. They are involved in various working situations, ranging from administrative work in a quiet and connected office environment, through travelling between technical installations in rugged industrial environments with varying network coverage. We assume that the companies where inspection is performed make an intensive use of ICT systems for registering information, tagging and controlling equipment. In the following, our scenario is structured in a set of scenes that relate to various working situations and contexts.

Scene 1 – Morning at home: The janitor checks his assignments for the day before he leaves home, using his company planning application on his handheld device. He is also running a video player on the device showing morning news on a screen in the kitchen. The first assignment is about fixing a ventilation system in a large building. He starts looking at information about the first assignment. There is little memory because the video player uses a lot. The home WLAN provides high capacity network connection. The device has been charging during the night and is still connected to outlet power, so power is abundant and the load on the server is low. In this situation, a thin client configuration is chosen as the initial configuration of the work planning application.

Scene 2 – Leaving home: The janitor shuts down the video player and prepares to leave home. This new situation raises a relevant context change: the memory available on the handheld becomes high. In order to increase application response time and reliability, the work planning application is reconfigured with a richer client caching data to save power on the handheld and to become less vulnerable to network instability.

Scene 3 – Driving: The janitor enters his car to go to the company building where the faulty installation is located. While he is driving the janitor wants to check more details, but since his eyes and hands are busy with the driving, he prefers hands-free user interface. The janitor selects tools and information for guiding the inspection assignment and initiates their downloading. The device is now connected through GPRS to the janitor company server. As the cost of using GPRS is high and the capacity of the network low, the downloading of the tools is postponed.

Scene 4 – Arriving at the customer: When the janitor arrives to the company site, he gets access to the company WLAN. He can now download tools. However the network cannot be regarded as trusted, and a VPN tunnel has to be established.

Scene 5 – Measurement: The janitor starts the inspection of the ventilation system. He starts the inspection application and is guided around in the building to measure temperature. During the work, he has to deal with different kinds of temperature sensors. Measurement is performed manually or automatically using Bluetooth. In the later case, various sensor drivers are needed depending on the sensor types. Drivers can be downloaded from the company equipment server. The building under inspection is large and the measurement collection has already lasted a long time. In order to reduce battery consumption, the measurement application switches to a stand-alone mode and

Table 1. Scenario: adaptation summary in a situation-action style

Scene	Relevant context and context changes	Adaptation
1	**Handheld:** available memory: low; high battery level **Network:** WLAN: high bandwidth, low cost	The initial configuration is selected. A thin client configuration is chosen.
2	**Handheld:** available memory: high	The application is reconfigured from thin to caching client. Assignment information is downloaded.
3a	**User needs:** hands-free mode	A hands-free UI is added.
3b	**User:** location: driving to customer **Network:** GPRS: medium bandwidth, high cost	The downloading of inspection tools is postponed
4	**User needs:** security policy **Network:** WLAN: high bandwidth, low cost	A VPN tunnel is established. The downloading that was postponed is started.
5a	**Infrastructure:** new sensor	The sensor drivers are downloaded and installed.
5b	**Handheld:** rapidly decreasing battery level **Network:** WLAN: high bandwidth, low cost	The application is reconfigured from a network connected mode to stand-alone mode. The data measurements are saved periodically
6	**User:** application priority **Handheld:** available memory: low **Network:** WLAN: high bandwidth, low cost	The data measurements are saved and the inspection application is suspended. The planning application is started.
7	**Infrastructure:** new computer	The inspection application is redeployed.

measurements are stored locally. However, the network coverage is good and measurements data are saved centrally periodically.

Scene 6 – Notification: During the measurement activity, the janitor is interrupted by a notification about a new task. The planning support application requires more resources than currently available on the handheld. In order to enable planning, measurements data are saved to the company equipment server, and the measurement application is partially suspended.

Scene 7 – Measurement analysis: When all measurements are collected, the janitor moves to the technical office where he can use a more powerful stationary computer to perform measurement analysis. When he enters the office, the janitor work session is automatically moved from the handheld to the stationary computer.

Table 1 summarizes the scenario in a situation-action style where each situation leads to an adaptation action. In that simple scenario, we observe that each situation requires taking into account various kinds of context. We also observe that various adaptation forms such as adaptation of functional richness, adaptation of behaviour and data deployment, and adaptation of the user interface modality, may take place.

3   Adaptation Effects

While Table 1 describes simple relations between situations and adaptation mechanisms, this section provides a deeper analysis demonstrating the complex dependencies between adaptation and context, and the effects of adaptation on system resources and offered service quality. We do not restrict to the single scenario, but generalize adding new context conditions that may occur under the janitor work.

Table 2 presents the analysis in a goal-oriented style. A goal describes a high-level behaviour objective that the self-adapting system should attempt to fulfil in order to maintain service usefulness and quality when context changes occur. Usually several adaptation mechanisms may be applied to achieve a goal. A classification according to goals allows us to present the relations between context and adaptation mechanisms in a concise way. Table 2 distinguishes between "primary context elements" i.e. the main triggers for adaptation, and "secondary context elements" that complement the primary elements when making a decision about adaptation. The "adaptation effects" describe the impact of adaptation: "(C)" indicates an impact on context, "(S)" on service quality, "(G)" on other goals, and "(A)" indicates an inferred new adaptation need.

Table 2. Adaptation analysis in a goal-oriented style

Goal	Context	Adaptation mechanism	Adaptation effect (s)
Maintain service availability	**Primary:** low power level **Secondary:** availability of external, handheld device or PC	Redeploy application session	(A) Adapt application configuration to new platform
	Primary: network coverage/no coverage	Redeploy application and data	(S) data integrity
Enhance operability	**Primary:** user activity, hands occupation **Secondary:** audio capabilities	Select UI modality (e.g. voice or text based UI)	(C) handheld resources consumption
	Primary: equipment, device and service extensions	Enrich application functionality	(C) handheld resources consumption
	Secondary: network coverage (e.g. Bluetooth)	Launch new application automatically depending on extension type	(C) handheld and network resources consumption
Control power consumption	**Primary | Secondary** user activity duration **Secondary | Primary** limited power resources	Adjust power demanding operations: network access	(A) Redeploy application; tune data synch. (C) network resources consumption
		Adjust power demanding operations: CPU frequency	(S) service response time

Table 2. (*continued*)

Goal	Context	Adaptation mechanism	Adaptation effect (s)
Optimize memory usage or Optimize CPU usage	**Primary** memory/CPU resources	Redeploy application (client / server split)	(S) service response time; data integrity (C) network resources consumption
		Select media type and richness adapted to resource	(S) service accuracy
	Primary memory/CPU resources **Secondary** priority of user tasks	Suspend low-priority applications	(G) service availability
Select a satisfactory network	**Primary** available networks (e.g. GSM, WiFi) **Secondary** user/application needs (e.g. cost, response time, security)	Hand over (switch) between networks	(C) resource consumption (S) cost and provided QoS
		Select a network adaptor adapted to network	(C) resource consumption
Optimize network usage	**Primary** network capacity	Redeploy application (client / server split)	(S) service response time, data integrity (C) power consumption
		Select appropriate time to perform operations (e.g. postpone task)	(G) service availability
		Adjust data richness; select media type; tune data synch.	(S) service accuracy
	Primary network security	Select the appropriate security model (e.g. VPN, encryption level)	(C) resource consumption (S) response time

4   Implications on System Architecture

By illustrating the interfering effects of service adaptation, the analysis presented in table 2 demonstrates the complexity of developing adaptive applications. In this section, we extract a set of implications on the architecture of self-adapting systems. These implications relate to the main functionality necessary for adapting applications: context monitoring, adaptation reasoning and reconfiguration.

Firstly, we observe the complexity related to context monitoring. Multiple context elements need to be taken into account. Further, these span from elementary elements, such as network cost, to more complex aggregated or derived elements, such as predicted location. Most of these elements are domain independent. We expect the set of relevant elements and the sources producing them to evolve in the same way as applications. This gives the following architectural implications: i1) *Context monitoring should be kept separate from the application and realized through reusable components or context middleware.* i2) *The context middleware should be extensible and support the addition of new elements and new forms of reasoning.*

Secondly, concerning adaptation reasoning, we observe multiple relations between context and adaptation mechanisms, and interfering effects of adaptation. During the generalization done in section 3, we found it difficult to capture all relations. We also expect that new relations will be introduced as applications and context monitoring evolve. Two main approaches [2] have been proposed for self-adaptation: internal approaches where adaptation is realized as part of the application using programming language features, and external approaches where adaptation mechanisms are realized by an application-independent middleware. The main drawback of internal approaches is the complexity introduced by intertwining adaptation and application behaviours. Also, they poorly support application and adaptation evolution. Given our observations, these drawbacks make internal approaches inappropriate in the context of mobile services, and thus: i3) *Adaptation mechanisms should be realized externally to the application.* External approaches require adaptations policies to be described separately from the applications. These policies are used by the middleware to reason and decide about adaptation. Three main approaches have been proposed for the description of policies. Two of them are respectively illustrated by table 1 and table 2: situation-action approaches [3] and goal-oriented approaches [4]. The third approach uses utility function that assign a utility value to each application variant as a function of application properties, context and goals [4]. The interfering effects of adaptation make the two first approaches inappropriate, and thus: i4) *Adaptation policies should be expressed using utility functions.*

Finally, concerning reconfiguration, we need to build adaptable applications. Two general approaches have been proposed [5]: parameterization supports fine tuning of applications through the modification of program variables, while compositional variability is specified at the component level allowing the modification of application structure and algorithms. Parameterization is an effective way to implement variability, but may also lead to a large set of variants and raise scalability issues, implying: i5) *Adaptable applications should be built on compositional variability combined with cautious use of parameterization.*

A main challenge given these implications is to develop effective and scalable solutions for handheld devices with restricted processing and memory capabilities.

References

1. MADAM "http://www.ist-madam.org/"
2. Oreizy, P. et al. "Architecture-based approach to self-adaptive software", IEEE Intelligent Systems and Their Applications, 1999, vol. 14 (3).
3. Garlan, D. et al. "Rainbow: Architecture-based self-adaptation with reusable infrastructure", IEEE Computer, 2004, vol. 37 (10).
4. Kephart, J.O. and Chess, D.M. "The vision of autonomic computing", IEEE Computer, 2003, vol. 36 (1).
5. McKinley, P.K. et al. "Composing adaptive software", IEEE Computer, 2004, vol. 37 (7).

Discovery of Stable Peers in a Self-organising Peer-to-Peer Gradient Topology

Jan Sacha, Jim Dowling, Raymond Cunningham, and René Meier

Distributed Systems Group, Trinity College, Dublin
{jsacha, jdowling, rcnnnghm, rmeier}@cs.tcd.ie

Abstract. Peer-to-peer (P2P) systems are characterised by a wide disparity in peer resources and capabilities. In particular, a number of measurements on deployed P2P systems show that peer stability (e.g. uptime) varies by several orders of magnitude between peers. In this paper, we introduce a peer utility metric and construct a self-organising P2P topology based on this metric that allows the efficient discovery of stable peers in the system. We propose and evaluate a search algorithm and we show that it achieves significantly better performance than random walking. Our approach can be used by certain classes of applications to improve the availability and performance of system services by placing them on the most stable peers, as well as to reduce the amount of network traffic required to discover and use these services. As a proof-of-concept, we demonstrate the design of a naming service on the gradient topology.[1]

1 Introduction

Recent measurements on peer-to-peer (P2P) systems show that the distribution of peer characteristics, such as their availability, bandwidth, or storage space, are highly skewed and often heavy-tailed or scale-free [1, 2, 3]. In particular, it has been shown that the uptime characteristics of peers are extremely diverse, and a large number of peers stay in the system for a relatively short time, which is commonly referred to as high "infant mortality" [4, 5].

At the same time, existing state-of-the-art P2P systems are often based on the assumption that all peers in the system have equal capabilities and that the distribution of resources between peers is uniform. Initial approaches using Distributed Hash Tables (DHTs), such as Chord [6], CAN [7] and Pastry [8], are examples of this assumption. These systems treat all peers as equals, and hence, low performance peers receive approximately the same amount of traffic as the highest performance peers.

A number of P2P systems address the heterogeneity of P2P environments by electing *super-peers* and assigning them extra responsibilities [9, 10, 11, 12]. However, these systems introduce the problem of super-peer election. Solutions based on flooding, random walking or other traditional election algorithms, potentially require communication with all peers in the network and thus do not

---

[1] This work was supported by the European Union funded "Digital Business Ecosystem" Project IST-507953.

F. Eliassen and A. Montresor (Eds.): DAIS 2006, LNCS 4025, pp. 70–83, 2006.

scale to large networks. Other solutions such as manual or static configuration of super-peers are inappropriate due to a lack of global knowledge of application characteristics.

This paper presents an approach where peers periodically measure their performance and stability properties, using a *utility* metric, exchange their measurements with neighbours, and construct a self-organising *gradient topology* that enables efficient searching for stable (high utility) peers in the network. We design and evaluate a search algorithm, called *gradient search*, that exploits the implicit information contained in the gradient topology and allows the efficient discovery of stable peers. We compare gradient search with random walking and with a probabilistic search strategy based on Boltzmann exploration, and we show that our approach provides superior performance. We also demonstrate that gradient search significantly reduces the message loss rate by preferentially forwarding messages through more stable peers.

The topology is designed to support certain classes of applications, such as P2P storage systems, or P2P registries, where system services are deployed on the most stable peers (super-peers), thus improving the stability and performance of these services. Our approach manages high rates of churn by exploiting stable peers to both provide system services and to route to these services using gradient search. As a proof-of-concept, we demonstrate the design of a sample naming service.

The remainder of the paper is organised as follows. Section 2 reviews related work. In section 3, we present an overview of the gradient topology and describe our neighbour selection algorithm that generates the topology. In section 4, we discuss search strategies for stable peer discovery in a gradient topology and we apply our approach to a sample naming service. In section 5, we describe our experimental setup and we analyse the results of the different search strategies. Section 6 concludes the paper.

2   Related Work

Recent research on P2P systems has been primarily focused on Distributed Hash Tables [6, 7, 8, 13], where the main goal is to provide efficient routing between any pair of peers. In our approach, we are focusing on searching for peers with particular properties in the system, and assuming that system services are placed on these peers, we provide a mechanism that allows the efficient discovery and consumption of these services.

A number of techniques have been developed for searching in unstructured P2P networks (e.g., Yang and Molina [14]). However, these techniques do not exploit any information contained in the underlying P2P topology, in contrast to our gradient search heuristic that takes advantage of the gradient topology structure to improve the searching performance. Morselli at al [15] proposed a routing algorithm for unstructured P2P networks that is similar to gradient searching, however, they address the problem of routing between any pair of peers rather than searching for reliable peers or services.

Many existing P2P systems adopt a super-peer structure to exploit stable and/or high performance peers. Yang and Molina [9] investigate general principles of designing super-peer-based networks, however, they do not provide any specific super-peer election algorithm. OceanStore [16] proposed to elect a primary tier "consisting of a small number of replicas located in high-bandwidth, high connectivity regions of the network" for the purpose of handling updates, however, no specific algorithm for the election of such a tier is presented. Brocade [10] improves routing efficiency in a DHT by exploiting resource heterogeneity, but unlike our approach, it doesn't address the super-peer election problem.

In Chord [6, 17], it has been shown that the load between peers can be balanced by assigning multiple *virtual servers* to high performance physical hosts. Similarly, Mizrak et al [12] proposed the use of high capacity super-peers to improve routing performance. However, these systems focus on load balancing, and do not allow the selection of potential super-peers from the set of all peers in the system.

Montresor [11] proposes a protocol for super-peer overlay generation, however, unlike our gradient topology, his topology maintains a discrete (binary) distinction between super-peers and client peers. In contrast, our novel approach introduces a continuous peer utility spectrum and thus allows the identification of high utility (super)peers. Our neighbour selection algorithm can be seen as a special case of the T-Man protocol [18] that generates a gradient topology, where the ranking function is based on peer utility. The advantage of such a utility ranking function is that applications built on top of the gradient topology can exploit more stable peers in the system.

3   Self-organising Gradient Topology

In this section, we introduce the concept of a gradient P2P topology and we outline its main properties. We present a neighbour selection algorithm that generates the gradient topology and we show that it is self-organising. The topology is used in the later sections by a searching algorithm that enables the discovery of stable peers in the system.

The gradient topology is a P2P topology where the highest *utility* peers are connected with each other and form the so called *core* of the system, while lower utility peers are located gradually farther from the core. Peer utility is application specific and measures the ability of a peer to maintain services or provide resources to the system. The core, which clusters the highest utility peers in the system, is therefore most suitable for maintaining system services and system data. Figure 1 shows a visualisation of a gradient topology with the core visible at the centre. The position of each peer in the topology is determined by the peer's utility.

The definition of the utility function depends on the application built on top of the gradient topology and it captures domain specific knowledge about peers. It measures the properties of peers that are desired or required by the application. For example, in a P2P storage systems, the utility of a peer may be defined as a peer's

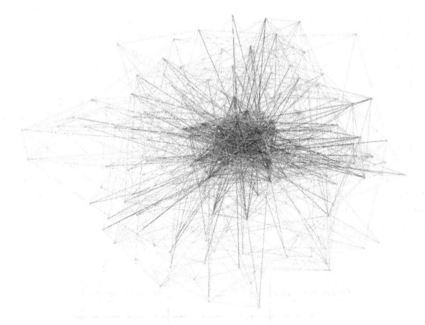

Fig. 1. Visualisation of a gradient topology

available bandwidth and local storage space. In a multi-media streaming application, the utility may be defined as a peer's latency and bandwidth, while in a grid computing system we may define the utility as a function of a peer's CPU load.

A very important property of the gradient topology is that the utility function is orthogonal to the neighbour selection algorithm, which generates the topology, and to the searching algorithm. The only assumption these algorithms make about the utility function is that every peer calculates some utility value.

In the experiments described later in this paper, we define peer utility as the peer's current *uptime*, and we use the uptime as a metric to measure peer stability. Our metric is based on the observation that high stability peers, on average, have a higher uptime value than low stability peers. More elaborate peer stability models will be studied in the future, in particular, metrics based on peer uptime history.

We also assume that the system runs in a cooperative environment, and that every peer is able to calculate its own utility. Future work will investigate the use of the gradient topology in an untrusted environment where malicious peers may provide incorrect utility information. We expect that this issue can be addressed by adopting one of the existing decentralised approaches to reputation or trust management.

3.1 Building a Gradient Topology

We have designed and evaluated a neighbour selection algorithm that generates the gradient topology in a completely decentralised P2P environment. Each peer maintains two sets of neighbours, a *similarity-based* set and a *random* set. Peers periodically gossip with each other and exchange their sets. On receiving both sets from a neighbour, a gossipping peer selects one entry whose utility level is closest to its own utility and replaces an entry in its similarity-based set. This behaviour clusters peers with similar utility characteristics and generates the core of the network surrounded by peers with gradually decreasing utility. In addition, a gossipping peer randomly selects an entry from the received random set and replaces a random entry in its random set. Connections to random peers allow peers to explore the network in order to discover other potentially similar neighbours. This greatly reduces the probability of more than one cluster of high utility peers forming in the network. Random connections also massively reduce the probability of the gradient topology partitioning due to excessive clustering. Figure 2 shows a neighbour selection algorithm being used by two peers, A and B, to exchange neighbour information during one round of gossipping.

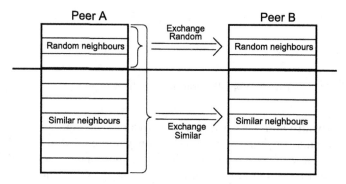

Fig. 2. Neighbourhood set exchange from Peer A to Peer B

In addition to the neighbour sets, each peer maintains a cache that stores estimated utility values of current neighbours. This cache is updated whenever a peer gossips with a neighbour.

Our initial evaluation of the neighbour selection algorithm, described in a separate paper [19], shows that the algorithm generates a P2P topology that has a gradient structure and a very small diameter (an order of 5-6 hops for 100,000 peers). The algorithm works well for a relatively small number of neighbours per peer (an order of 20). Figure 1 above shows a visualisation of a sample gradient topology created using the described neighbour selection algorithm.

The emergence of the gradient topology is an example of self-organisation. Peers are independent, have limited knowledge about the system and interact with a limited number of neighbours. There are no centralised components. The peers estimate their microscopic properties, i.e., their utility, and through the exchange of information with neighbours the peers build a P2P topology that has global, macroscopic properties, i.e., the gradient structure. The resultant topology is based on peer utility characteristics, which contrasts with many other P2P systems where the topology is based on random peer identifiers.

4   Discovery of Stable Peers

In this section, we present a heuristic search algorithm, which we call gradient search, based on the gradient topology, that enables the discovery of high utility peers in the system. The algorithm exploits the information contained in the gradient topology to limit the search space to a relatively small subset of peers and to achieve a significantly better search performance than traditional search techniques, such as random walking, which require the communication with potentially all peers in the system.

The goal of the search algorithm is to deliver a message from any peer in the system to a high utility peer in the core, i.e., to a peer with utility above a *threshold*. The value of the threshold is assigned by a peer that initiates the search and is included in the search message. The threshold values are application specific and can vary between services. Peers below the specified utility threshold forward messages to their neighbours. Each message is associated with a time-to-live (TTL) value that determines the maximum number of hops the message can be propagated. The messages are never duplicated.

In gradient search, a peer greedily forwards messages to its highest utility neighbour. Thus, messages are forwarded along the utility gradient, as in hill climbing and other similar techniques. It is important to note that the gradient search strategy is generally applicable only to a gradient topology. It relies on a certain structure of the P2P overlay, in particular, it assumes that a higher utility peer is closer to the core in terms of the number of hops than a lower utility peer. The maintenance of the gradient structure introduces extra overhead, however, the cost of topology maintenance is generally constant per peer, since the neighbour selection algorithm is performed periodically, and potentially can be lower than the cost of frequent and expensive searches.

In a greedy search strategy, where messages are always forwarded to the highest utility peer, messages may oscillate around peers with a locally maximal utility. To prevent message looping, we append a list of visited peers to each message, and we add a constraint that messages are never forwarded to already visited peers. Local maxima should never occur in an idealised gradient topology, however, every P2P system is under constant churn and the topology can always contain local deviations.

We compare gradient search with a probabilistic search strategy where a peer, x, selects the next-hop destination for a message with probability, P_x, given by the Boltzmann exploration formula [20]:

$$P_x(a) = \frac{e^{(U(a)/T)}}{\sum_{i \in N_x} e^{(U(i)/T)}}$$

where $P_x(a)$ is the probability that x selects neighbour a, $U(a)$ is the estimated utility of peer a, N_x is the set of x's available neighbours, and T is a parameter of the algorithm called the temperature. Setting T close to zero causes the algorithm to be more greedy and deterministic, as in gradient search, while if T grows to infinity, all neighbours are selected with equal probabilities similar to random walking. Thus, the temperature enables a trade-off between exploitative (and deterministic) routing of messages towards the core, and random exploration that enables searches to escape local maxima.

Routing messages steeply towards the core, as in the gradient search, or Boltzmann search with a low temperature value, has the advantage over random walking that subsequent peers on a message's path are more and more stable, and therefore, the probability of message loss decreases.

4.1   Applying the Gradient Search

We demonstrate the use of the gradient topology by sketching out the design of a sample naming service. The naming service supports registration, unregistration, and querying of names. We show that all of these operations can be implemented easily using gradient searching.

One of the first decisions when designing a naming service is where to store the name entries, i.e., the mapping between the names and the objects associated with them. We assume that a centralised solution, where all information is stored by one peer is unacceptable due to reliability and performance reasons. Another extreme, a fully decentralised solution, where all peers participate in the replication of the naming service, has a drawback that the use of low performance peers may degrade the performance of the entire system. For this reason, it is preferable to choose a group of super-peers and use them to host the naming service. However, this introduces the problem of super-peer selection from the set of all peers in the system.

This problem can be solved using the gradient topology and gradient search. We define the utility function so that it describes the requirements for our super-peers, for example as some peer stability metric (e.g. uptime). If we expect that the size of the naming service is significantly large, we may extend the utility metric to include the peer storage space, and potentially, network bandwidth. Given the utility function, the gradient topology can then be generated by the peers in the system.

In order to create the first replica of the service, the owner of the service decides on the utility threshold required for the naming service replica, searches for a peer above the threshold, and requests a replica placement. Subsequent replicas are created in a similar way. Whenever a peer updates the naming service, either by inserting, removing, or modifying an entry, the update request is routed to the core using the gradient search and the update is performed on one of the replicas of the naming service. The replicas need to be synchronised after they are modified. The synchronisation method depends on the replication scheme used, and exact details of the synchronisation algorithm are beyond the scope of this paper. However, we assume that some probabilistic gossip-based approach can be efficiently adopted, since in the gradient topology replicas are located close to each other in the core, and hence, the update messages do not need to be propagated to low-utility peers outside of the core.

The query operation is perhaps the most important for the performance of the system since we expect that most naming services are much more frequently queried than updated, similarly as the update can be implemented using gradient searching. A query is routed to the core where it can be resolved by any naming service replica (see Figure 3). No synchronisation is needed. For subsequent requests, peers may cache known replica addresses and contact them directly.

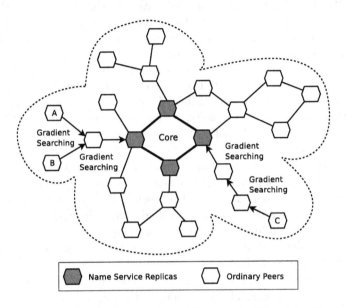

Fig. 3. Sample Naming Service built on top of the Gradient Topology. Gradient searching is used by Peers A, B, and C to discover and access instances of the naming service.

We believe that our approach based on the gradient topology and gradient searching can be used to build other classes of applications, such as a P2P storage system, a P2P distributed database, or a P2P multicast application.

5   Experimental Evaluation

In this section, we describe our experimental setup and present the results of search experiments on the gradient topology. In the experiments we compare the performance of gradient search, random walking, and Boltzmann search by measuring the three properties for each of the three search algorithms. Firstly, we calculate the average number of hops in which the algorithm delivers a message from a random peer in the network to the core, i.e., to a peer above a certain utility threshold. Next, we measure the average message loss rate of the sent messages. Finally, we calculate the average utility of peers that are used as hops when forwarding messages.

We perform three experiments to simulate the gradient topology. In the first experiment, we increase the number of peers in the system while keeping a constant peer churn rate. In the second experiment, we keep the network size constant, however, we increase the peer churn rate over time. In the last experiment, the number of peers and the churn rate are fixed, but we increase the message TTL.

We ran our experiments on a Pentium 4 machine with a 3GHz processor and 3GB RAM under Debian Linux. We evaluate the search algorithms in a Java-based discrete event simulator. An individual experiment consists of a set of peers, connections between peers, and messages passed between peers. We assume all peers are mutually reachable, i.e., any pair of peers can establish a connection. We also assume that it takes exactly one time step to pass a message between a pair of connected peers. We do not model network congestion, however, we limit the maximum number of concurrent connections per peer. In order to reflect network heterogeneity, we limit the number of peer connections according to the Pareto distribution with an exponent of 1.5 and a mean of 20 connections per peer.

The simulated P2P network is under constant churn. Every new peer is assigned a session duration, measured in simulation steps, according to the Pareto distribution with an exponent of 1.5. The session duration determines the time step when a peer leaves the system. We calculate the churn rate as the fraction of peers that leave (and join) the system at one step of the simulation. Over the lifetime of a running system, the average churn rate is equal to the inverse of the expected peer session time.

We use a central bootstrap server that stores 1000 addresses of peers that have recently joined the network. The list includes "dangling references" to peers that may have already left the system. Every joining peer receives an initial random set of neighbours from the bootstrap server. A peer discovers other peers in the system by gossipping with neighbours at every step of the simulation. If a peer becomes isolated from the network (i.e., has no neighbours), it is bootstrapped again. Our experience shows that if a peer maintains 10 random connections, the possibility of isolation is extremely low.

We start each individual experiment from a network consisting of a single peer. The number of peers is increased by one percent at each time step, until the network grows to the size required by the experiment. Afterwards, the network is still under continuous churn, however, the rate of arrivals is equal to the rate of departures and the number of peers in the system remains constant.

At each turn, a number of randomly selected peers emit messages, and all peers attempt to either deliver or forward messages that they hold in their buffers. If a peer's utility is higher than a defined utility threshold, all messages in its buffer are delivered. Otherwise, each message is forwarded to one of the peer's neighbours selected by the current search policy. When the TTL value of a message drops to zero, the message is discarded. Additionally, if a peer leaves the system, all messages that it currently stores in its buffer are lost.

We examine peer churn rates between 0 and 0.1, where the value of 0.1 corresponds to a configuration where 10% of all peers leave the system at every step of the simulation. In physical time, if a discrete time step was 10 seconds, such churn rate would correspond to roughly 1000 peer departures per second for a 100,000 peer network. We have observed that for extreme churn rates, such as 0.1 and higher, the network topology depends heavily on the bootstrapping method.

For the purpose of the simulation, in all experiments, we set the utility threshold to a value that corresponds to 1% of highest utility peers. In Boltzmann searching we compare two temperatures: 1000 and 100. The TTL value is set to 100 hops if not stated otherwise.

5.1 Evaluation Results

The experimental results reveal that gradient search exhibits better performance than Boltzmann searching and random walking, in terms of number of hops and message loss rate, when routing messages from a random peer to the core.

Figure 4(a) shows the average hop count for delivered messages as a function of the network size. The churn rate was fixed at 0.01. We can see that gradient search performs better than other search strategies, and that the message hop count increases together with the Boltzmann temperature. For the random walk, the hop count grows more slowly than for gradient search with increasing network size. This can be explained by the fact that the average number of high utility peers is a fixed percentage of the network size, and hence, the probability of high utility peer discovery by random walking is a function of this percentage. For gradient search, the hop count increases with the network size, since the average distance from a peer to the core increases. We can also see that the two Boltzmann approaches, with different temperatures, converge as the network size grows. This is due to the growing average utility (uptime) of peers in the system, which results in a decreasing relative difference between the Boltzmann temperatures.

Figure 4(b) shows the average message loss rate as a function of the network size with a churn rate of 0.01, and Figure 5(a) shows the average message loss rate as a function of the churn rate for a network of 10,000 peers. Both figures demonstrate that the message loss rate is lowest for the gradient search, and that it grows as the Boltzmann temperature is increased.

Better performance of the gradient search results from two facts. First, as shown in Figure 4(a), the message path is shorter in gradient searching than in other search strategies, and therefore, the probability that a message is lost by forwarding peers, or that the message exceeds its TTL value, is lower. Second, as confirmed by measurements reported below, the stability of peers used for forwarding messages in the gradient search is higher, which additionally reduces the message loss probability. For random walking the message loss rate is nearly equal for all network sizes, which is due to the fixed percentage of high utility peers in the system.

Figure 5(b) presents the message loss rate as a function of the churn rate with a distinction between message loss caused by exceeded message TTL and message loss caused by peers leaving the system. The total message loss rate is calculated as a sum of the two mentioned loss rates. The figure shows that for random walking the message loss rate attributed to peers leaving the system

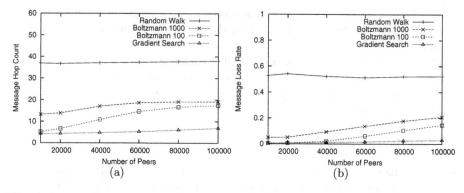

Fig. 4. Average hop count of delivered messages (a) and average message loss rate (b) as function of network size with a churn rate of 0.01 and TTL set to 100

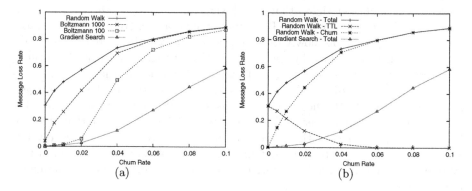

Fig. 5. Message loss rate as a function of peer churn rate. (a) Comparison between random walk, Boltzmann search, and gradient search. (b) Comparison between message loss rates attributed to exceeded message TTL and message loss attributed to peer churn. For gradient search, nearly 100% of the observed message loss is caused by peer churn (network size is 10,000 and TTL=100).

grows together with the churn rate. At the same time, the message loss rate attributed to exceeded TTL decreases with growing churn, which means that for higher churn rates messages are more likely to be lost by leaving peers than by exceeding their TTL values. For gradient search, nearly 100% of the total message loss is caused by churn.

Figure 6(a) shows the message loss rate as a function of message TTL. We can see that the overall message loss decreases when TTL grows. For random walking, as the TTL is increased, messages are lost more often due to churn, i.e., because of peers leaving the system. As a consequence, the message loss rate does not converge to zero. On the contrary, for the gradient search, the message loss rate becomes negligible for TTL values above approximately 50 hops.

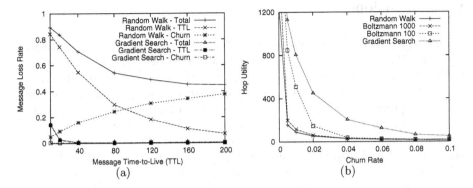

Fig. 6. (a) Message loss rate as a function of message TTL for 10,000 peers and 0.01 churn rate. The graph shows a distinction between message loss caused by exceeded message TTL and message loss caused by peers leaving the system. (b) Average utility of peers forwarding messages (hop utility). The average utility of all peers in the system, measured as uptime, decreases with the churn rate. Gradient search achieves better hop utility by forwarding messages to the highest utility peers (network size is 10,000, TTL=100).

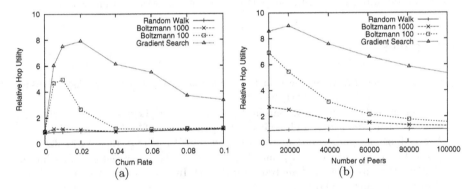

Fig. 7. Average relative utility of peers forwarding messages (relative hop utility) as a function of churn rate (a) and network size (b). The utility is scaled so that the value of 1 corresponds to the average utility among all peers in the system.

Figures 6(b), 7(a), and 7(b) demonstrate the average utility of peers used for forwarding messages in different searching strategies. In all cases we can see that the average hop utility is highest for gradient search and lowest for random walks. This result is consistent with the observation that for gradient search the message loss rate is lower than for the other strategies. In Figures 7(a) and 7(b) the utility is scaled in such a way that the average utility over all peers in the system is 1. As expected, for random walking the average path utility is 1. Figure 6(b) shows also that the average peer utility (measured as uptime) grows steeply when the churn rate approaches zero.

6   Conclusions

In this paper, we have described the gradient topology and the gradient search algorithm that allow peers to efficiently discover peers with particular attributes in the system, i.e., high utility peers. The topology can be used to improve the availability and performance of system services by placing them on the highest utility peers, as well as to reduce the amount of network traffic required to discover and use these services. The topology enables a trade-off between centralisation and decentralisation, in the sense that it allows the selection of a subset of high utility peers for supporting application services rather than distributing the services equally between all peers. We demonstrate the usability of our approach by designing a sample naming service on top of the gradient topology.

The evaluation of our work shows that gradient search achieves significantly better performance than random walking. Our results agree with the no-free lunch theorem for search [21], that states that no generalised search algorithm, such as random walking, can out-perform a specific search algorithm that makes use of suitable domain knowledge. The gradient topology contains implicit knowledge of peers' utilities and this knowledge is exploited by our gradient search algorithm, enabling its significant performance gains over random walking.

References

1. Sen, S., Wong, J.: Analyzing peer-to-peer traffic across large networks. Transactions on Networking **12** (2004) 219–232
2. Gummadi, K.P., Dunn, R.J., Saroiu, S., Gribble, S.D., Levy, H.M., Zahorjan, J.: Measurement, modeling, and analysis of a peer-to-peer file-sharing workload. In: Proceedings of Symposium on Operating Systems Principles. (2003) 314–329
3. Pouwelse, J., Garbacki, P., Epema, D., Sips, H.: The bittorrent p2p file-sharing system: Measurements and analysis. In: the 4th International Workshop on Peer-To-Peer Systems. (2005)
4. Bhagwan, R., Savage, S., Voelker, G.M.: Understanding availability. In: the 2nd International Workshop on Peer-to-Peer Systems. (2003)
5. Rhea, S., Geels, D., Roscoe, T., Kubiatowicz, J.: Handling churn in a dht. In: Proceedings of the USENIX 2004 Annual Technical Conference. (2004) 127–140
6. Stoica, I., Morris, R., Karger, D., Kaashoek, M.F., Balakrishnan, H.: Chord: A scalable peer-to-peer lookup service for internet applications. SIGCOMM Computer Communication Review **31**(4) (2001) 149–160
7. Ratnasamy, S., Francis, P., Handley, M., Karp, R., Schenker, S.: A scalable content-addressable network. In: Proceedings of the Conference on Applications, Technologies, Trchitectures, and Protocols for Computer Communications. (2001) 161–172
8. Rowstron, A.I.T., Druschel, P.: Pastry: Scalable, decentralized object location, and routing for large-scale peer-to-peer systems. In: Proceedings of the 18th International Conference on Distributed Systems Platforms. (2001) 329–350
9. Yang, B., Garcia-Molina, H.: Designing a super-peer network. In: Proceedings of the 19th International Conference on Data Engineering. (2003) 49–60

10. Zhao, B.Y., Duan, Y., Huang, L., Joseph, A.D., Kubiatowicz, J.D.: Brocade: Land-mark routing on overlay networks. In: Proceedings of the 1st International Work-shop on Peer-to-Peer Systems. (2002) 34–44

11. Montresor, A.: A robust protocol for building superpeer overlay topologies. In: Pro-ceedings of the 4th International Conference on Peer-to-Peer Computing. (2004) 202–209

12. Mizrak, A.T., Cheng, Y., Kumar, V., Savage, S.: Structured superpeers: Leveraging heterogeneity to provide constant-time lookup. In: Proceedings of the 3rd IEEE Workshop on Internet Applications. (2003) 104–111

13. Manku, G.S., Bawa, M., Raghavan, P.: Symphony: Distributed hashing in a small world. In: Proceedings of the 4th USENIX Symposium on Internet Technologies and Systems. (2003) 127–140

14. Yang, B., Garcia-Molina, H.: Improving search in peer-to-peer networks. In: Pro-ceedings of the 22nd International Conference on Distributed Computing Systems. (2002) 5–14

15. Morselli, R., Bhattacharjee, B., Srinivasan, A., Marsh, M.A.: Efficient lookup on unstructured topologies. In: Proceedings of 24th ACM Symposium on Principles of Distributed Computing. (2005) 77–86

16. Kubiatowicz, J., Bindel, D., Chen, Y., Czerwinski, S., Eaton, P., Geels, D., Gummadi, R., Rhea, S., Weatherspoon, H., Weimer, W., Wells, C., Zhao, B.: Oceanstore: An architecture for global-scale persistent storage. In: Proceedings of the 9th international Conference on Architectural Support for Programming Languages and Operating Systems. (2000) 190–201

17. Rao, A., Lakshminarayanan, K., Surana, S., Karp, R., Stoica, I.: Load balancing in structured p2p systems. In: the 2nd International Workshop on Peer-to-Peer Systems. (2003)

18. Jelasity, M., Babaoglu, O.: T-man: Gossip-based overlay topology management. In: the 3rd International Workshop on Engineering Self-Organising Applications. (2005)

19. Sacha, J., Dowling, J.: A self-organising topology for master-slave replication in p2p environments. In: Proceedings of the 3rd International Workshop on Databases, Information Systems and Peer-to-Peer Computing. (2005) 52–64

20. Sutton, R.S., Barto, A.G.: Reinforcement Learning: An Introduction. MIT Press, Cambridge, MA (1998)

21. Wolpert, D.H., Macready, W.G.: No free lunch theorems for search. IEEE Trans-actions on Evolutionary Computation 1(1) (1997) 67–82

On the Value of Random Opinions in Decentralized Recommendation

Elth Ogston, Arno Bakker, and Maarten van Steen

Department of Computer Science
Vrije Universiteit
De Boelelaan 1081a
1081 HV Amsterdam
The Netherlands
{elth, arno, steen}@cs.vu.nl

Abstract. As the amount of information available to users continues to grow, filtering wanted items from unwanted ones becomes a dominant task. To this end, various collaborative-filtering techniques have been developed in which the ratings of items by other users form the basis for recommending items that could be of interest for a specific person. These techniques are based on the assumption that having ratings from similar users improves the quality of recommendation. For decentralized systems, such as peer-to-peer networks, it is generally impossible to get ratings from all users. For this reason, research has focused on finding the best set of peers for recommending items for a specific person. In this paper, we analyze to what extent the selection of such a set influences the quality of recommendation. Our findings are based on an extensive experimental evaluation of the MovieLens data set applied to recommending movies. We find that, in general, a random selection of peers gives surprisingly good recommendations in comparison to very similar peers that must be discovered using expensive search techniques. Our study suggests that simple decentralized recommendation techniques can do sufficiently well in comparison to these expensive solutions.

1 Introduction

Many successful recommendation systems are based on the idea of *collaborative filtering (CF)* [6]. In collaborative filtering, two users who have liked the same things in the past are assumed to like similar things in the future. A user's preference for a new item, such as a movie or a book, can therefore be predicted by examining ratings of that item made by users that previously had similar opinions. Traditionally, CF algorithms operate on complete knowledge, that is, the ratings of all users are known in one location. This makes it easy to discover the similar users needed to make the predictions. This, however, also makes these algorithms hard to employ in a decentralized context, where not all users' ratings can be available at all locations. In this paper we investigate how well CF algorithms operate on partial knowledge; that is, how many similar users does an algorithm actually need to produce good recommendations for a given user, and how similar must those users be.

We consider the example of a network of millions of interconnected personal video recorders. In the near future, these devices will not just be able to receive and record

F. Eliassen and A. Montresor (Eds.): DAIS 2006, LNCS 4025, pp. 84–98, 2006.

programs from satellite or the ether but also over the Internet. As a result, they will make more content available to the user than ever before, creating the need for a recommendation system that helps the user to decide what to watch. To build a decentralized recommendation system for these recorders we need to answer the question: what knowledge they need to achieve good quality recommendations for their users and how to obtain it?

In the context of personal video recorders, there are a number of related tasks for which recommendation systems can be used. Recommendation information can be used to augment an electronic program guide by adding a predicted rating to each item. Alternatively, it can be used to rank the items currently available for a user to watch (i.e., present the user with a Top-N of programs to watch). Both of these tasks require calculating accurate recommendations for an entire set of items. We conjecture that in a network that offers large amounts of content a simpler recommendation task might be sufficient. In this situation users are more likely to be interested in a list of some programs which they are certain to enjoy, rather than knowing ratings for all programs, or identifying the absolute best of the currently accessible programs. Simply discovering *some* good programs creates an easier recommendation task. Firstly, it requires an algorithm that need only accurately rate programs the user will find good, rather than having to accurately predict ratings in the entire rating range. Secondly, an absolute ordering of programs is not required. Finally, only a sufficiently large number of good programs must be identified, it does not matter if some are missed. This task is more suitable for a decentralized setting in which a Top-N recommendation can never be fully correct due to the fact that not all programs or ratings data are available to each user.

The main contribution of this paper is that we show for the well-known MovieLens data set [10] that sufficiently good recommendations can be made based on the ratings of a relatively small number of random users. We believe this to be an important result in light of the various attempts to port CF solutions to decentralized systems. Based on our experiments we conjecture that simple solutions are good enough.

The remainder of the paper is organized as follows. In Section 2 we present background on collaborative filtering algorithms and our system model. Section 3 describes our experiments studying the effects of the number and type of users on recommendation quality for the MovieLens data set. We present conclusions in Section 4.

2   Background and System Model

The amount of information made available through computer networks often means that people need to be selective about what content they spend their time on. This is especially true in future video-on-demand systems where so many videos are available that it is infeasible to even browse through them all. Given such an overabundance of options, recommendation systems can help people make choices by aggregating opinions on what others have found, in their experience, to be valuable. In the simplest case such recommendations can take the form of a single joint rating which is given to all users. A group of people can, however, have very different opinions about the value of an item. More advanced algorithms thus provide personalized predictions by filtering the opinions upon which a recommendation is made. This is done on the principle that users that have exhibited similar opinions on items in the past are likely to continue to have similar opinions on new items [7, 1].

At an abstract level the problem of collaborative-filtering considers a set of N users, $U = \{u_1,\ldots,u_N\}$ and a set of M items $X = \{x_1,\ldots,x_M\}$. Each user provides ratings, taken from a set of possible values, V, the rating scale, for a subset of the items in X. These ratings form an $N \times M$ user-item matrix, R, where the entry $r_{i,j}$ is the rating of user u_i for item x_j, or empty if that rating is unknown. The basic recommendation task is to predict a rating value for a given empty element $r_{i,j}$ based on the known values in R. This is done by means of a prediction function, f, where $f(R,i,j) \mapsto V$.

The prediction function usually performs two tasks. First, it *selects* rows from the matrix which correspond to data which is most likely to accurately predict $r_{i,j}$. Second, it *aggregates* the information in these rows to calculate an actual value for $r_{i,j}$. When the user-item matrix is used as the input to f, the rows selected correspond to users that are similar to user u_i. This is called *user-based* collaborative filtering. The item-user matrix, $R^\top$, can also be used as the input to the prediction function, thus calculating $f(R^\top,j,i)$. In this case the rows selected correspond to data items that have received similar ratings to the item x_j. This is called *item-based* collaborative filtering [8]. Exactly how f performs the selection and aggregation tasks is the subject of many studies on which heuristics lead to the best recommendations [2, 1, 8].

In our study, we assume an architecture in which each user has a personal networked video recorder by which he or she rates content. These personal devices can exchange gathered ratings with the devices of other users via the network, and use them to make personal predictions to their respective users using a given prediction function f. As the network grows, it becomes infeasible to distribute all ratings, i.e. the full matrix R, to all recorders. The video recorder for user u_i must therefore base its predictions on a submatrix of R denoted R_i. In this paper, this submatrix R_i will consist of u_i's own ratings and the ratings of a specific set of other users, called u_i's *peer group*, as described in Section 3.1.

Following the above, there are five factors that can influence the quality of the predictions in decentralized algorithms. In addition to (1) the size and (2) composition of the peer group of each user, the quality of prediction will be affected by the properties of function f itself. In particular, it depends on f's (3) selectiveness in choosing rows of the ratings matrix to consider, (4) the sophistication of the method by which aggregation is performed, and (5) whether the function considers user-based or item-based correlations. We study the effects of these five factors. As we shall see, the differences between simple and sophisticated approaches are small enough to raise the question of whether we need sophisticated algorithms at all.

3   Experiments

We present an analysis study in which we examine the effects of the five factors identified in the previous section on the quality of decentralized peer-to-peer recommendation algorithms. We first introduce our methodology and the data set we consider in Section 3.1. Next, we study the effect of peer-group size and composition in isolation from other factors, by using rudimentary prediction functions in Section 3.2. The analysis is repeated with sophisticated prediction functions from the well-known CF algorithms in Section 3.3. Section 3.4 analyzes the suitability of the well-known algorithms for the task of identifying just some good items to recommend to a user (as opposed to the absolute best available). Section 3.5 repeats the analysis of Section 3.4 for the PocketLens peer-to-peer recommendation algorithm proposed in [4].

3.1 Experiment Methodology

For our experiments we organize the users' personal video recorders into a peer-to-peer overlay. The personal recorder for user u_i will make its predictions on the submatrix R_i, consisting of the ratings of the peers it is connected to in the peer-to-peer overlay and its own ratings. To test the influence of the five factors, we vary the number and type of peers u_i is connected to and the prediction functions used.

The users' personal devices are organized into overlays as follows. Each of the nodes in the overlay stores the ratings data for a single user, that is, the node for user u_i stores the ith row of R. Nodes connected by directed *links* to other nodes, called their *neighbors*, thus forming a peer-to-peer overlay network. The set of links of each node is called its *neighbor cache* which has a size c. Only the ratings data stored at a node's neighbors is available as input to the prediction function f. Note that because links are directed, more than c nodes can use the ratings of any particular user.

In addition to varying c, we consider two contrasting peer-to-peer overlay topologies. In the first, neighbor caches contain links to random nodes, creating a *random overlay*. In the second, neighbor caches contain links to the nodes to which a node is most similar, given a similarity function d for rating data, creating a *best-neighbors overlay*. Given the base assumption of collaborative filtering that ratings from similar users provide the best quality recommendations, these two cases represent a worst-case and a best-case scenario, respectively.

A best-neighbors overlay can be constructed in a decentralized fashion, for instance by using a gossiping protocol such as Cyclon/Vicinity [11]. Nodes exchange their rating data and compute the similarity to the other peers using the given similarity function d. By remembering the best candidates so far, while continuing to exchange preferences with other peers, each node will eventually fill its neighbor cache with the nodes most similar to it. As running such a protocol is more expensive in terms of network usage than discovering random peers, the random and best-neighbor overlays also represent the cheap and expensive solution respectively. We use Pearson's correlation using significance weighting [2] as the similarity function to define best-neighbors overlays in all our experiments. Following Herlocker *et al.*'s conclusions for the MovieLens data set we set the significance weighting parameters to *minCommonItems*=2 and *maxCommonItems*=100 for all experiments. Negative correlations are not considered.

We evaluate the performance of each algorithm for differing values of c and the two topologies using the MovieLens data set [10]. This data set consists of 100,000 ratings, on a scale of 1 to 5 stars, of 1,682 movies made by 943 users. Each user rates at least 20 items, but the data set is still sparse: 94% of the user-item space has no rating. For evaluating the performance we partition this data into a training set and a test set. The training set forms the matrix R, constituting the users' ratings used to populate the

Table 1. Summary of the ratings in the training and test set

Ratings	Count in Training Set	Count in Test Set
1*	5568	542
2*	10375	995
3*	24721	2424
4*	30858	3316
5*	19048	2153
Total	90570	9430

nodes in the overlay. The test set consists of 10 randomly chosen movies per user as summarized in Table 1.

Each experiment consists of constructing the peer-to-peer overlay using the training set and then attempting to make predictions for the 9430 withheld (user,movie) pairs. Our experiments thus measure algorithm performance in making 9,430 predictions based on 90,570 ratings. In particular, each node will attempt to predict the rating its user u_i would give to the 10 withheld items based on its R_i matrix, consisting of the ratings of the user and those of its neighbors. The resulting predictions are compared to the 9430 actual ratings in the test set using several metrics. The experiments are conducted using the CoFE collaborative filtering engine [5] that implements centralized user-based collaborative filtering. We extended CoFE to support item-based recommendation and the rudimentary recommendation algorithms.

We use the following metrics to evaluate predictions. Initially, we consider the *mean absolute error (MAE)* metric [9]. Given a list L of H user-item pairs (u_{i_1}, x_{j_1}), ..., (u_{i_H}, x_{j_H}), a corresponding list A of actual user ratings for these user-item pairs $r_{i_1 j_1}$, ..., $r_{i_H j_H}$ with $r_{i_k j_k} \in V$, and a corresponding list P of *unrounded*[1] predictions of the ratings for the user-item pairs $r^*_{i_1 j_1}$, ..., $r^*_{i_H j_H}$ with $r^*_{i_k j_k} \in V$, the mean absolute error is given by:

$$MAE = \frac{\sum_{k=1}^{H} |r^*_{i_k j_k} - r_{i_k j_k}|}{H}$$

Associated with MAE is the *coverage* metric which measures what fraction of the predictions attempted actually returned a result. Predictions for user u_i and movie x_j may fail because, for example, none of the user's neighbors actually rated x_j.

Mean absolute error is a rough estimation of the overall accuracy of an algorithm. It considers errors in any part of the ratings scale to be equal. For our stated purpose of identifying a set of some good items, however, errors at the top end of the scale become more important than errors elsewhere in the scale. In order to measure recommendation accuracy more precisely we will use the standard information-retrieval metrics *recall* and *precision* in Section 3.4. Recall and precision compare, for a particular query q, the set of selected items S_q, which were returned in reply to q, and the set of relevant items T_q, which contains all items that are correct replies to q. Recall measures the fraction

---

[1] Users rate and see predictions as integer values, but for the calculation of prediction-performance metrics the unrounded predictions returned by the recommendation algorithms are used.

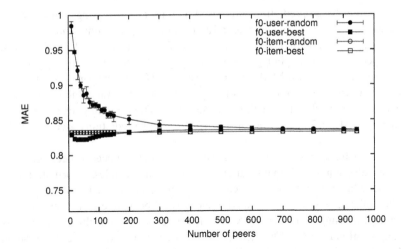

Fig. 1. Recommendation quality for the four rudimentary algorithms. For the random overlays, values are averaged over three runs. The vertical errorbars show the minimum and maximum value obtained in these three runs. Note that the y-axis starts at 0.72.

of correct replies to q that actually appeared in the selected set: $|S_q \cap T_q|/|T_q|$. Precision measures, for the selected set, the fraction of correct replies it contains: $|S_q \cap T_q|/|S_q|$.

3.2 Rudimentary Recommendation Algorithms

In this section we establish a baseline for the effect of varying peer-group size and composition. We also look at the underlying differences between user-based and item-based algorithms. We consider a rudimentary prediction function, f_0. This function performs no selection on its input matrix. To predict a rating for user u_i of an item x_j it simply computes the mean value of the relevant column in the input matrix. More specifically, when given a user-item matrix R, f_0 calculates a user-based prediction by computing the average of the rating for item x_j as given by the nonempty entries in column j (that is, from users who have rated x_j). When given an item-user matrix, f_0 calculates an item-based prediction by computing the average over the values for items rated by user u_i.

Figure 1 shows recommendation quality in terms of MAE versus the size c of a user's peer group (i.e., its neighbors). We consider four different inputs to f_0. In the user-based cases, the input consists of the submatrix R_i as constructed from the peer group. In the item-based cases, the input is $R_i^\top$, the transposition of R_i. The x-axis shows the effect of having more or less ratings data available to f_0; the random and best-neighbors variants show the effect of the quality of the information available.

The first thing to note when analyzing Figure 1 is the scale of the y-axis. MAE values range from 0.82 to 0.99. An MAE of 1 means that predictions are, on average, one star off from the actual ratings given by users. From this perspective, a difference in MAE 0.17 is fairly insignificant, and we could say that all four algorithms perform fairly well. It is interesting to note that the best reported MAE for an algorithm on this data set is 0.72 [8].

Because item-based predictions are based on a user's own ratings, and f_0 does not select among these ratings, the item-based algorithms simply recommend the average of a user's ratings for all predictions. Therefore, the results are independent of the network type and peer-group sizes. For group sizes of over 200 these item-based algorithms actually produce the lowest MAE of all algorithms, 0.83. Such a small MAE indicates that users tend to give similar ratings to all the movies they rate. Table 1 shows that, in general, this is fairly true for this data set: the average rating over the whole data set (training+test) is 3.53 and using this value for all predictions gives an MAE of 0.94.

For the user-based best-neighbors algorithm, in which the peer-to-peer network performs user selection, we see that smaller group sizes, in which less information is available, produce better results. This indicates that some users are better predictors of each other than others, and therefore selection can have a positive effect. It also shows the disadvantage of using averaging, by which mediocre opinions can drown out good ones, in the aggregation function. The fact that this algorithm performs better than the others only for groups sizes under 200 indicates that the number of very similar neighbors per peer is fairly small. The small difference between good performance and bad again indicates that all peers are similar enough to provide acceptable predictions.

We also calculated the coverage values for the four algorithms. The item-based algorithms are always able to make predictions for all items. For the user-based best-neighbors algorithm coverage was about 1.0 for all group sizes showing that nodes' best neighbors practically always had at least one rating for their movies in the test set. This could indicate that nodes with a large numbers of ratings tend to be chosen more often as best neighbors. For random groups coverage was as low as 0.69 for a group size of 10 but rose quickly to 0.98 or higher for group sizes over 100.

Given the overall small differences in MAE it could be said that even small groups of randomly chosen neighbors produce sufficiently good recommendations. This leads to the interesting conclusion that we need only consider small groups of users, and their exact composition may not be that critical. Note, however, that the difference in terms of MAE between the best performing algorithm to date and the trivial algorithm that always predicts the average rating is only two tenths of a star. This makes MAE an un-intuitive metric for measuring recommendation performance. The trivial algorithm does not provide user-specific recommendations nor does it accurately predict which movies are very good or very bad. Therefore, a metric judging this algorithm's performance should clearly indicate that it performs poorly. For now, we continue to use MAE as it is a standard metric that, although subtly, gives a decent indication of the general performance difference between algorithms. We return to the issue of performance metrics in Section 3.4.

3.3 Sophisticated Recommendation Algorithms

The experiments with a simple prediction function, f_0 provided some initial insight into the effect of decentralization on recommendation quality. By removing the selection task from the prediction function we were able to examine the situation where all peer selection (if any) is done by the peer-to-peer protocol. In this section we reintroduce (additional) selection by the prediction function. Letting the prediction function make the selection is to be preferred provided quality does not suffer much, as it is a local operation on the matrix R_i rather than a search operation on the network.

Advanced prediction functions use two types of selection: (1) choosing from the matrix those ratings of a user that are of interest, and (2) judging the relative importance of the ratings chosen. This second selection is accomplished by assigning weights to the input ratings. For this experiment we use a prediction function f_1 that was designed by Herlocker *et al.* [2] to optimize user-based prediction accuracy. This prediction function performs both types of additional selection. First, when asked to make a prediction for item x_j for user u_i, it selects from the matrix R_i supplied by the peer-to-peer overlay the ratings of x_j as made by the z users most similar to u_i, thus creating a rating vector $\vec{r}$. To calculate the similarity it uses the same function as the best-neighbors overlay (Pearson's correlation with significance weighting).

Second, when making the actual prediction for item x_j it weights the rating of the z users most similar to u_i with their similarity value. In short, in addition to any selection by the peer-to-peer network, f_1 limits the set of opinions to consider to z and weights those opinions based on just how similar they are in absolute terms. In this experiment we use a parameter set shown by Herlocker to be optimal for user-based predictions on this data set [2], in particular, z is set to 60 and the Pearson significance weighting parameters are set to $minCommonItems=2$ and $maxCommonItems=100$, as before.

Figure 2 shows data for the experiment from the previous section repeated with prediction function f_1. The first two plots in Figure 2 (using the dark symbols) show results for user-based prediction using f_1 on random and best-neighbors overlays. For comparison, the f_0 results for user-based prediction on the best-neighbors overlay are also shown. For both overlays, f_1 improves predictions over f_0. For the random overlay, f_1 bases predictions only on the more similar users in the random input set. For small

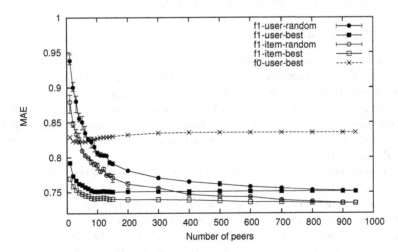

Fig. 2. Recommendation quality for the sophisticated algorithms. For the random overlays, values are averaged over three runs. The vertical errorbars show the minimum and maximum value obtained in these three runs. Note that the y-axis starts at 0.72.

group sizes this results in very little data with which to make predictions, but it is very effective for larger group sizes. The additional ability to weight these inputs relative to each other allows f_1 on a random overlay to outperform f_0 on a best-neighbors overlay for group sizes over 100. Using a best-neighbors overlay to provide f_1 with higher quality input improves recommendation, especially for smaller groups. The difference between the f_1 user-based best-neighbors and the f_0 user-based best-neighbors curves shows how valuable weighting input results can be.

The second two plots in Figure 2 (using the open symbols) show results for item-based prediction using f_1 on random and best-neighbors overlays. Interestingly, even though f_1 was not designed as an item-based prediction function, the results improve slightly on those for user-based predictions. This indicates that there may be more similarity between items than between users in the data sets, though the imprecision of the MAE metric precludes hard conclusions. It should be noted that the item-based best-neighbors algorithm is in fact a hybrid item-based/user-based approach, with user-based selection taking place within the peer-to-peer network and item-based selection taking place within the prediction function.

We also examined the coverage of the algorithms using f_1. This was slightly lower than the coverage using f_0, especially for predictions based on random groups of users, but still above 0.93 for all algorithms for a group size of 100 or more.

Overall, this experiment shows that for a more sophisticated prediction function making item-based predictions in a best-neighbors network produces the best MAE values. The differences between the algorithms are, however, fairly small. In general, it appears that performing selection within the prediction function, even out of a small amount of random input, is more effective than performing selection within the peer-to-peer network. This again indicates that peer-to-peer networks that provide users with small amounts of random ratings information from other users might be a sufficient basis for decentralized-recommendation algorithms.

3.4   Identifying Good Programs

Our measurements of mean absolute error in Section 3.3 give an indication of the relative quality of our recommendation methods. MAE, however, provides only a general measure of overall quality. As described in the introduction, in the context of a personal video recorder we are most interested in being able to produce accurate recommendations for movies at the five-star end of the ratings scale. To investigate recommendation behavior in more detail, we employ the standard information-retrieval metrics precision and recall (see Section 3.1), as follows.

For the user-item pairs in the test set, we separate the list of returned predictions P, according to prediction value, into the sublists P_{1*}, P_{2*}, P_{3*}, P_{4*} and P_{5*}. We also divide the actual ratings of the test set in a similar manner into A_{1*}, A_{2*}, A_{3*}, A_{4*} and A_{5*}. Thus, P_{5*}, for instance, contains all of the five-star predictions ($r^*_{i_k j_k} = 5$) and A_{5*} contains all the actual five-star ratings in the test set ($r_{i_k j_k} = 5$). The user-item pairs (u_{i_k}, x_{j_k}) that correspond to the predictions and ratings in P_{5*} and A_{5*} can be viewed as a selected-items set S_{5*} and a relevant-items set T_{5*}, respectively, for the query "find all five-star movies for each user". This allows us to calculate precision and recall per

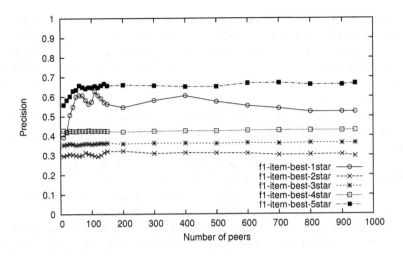

Fig. 3. The 1–5 star precision of f_1 item-based for differing numbers of similar peers

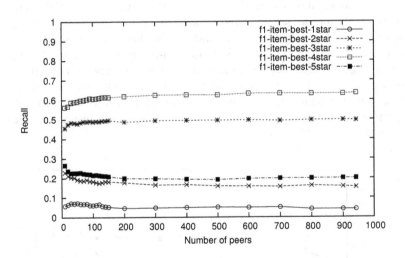

Fig. 4. The 1–5 star recall of f_1 item-based for differing numbers of similar peers

rating value. Note that precision and recall are computed only over the predictions that could actually be made (see the discussion of the coverage metric in Section 3.1).

We use these new metrics to analyze the best performing according to MAE, the f_1 item-based best-neighbors algorithm, in Figures 3 and 4. The figures establish that items with different values in the ratings scale are not, in fact, treated equally by the algorithm. In general, precision is higher for items at the extremes for the rating scale, while recall is higher for items in the middle of the rating scale. This tradeoff between recall and precision is not unusual, increasing precision requires an algorithm to be more picky about the replies it chooses, which tends to decrease recall.

Figures 3 and 4 indicate that this algorithm tends to predict extreme ratings values only when the rating is fairly clear, and otherwise chooses a safer prediction in the middle of the scale. This is in line with the fact that the algorithm does aggregation by taking a weighted average of ratings. Items with mixed reviews should thus tend to be given mediocre predicted ratings, while items which everyone liked or disliked can be given extreme ratings.

Fortunately, for the task of recommending some good items, we are most interested in having a high precision for five-star items, as is the case. Five-star recall is less important, as long as it is high enough for a query for five-star items to produce some answers. Five-star recall for the test set is 20 percent for this algorithm at a group size of 200. An average user rates about 21% of movies with five stars, so in the collection of 1682 movies there are about 357 movies he will like. If we use the recall for the test set as an estimate for recall on the whole data set, the algorithm recalls 20% of these 357 enjoyable movies, yielding roughly 71 movies to watch. At 1.5 hours per movie, this translates to 107 hours of viewing pleasure. A video-on-demand system is likely to give access to even more content.

Comparing the performance of the four f_1 algorithms from Section 3.3, we find that using a best-neighbors overlay instead of a random one results in higher precision values, especially for one-star and five-star items and groups smaller than 200. In particular, one-star precision is up to 24 percentage points higher and five-star precision is 11 percentage points higher for the item-based best-neighbors algorithm. For the user-based best neighbors algorithm these values are 28 percentage points and 8 percentage points, respectively. This higher precision does not come at the cost of a lower recall, which remains practically the same for these extremes. Recall for the other values increases up to 6 percentage points. Figure 5 and 6 show precision, respectively recall for f_1 item-based using a random overlay.

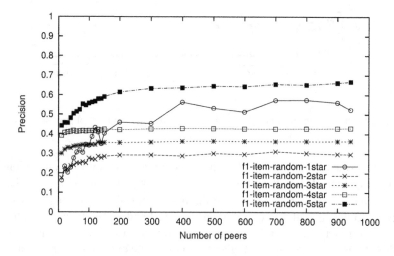

Fig. 5. The 1–5 star precision of f_1 item-based for differing numbers of random peers. Values are averaged over three runs.

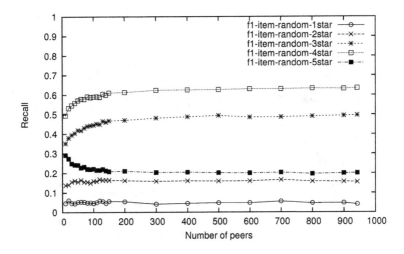

Fig. 6. The 1–5 star recall of f_1 item-based for differing numbers of random peers. Values are averaged over three runs.

In general, making item-based in place of user-based predictions results in higher precision for five-star ratings. The item-based best-neighbors algorithm improves this precision by an average of 8 percentage points over the user-based best-neighbors algorithm for all group sizes. This is, however, at the cost of recall, which we found to be up to 10 percentage points lower for five-star predictions. Meanwhile recall on four-star and three-star items improves slightly, indicating that item-based prediction gives higher five-star precision because it has a greater tendency to give predictions from the middle of the scale. One-star precision decreases around 8 percentage points, its recall went down by 3 percentage points on average.

Precision results may be affected by the fact that there are a very small number of one-star items in the data set, due to the way user opinions were gathered. A data set with a more even distribution of ratings might result in slightly worse precision results. On the other hand, in a video-on-demand network, users are also likely to watch and rate a majority of items at the upper end of the scale.

For the task of recommending good items, predictions that are slightly off will probably not be noticed, while predictions that are very wrong could undermine a user's faith in the recommendation system. A list of good items to watch should ideally contain only five-star items. A user will probably also be glad to watch four-star items, but will be annoyed to find one-star or two-star items in the list. We thus introduce a further metric, *adapted top precision (ATP)*, which measures precision for the query "find five-star movies for each user" but also considers a four-star prediction a valid answer. Formally, $ATP = |S_{5*} \cap (T_{4*} \cup T_{5*})|/|S_{5*}|$. Figure 7 shows ATP for each of the four f_1 algorithms. All four algorithms perform well on this metric. Even the worst performing algorithm at the smallest group size still returns 77% four- or five-star items when asked for five-star items.

Overall, the experiments in this section confirm the conclusions we made in Section 3.3. The item-based best-neighbors algorithm generally produces the best

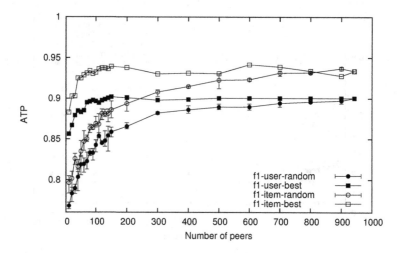

Fig. 7. Adapted top precision for differing numbers of peers. For the random overlays, values are averaged over three runs. The vertical errorbars show the minimum and maximum value obtained in these three runs. Note that the y-axis starts at 0.76.

recommendations, especially from the perspective of simply finding good items. But again, results for item-based prediction on a random network are not that much worse. We also still find that increasing group size improves results, but that small groups can still produce good recommendations. As an example, when given the task of finding a set of items which are predicted to have five-star ratings, for a group size of 200, the item-based best-neighbors algorithm returns 425 five-star items, 179 four-star items, 26 three-star items, 9 two-star items, and 5 one-star items. The item-based random algorithm returns 444 five-star items, 202 four-star items, 53 three-star items, 14 two-star items and 10 one-star items.

3.5   Comparison to PocketLens

PocketLens is an item-based prediction algorithm designed specifically for a peer-to-peer setting. In [4], Miller *et al.* evaluated the performance of PocketLens using several different underlying overlays: a Gnutella-based random overlay, a best-neighbors overlay, and two Distributed-Hash Table-based overlays. The performance of each overlay was tested using a non-standard version of the MovieLens data set with twice as many items. They found the best MAE performance was achieved by the random overlay and with sufficient coverage (already 90% for groups of just 65 peers). Their measurements thus support our conclusion that random overlays can be used for decentralized CF algorithms. We show it holds for the standard MovieLens data set and for user-based algorithms, and when measured using more expressive metrics. In addition, we provide a detailed examination of why random overlays can be used.

To examine how PocketLens performs on the new task of recommending some good items we repeat the analysis from the previous section for this algorithm. Figure 8 compares the adapted top precision measure for the PocketLens prediction function on a

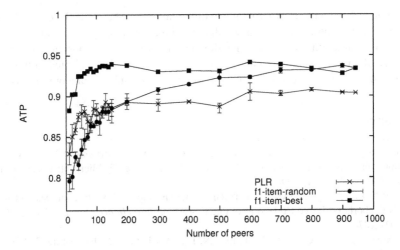

Fig. 8. Adapted top precision for PocketLens compared to f_1 item-based predictions. For the random overlays, values are averaged over three runs. The vertical errorbars show the minimum and maximum value obtained in these three runs. Note that the y-axis starts at 0.76.

random overlay with the most similar algorithm we studied, the item-based f_1 prediction function on a random overlay. We also plot the results for item-based f_1 on a best-neighbors overlay, the algorithm which produced the best ATP above.

The PocketLens prediction function performs better than f_1 on the random overlay for group sizes smaller than 300, but fails to improve its predictions for larger group sizes. In a more detailed exploration of this behavior we found that PocketLens produces high five-star precision values in this range, but that this is at the cost of low five-star recall. For a group size of 100, for instance, PocketLens has a five-star recall value of 0.07 while the item-based f_1 algorithm has a recall of 0.22. Overall, we found that PocketLens produces lower recall for all ratings except for four-stars, indicating that it has a much greater tendency to guess that items will be rated four-stars, which is the rounded average ratings value for the data set (see Section 3.2).

4   Conclusions

Our experiments with the MovieLens data set bring us to the conclusion that the neighbors from which a peer receives ratings data may not be critical to the quality of peer-to-peer recommendations. That is, neither the number of neighbors nor selecting the most similar really matters. If a peer has access to ratings from a few hundred, randomly chosen other nodes, we see that reasonable recommendations can be obtained. This is a notable result in light of the various attempts to port existing centralized collaborative-filtering algorithms to peer-to-peer networks. We conjecture that there may be no need to incur the added costs of structuring a network in order to improve recommendations.

Whether these results can be generalized remains to be seen. The quality of recommendations provided by any algorithm is highly dependent on the quality of the input ratings data, which in turn, strongly depends on the rating behavior of users [3]. To this end, we plan to extend our experiments to other data sets. There may be circumstances in which selecting best neighbors is worth the trouble. For example, our current experiments show that quality of recommendation does improve if neighbors are *not* selected randomly, albeit by a small amount. Thus, although the results presented in this paper are promising, further research is needed in order to truly substantiate our claims.

References

1. BREESE, J., HECKERMAN, D., AND KADIE, C. Empirical Analysis of Predictive Algorithms for Collaborative Filtering. Tech. Rep. MSR-TR-98-12, Microsoft Research, Redmond, WA, USA, May 1998.
2. HERLOCKER, J., KONSTAN, J., AND RIEDL, J. An Empirical Analysis of Design Choices in Neighborhood-Based Collaborative Filtering Algorithms. *Information Retrieval 5*, 4 (Oct. 2002), 287–310.
3. HERLOCKER, J., KONSTAN, J., TERVEEN, L., AND RIEDL, J. Evaluating Collaborative Filtering Recommender Systems. *ACM Transactions on Information Systems 22*, 1 (Jan. 2004), 5–53.
4. MILLER, B., KONSTAN, J., AND RIEDL, J. PocketLens: Toward a Personal Recommender System. *ACM Transcations on Information Systems 22*, 3 (July 2004), 437–476.
5. OREGON STATE UNIVERSITY. COllaborative Filtering Engine version 0.4. http://eecs.oregonstate.edu/iis/CoFE/, Sept. 2005.
6. RESNICK, P., IACOVOU, N., SUCHAK, M., BERGSTROM, P., AND RIEDL, J. GroupLens: An Open Architecture for Collaborative Filtering of Netnews. In *Proceedings 1994 ACM Conference on Computer Supported Cooperative Work* (Chapel Hill, NC, United States, Oct. 1994), pp. 175–186.
7. RESNICK, P., AND VARIAN, H. Recommender systems. *Communications of the ACM 40*, 3 (1997), 56–58.
8. SARWAR, B., KARYPIS, G., KONSTAN, J., AND RIEDL, J. Item-Based Collaborative Filtering Recommendation Algorithms. In *Proceedings 10th International Conference on the World Wide Web (WWW10)* (Hong Kong, Hong Kong, May 2001), pp. 285 –295.
9. SHARDANAND, U., AND MAES, P. Social Information Filtering: Algorithms for Automating "Word of Mouth". In *Proceedings 1995 ACM SIGCHI Conference on Human Factors in Computing Systems* (Denver, CO, USA, May 1995), pp. 210–217.
10. UNIVERSITY OF MINNESOTA. GroupLens Home Page. http://www.grouplens.org/, Sept. 2005.
11. VOULGARIS, S., AND VAN STEEN, M. Epidemic-style Management of Semantic Overlays for Content-Based Searching. In *Proceedings 11th International Euro-Par Conference* (Lisbon, Portugal, Aug. 2005), pp. 1143–1152.

Information Agents That Learn to Understand Each Other Via Semantic Negotiation

Salvatore Garruzzo and Domenico Rosaci

DIMET, Università Mediterranea di Reggio Calabria
Via Graziella, Località Feo di Vito
89060 Reggio Calabria, Italy
{salvatore.garruzzo, domenico.rosaci}@unirc.it

Abstract. A key issue in Distributed Applications, that widely use Information Agents for implementing several typologies of services, is that of making reciprocally understandable the meaning of terms contained in the exchanged messages, in those cases where agents use different, heterogeneous ontologies. A possible way for facing this issue is offered by the *semantic negotiation*, a framework in which agents try to understand each other by negotiating the semantic of the terms. Several models and protocols of semantic negotiation have been proposed in the last years. However, most of these approaches are not able to support semantic negotiation without requiring agents either to share knowledge or to use a global common ontology, and none of them provides a semantic negotiation protocol that allows the whole agent community to contribute to the semantic understanding process between each agent pair. In this work, we propose the HIerarchical SEmantic NEgotiation (HISENE) protocol, based on the idea that an agent a should be able to partition the set of the other agents on the basis both of their personal expertise of the application domain, as well as on the particular capability that each of them shows in understanding a. We also give an implementation of the proposed protocol in the standard Java Agent DEvelopment Framework (JADE).

1 Introduction

In human discussions, the meaning of terms contained in the statements are not always reciprocally clear for both the interlocutors. Often, one of them uses a term that the other one either does not understand or considers ambiguous. Generally, human beings try to solve these situations by *negotiating* the semantics of the involved terms, where the negotiation implies several operations performed by the two interlocutors as, for instance, a query that one of them could pose for having a description of a non-understood term, a response provided by the other interlocutor, containing the requested description, etc. This scenario, very usual in human context, has today a counterpart in Distributed Applications field, where distributed software entities, generally called *information agents*, operates on the behalf of human beings to perform operations that would be

F. Eliassen and A. Montresor (Eds.): DAIS 2006, LNCS 4025, pp. 99–112, 2006.

too onerous to be completed manually, as information searching, e-commerce and e-learning activities, software exchanging and so on. On the one hand, each information agent generally stores an internal representation, called *ontology*, of the domain of interest for its human owner. On the other hand, agents communicate between each other in a distributed Multi-Agent System (MAS) to perform their activities. As an example, consider the case of an e-commerce scenario in which an agent, operating on the behalf of a human customer, negotiates for a product with another agent operating on the behalf of a human seller. This communication is performed effectively in the case the two agents share the same ontology, i.e. if both of them know the same terms and give the same meanings to the terms. Otherwise, the problem arises for an agent interpreting some terms unknown or ambiguous contained in messages arriving from the other agent. It is important to consider that nowadays communications among agents have become a key issue for the development of the whole Web, and not just some particular application domain as e-commerce and e-learning. A suitable example for understanding this fact is represented by the general case of Web Services, that can be viewed as (server) agents that provide services to other (client) agents. It is necessary that, as Web Services become more prevalent, client agents should be able to compose together disparate Web Services. However, in order to enable such compositions, it is not enough just agreeing on common protocols (e.g. SOAP) but also the messages' contents need to be mutually understandable: this means that there should be an agreement on the semantics of the terms used in the messages.

Although we have observed over the last years an important evolution towards the standardization of agent communication languages (ACL's), as KQML [5] and FIPA ACL [6], it is worth to point out that the focus of these standards is mainly on the syntax of messages and the semantics of performatives, while the semantics of the content of a message is specified by the ontology which is used. This means that, in order to correctly understand the content of a message, the receiving agent has to understand the terms contained in the ontology of the sending agent. In a MAS, this is possible if either all the agents share the same ontology, or every agent knows each other's ontology. However, none of these situations are desirable, since: (i) every agent generally deals with its own particular task and thus requires its own specialized ontology; (ii) making every agent of an open MAS, whose size can quickly increase in time, always acquainted with every other agent's ontology would lead to a untenable situation.

A possible way of facing the problem to solve the difficulties of an agent in understanding the messages coming from other agents having different ontologies is offered by the *semantic negotiation*. This is a process by which agents in an agent community try to reach mutually acceptable definitions (i.e., mutually acceptable agreements on terms).

Several models and protocols of semantic negotiation have been proposed in the last years [2, 4, 7, 11, 12]. However, most of these approaches are not able to support semantic negotiation without requiring agents either to share knowledge or to use a global common ontology, and none of them provides a semantic negotiation protocol that allows the whole agent community to contribute to the semantic understanding process between each agent pair. In this work, we introduce the idea that two agents involved in a communication process can require the help of other agents in order to solve possible understanding problems. In this context, the notion of *expertise* of an agent introduces a measure of the capability of the agent to explain non-understood terms to each other agent. Moreover, we also define the notion of *understanding capability* of an agent a with respect to another agent b, that measures the capability of a to explain terms that b does not understand. Therefore, the expertise of an agent a is the capability of a to effectively explain non-understood terms to the whole community, while the understanding capability with respect to b is relative to the only agent b. These two notions allow the possibility to introduce the synthetic measure of *negotiation degree*, defining the potential capability of a to negotiate the semantic of terms belonging to b. Therefore, in our framework, an agent can ask help to other agents for understanding a term on the basis of their negotiation degree; for this purpose, he groups the agents in different *partitions* $p_1, p_2, .., p_n$, ordered by a decreasing level of negotiation degree. We propose a semantic negotiation protocol, called *HIerarchical SEmantic NEgotiation* (HISENE), that is suitable to be applied for implementing such a semantic negotiation in the standard Java Agent DEvelopment Framework (JADE) [8]. An important advantage that this protocol introduces is that each agent can contact the other agents in different stages, by following the rational criteria of firstly negotiating with the agents belonging to the partition p_1, contacting agents of the partition p_2 only if none of the agents in p_1 is able to positively answer, then contacting agents of the partition p_3 only if none of the agents in p_2 succeeds, and so on. Moreover, each contacted agent can start, in its turn, another semantic negotiation, in order to understand unknown term; however, in order to avoid the presence of a loop, each term is processed only once by each agent. This leads to use in an efficient way the network communication resources. The plan of the paper is the following: Section 2 describes some related work; Section 3 gives some preliminary notions on the JADE framework; Section 4 deals in detail with the HISENE protocol, while Section 5 describes a simple example of how HISENE works; Section 6 draws some final conclusions. The Appendix describes the JAVA implementation of the main components composing the package HISENE, built on top of the JADE framework.

2   Related Work

In a MAS, each agent is specialized in solving a particular task, so it requires its own ontology. In order to allow agents having different ontologies to understand each other, some approaches have proposed in the past the use of a *common shared ontology*. As an example, the approach proposed in [11] provides the agents with a set of shared concepts, in which they can express their private knowledge. The communication vocabulary is formalized as an ontology, shared by the entire MAS, and in which every private concept of each individual agent can eventually be defined. Concept names used in an agent's private ontology, are not understandable to other agents. However, their definitions in terms of ground concepts are understandable. The use of definition terms, instead of the concepts, enables optimal communications between agents.

Moreover, the approach presented in [2] introduces a computational framework for the detection of ontological discrepancies between two agents in multi-agent systems. In this method, presuppositions are extracted from the sender's messages, expressed in a common vocabulary, and compared with the recipient's ontology, which is expressed in type theory. Discrepancies are detected by the receiving agent if it notices type conflicts, particular inconsistencies or ontological gaps. Depending on the kind of discrepancy, the agent generates a feedback message in order to establish alignment of its private ontology with the ontology of the sender. The dialogue framework is based on a simple model of interaction.

Another approach using a common knowledge is that presented in [12], where authors introduce a machine learning methodology and algorithms for multi-agent knowledge sharing and learning in a peer-to-peer setting. Agents can use a set of shared concepts in which they can express their private knowledge.

The work [7] proposes to consider the use of shared keys to solve the problem of using different names for the same object; in particular, a probabilistic matching approach is introduced. Semantic negotiation is described as a process by which a client and a service can negotiate mutually shared references.

There are some other approaches that do not require the use of a shared ontology. As an example, in [4], to allow agents to interoperate, authors have developed a matchmaking system that, rather than requiring agents to share ontologies, exploits an agent-independent, domain-specific ontology, called a *global ontology*. Besides the global ontology, the proposed system, when an agent joins the platform, applies an information-extraction engine to the agent's code to extract useful information, that includes recognized names of concepts the agent uses (e.g. class names, parameter names, etc.). Instead of having a shared ontology, the proposed system maintains a mapping of the local ontologies of all agents to the independent global ontology. The main difference between this approach and a shared ontology approach is that an agent's programmer does not need to know anything about any other agent's local ontology, nor he does need to know about the global ontology, but it is the system that does the necessary mapping.

The main difference between the approaches described above and that one we propose in this paper is that in our approach, agents do not need to share either a common ontology or to maintain a global ontology, in order to understand each other, but they try to solve their understanding problems availing the help of other agents that are considered experts in the involved domain and that have similar ontologies. Obviously, by using this approach, the understanding can be obtained only by waiting that the agent community evolves in time, allowing the formation of expert agents and understanding relationships among agents, due to the continuous interaction. The main advantage that our method presents is that the mutual understanding among agents is not statically related to a global ontology, but it can dynamically improve by following the agent interactions and monitoring the agent communications.

Other approaches exist in the literature, that we consider alternative to our one. As an example, in [3], the problems brought by the schema heterogeneity in Digital Libraries are discussed. The proposed architecture integrates the ontology, agent and P2P technologies together to support the schema mapping. The goal is to allow agents embedded in different libraries to communicate semantically. As another example, in [1], authors present a technique to generate elementary speech act sequences in a dialogue game between an electronic assistant and a computer user. The work focuses on the conversational process of the understanding of the meaning of a vocabulary shared by two dialogue participants, where the computer interface is considered to be a cooperative agent. Another proposal is that contained in [10]. In this work, agents in an open agent system jointly agree on an axiomatic semantics for the agent communications language utterances they will use to communicate. This work assumes that the agents involved all start with a common semantic space, and then together assign particular locutions to specific points in this space. Such a structure would not appear to permit an incremental construction of the semantic space itself.

3   Preliminaries

Agents in a multi-agent system can communicate by means of messages. Information inside a message is represented as a *content expression* consistent with a proper content language and encoded in a proper format. Taking into account that agents have their own way of internally representing the information, it is quite clear that the representation used in a content expression is not suitable for the inside of an agent. For this reason, agents need to convert their internal representation into a content expression representation, and vice versa. Moreover, the problem of different ontology explained in Section 1 determines the impossibility of message understanding.

JADE is a software framework fully implemented in Java language to realize distributed multi-agent systems complied with the FIPA specifications. JADE offers a number of advantages such as: (*i*) each agent "lives" in a runtime environment on a given host; (*ii*) communications are held by means of ACL messages; (*iii*) information can be represented as an instance of an application-specific class (a Java object). Moreover, the support for content languages and ontologies provided by JADE is designed to automatically perform all the above conversion operations, thus allowing developers manipulating information within their agents as Java objects.

In order for JADE to perform the proper semantic checks on a given content expression it is necessary to classify all possible elements in the domain of discourse (i.e. elements that can appear within the content of an ACL message) according to their generic semantic characteristics. This classification is derived from the ACL language defined in FIPA which requires that the content of each ACLMessage must have a proper semantics according to the performative of the

ACLMessage. The JADE *content reference model* considers only four types of elements which can be used as meaningful content of an ACL message, namely:

Predicates, that are boolean expressions saying something about the status of the world. As an example, the expression

$(studies - in\ (Student : name\ Jim)(University : name\ MIT))$

states that "the student Jim studies in the University MIT". Generally, inside predicates there are referenced some expressions called *concepts*, that indicate entities with a complex structure e.g. $(Student : name\ Jim : age\ 21)$.

Agent Actions, indicating actions that can be performed by some agents, e.g. $(sell\ (Book : title\ ``AnnaKarenina")\ (Person : name\ Jim))$

states that the person Jim sells the book "Anna Karenina".

Identifying Relational Expressions (IRE), that are expressions that identify the entities for which a given predicate is true, e.g. $(all\ ?x\ (studies - in\ ?x\ (University : nameMIT)$ identify all the students for which the predicate $(studies - in\ (Student : name\ x)(University : name\ MIT))$ is true.

ContentElement Lists, that are lists of elements of the above three types.

In the following, we introduce a technique for supporting semantic negotiations among JADE agents that uses the ontology support libraries.

4   The HISENE Protocol

In our framework, we suppose that an integer coefficient e_i, called *expertise coefficient* (that we will call in the following e-coefficient, for shortly) of i, is associated with any agent i of the MAS, representing the degree of expertise that the whole agent community gives to i. Moreover, another integer coefficient u_{ij}, called *understanding capability coefficient* (that we will call in the following u-coefficient, for shortly) of j with regards to i, is associated with each pair of agents (i, j), representing the degree of understanding that the agent j presents with regards to the agent i. Each agent i stores all the u-coefficients in a local database, called *Understanding Coefficient DataBase* ($UCDB_i$), while all the e-coefficients are stored in a global database called *Expertise Coefficient DataBase* ($ECDB$), by means of a yellow pages service provided by a specific agent.

These two coefficients are used by each agent i of the MAS to determine a partitioning in the set of the agents belonging to the MAS. We call AS_i the set of all the agents belonging to the MAS, except the agent i. We call AS_i^k, $k = 1, 2, .., p_i$, the k-th partition determined by the agent i in the agent set AS_i. The agent i decides how many partitions p_i have to be considered; moreover, the criterium for assigning each agent j, belonging to AS_i, to a partition AS_i^k, is represented by a function $p(j)$ that receives the agent j as input and yields as output, on the basis of the overall *negotiation degree* of j, the number of the partition which j has to be assigned to. More in particular, the agent i assigns a weight w_e^i (resp. w_u^i) to the e-coefficient (resp. u-coefficient), representing the importance the agent i gives to the expertise (resp. understanding capability), defines a threshold parameter t_k for each partition $k = 1, 2, ..p_i$, and then

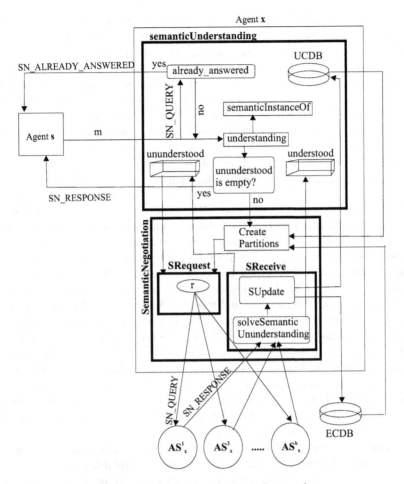

Fig. 1. Semantic Negotiation's Protocol

computes the *negotiation degree* n_{ij} of j as $w_e^i \cdot e_j + w_u^i \cdot u_{ij}$. Then, the function $p(j)$ is calculated as: $p(j) = z$ if $t_{z+1} \leq n_{ij} < t_z$.

Now, we describe the protocol (see Fig. 1) supporting the semantic negotiation followed by an agent x that receives a message m from another agent s.

This message can be an *ordinary* ACL message (i.e., a message with performative INFORM, QUERY_IF, PROPOSE, etc.) or a *semantic negotiation message* (i.e., a message with either performative SN_QUERY_FOR, or SN_RESPONSE, or SN_UNKNOWN or SN_ALREADY_ANSWERED). In the case of an ordinary message, the message's content is composed by a list of r content elements $e_1, e_2, .., e_r$ (see Section 3), where in the case of a semantic negotiation message we have three possibilities: (i) the messages's performative is SN_QUERY: In this case, the content is composed by an AID indicating the agent ia that is interested to the query's result (this agent could be different from the sender s of the message, because the sender could simply be an agent that received in its turn the query from ia and, not being capable to answer the request, decided to request the help of x); (ii) the message performative is SN_RESPONSE: In this case, the content of the message is a list of pairs $(e_1, sl_1), (e_2, sl_2), .., (e_r, sl_r)$ where e_i is a content element in the ontology of x and sl_i is a list of content elements synonyms of e_i in the ontology of the messages's sender: these synonyms could help x to understand e_i; (iii) the message performative is SN_UNKNOWN, meaning that s says that it is unable to give an answer to a previous request of x, or SN_ALREADY_ANSWERED, meaning that s has already answered to a previous request of x: In this case, the content of the message is void.

In order to understand the content of the message m, the agent x executes a *semanticUnderstanding* behaviour. This latter operates as follows:

1. If the message's performative is SN_QUERY, x first invokes the boolean function *already_answered*(m). This function returns *true* if all the content elements belonging to the message's content have already been processed in response to previously received SN_QUERY messages having as interested agent the same one specified in m; otherwise (i.e. if there are only some content elements already processed for that interested agent) these elements are deleted from the message and the function returns *false*. If the function *already_answered*(m) returns *true*, the behaviour is completed and a message with performative SN_ALREADY_ANSWERED is sent to s; otherwise, it continues as follows: First, the function *understanding*(m) is executed. This function, for each content element e_i, $i = 1, 2, .., r$ contained in m, determines if e_i is an instance of some schema S_k, $k = 1, .., n$ belonging to the x's ontology. This check is performed by invoking, for each pair $(e_i, S_k), i = 1, .., r$, $k = 1, .., n$ the boolean function *semanticInstanceOf*(e_i, S_k) that returns *true* if e_i is (semantically) an instance of S_k.

   The function *semanticInstanceOf* performs a schema matching between the schema of e_i and S_k, and can be implemented by using one of the several schema-matching methods existing in the literature as, for instance, those proposed in [9]. The function *understanding*(m) for each content element e_i that matches with at least one of its schemas, inserts into a list *understood* the pair (e_i, sl_i), where sl_i^l is the l-th schemas of the x's ontology matching with e_i, and inserts into another list *ununderstood* each element e_i that does not matches with any of its schemas S_k; then, if the list *ununderstood* is empty, the behaviour *semanticUnderstanding* sends a message with performative SN_RESPONSE to the agent s, containing as content all the elements of the list *understood*; otherwise, if some elements are present into *ununderstood*, the behaviour *semanticNegotiation* is executed for trying to understand the meanings of these elements.

2. When the *semanticNegotiation* behaviour is executed, another function *createPartitions* is firstly invoked. This function reads the e-coefficients (resp. u-coefficients) from $ECDB$ (resp. $UCDB$) and, on the basis of the partition weights set by the agent owner, determines the agent partitions. Then, SRequest and SReceive behaviours are executed. SRequest is a OneShotBehaviour that, for each partition level k, sends a message r to each agent

contained in the k-th partition, until either the list *ununderstood* becomes empty or a timeout t_1 is reached. r contains SN_QUERY as performative and the content element list *ununderstood* as content. SReceive is a CyclicBehaviour in which the agent x waits for messages containing a performative SN_RESPONSE, arriving from the contacted agents belonging to the $AS_x^1, AS_x^2, .., AS_x^k$. As said above, each received message m_a arriving from an agent a has as content a list of pairs $(e_1, sl_1), (e_2, sl_2), .., (e_h, sl_h)$ where e_i is a content element belonging to *ununderstood* and sl_i is a list $[s_i^1, s_i^2, .., s_i^l]$ of content elements synonyms of e_i, thus they are l possible meanings for e_i. Therefore, the function $solveSemanticUnunderstanding(e_i, s_i^g)$, $g = 1, 2,$ $.., l$ is called for each pair (e_i, s_i^g): this function, if at least one s_i^g is an instance of some schemas belonging to the x's ontology, performs two operations: (i) deletes e_i from the list *ununderstood*, (ii) adds s_i^g to the list sl_i contained in *understood*.

Finally, the function *SUpdate* is called, that increases of one unit both the u-coefficient u_{xa} and the e-coefficient e_a.

5   An Application Example: Agents That Buy and Sell

In this Section, we present an application of the semantic negotiation technique we have previously described to the simple situation of a small e-commerce agent community, composed by four agents, denoted by $a1, a2, a3, a4$. Figure 2 shows the evolution of the community during three consecutive semantic negotiation stages represented in subfigures 2.A, 2.B and 2.C. In each subfigure, the global database $ECDB$ is represented by a row vector containing the four expertise coefficients $e_{a1}, e_{a2}, e_{a3}, e_{a4}$, associated to $a1, a2, a3$ and $a4$, respectively, while the four local databases $UCDB$ are synthetically represented by a matrix $UCDB$ where each element $UCDBij$ contains the u-coefficient u_{ij}. At the beginning, both the understanding capability and expertise coefficients are equal to 0. We also suppose that all the agents give the same importance both to the understanding capability and the expertise, therefore all the weights w_e and w_u are equal to 0.5. Furthermore, each subfigure represents each message sent by an agent i to an agent j by an arrow oriented from i to j. A thin line is used to represent ordinary messages, while a double line is exploited for the semantic negotiation messages. Each arc is labelled with the message's content. Due to layout reasons, we omit to represent the negotiation messages with performative SN_UNKNOWN or SN_ALREADY_ANSWERED.

In Fig. 2.A, we see that the agent $a1$ sends a PROPOSE message to $a2$, containing a predicate that says he desires to sell by auction a book having the title "Anna Karenina", with initial price equal to 13 US dollars, with a reservation price (i.e., the lowest price $a1$ accepts for selling the book, that is obviously secret), and with the possibility (represented by the element *purchase_now*) for a buyer to purchase immediately the book without participating to the auction, paying a price equal to 15 US dollars. The agent $a2$ receives the message, but it is unable to understand the terms *reservation* and *purchase_now*, since they are

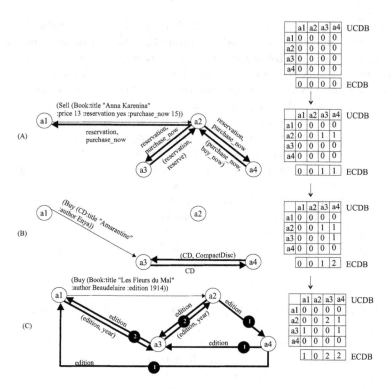

Fig. 2. An example of Semantic Negotiation

not present in his ontology. Then, he decides to exploit the semantic negotiation protocol and, since both the understanding capability and expertise coefficients are equal to 0, the only agent partition that he can build is AS^0_{a2} containing all the other agents $a1$, $a3$ and $a4$. Suppose that when the timeout of $a2$ is reached (*i*) only $a3$ and $a4$ have sent a SN_RESPONSE message (*ii*) $a3$ proposes, as a synonym of *reservation*, the term *reserve* (*iii*) $a4$ provides the term *buy_now* for explaining the term *purchase_now*. Now, suppose the ontology of $a2$ contains both *reserve* and *buy_now*: in this case, it is now able to completely understand the message of $a1$ and to respond to it in an adequate way. Moreover, both the u-coefficients $u_{a2,a3}$, $u_{a2,a4}$, and the e-coefficients e_{a3}, e_{a4} become equal to 1.

The subfigure 2.B shows the agent $a1$ sending a PROPOSE message to $a3$, saying that he desires to buy a CD having title "Amarantine" of the author "Enya". However, $a3$ does not understand the term CD and thus he decides to exploit the semantic negotiation protocol. First, he builds the two partitions $AS^0_{a3} = \{a4\}$ and $AS^1_{a3} = \{a1, a2\}$ since $p(a4) = 0.5 \cdot 1 + 0.5 \cdot 0 = 0.5$ and $p(a1) = p(a2) = 0$. Then, $a3$ begins the semantic negotiation only with a_4 and receives a SN_RESPONSE message by this latter that explains that a synonym for CD is $CompactDisc$, that we suppose to be present in the ontology of $a3$.

Then, $a3$ can end the semantic negotiation process, since he is now able to understand the message of $a1$. As a consequence of this process, the e-coefficient e_{a4} becomes equal to 2 and the u-coefficient $u_{a3,a4}$ becomes equal to 1.

In the subfigure 2.C is depicted the next situation, in which the agent $a1$ sends to $a2$ a PROPOSE message, saying that he desires to buy a book with title "Les Fleurs du Mal", with author "Beaudelaire" and edition 1914. Since $a2$ does not understand the term *edition*, he decides to exploit the semantic negotiation protocol, and he first constructs the partitions $AS_{a2}^0 = \{a4\}$, $AS_{a2}^1 = \{a3\}$ and $AS_{a2}^2 = \{a1\}$, since $p(a4) = 0.5 \cdot 1 + 0.5 \cdot 2 = 1.5$, $p(a3) = 0.5 \cdot 1 + 0.5 \cdot 1 = 1$ and $p(a1) = 0$. Then, $a2$ first asks the help of $a4$, but this latter is not able to autonomously provide an explanation for the term *edition*, then he sends a semantic negotiation message to both $a1$ and $a3$. The black circle labelled with 1 on the arc involved above means that all these arcs are related to the first attempt of negotiation of $a2$. Suppose that both these messages do not arrive to their destination due to a break of the connections $a4$-$a3$ and $a4$-$a1$. When the timeout of $a2$ for $a4$ is reached, $a2$ begins a new semantic negotiation with $a3$ that, in its turn, is not able to provide an explanation for the term *edition*, and thus he requires the help of $a1$ and $a4$. $a4$ is not able to be reached, due to the connection's break, while $a1$ responds with a synonym *year* for *edition*. This leads to set to 1 both the expertise e_{a1} and the understanding capability $u_{a3,a1}$. Now, $a3$ is able to send to $a2$ the explanation *year* for the term *edition* and, supposing *year* to be in the ontology of $a2$, the semantic negotiation of $a2$ can be terminated. All the arcs involved in this second negotiation tentative of $a2$ contains a black circle labelled with 2. As a consequence of the negotiation process, both e_{a3} and $u_{a2,a3}$ become equal to 2.

Now, observe the final situation represented in the tables $UCDB$ and $ECDB$ of the subfigure 2.C. The most "expert" agents are $a3$ and $a4$, and this is completely justified by the fact that they have solved for two ways semantic understanding's problems. The $UCDB$ rows corresponding to agents $a1$ and $a4$ have all their elements equal to 0, reflecting the fact that no other agents have helped them to understand any terms. The agent $a2$ has been helped 2 times by $a3$ and 1 time by $a4$, and this is represented by the corresponding values in the $UCDB$ row of $a2$. The agent $a3$ has been helped once by $a1$, and this is represented by the only one no zero coefficient in the $UCDB$ row of $a3$.

6   Conclusions

Semantic negotiation is a powerful framework for solving understanding problems among agents having personal ontologies that are not completely homogeneous. However, a key problem in semantic negotiation protocol is making the right choice of the agents with which it is most suitable to negotiate. In this work, we present a semantic negotiation protocol that makes effective the process of selecting the negotiation partners, by defining two measures, called expertise and understanding capability, that reflects two of the most important features that should be considered in making this selection, that are (i) the capability of an agent to respond to semantic negotiation answers arriving from whatever agent, representing the degree of expertise that the agent has in the community and (*ii*) the capability of an agent to respond to semantic negotiation answers arriving from a particular other agent, that defines the degree of comprehension that the former agent has with respect to the latter one. We define an agent negotiation protocol that allows to compute these measures by observing the results of the agent negotiation. Furthermore, we have implemented this protocol in the JAVA language as component of the middleware JADE, giving the possibility to use it for realizing JADE agents able to negotiate the semantic of the terms. Our ongoing research deals with the possibility of including in the protocol more sophisticated features as, for instance, the possibility that an agent gives a negative feedback when he receives a unsatisfactory response by another agent.

References

1. R.-J. Beun and R.M. van Eijk. A Cooperative Dialogue Game for Resolving Ontological Discrepancies. In *Workshop on Agent Communication Languages*, pages 349–363, 2003.
2. R.-J. Beun, R.M. van Eijk, and H. Prust. Ontological Feedback in Multiagent Systems. In *AAMAS '04: Proceedings of the Third International Joint Conference on Autonomous Agents and Multiagent Systems*, pages 110–117, Washington, DC, U, 2004. IEEE Computer Society.
3. H. Ding and I. Sølvberg. Towards the schema heterogeneity in distributed digital libraries. In *ICEIS (5)*, pages 307–312, 2004.
4. D.W. Embley. Toward Semantic Understanding: An Approach Based on Information Extraction Ontologies. In *CRPIT '04: Proceedings of the fifteenth conference on Australasian database*, pages 3–12, Darlinghurst, Australia, Austra, 2004. Australian Computer Society, Inc.
5. T. Finin, R. Fritzson, D. McKay, and R. McEntire. KQML as an agent communication language. In *Proceedings of the 3rd International Conference on Information and Knowledge Management (CIKM'94)*, pages 456–463, Gaithersburg, Maryland, USA, 1994. ACM Press.
6. http://www.fipa.org, 2005.
7. R. Guha. Semantic Negotiation: Co-identifying objects across data sources. In *AAAI '04 Spring Symposium Series: Proceedings of the Semantic Web Services*, March 2004.
8. http://www.jade.tilab.org, 2005.
9. E. Rahm and P.A. Bernstein. A survey of approaches to automatic schema matching. *VLDB Journal: Very Large Data Bases*, 10(4):334–350, 2001.
10. C. Reed, T.J. Norman, and N.R. Jennings. Negotiating the Semantics of Agent Communication Languages. *Computational Intelligence*, 18(2):229–25, 2002.
11. J. van Diggelen, R.-J. Beun, F. Dignum, R.M. van Eijk, and J.-J.Ch. Meyer. Optimal communication vocabularies and heterogeneous ontologies. In R.M. van Eijk, M.-P. Huget, and F. Dignum, editors, *Developments in Agent Communication*, LNAI 3396. Springer Verlag, 2004.
12. A.B. Williams. Learning to Share Meaning in a Multi-Agent System. *Autonomous Agents and Multi-Agent Systems*, 8(2):165–193, 2004.

Appendix: The Package jade.hisene

In this Appendix we present a java implementation of the semanticUnderstanding behaviour (see Fig. 3) and the semanticNegotiation behaviour (see Fig. 4) as described in Section 4. These behaviours are part of the jade.hisene package that we are writing and which is in an advanced state of development. Due to the length of the code we don't present the private methods. However, they are of a simple implementation.

```java
package jade.hisene;
import jade.core.*;
import jade.core.behaviours.OneShotBehaviour;
import jade.lang.acl.ACLMessage;
...

public class semanticUnderstanding extends OneShotBehaviour {
    private ACLMessage msg;
    private List understood, ununderstood;

    public semanticUnderstanding (Agent a, ACLMessage msg) {
        super(a);
        this.msg = msg;
    }

    public void action() {
        if (msg.getPerformative() == Semantic.SN_QUERY && alreadyAnswered(msg)){
            ACLMessage reply = msg.createReply();
            reply.setPerformative(Semantic.SN_ALREADY_ANSWERED);
            reply.setContent(msg.getContent());
            myAgent.send(reply);
        } else {
            understanding(msg);
            if (!ununderstood.isEmpty()) {
                ACLMessage sn_query_msg;
                sn_query_msg = setUnderstood(msg, understood);
                sn_query_msg = setUnunderstood(msg, ununderstood);
                sn_query_msg.setPerformative(Semantic.SN_QUERY);
                ((Semantic)parent).addSubBehaviour(new semanticNegotiation(myAgent, sn_query_msg));
            } else {
                ACLMessage reply = msg.createReply();
                reply.setPerformative(Semantic.SN_RESPONSE);
                reply.setContent(msg.getContent());
                reply = setUnderstood(reply, understood);
                myAgent.send(reply);
            }
        }
    }
    // Private Methods Section
    ...
}
```

Fig. 3. The semanticUnderstanding behaviour

```
package jade.hisene;
import jade.core.*;
import jade.core.behaviours.*;
import jade.lang.acl.ACLMessage;
...


public class semanticNegotiation extends ParallelBehaviour{

    private ACLMessage msg;
    private Stack partitions;
    private Behaviour srequest = new SRequest(myAgent, msg, partitions);
    private Behaviour sreceive = new SReceive(myAgent, msg);

    public semanticNegotiation (Agent a, ACLMessage msg) {
        super(a, WHEN_ANY);
        this.msg = msg;
    }

    public void onStart() {
        createPartitions();
        addSubBehaviour(srequest);
        addSubBehaviour(sreceive);
    }

    public int onEnd() {
        removeSubBehaviour(sreceive);
        ACLMessage reply = msg.createReply();
        reply.setPerformative(Semantic.SN_RESPONSE);
        reply.setContent(msg.getContent());
        myAgent.send(reply);
        return 0;
    }
    // Private Methods Section
    ...
}
```

Fig. 4. The semanticNegotiation behaviour

Discovering Semantic Web Services with Process Specifications

Piya Suwannopas and Twittie Senivongse

Department of Computer Engineering, Chulalongkorn University
Phyathai Road, Pathumwan, Bangkok 10330 Thailand
piya.su@student.chula.ac.th, twittie.s@chula.ac.th

Abstract. Service discovery is one of the crucial issues for service-oriented architectural model. Recently the trend is towards semantic discovery by which semantic descriptions are the basis for service matchmaking instead of simple search based on service attributes. OWL-S is a widely adopted semantic specification for Web Services which comprises three profiles. Among those, process model is the profile that describes dynamic behaviour of Web Services in terms of functional aspects and process flows, and is generally aimed for service enactment, composition, and monitoring. This paper presents a new approach to use OWL-S process model for service discovery purpose. A Web Service can have its internal process described as an OWL-S process model specification, and a service consumer can query for a Web Service with a particular process detail. Matchmaking will be based on flexible ontological matching and evaluation of constraints on the functional behaviour and process flow of the Web Service. The architecture for process-based discovery is also presented.

1 Introduction

Service discovery is an important part of service-oriented computing in which services, as building blocks for building applications, are provided and distributed in large-scale open environment [1]. Provided services will publish generalised descriptions of their capability to a matchmaker whereas service consumers consult the matchmaker to identify potential services that most closely satisfy their needs. The effectiveness of service discovery relies on the richness of service metadata and the matchmaking mechanism that utilises the expressiveness of the metadata. Current Web Services Standards realise this concept and provide UDDI [2] as a standard registry that performs matchmaking based on matching of syntactic service attribute values.

From our previous study [3], a service description model has been defined as a result of an empirical survey about service advertisements on the Internet (Fig. 1). The model shows that service advertisements should reflect different aspects of service capabilities; some are simple characteristics and may be in the form of simple attributes whereas some are more complex capabilities and require some specification languages to express them. (Those highlighted in Fig. 1 have no correspondences in

F. Eliassen and A. Montresor (Eds.): DAIS 2006, LNCS 4025, pp. 113–127, 2006.
© IFIP International Federation for Information Processing 2006

UDDI.) This model is generic, meaning that it is independent from any specific representation languages and can be used simply for information or for other purposes such as automatic service discovery or composition.

One way to enrich service metadata is by using ontology languages to represent service descriptions. This approach is gaining a lot of attention in Web Services community as ontology languages are expressive for describing several aspects of service capabilities and ontological reasoning also provides a way to infer more about the capabilities. Semantic Web Services are Web Services in which ontologies ascribe meanings to published service descriptions so that software systems representing prospective service consumers can interpret and invoke them [4]. With this vision, the Web Ontology Language for Services (OWL-S) consortium contributes with an OWL-S specification [5] which is the building block for encoding rich semantic service descriptions in a way that builds naturally upon OWL language. OWL-S consists of three profiles, namely service profile, process model, and service grounding. Service profile defines basic and functional properties of the service as well as functional behaviour. Process model details service operation in terms of functional behaviour, control structure, and data flow structure required to execute the service. Service grounding specifies details of how to access the service by mapping from an abstract service specification (process model) to concrete specification (WSDL). It can be seen that OWL-S and the model in Fig. 1 share some characteristic; they both model services with simple attributes and more complex specifications.

Our previous work [6] proposes an integrated service profile that corresponds to the model in Fig. 1. The integrated service profile is a collection of ontology-based profiles for services, including the attribute, structural, behavioural, and rule profiles,

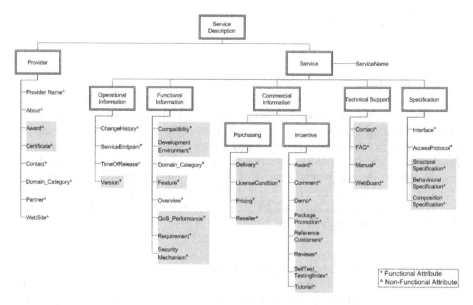

Fig. 1. Service description model from survey [3]

and it overlaps with OWL-S. This paper extends the integrated service profile with the focus on the composition specification of a service. Composition specification shows how simple components are composed into a service and may be expressed as a hierarchy of goal and subgoals or as a workflow of tasks for service execution [1]. This paper is interested in describing the composition specification as a workflow and we borrow OWL-S process model to represent the workflow specification.

OWL-S process model is found in use by researches in service composition and workflow coordination and monitoring, but it can also be used for in-depth analysis for matchmaking to see whether the service meets process constraints required by the service consumer. This is to check a dynamic aspect of the service. For example, the service consumer may want to find a software store with a workflow such that, after processing the purchase order of the customer, the store registers the customer for the software training programme. The store service with such automatic registration for training should be preferable to ones without training. Sometimes the flow may have a constraint such that automatic training registration is available only if the purchase is worth more than 0.5 million bahts (Thailand currency). Such a constraint will have to be taken into account during matchmaking. Here we present an example of the services using OWL-S process model to describe their internal processes. A service consumer can issue a process-based query. The services are queried on their functional behaviour and flow of their process. Ontological reasoning and evaluation of the rule-based constraints on the behaviour and process flow are considered.

The rest of the paper starts with Section 2 that discusses related work. Section 3 outlines the constructs of OWL-S process model for process specification. Section 4 gives an example of the process specifications of three services described using OWL-S process model. Matching criteria are summarised in Section 5 and used in Section 6 to consider matching for a query. Section 7 presents a process-based discovery framework and Section 8 concludes the paper.

2   Related Work

Semantics-based service discovery is accomplished mainly by the use of ontology to describe service capabilities. Web Services Modeling Ontology (WSMO) [7] provides a framework for describing semantic Web Services with Web Services Modeling Language (SWML) [8] as a formal language that realises the framework. WSML defines semantics in terms of four elements: ontologies, goals, Web Service descriptions, and mediators. Ontologies provide vocabularies, concepts, instances, and axioms that will be used by other elements. Goals are similar to queries. Web Service descriptions describe capability in terms of assumption, precondition, postcondition, effect, and allow for interface and orchestration specifications. As WSMO shares with OWL-S the vision that ontologies are essential to support automatic discovery, it is possible for our work to adopt either of their process-related specifications. However, at the moment OWL-S can be implemented without stipulating framework and several tools exist. We adopt OWL-S process model for process specification in this paper.

Most of research work in service discovery area focuses on search based on a particular aspect of the service and little is found to concentrate on process-based discovery. UDDI version 4 is incorporating an ontology-based taxonomy for the standard categories of Business Entity and Business Service entries that are registered with UDDI [9]. This will allow UDDI to be able to look for the businesses or services of a specialised or generalised category. The work in [10] shows how ontology describing general knowledge of a particular service domain can be used for search. The work in [11], [12] focuses on searching functional behaviour but they do not consider search with behavioural constraints. In [13], an efficient search algorithm is devised for services described by OWL-S but the search considers only the OWL-S service profile. In [14], process ontology is used as a basis for service discovery. The process ontology is described by the service process, constituent subtasks, connection ports between subtasks and connection mechanisms, and exceptions within the process. The query is done by a PQL language. Unlike our approach, the process ontology in this work follows the goal-subgoal model of service composition, not the workflow model, and it does not accommodate for process constraints.

Service discovery and service composition share a characteristic such that both aim to identify services that can satisfy users' requirements. Nevertheless, service discovery tends to identify individual services that can answer to a particular query, whereas service composition identifies a group of services that can work together to satisfy a certain goal. In the area of Web Service composition, OWL-S process model is used in several researches for describing Web Services. In [15], an AI planner called OWLS-Xplan is proposed to compose Web Services. An OWL-S process model is used to specify input, precondition, output, and effect of the goal (i.e. the composite service) and of the individual Web Services to be composed. The goal in OWL-S process model will be translated into a planning domain description in PDDL in order for the planner to generate a plan sequence as a workflow of individual Web Services. The work in [16] integrates an OWL reasoner with an AI planner and shows how OWL or SWRL [17] is used to encode the preconditions and effects of the Web Services in the composition process. The Web Services are also described by OWL-S process model. By using OWL, the composition gains the reasoning power of OWL in the evaluation of the preconditions and the update of the effects that have impacts on real world knowledge. Although these researches above conduct some analysis on OWL-S process model, they concern the functional behaviour part of the process model in service composition. In our work, we focus on analysing not only the functional behaviour part but also the workflow part of individual Web Services in order to find any single services that can satisfy the query.

3   OWL-S Process Model

This section briefly describes the constructs of OWL-S process model that are of interest to this paper. A particular service is described by a service model and a process is a subclass of the service model. Fig. 2 shows OWL-S process ontology [5] with the classes and properties that altogether describe how a service works. A process describes its functional behaviour by specifying inputs, outputs, preconditions, and effects (IOPE) of its performance. As the name implies, a precondition is a logical expression which must hold for the process to be successfully invoked. Local refers to an auxiliary parameter that is bound to the precondition and is useful for determining the logical value of the precondition. Result refers to a coupled output and effect and can be constrained by an incondition property which specifies the logical condition under which the result occurs; hence the corresponding output and effect become conditional output and conditional effect. Result variable is also an auxiliary parameter that is bound to a result and useful for determining the associated incondition.

The process is further described as a composition of subprocesses. The subprocess can be atomic, composite, or simple process. An atomic process is one which has no further subprocesses, is directly invocable, and executes in a single step. A composite process is decomposed into other non-composite or composite processes. The decomposition can be specified by using control constructs, i.e. sequence, split, split-join, any-order, choice, if-then-else, iterate, repeat-while, repeat-until. A simple process is an abstraction that provides a view of some atomic process or a simplified representation of some composite process and is not invocable.

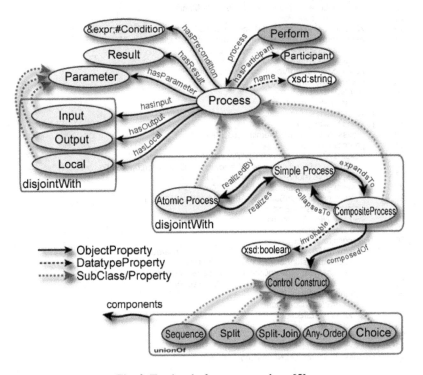

Fig. 2. Top level of process ontology [5]

Since the constraints in OWL-S process model – either the preconditions, the conditions of the results, or the guards on the control flow – are represented as logical formula, these logical expressions are treated as literals – either XML literals or string literals. Therefore several languages can be used to express these constraints (e.g. SWRL, RDF, KIF, PDDL). In this paper we represent such process constraints with SWRL rule expressions.

4 Process Specifications

Bank loan service is used as an example for process-based discovery. Fig. 3 shows the first part of the process specification of a loan service S_1 written in OWL-S process model. This part describes the functional behaviour of S_1.

```
1.    <process:CompositeProcess rdf:ID="LoanService">
2.      <process:hasInput>
3.        <process:Input rdf:ID="CustomerInfo"/>
4.      </process:hasInput>
5.      <process:hasOutput>
6.        <process:Output rdf:ID="LoanInterestRate"/>
7.      <process:hasOutput/> ...
8.      <process:hasLocal rdf:resource="#IncomePerMonth"/>
9.      <process:hasPrecondition>
10.       <expr:SWRL-Condition rdf:ID="IncomeCondition">
11.         <expr:expressionLanguage rdf:resource="&Expression.owl#SWRL"/>
12.         <expr:expressionBody rdf:datatype="Literal">
13.         swrlb:greaterThanOrEqual(#IncomePerMonth,10000) →
14.         hasIncomeStatus(#ValidIncome,"xsd:True")
15.         </expr:expressionBody>
16.       </expr:SWRL-Condition>
17.     </process:hasPrecondition>
18.     <process:hasResultVar rdf:resource="#LoanAmount"/>
19.     <process:hasResult>
20.       <process:Result rdf:ID="PremiumLoanResult">
21.         <process:inCondition>
22.         <expr:SWRL-Condition rdf:ID="PremiumLoanCondition">
23.           <expr:expressionLanguage rdf:resource="&Expression.owl#SWRL"/>
24.           <expr:expressionBody rdf:datatype="Literal">
25.           swrlb:greaterThan(#LoanAmount,300000) →
26.           hasPremiumLoanStatus(#PremiumLoanStatus,"xsd:True")
27.           </expr:expressionBody>
28.         </expr:SWRL-Condition>
29.         </process:inCondition>
30.         <process:hasEffect>
31.           <expr:SWRL-Condition rdf:ID="PremiumCreditCardCondition">
32.           <expr:expressionBody rdf:datatype="Literal">
33.           → chargedPremiumCreditCard(#LoanService, #PremiumCreditCardFee)
34.             swrlb:equal(#PremiumCreditCardFee, 0)
35.           </expr:expressionBody>
36.         </expr:SWRL-Condition>
37.         </process:hasEffect>
38.       </process:Result>
39.     </process:hasResult>
40.     <process:hasResult>
41.       <process:Result rdf:ID="NormalLoanResult">
42.         ...
```

Fig. 3. Functional behaviour of S_1 in OWL-S process model

From the figure, the service requires customer information as an input (line 2-4), and gives loan interest rate as an output (line 5-7). The service has a precondition such that the consumer needs to have income at least 10,000 bahts per month in order to use the service (line 9-17). The effects of this service are conditional, depending on the loan amount. If the loan is more than 300,000 bahts, it is a premium loan (line 21-29) and the consumer is entitled to apply for a premium credit card. This effect is further constrained by the annual credit card fee which is equal to 0 (line 30-37). On the other hand, if the loan is not more than 300,000 bahts, it is a normal loan (line 41) and the credit card effect will be subject to the annual fee. Note that all the constraints are expressed as SWRL rules.

The second part of the process specification of S_1 involves its workflow. This is depicted in Fig. 4. Suppose, in general, a loan service is composed of several classes of loan approval. Department approval process is performed when the loan amount is small or the loan is not critical and the decision can be made by the loan department manager. Branch approval process is performed when the loan is more critical but the decision can still be made within the branch by the branch manager. Otherwise the loan application has to be approved at the head quarter. The bank will maintain loan history of the customers for future reference.

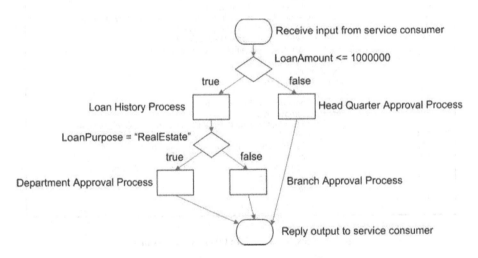

Fig. 4. Process flow of service S_1

Fig. 5 shows a snippet of OWL-S process specification for Fig. 4. The first guard condition checks whether the loan amount is less than or equal to 1 million bahts (line 64-72). The second guard condition determines whether the purpose of loan is for real estate (line 88-96).

For further comparison, we assume there are two more candidate services S_2 and S_3. These two services exhibit the same functional behaviour as S_1 (c.f. Fig. 3) but they have a slightly different workflow as in Fig. 6 and Fig. 7 respectively.

```
62.    <process:composedOf>
63.     <process:If-Then-Else rdf:ID="LoanAmount_If-Then-Else">
64.      <process:ifCondition>
65.       <expr:Condition rdf:ID="LoanAmountCondition">
66.        <expr:expressionLanguage rdf:resource="&Expression.owl#SWRL"/>
67.        <expr:expressionBody rdf:datatype="Literal">
68.         swrlb:lessThanOrEqual(#LoanAmount,1000000) →
69.         hasLoanAmountStatus(#SmallLoanAmount,"xsd:True")
70.        </expr:expressionBody>
71.       </expr:Condition>
72.      </process:ifCondition>
73.      <process:then>
74.       <process:Sequence rdf:ID="Bank_Sequence">
75.        <process:components>
76.         <process:ControlConstructList rdf:ID="LoanHistory_ControlConstructList">
77.          <list:first>
78.           <process:Perform rdf:ID="LoanHistoryPerform">
79.            <process:process>
80.             <process:AtomicProcess rdf:ID="LoanHistoryProcess"/>
81.            </process:process>
82.           </process:Perform>
83.          </list:first>
84.          <list:rest>
85.           <process:ControlConstructList rdf:ID="Bank_ControlConstructList">
86.            <list:first>
87.             <process:If-Then-Else rdf:ID="Purpose_If-Then-Else">
88.              <process:ifCondition>
89.               <expr:Condition rdf:ID="PurposeCondition">
90.                <expr:expressionLanguage rdf:resource="&Expression.owl#SWRL"/>
91.                <expr:expressionBody rdf:datatype="Literal">
92.                 swrlb:equal(#LoanPurpose,"RealEstate") →
93.                 hasPurposeStatus(#RealEstatePurpose,"xsd:True")
94.                </expr:expressionBody>
95.               </expr:Condition>
96.              </process:ifCondition>
97.              <process:then>
98.               <process:Sequence rdf:ID="Department_Sequence">
99.                <process:components>
100.                <process:ControlConstructList rdf:ID="Department_ControlConstructList">
101.                 <list:first>
102.                  <process:Perform rdf:ID="DepartmentApprovalPerform">
103.                   <process:process>
104.                    <process:AtomicProcess rdf:ID="DepartmentApprovalProcess"/>
105.                   </process:process>
106.                  </process:Perform>
107.                     ...
```

Fig. 5. Process flow of S_1 in OWL-S process model

5 Matching Criteria

To determine whether a process specification of a service can fulfill a service consumer's needs, matchmaking will perform ontological matching on the concepts
within the specification and evaluate constraints on the functional behaviour and the
guards on the control constructs in order to determine the actual behaviour of the
service. Several matching criteria are defined:

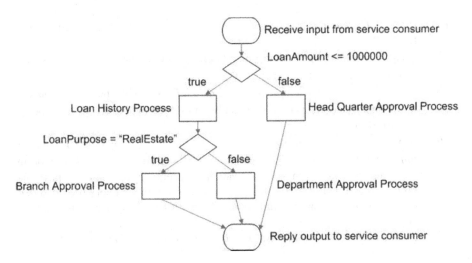

Fig. 6. Process flow of service S_2

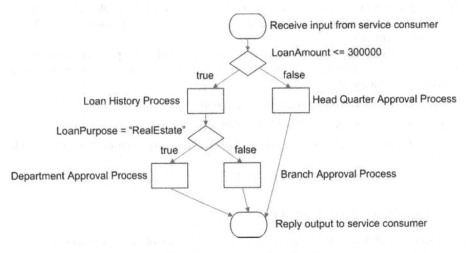

Fig. 7. Process flow of service S_3

5.1 Matching Ontological Concepts

Matching by subsumption and equivalence is the basis for matching ontological concepts in the query and the process specification. This approach is based on the IS-A taxonomy of the concepts shared within the service domain and has been adopted in literature including [10], [18], [6].

Let C_Q be the concept specified in the query and C_P be the concept in the process specification:

(i)   *If $C_Q \equiv C_P$ then C_P is an exact match for C_Q, where $\equiv$ means is equivalent to.*

(ii) *If $C_P \sqsubseteq C_Q$ then C_P is a specialised match for C_Q, where $\sqsubseteq$ means is subsumed by (i.e. C_P is more specific than C_Q).*

(iii) *If $C_Q \sqsubseteq C_P$ then C_P is a generalised match for C_Q.* This means the concept in the query is more specific than, and is subsumed by, the one in the process specification.

(iv) *If $(C_Q \not\sqsubseteq C_P) \wedge (C_P \not\sqsubseteq C_Q) \wedge (C_Q \sqsubseteq C_C) \wedge (C_P \sqsubseteq C_C)$ then C_P is a partial match for C_Q, where $\not\sqsubseteq$ means is not subsumed by* and C_C is a node in the same IS-A taxonomy. This means it is acceptable for the concept in the process specification to be a match for the concept in the query provided that the two concepts have common characteristics through a common parent concept.

(v)   *If none of the above relationships exist then C_P is a failed match for C_Q.*

5.2 Matching Numerical Ranges

Matching two numerical ranges compares the ranges of the possible values that are defined in the constraints. The degree of matching for numerical ranges can be determined as described below.

Let N_Q be a nonempty set of numerical range values of the expression in the query (E_Q), and N_P be a nonempty set of numerical range values of the expression in the process specification (E_P):

(i)   *If $N_P \subseteq N_Q$ then E_P is an exact match for E_Q*

(ii) *If $N_Q \subseteq N_P$ then E_P is a plug-in match for E_Q*

(iii) *If $(N_P \cap N_Q \neq \phi) \wedge (N_P \not\subseteq N_Q) \wedge (N_Q \not\subseteq N_P)$ then E_P is a weak match for E_Q*

(iv) *If $N_P \cap N_Q = \phi$ then E_P is a failed match for E_Q*

5.3 Matching Logical Constraint

The service will match to the query if, by applying a set of values obtained from the query into the rule expression, the rule evaluation hits and returns true as a result. The expression in the head atom of the rule may be a numerical constraint or constraint on some data values, and these may require ontological reasoning, numerical computation, and also rule reasoning. We consider a match only when such evaluation returns true.

5.4 Matching Process Model

To check whether a process specification satisfies the query, we consider matching on all aspects of the functional behaviour and the processes within the workflow. For each aspect, it may need to perform ontological matching (Section 5.1) before considering other kind of constraint matching (Sections 5.2-5.3). The process specification will match the query if it satisfies the following:

(i)   *input, unconditional output, unconditional effect, and process without guard satisfy ontological match in Section 5.1, and*

(ii)   *precondition, conditional output, conditional effect, and process with guard satisfy relevant matching criteria in Section 5.2-5.3*

In other words, let $\mathbb{R}_Q$ and $\mathbb{R}_P$ be the sets of functional behaviour and workflow processes (with and without constraints) within the query and the process specification respectively:

$ProcessModelMatch(\mathbb{R}_Q, \mathbb{R}_P) = $ true $\Leftrightarrow$

$$(\mathbb{R}_Q \subseteq \mathbb{R}_P) \wedge (\forall i, \exists j : (i \in \mathbb{R}_Q) \wedge (j \in \mathbb{R}_P) \wedge (i \ominus j))$$

where $\ominus$ means having a kind of match as in Sections 5.1-5.3.

6 Process-Based Discovery

Assume a service consumer wants to apply for a 400,000-baht loan with a bank in order to buy a house. The consumer wants the bank that allows a loaner to apply for a credit card with no annual fee and approve the loan application at loan department level. This is to ensure that the loan process is quick. The consumer earns 20,000 bahts a month.

We present a query ($\mathbb{Q}$) as a collection of relation expressions. A relation expression is in the form of *property(subject, object)* which corresponds to an RDF statement *<subject, property, object>*. For a constraint that relates to a numerical value, such numerical constraint is represented as *property(argument, relationaloperator, literalvalue1, [literalvalue2,] unit)*. For the example above, the relation expressions are superscripted by symbols *C, E, G, and P* which refer to precondition, effect, guard, and process respectively:

$\mathbb{Q} = \{$hasIncomePerMonth(IncomePerMonth, 20000$)^C$,

hasPremiumCreditCardFee(PremiumCreditCardFee, Equal, 0, baht$)^E$,

hasLoanAmount(LoanAmount, 400000$)^G$,

hasLoanPurpose(LoanPurpose, Housing$)^G$,

hasProcess(Process, DepartmentApprovalProcess$)^P\}$

To determine whether a service is a match, its process specification will also be treated as a collection of relation expressions in order to check against the set of relation expressions of the query. The rule expressions embedded in the process specification will be extracted and translated into a rule language in order to use a rule reasoning engine to check whether the rule is satisfied. In our implementation, SWRL rule will be translated into Jess script in order to use Jess engine [19].

If we look at S_1 and the query, to check whether the precondition holds for the query, we use the criterion to match numerical ranges (Section 5.2) and the consumer's income is an *exact match* and hence valid to use the service. To check the effect, we have to determine what S_1 will give as an effect since it is conditional. We first check the incondition by using matching of numerical ranges on the loan amount and the premium credit card effect is satisfied with an *exact match*. Then we use again the numerical range matching criterion to check whether the premium credit card offers 0 baht annual fee. This also returns an *exact match*. When all aspects of the functional behaviour of S_1 match to the query, S_1 is a potential service but we have to check further on its process flow. (In this example, the functional behaviour of S_2 and S_3 also matches to the query because we assume earlier that all three services exhibit the same functional behaviour.)

To consider the workflow of the service, we associate each process with guards that determine its performance. For example, the rules for all approval processes within the process specification of S_1 are listed below:

!hasLoanAmount(LoanAmount, LessThanOrEqual, 1000000, baht) →
    hasProcess(Process, HeadQuarterApprovalProcess);
hasLoanAmount(LoanAmount, LessThanOrEqual, 1000000, baht) →
    hasProcess(Process, LoanHistoryProcess);
hasLoanAmount(LoanAmount, LessThanOrEqual, 1000000, baht),
    hasLoanPurpose(LoanPurpose, RealEstate) →
    hasProcess(Process, DepartmentApprovalProcess);
hasLoanAmount(LoanAmount, LessThanOrEqual, 1000000, baht),
    !hasLoanPurpose(LoanPurpose, RealEstate) →
    hasProcess(Process, BranchApprovalProcess);

To check whether S_1 performs the requested process under the context of a particular query, we check whether the associated guards fire. This is possible when the information necessary for evaluating the guards can be obtained from the service consumer or from the process specification itself. In this example, the consumer requests for a department approval process. The first guard on loan amount fires with *exact match* by considering numerical ranges matching against the loan amount of the consumer. For the second guard on loan purpose, we first use ontological matching (Section 5.1) to check the ontological value RealEstate. Assume that there is a domain ontology which defines an IS-A taxonomy for RealEstate with subconcepts such as Housing and Land. S_1's purpose will be a *generalised match*, and by matching logical constraints (Section 5.3), this second guard will also fire. Therefore, S_1 will perform department approval process under the constraints placed by the query. When S_1 matches with all aspects defined in the query, it will be returned as a match to the consumer. With this approach, S_2 will fail to match the query because the consumer's loan purpose will not cause the loan purpose guard associated with its department approval process to fire. Similarly, S_3 will also fail to match the query because the consumer's loan amount does not satisfy the loan amount guard associated with its department approval process.

Process-based discovery is effective when a shared process ontology of a particular service domain is assumed. The shared process ontology defines common pattern of the process within a domain which includes internal tasks and relevant conditions. This approach is possible as the concept of business process patterns exists [20], [21]. Service providers should publish process specifications that are derived from the domain process ontology, and service consumers should have some knowledge about the behaviour and workflow of the domain in order to compose an effective query. In our example, it should be commonly known that a bank loan process usually involves several classes of approval, and factors that influence the approvals include loan amount, loan purpose, and earning capability of the loaner. Although this process is internal to the bank, it is not classified business information since bank staff would normally give such information to the loaners. With a shared process ontology, the service consumer can submit a query without having to know other details of the candidate Web Services which may be considered as classified business rules; in our case, the service consumer does not need to know that the bank with a process specification such as S_1 has set a boundary of 1 million bahts for a head quarter approval. Process specifications are maintained by service providers; our approach does not require service consumers to have access to them.

7 Discovery Framework

The agent-based discovery framework in our previous work [6] is extended to accommodate process-based discovery. We develop the components within the architecture in Fig. 8 while also adopting existing ontology-based tools and rule engine.

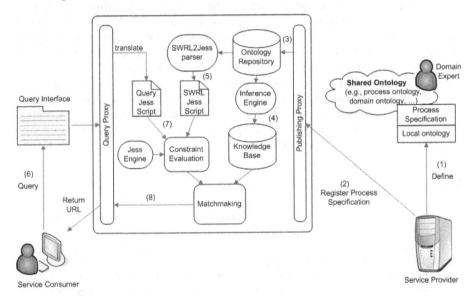

Fig. 8. Process-based discovery framework

In the figure, a service provider will define the process specification of the service as well as any necessary local ontology (1), using an ontology editor (e.g. Protégé). The definition may be based on shared ontology of the domain, which is defined by service domain experts. The service provider maintains the process specification and the local ontology, but also registers the specification with the agent via the publishing proxy (2). The publishing proxy will store the URL of the process specification and local ontology in the ontology repository (3). The agent may preprocess to extract knowledge and to reason from the shared ontologies prior to the matchmaking by using an inference engine (e.g. Jena [22]); the results are stored in a knowledge base

(4). At discovery time, the process specification will be processed and rule constraints are extracted and translated into a rule script by a parser (i.e. SWRL2Jess parser) (5). The agent can provide the service consumers with a GUI template that corresponds to the process ontology of the domain so that the consumers can specify query onto the process specifications more easily (6). Internally, the query will be translated into RDF-based relation expressions and will pass through the query proxy. Rule constraints in the query are translated into a rule script so that it is evaluated against constraints in the process specification (7). The constraint evaluation module is integrated with a rule engine (e.g. Jess engine). Matchmaking module considers matching criteria and reports the result in an XML document which will be returned to the consumer (8).

8 Conclusion

We present a new approach to service discovery by using OWL-S process model to model functional behaviour and workflow of the services and querying on such process specifications. Constraints can be placed on the functional behaviour and guard the flow of process execution. Matchmaking uses ontological reasoning and constraints evaluation to determine the actual behaviour of the services. Service consumers can then look for the services with a satisfied internal process.

The example in this paper shows a query concerning if-then-else and sequence constructs. Query based on other constructs is also meaningful and possible. We are in the process of finishing the integration of process-based discovery with the framework in [6] so that the integrated service profile is more complete and fits well with the service description model in Fig. 1.

References

1. Huhns, M. N., Singh, M. P.: Service-Oriented Computing: Key Concepts and Principles. IEEE Internet Computing. January-February (2005) 75-81
2. uddi.org: UDDI: Universal Description, Discovery, and Integration of Web Services (Online). (2002). http://www.uddi.org
3. Tapabut, C., Senivongse, T., Futatsugi, K.: Defining Attribute Templates for Descriptions of Distributed Services. In: Proceedings of 9th Asia-Pacific Software Engineering Conference (APSEC 2002), Gold Coast, Australia, December (2002) 425-434
4. Burstein, M. et al.: Semantic Web Services Architecture. IEEE Internet Computing. September-October (2005) 72-81
5. OWL-S Coalition. OWL-S 1.1 Release (online). http://www.daml.org/services/owl-s/1.1/
6. Sriharee, N., Senivongse, T.: Matchmaking and Ranking of Semantic Web Services Using Integrated Service Profile. To be published in International Journal of Metadata, Semantics and Ontologies, Vol. 1, No. 2, Inderscience Publishers
7. WSMO. Web Services Modeling Ontology (online). (2004). http://www.wsmo.org
8. Bruijn, D.J., Lausen, H., Polleres, A., Fensel, D.: The Web Service Modeling Language WSML: An Overview. DERI Technical Report, June 16 (2005)

9. Paolucci, M., Sycara, K.: UDDI Spec TC V4 Proposal Semantic Search (online). (2004). http://www.oasis-open.org/committees/uddi-spec/doc/req/uddi-spec-tc-req029-semanticsearch-20040308.doc
10. Trastour, D., Bartolini, C., Gonzalez-Castillo, J.: A Semantic Web Approach to Service Description for Matchmaking of Services. In: Proceedings of the International Semantic Web Working Symposium (SWWS'01) (2001)
11. Paolucci, M. et al.: Semantic Matching of Web Services Capabilities. In: Proceedings of the 1st International Semantic Web Conference (ISWC 2002), Sardinia (Italy), Lecture Notes in Computer Science, Vol. 2342. Springer Verlag (2002)
12. Sivashanmugan, K., Verma, K., Sheth, A., Miller, J.: Adding Semantics to Web Services Standards. In: Proceedings of the International Conference on Web Services (2003)
13. Srinivasan, N., Paolucci, M., Sycara, K.: An Efficient Algorithm for OWL-S Based Semantic Search in UDDI. In: Proceedings of 1st International Workshop on Semantic Web Services and Web Process Composition (SWSWPC 2004), San Diego, CA, USA, July 6, (2004)
14. Klein, M., Bernstein, A.: Searching for Services on the Semantic Web Using Process Ontologies. The Emerging Semantic Web – Selected papers from 1st Semantic Web Working Symposium. I. Cruz et al. (Eds.) IOS press, Amsterdam (2002) 159-172
15. Klusch, M., Gerber, A., Schmidt, M.: Semantic Web Service Composition Planning with OWLS-Xplan. In: Proceedings of 1st Intl. AAAI Fall Symposium on Agents and the Semantic Web, Arlington, VA, USA, AAAI Press (2005)
16. Sirin, E., Parsia, B.: Planning for Semantic Web Services. In Proceedings of Semantic Web Services Workshop at 3rd International Semantic Web Conference (ISWC'04) (2004)
17. Horrocks, I., Patel-Schneider, P.F., Boley, H., Tabet, S., Grosof, B., Dean, M.: SWRL: A Semantic Web Rule Language combining OWL and RuleML. (Online). (2003). http://daml.org/2003/11/swrl/
18. Li, L., Horrocks, I.: A Software Framework for Matchmaking Based on Semantic Web Technology. In: Proceedings of 12th International World Wide Web Conference (2003)
19. Jess the Rule Engine for the JAVA™ Platform. (online). http://herzberg.ca.sandia.gov/ jess
20. Havey, M.: Essential Business Process Modeling. O'Rielly (2005)
21. Barros, O. H.: Business Information System Design Based on Process Patterns and Frameworks. (online). (2004). http://www.bptrends.com
22. Jena Semantic Web Framework: Jena. (online). http://jena.sourceforge.net/ index.html

Towards Building a Semantic Grid for E-Learning

Wenya Tian[1,2] and Huajun Chen[2]

[1] Information Technology Department, Zhejiang Economic & Trade Polytechnic,
Hangzhou 310018, China
[2] Grid Computing Lab, College of Computer Science, Zhejiang University,
Hangzhou 310027, China
Tianweny@163.com, huajunsir@zju.edu.cn

Abstract. In an E-learning scenario, educational resources, such as course documents, videos, test-bases, courseware, and teacher information etc., are shared across different schools. DartGrid is built upon several techniques from both Semantic Web and Grid research areas, and is intended to offer a semantic grid toolkit for data integration. In this paper, a Semantic Grid for E-leaning based on DartGrid is introduced, and it provides a Semantic-based distributed infrastructure for E-learning resource sharing. We explore the essential and fundamental roles played by RDF semantics for e-learning, and implement a set of semantically enabled tools and grid services for E-learning such as semantic browser, ontology service, semantic query service, and semantic registration service.

1 Introduction

Facilities to put machine-understandable data on the Web are becoming a high priority for many communities. The Semantic Web is an effort to improve the current Web by making Web resources machine-understandable because current Web resources do not reflect machine-understandable semantics [5,6]. The Semantic Web [3] provides a common framework that allows data to be shared and reused across applications, enterprises, and community boundaries. It is based on the Resource Description Framework (RDF), which integrates a variety of applications using XML as syntax and URIs for naming.

The Grid [1] is aimed to connect a wide variety of geographically distributed resources such as Personal Computers, workstations and clusters, storage systems, data sources, databases and special purpose scientific instruments and presents them as an integrated resource, and it is a technology that enables distributed computing resources to be shared, managed, coordinated, and controlled.

The Semantic Grid [4] is an Internet-centered interconnection environment that can effectively organizes, shares, clusters, fuses, and manages globally distributed versatile resources based on the interconnection semantics. In short, the Semantic Grid [7] vision is to achieve a high degree of easy-to-use and seamless automation to facilitate flexible collaborations and computations on a global scale, by means of machine-understandable knowledge both on and in the Grid.

F. Eliassen and A. Montresor (Eds.): DAIS 2006, LNCS 4025, pp. 128–137, 2006.

In an E-learning scenario nowadays, educational resources, such as course documents, videos, test-bases, courseware, and teacher information etc, are shared across different colleges. Typically, teachers from many colleges in different district collaborate with each other for teaching. E-learning is the result of the development of modern information technology, and it is the primary method of building life long people education system during the knowledge economy age. E-learning gives students the freedom to study anytime and anywhere and is widely developed and deployed in our country recently. In E-learning, we often need to integrate E-learning services across distributed, heterogeneous, dynamic "virtual organizations" formed by the disparate education resources within a single enterprise and/or from external education resource sharing via service provider relationships. This integration can be technically challenging because of the need to achieve various qualities of E-learning service when running on top of different scholastic platforms.

DartGrid[1] is a data integration toolkit using technologies from semantic web and grid, and is intended to offer a generic semantic infrastructure for building database grid applications. Roughly speaking, DartGrid is a set of semantically enabled tools and grid services such as *semantic browser, semantic mapping tools, ontology service, semantic query service, semantic registration service*, that support the development of database grid applications.

In this paper, a Semantic Grid for E-leaning based on DartGrid is introduced, and it provides a Semantically distributed infrastructure for E-learning scenarios aforementioned. We explore the essential and fundamental roles played by RDF semantics for E-learning grids, and implement a set of semantically enabled tools and grid services for E-learning resource sharing such as semantic browser, ontology service, semantic query service, and semantic registration service.

This paper is outlined as below: Section 2 introduces the architecture and the core components of a Semantic Grid for E-leaning from technical perspective. Section 3 introduces a working scenario for the E-learning grid application. Section 4 mentions some related works. Section 5 gives the summary.

2   Layered Architecture and Core Grid Services

2.1   Technical Approach

2.1.1   RDF

At the present time, the most popular languages for representing data semantics are RDF framework and OWL language, which is proposed in Semantic Web research area and standardize-ed by W3C organization. The Resource Description Framework (RDF) is a language for representing web information in a minimally constraining, extensible, but meaningful way.

The RDF structure is generic in the sense that it is based on the directed acyclic graph (DAG) model. RDF is based on the idea of identifying things using Web identifiers (called Uniform Resource Identifiers, or URIs), and describing resources in terms of simple statements about the properties of resources. Each statement is a

---

[1] DartGrid Official Website: http://ccnt.zju.edu.cn/projects/dartgrid

triplet consisting of a subject, a property and a property value (or object). For example, the triple ("http://example.org", ex:createdBy, "Wenya") has the meaning of "http://www.example has a creator whose value is Wenya".

RDF also provides a means of defining classes of resources and properties. These classes are used to build statements that assert facts about resources. While the grammar for XML documents is defined using DTD or XSchema, RDF uses its own syntax (RDF Schema or RDFS) for writing a schema for resources. RDFS is expressive and it includes subclass/superclass relationships as well as constraints on the statements that can be made in a document according to the schema. The generic structure of RDF makes data interoperability and evolution easier to handle different types of data can be represented using the common graph model, and it offers greater value for data integration over disparate web sources of information. OWL is an extension of RDF/RDFS and supports more sophisticated knowledge representation and inference.

In our work, RDF is used to describe E-Learning data semantics.

2.1.2 OGSA/WSRF and the Globus Toolkit

OGSA/Web Service Resource Framework focuses on service- oriented architecture for grid application. In a grid, computational resources, storage resources, networks, programs, databases, and the like are all represented as services. A service-oriented view allows us to address the need for standard interface definition mechanisms, local/remote transparency, and adaptation to local OS services, and uniform service semantics.

The open source Globus Toolkit [20] is a fundamental enabling technology for the "Grid," letting people share computing power, databases, and other tools securely online across corporate, institutional, and geographic boundaries without sacrificing local autonomy. The toolkit includes software services and libraries for resource monitoring, discovery, and management, plus security and file management.

The Globus Toolkit is built to remove obstacles that prevent seamless collaboration. Its core services, interfaces and protocols allow users to access remote resources as if they were within their own machine room while simultaneously preserving local control over who can use resources and when. The toolkit components that are most relevant to OGSA are the Grid Resource Allocation and Management (GRAM) protocol and its "gatekeeper" service, which provides for secure, reliable, service creation and management [22]; the Meta Directory Service (MDS-2) [21], which provides for information discovery through soft state registration [23, 11], data modeling, and a local registry ("GRAM reporter" [22]); and the Grid Security Infrastructure (GSI), which supports single sign on, delegation, and credential mapping.

In our work, the E-Learning services conform to the OGSA/WSRF specification, and are implemented upon Globus 4 toolkit. Globus 4 is also used as the service container for the E-learning grid application.

2.2 Layered Architecture

Fig.1. illustrates the layered architecture of E-learning Semantic Grid.

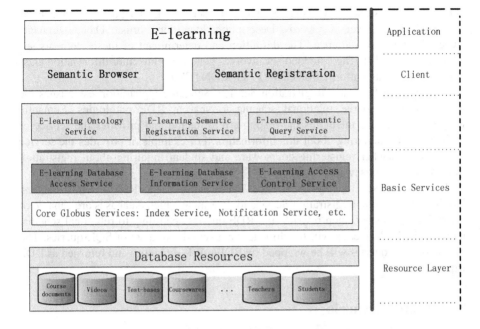

Fig. 1. Layered Architecture of E-learning Semantic Grid

At the basic service layer, three services are implemented.

1. E-learning Database Access Service. It supports the typical remote operations on educational resource contents, such as course documents, videos, test-bases, courseware, and teacher information etc. It also includes querying an education resources, insertion an education resources, deletion an education resources, and modification an education resources.

2. E-learning Database Information Service. It supports inquiring about meta information of the educational data resources such as DBMS descriptions, privilege information, statistics information that includes CPU utilization, available storage space, active session number etc..

3. E-learning Access Control Service. This service is developed for access control in E-learning Semantic Grid. For example, it provides the service of authorizing or authenticating students to access courseware resource.

We mainly contribute to the semantic service level. The services at this level are mainly designed for RDF-based relational schema mediation and semantic query processing.

1. E-learning Ontology Service. This service is used to expose the shared onto-logies that are defined by RDF/OWL languages. The ontologies are used to mediate heterogeneous relational databases. For example, there are two parts in the courseware ontology. One part is defined based on CELTS or IMS. The other part is

defined as an extended set (Fig. 3.).The core set of CELTS has 11 elements as follows: Title, Subject, Keywords, Description, Identifier, Format, Date, Language, Type, Creator and Audience. The definition and determinant of these elements see also CELTS40 [18]. The extended set involves general architecture information class (FRAME) and page information class (PAGECONTENT).

2. E-learning Semantic Registration Service. Semantic registration establishes the mappings from source relational schema to sharing RDF ontologies. Semantic Registration Service maintains the mapping information and provides the service of registering and inquiring about this information. For example, it provides the service that enables teacher registering courseware and student inquiring about registration information of courseware.

3. E-learning Semantic Query Service. This service accepts RDF semantic queries, inquires of Semantic Registration Service to determine which databases are capable of providing the answer, then rewrites the RDF queries according to relational schema, namely, the RDF queries will be ultimately converted into a set of SQL queries. The results of SQL queries will be wrapped by RDF/OWL semantics and returned as RDF triples.

3 Working Scenario

3.1 Typical Use Cases of E-Learning Semantic Grid

Generally, there are two kinds of user roles in E-learning Semantic Grid, they are: Local Database Administrator (such as teachers), and Normal User (such as students). Fig.2. illustrates the relationship between these user roles and the core components of E-learning Semantic Grid.

Local Database Administrator (such as teachers). Education resources can be dynamically added into the sharing cycle of an e-learning semantic grid. E-learning Semantic Grid provides the education resource provider (such as a teacher) with a Semantic Mapping Tool. After a database grid service is setup, the teacher can use semantic mapping tool to register his database to the semantic grid. Typically, the mapping tool retrieves the e-learning ontologies from ontology service, and gets the relational schema from database grid service. Then the DBA can visually map the relational schema to e-learning ontologies. For example, the process that a teacher registers a courseware to the Semantic Registration Service is as follows:

1. Obtain the local database resource schema;
2. Obtain the domain ontologies on the ontology service;
3. Establish the semantic relational mapping between the local database resource schema and the sharing ontologies;
4. Submit the registering information to the semantic registration service.

Section 3.2.2 introduces the semantic mapping tool in more details.

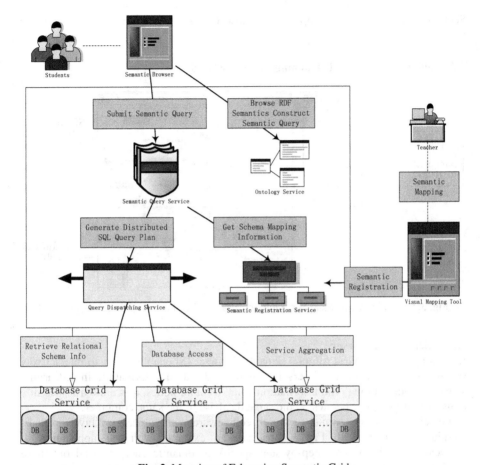

Fig. 2. Mapping of E-learning Semantic Grid

Normal User (such as a student) for normal users, E-learning Semantic Grid offers an intelligent user interface called Semantic Browser [8]. It is a visual interface enabling the user to graphically browse the RDF/OWL semantics and visually construct a RDF semantic query. For example, the process that a student inquires about a courseware is as follows:

1. User browser the e-learning ontology by using the semantic browser;
2. User visually construct a semantic query;
3. User submit the query to a semantic query service;
4. The semantic query service accesses the Semantic Registration Service to query the workable database resource and gets the schema mapping information;
5. The semantic query service generates the distributed SQL Query plan;
6. The semantic query service gets the data information from the idiographic database;
7. Return the result to the student.

Section 3.2.1 gives an example about how to construct a semantic query using this tool.

3.2 Semantic Tools for E-learning Semantic Grid

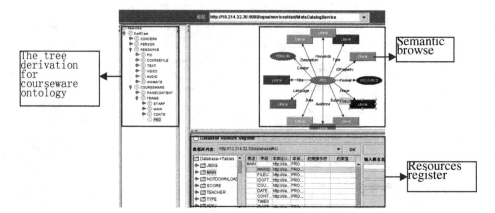

Fig. 3. Semantic Browser and Semantic Registration Tool For E-learning Semantic Grid

3.2.1 Semantic Browser

E-learning Semantic Grid offers a semantic browser [8] enabling user to interactively specify a semantic query. Users can search education information in E-learning semantic grid. Although the information come from all nodes, it is done transparently to users as if the user operates on the same database of the same computer.

For example, a user wants to search courseware with subject as "Java" from E-learning Semantic Grid. Fig 3 illustrates an example with our application. It showcases how users can step-by-step specify a semantic query to find out those needed courseware. In the first step (the left part of the Fig.3.), the user selects the courseware class and its subject property. In the second step, the user inputs a constraint which specifies that the name of the subject as "Java". The Semantic Browser constructs the semantic query automatically. Here the query language is Q3 [15], a database query language like SQL semantically defined by Grid Computing Lab of ZheJiang University. It is a visual process to write q3 in Semantic Browser.

The Q3 language is as following:

```
[q3:context
  [q3:prefix(tcm:http://dart.zju.edu.cn/tcm)
   q3:variable{
     ?x1 a tcm:PRO
   }
  ]
 q3:pattern ()
 q3:constraint{
   ?x1.tcm:Subject="Java"
 }]
```

At last, the result (the above of the right part of Fig.3.) records come from all databases of different nodes.

3.2.2 Semantic Registration

The task of defining semantic mapping from local relational schema to RDF ontologies is burdensome and erroneous. E-learning Semantic Grid offers a visual tool to facilitate the task of defining semantic mappings. As Fig.3 displays, the user can use the registration panel (the below of the right part in the fig.3) to view the table and column definition of the relational database, and use the semantic browsing panel (the above of the right part in the fig.3) to browse the RDF ontologies graphically. The user can then specify which RDF class one table should be mapped onto and which RDF property one table column should be mapped onto. After finishing the mapping, the tool automatically generates a registration entry in RDF/XML format, and submits it to the semantic registration service.

For example, a teacher wants to register courseware recourses. The Semantic Registration tool directly registers courseware resources to the Semantic Registration Center. It is a semantic mapping from the local courseware resources to the sharing semantic ontology.

During the registration, mapping information is written into a semantic registry. The courseware resource content itself is not uploaded to the registration center or any other centralized node. When the user searches resources, the Semantic Registration Center will look up the result from the resource registration table. User will download and browse the corresponding resources from the data node by linking it directly. The way it works is very similar to other P2P mode. The registration interface shows as Fig.3.

4 Related Work

There are a lot of relevant works. Within the domain of Grid research, there are many efforts about accessing and integrating e-learning database under the grid framework. Typical example is Realcourse [2]. Realcourse is a successful application of distributed computing [13] technology in a geographically wide area. Different from some traditional distributed fault-tolerant services like ISIS [14], Realcourse emphasizes giving clients access to the service with reasonable response time. For most cases, it means as much of the time as possible.

In [12], it is clear that standards like LOM, or Dublin Core are gaining importance. They provide more information on the learning material that is to be found in the web. However, their simple structure prevent them being used for modeling more complex knowledge. [10] Explains how Semantic Web technologies based on ontologies can improve different aspects of the management of E-Learning resources. Indeed, ontologies are a means of specifying the concepts and their relationships in a particular domain of interest. Web Ontology languages, like OWL, are specially designed to facilitate the sharing of knowledge between actors [17] in a distributed environment. We wish to emphasize here that Web Ontology languages have various advantages.

The significant difference, compared with others, is the RDF-based and semantic-web-oriented approach adopted in the Semantic Grid for E-learning. The Semantic Grid for E-learning complements those efforts with a semantic infrastructure for building database grid application and this infrastructure can provide information and knowledge services as other conventional portals. In addition, the use of multiple servers can semantically assist users in formulating their problem description, searching possible solutions on the Grid.

5 Summary and Future Work

The Semantic Grid will play a very important role for the wide acceptance of the Grid [9]. It will provide enhanced support for end users to access heterogeneous Grid services and resources by understanding their domain problems and providing solutions. We present a Semantic Grid for E-leaning based on DartGrid, and also put forward a dynamic, extensible Semantic-based distributed infrastructure for E-learning scenarios. We explore the essential and fundamental roles played by RDF semantics for e-learning resource sharing, and implement a set of semantically enabled tools and grid services for E-learning such as semantic browser, ontology service, semantic query service, and semantic registration service.

There are more works need to be done in this area. Semantic Grid for E-leaning, a DartGrid application, has many obvious attributes as a good test bed. As a typical DartGrid application by its nature, it stores various data classes that can be collected easily. Plus, the test result can be verified easily. The system needs to be further tested with more data classes and more grid nodes. More features are needed for the education resource management. In the meantime, DartGrid itself also needs to be continuously improved for perfection. Now we have a working prototype of an open education resource management system. The next step is to make it more powerful by fine-tuning its operability. As far as education is concerned, it is important to manage all education resources via the semantic grid for E-learning.

Acknowledgements

We gratefully acknowledge helpful discussions with other members in the Grid Computing Lab of Zhejiang University. This work is co-funded by subprogram of China 973 project (NO. 2003CB316906), a grant from Program for New Century Excellent Talents in University of Ministry of Education of China (NO. NCET-04-0545), China NSF program (NO. NSFC60503018), and Zhejiang Provincial Natural Science Foundation of China (NO. Y105463) .

References

1. I. Foster, C. Kesselman, The Grid, Blueprint for a New Computing Infrastructure, Morgan Kaufmann, San Francisco, USA, 1998
2. Jinyu Zhang, Xiaoming Li, The Model, Architecture and Mechanism Behind Realcourse, ISPA 2004, LNCS 3358, pp. 615–624, 2004.

3. http://news.11138.com/2001/sw/
4. H Zhuge, Semantic Grid: Scientific Issues, Infrastructure, and Methodology, Communication of the ACM Vol. 48, No. 4(2005) 197
5. T. Berners-Lee, J. Hendler, O. Lassila, Semantic Web, Sci. Am. 284 (5) (2001) 34–43.
6. J. Hendler, Agents and the semantic web, IEEE Intell. Syst. 16 (2) (2001) 30–37.
7. D. de Roure, N. R. Jennings and N. Shadbolt (2003) "The Semantic Grid: A future eScience infrastructure" Int. J. of Concurrency and Computation: Practice and Experience 15 (11)
8. Yuxin Mao, ZhaohuiWu, Huajun Chen. Semantic Browser: an Intelligent Client for Dart-Grid. Proceedings of International Conference on Computational Science (Lecture Notes in Computer Science, vol. 3036) , Springer:Berlin, 2004; 470-473.
9. M. Li, P. van Santen, D.W. Walker, O.F. Rana, M.A. Baker,SGrid: a service-oriented model for the Semantic Grid, Future Generation Computer Systems 20 (2004) 7–18
10. Ljiljana Stojanovic, Steffen Staab, and Rudi Studer. E-learning based on the semantic web. In WebNet2001 - World Conference on the WWW and Internet, Orlando, Florida, USA, 2001.
11. Zhang, L., Braden, B., Estrin, D., Herzog, S. and Jamin, S., RSVP: A new Resource ReSerVation Protocol. In IEEE Network, (1993), 8-18
12. Jan Brase and Wolfgang Nejdl. Ontologies and Metadata for eLearning, pages 579–598. Springer Verlag, 2003.
13. George Coulouris, Jean Dollimore, Tim Kindberg, Distributed System Concepts and Design (Third version), ISBN 7-111-11749-2, China Machine Press
14. Birman, K.P. (1993). The process group approach to reliable distributed computing. Comms. ACM, Vol. 36, No. 12, pp. 36-53
15. Huajun Chen, Zhaohui Wu, Guozhou Zheng, Yuxing Mao. DartGrid: a Semantic-based Approach for Data Integration Using Grid as the Platform
16. Christian Bizer, Andy Seaborne. D2RQ -Treating Non-RDF Databases as Virtual RDF Graphs. Presented at the 3rd International Semantic Web Conference (ISWC2004),November 2004.
17. Rudi Studer Steffen Staab, Hans-Peter Schnurr and York Sure. Knowledge processes and ontologies. IEEE Intelligent Systems, 16(1), 2001.
18. China ELearning Technology Standardization Committee, Education Informationize Technology Standard□http://www.celtsc.edu.cn sub standard CELTS-40
19. Foster, I. and Kesselman, C. Globus: A Toolkit-Based Grid Architecture. In Foster, I. and Kesselman, C. eds. The Grid: Blueprint for a New Computing Infrastructure, Morgan Kaufmann, 1999, 259-278.
20. http://www.globus.org/toolkit/about.html
21. Czajkowski, K., Fitzgerald, S., Foster, I. and Kesselman, C., Grid Information Services for Distributed Resource Sharing. In 10th IEEE International Symposium on High Performance Distributed Computing, (2001), IEEE Press, 181-184
22. Czajkowski, K., Foster, I., Karonis, N., Kesselman, C., Martin, S., Smith, W. and Tuecke, S. A Resource Management Architecture for Metacomputing Systems. In 4th Workshop on Job Scheduling Strategies for Parallel Processing, Springer-Verlag, 1998, 62-82.
23. Raman, S. and McCanne, S. A Model, Analysis, and Protocol Framework for Soft State-based Communication. Computer Communication Review, 29 (4). 1999.

A Code Migration Framework for AJAX Applications

Arno Puder

San Francisco State University
Computer Science Department
1600 Holloway Avenue
San Francisco, CA 94132
arno@sfsu.edu

Abstract. AJAX (Asynchronous JavaScript and XML) defines a new paradigm for writing highly interactive web applications. Prominent web sites such as Google Maps have made AJAX popular. Writing AJAX applications requires intimate knowledge of JavaScript since it is difficult to write cross-browser portable JavaScript applications. In this paper we first discuss the benefits of AJAX compared to other technologies such as Java applets. Then we propose a code migration framework that allows the programmer to write AJAX applications in Java. The Java application is automatically translated to JavaScript and migrated to the browser for execution. Our approach requires no knowledge of JavaScript. As web applications are written in Java, the developer benefits from powerful debugging tools that are not available for JavaScript. We have implemented a prototype that demonstrates the feasibility of our ideas. The prototype is available under an Open Source license.

1   Motivation

The initial intend of the World-Wide Wide (WWW) was to give access to remote documents. This document centric view soon proved to be insufficient as eCommerce recognized the potential of the new media. Subsequently, HTML was extended to allow the description of user interfaces based on web forms. The web browser thus assumed the role of a generic client that is capable to render *a priori* unknown user interfaces. The technologies of the WWW therefore have changed from being document centric to operational interaction centric. Numerous technologies came into existence to facilitate the development of web applications. Java Server Pages (JSP), PHP Hypertext Processor (PHP), and Struts are only few of those technologies.

Despite these new technologies, the user is very much aware of latencies because web applications are still based on web pages (i.e., user interfaces) being loaded from a remote web server. A light-weight scripting language called JavaScript was introduced by Netscape in 1995 mainly for doing some user input validation that does not require interaction with a remote web server. This can already be seen as the first step towards migrating part of the application logic to the web browser.

F. Eliassen and A. Montresor (Eds.): DAIS 2006, LNCS 4025, pp. 138–151, 2006.

Other technologies such as Java applets have attempted to become a standard for client-side processing, but they could not establish themselves mostly because of political issues between different vendors. The lowest common denominator today for writing client-side applications that can run inside any web browser without requiring any additional browser plugins is thus JavaScript. It is in this context that AJAX (Asynchronous JavaScript and XML) has emerged as a new paradigm for writing highly-interactive web applications.

At the core of AJAX is JavaScript and writing an AJAX application thus requires intimate knowledge of JavaScript. Matters become more complicated by the fact that writing portable JavaScript that runs in all major browsers such as Internet Explorer (IE) or Firefox is a daunting task. One of those problems is the lack of powerful development tools for JavaScript. This paper introduces a new approach for facilitating the creation of AJAX application based on a code migration framework. The outline of this paper is as follows: Section 2 gives a proper definition of AJAX and also discusses the difficulties in writing an AJAX application. Section 3 introduces our code migration framework. Section 4 discusses our prototype implementation while in Section 5 we discuss related work. Section 6 finally provides a conclusion and an outlook.

2   AJAX

In this section we first provide an introduction to AJAX (Section 2.1), explain the benefits of AJAX (Section 2.2), and finally why it is so difficult to write AJAX applications (Section 2.3).

2.1   Overview of AJAX

The term AJAX was first coined in [5]. The author of this article attempted to describe a new class of web applications that differ significantly from previous technologies such as PHP, JSP, or Struts. Figure 1 demonstrates this difference. The left side of this figure shows the traditional way of implementing web applications. The web browser is used for rendering the user interface, typically a web form that the user can populate. Apart simple input validation, no processing happens during this phase. Once the user presses the submit button, the form is sent via an HTTP request to the server. Upon unmarshalling the data, the web application running on the side of the web server computes a new HTML page that is sent back to the browser. While the browser is waiting for that response, the user cannot use the interface.

The right hand side of Figure 1 shows how AJAX changes this picture. The main difference is that AJAX application make use of the JavaScript interpreter that is contained in every popular web browser. Part of the application logic is thus implemented in JavaScript and executed on the side of the client. All browsers support the so-called XMLHttpRequest object that allows JavaScript to issue a HTTP request to the remote web server. The user can continuously interact with the application as shown in the figure. Event handler invoke appropriate JavaScript functions that use the DOM (Document Object Model) to

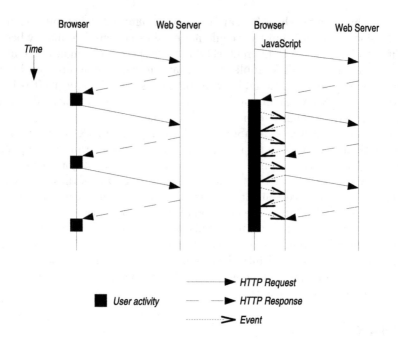

Fig. 1. Traditional web application vs. AJAX

make fine-grained updates to the user interface without requiring complete page reloads as in the traditional model.

The asynchronous nature of AJAX applications refers to the fact that the JavaScript code may issue HTTP requests independent of user interaction. This makes it possible to do processing in the background without the user having to wait for a response from the web server. All parameters and responses have to be marshalled in a way so they can be piggy-backed on HTTP requests and responses. One obvious choice is XML as all popular browsers include XML parsers that make the marshalling and unmarshalling of parameters relatively simple.

2.2   AJAX vs. Other Technologies

AJAX allows the execution of application logic inside the browser. This increases interactivity of web application dramatically compared to the submit-and-page-reload paradigm. By doing so, AJAX applications get closer to the look-and-feel of desktop applications and some analysts already foresee the browser as the next-generation desktop replacement that could even threaten Microsofts monopoly. Whether or not this vision will come true, it can certainly be expected that more and more web applications will want to employ AJAX technologies.

AJAX makes use of the fact that JavaScript interpreters are ubiquitous in all popular web browser. Moving application logic to the client side is not new. One of the promises of the Java programming language was to enable web applications in a similar way as AJAX through Java applets. A Java applet is a Java application running inside the browser. It is therefore possible to achieve the same effect with applets as with AJAX applications. While Java is a much more mature language than JavaScript with a more powerful GUI library, the major downside of applets is that they require a Java Runtime Environment (JRE) plugin for the respective browser. This requires the end-user to download the plugin which creates an additional burden for the end-user.

Given a choice, end-users either intentionally or unintentionally choose not to install additional software if they have an already existing solution and the benefits of the alternative are not immediately apparent. As a specific example of the reluctance of end-users to explicitly install software can be seen by the proportion of Windows users who use IE, despite security issues compared to other browsers. IE currently owns more than 85% of the market share (see [9]), primarily because it is bundled along with Windows. If end-users are reluctant or simply do not bother to use easy-to-install software such as alternate web browsers, they are usually not willing to install a Java Runtime Environment. This accounts for the fact that AJAX has become so popular because it only uses the lowest common denominator available in virtually all web browsers.

2.3 Writing AJAX Applications

As outlined above, writing AJAX applications therefore requires JavaScript to achieve the interactiveness desired by the latest generation of web applications. JavaScript was created by Netscape and was first incorporated in Netscapes browser version 2.0. The rationale behind JavaScript was to make Navigator's newly added Java support more accessible to non-Java programmers. The design goals of JavaScript therefore focused on a loosely-typed scripting language suited the environment and audience, namely the few thousand web designers and developers back in 1995 who needed to be able to tie into page elements without a bytecode compiler or knowledge of object-oriented software design.

Microsoft released a port of JavaScript called JScript with IE 3.0. JScript was one revision behind Navigator's JavaScript that made it difficult already back then to write cross-browser portable JavaScript. In 1997, the European Computer Manufacturers Association (ECMA) standardized a universally supported core functionality called ECMAScript (see [3]). Despite this standardization effort, support for JavaScript is not as homogeneous as one might wish. Writing portable JavaScript for all major browsers still requires intimate knowledge of the different object models.

There are many pitfalls that a JavaScript programmer has to deal with today. First and foremost, there are no powerful development tools available for JavaScript. Mozilla offers a debugger, but IE merely indicates by an alert icon in the status bar when something went wrong. Other issues in creating JavaScript applications has to do with differences in the JavaScript object model supported by various browsers. Sometimes events such as mouse events are offered from inner-most nested elements to top-level elements (called *Event Bubbling* and supported by IE); sometimes events are offered elements in the reverse order (called *Event Capturing* and supported by Netscape/Mozilla). Advanced event models such as Event Listeners that allow the registration of multiple listeners for one particular event are not supported sufficiently in IE. The author of [6] gives a more comprehensive list of issues.

This is only a short list of the problems that one will likely encounter when developing AJAX applications. These issues combined with the fact that JavaScript supports object-oriented programming only through conventions and clever programming tricks (e.g., to achieve the effect of inheritance one has to change the prototype of the derived class) will place a high burden on anyone interested in creating AJAX applications. The main idea of this paper is that a programmer can write an AJAX application without requiring any knowledge of JavaScript. Our approach is outlined in the following.

3   Framework

This section gives a detailed description of our framework. At its core is a code migration framework that shields the programmer from the complexities of writing JavaScript applications. A developer can write an AJAX web application in Java benefiting from powerful and mature tools and then migrate the code to JavaScript. In Section 3.1 we briefly state our assumptions that guide the design of our framework. Section 3.2 then introduces XMLVM, an XML-based programming language that is at the core of our code migration framework. Section 3.3 then shows how to create JavaScript out of XMLVM. In Section 3.4 we finally describe the underlying architecture of our framework.

3.1   Assumptions

Before describing the details of our approach, we first explicitly state the assumptions that will influence some design decisions of our framework:

Universal access: We assume that potentially any user in the WWW might be using the web application.

No special browser plugins: In order to support universal access, we do not assume any special browser plugins such as the Java Runtime Environment.

Web applications using Java: We assume that the programmer is using Java (not JavaScript) as the programming language of choice to write his or her web application.

Self-contained applications: For now, we only consider self-contained applications that have no dependencies to external resources such as databases.

No JavaScript knowledge necessary: The programmer does not need to know any JavaScript in order to develop AJAX-enabled web applications.

The reason for assuming universal access to a web application is that it is generally much simpler to develop a web application for a closed environment.

Corporate intranets for example typically enforce the use of a particular desktop configuration. AJAX should only be considered in heterogeneous environments. The assumptions stated above basically lead to a development environment where the programmer is shielded from JavaScript. Since we do not assume any special browser plugins, but yet allow the programmer to implement his or her program in Java, we need a code migration framework that can translate and migrate the Java application to JavaScript.

3.2 XMLVM

As a first step towards our code migration framework for AJAX applications, we begin by defining an XML-based programming language. In this section we focus on describing the details of this language and defer the usage of this language to a subsequent section. Since this XML-based programming language is based on the Java virtual machine, we call this language XMLVM. XMLVM basically allows us to represent the contents of a class file (i.e., the output generated by a Java-compiler) through XML. Another way to look at XMLVM is that it defines an assembly language for the Java virtual machine using XML for the syntax. The object model of XMLVM is consequently based on the object model of Java. The virtual machine model of XMLVM is shown in Figure 2.

The XMLVM program shown in Figure 2 contains the instructions of a method to be executed. These instructions are essentially the byte code instructions supported by the Java virtual machine. The virtual machine maintains an instruction pointer to the next instruction to be executed. Upon entering a method, a new frame consisting of a stack and local variables is created. This frame will be deleted upon exiting the method. The virtual machine maintains a pointer to

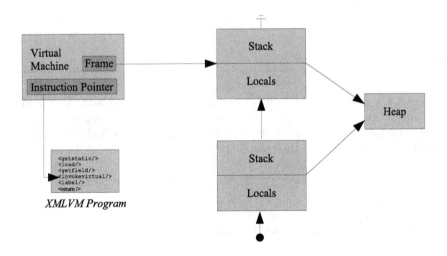

Fig. 2. XMLVM Virtual Machine Model

the current frame (which represents the most nested method call). A method has only access to its own stack and local variables as well as the global heap. The actual parameters of a method are automatically stored in the local variables. Besides the stack frames, the virtual machine maintains a garbage collected global heap where a program can allocate new objects. The following template shows the general structure of any XMLVM program:

```
1 <xmlvm>
2   <class ...>
3     <field .../>
4     <method ...>
5       <signature>...</signature>
6       <code>...</code>
7     </method>
8   </class>
9 </xmlvm>
```

An XMLVM program consists of one class. Every class can have one or more fields and methods. The attributes of the XML-tags, that are not shown in the template above, give more details such as identifiers or modifiers. A method is defined through a signature and the actual implementation, denoted by the tags <signature> and <code> respectively. Consider the following simple Java-class:

```
1 // Java
2 class Calc {
3     int x;
4     void add(int y)
5     {
6         x += y;
7     }
8 }
```

Class Calc has one field called x and one method called add. The method adds the actual parameter given to it to the field x. Although this is a very simple example, it allows us to show all basic aspects of an XMLVM program. The following XML shows the representation of class Calc in XMLVM:

```
1 <xmlvm>
2   <class name="Calc">
3     <field name="x" type="int"/>
4     <method name="add" stack="3" locals="2">
5       <signature>
6         <return type="void"/>
7         <parameter type="int"/>
8       </signature>
```

```
 9        <code>
10          <load type="Calc" index="0"/>
11          <dup/>
12          <getfield class-type="Calc" type="int" field="x"/>
13          <load type="int" index="1"/>
14          <add/>
15          <putfield class-type="Calc" type="int" field="x"/>
16          <return/>
17        </code>
18      </method>
19    </class>
20 </xmlvm>
```

It should be emphasized again that the above XMLVM program is essentially an XML-representation of the contents of the Calc.class class file. The top-level tags are identical to the XML-template shown earlier. The <method>-tag has two attributes: stack and locals. stack tells the virtual machine the maximum stack-size needed for this method. In this example, method add will never push more than 3 elements at the same time onto its stack. The locals attribute tells the virtual machine how many local variables are needed for this method. The first local variable always represents the this-pointer. The next local variables represent the actual parameters. Since method add has only one input parameter and no additional local variables, the locals attribute is 2. Note that the Java compiler computes the values for stack and locals and stores them in the class file.

The more interesting part of the XMLVM-program shown above is the actual implementation of method add. The <load> instruction pushes the this-pointer referred to by local variable with index 0 onto the stack. Instruction <dup> duplicates the top of the stack so that the this-pointer now is pushed twice on the stack. <getfield> pushes the current value of field x onto the stack. Since every instance of class Calc has its own field x, <getfield> needs a reference to the instance whose field x should be pushed onto the stack. This reference has to be on the top of the stack. <getfield> pops off the reference and replaces it with the value of field x. After this instruction, the stack contains the this-pointer and the value of field x.

The next instruction <load> pushes the actual parameter y (referenced through local variable index 1) onto the stack. The top two elements of the stack are now the values to be added. The following instruction <add> pops off the last two values and pushes their sum back onto the stack. At this point, the stack contains the this-pointer as well as the sum. The <putfield> instruction works similarly as the <getfield> instruction, except that a value is written back to a field. After this instruction, the stack is empty. The final instruction <return> exits the method.

The XMLVM instruction set feature a mix of low-level and high-level virtual machine instructions. Next to the low-level instructions mentioned above, there exist high-level instructions such as new (for instantiating new objects)

Table 1. Representative XMLVM instructions

Instr.	Stack
<add>	$\ldots, value_1, value_2 \Rightarrow \ldots, result$
<getfield>	$\ldots, objref \Rightarrow \ldots, value$
<putfield>	$\ldots, objref, value \Rightarrow \ldots$
<load>	$\ldots \Rightarrow \ldots, value$
<new>	$\ldots \Rightarrow \ldots, objref$
<invokevirtual>	$\ldots, objref, [arg_1, [arg_2, \ldots]] \Rightarrow \ldots$

and invokevirtual (invoke a virtual method). These instructions go beyond the capabilities of normal (hardware) machine languages and therefore require substantial runtime support. Table 1 gives an overview of some of the instructions found in XMLVM. The table shows how the instructions introduced in this section affect the stack by showing the stack before and after the respective instruction.

3.3 Language Transformation

As stated earlier, XMLVM can be seen as an assembly language for the Java virtual machine. The difficult part is done by a Java compiler. Once a class file has been created as the result of the compilation process, it can be easily translated to XMLVM simply by analyzing the contents of the class file. The next step consists in translating XMLVM to JavaScript. This translation can be done by an XSL-stylesheet that maps XMLVM-instructions one-to-one to the target language. Since XMLVM is based on a simple stack-based machine, we simply mimic a stack-machine in the target language. An example helps to illustrate this approach. The XMLVM instruction <add> introduced earlier pops off two values and pushes the sum back onto the stack. Here is the XSL-template that creates JavaScript code for this instruction:

```
1 <xsl:template match="add">
2       <xsl:text>
3             __op2 = __stack[--__sp];
4             __op1 = __stack[--__sp];
5             __stack[__sp++] = __op1 + __op2;
6       </xsl:text>
7 </xsl:template>
```

We mimic the virtual machine of XMLVM via the variables __locals (for local variables), __stack (for the stack), and __sp (for the stack pointer). Variables __op1 and __op2 are used as temporary variables needed by some XMLVM-instructions. Those variables are declared for every method. The code below represents the JavaScript version of the class Calc introduced in Section 3.2:

```
1 // JavaScript generated by stylesheet
2 function Calc()
3 {
4   this.x = null;
5
6   this.add = function( __arg1)
7   {
8     var __locals = new Array(2);
9     var __stack = new Array(3);
10    var __sp = 0;
11    var __op1;
12    var __op2;
13    __locals[0] = this;
14    __locals[1] = __arg1;
15    __stack[__sp++] = __locals[0];
16    __op1 = __stack[__sp - 1];
17    __stack[__sp++] = __op1;
18    __op1 = __stack[--__sp];
19    __stack[__sp++] = __op1.x;
20    __stack[__sp++] = __locals[1];
21    __op2 = __stack[--__sp];
22    __op1 = __stack[--__sp];
23    __stack[__sp++] = __op1 + __op2;
24    __op2 = __stack[--__sp];
25    __op1 = __stack[--__sp];
26    __op1.x = __op2;
27    return;
28  }
29 }
```

The JavaScript code was generated automatically by applying an appropriate XSL-stylesheet to the XMLVM version of class Calc. As can be seen, there is a natural mapping from XMLVM to JavaScript. The intention is not to generate readable code, but correct code that uses the API of the target language. It should also be obvious that the above JavaScript code will be less efficient than the original Java program. Our assumption is that we do not migrate computational heavy applications to the browser. By carefully designing the XSL-stylesheet one can generate portable JavaScript.

3.4 Architecture

The description of the architecture that is to follow in this section, explains how XMLVM is embedded in an infrastructure for the code migration framework. As shown in Figure 3, the main component is a Web Container that serves as an HTTP server towards the web browser. The URL used to contact the Web Container encodes a bootstrap web page as well as the application that is to be executed as an AJAX application. As shown in Figure 3, the web page index.html will be returned to the browser. This page has the following simple structure:

```
1 <html>
2   <head>
3     <script type="text/javascript" src="xmlvm.js"/>
4   </head>
5   <body onLoad="bootXMLVM()">
6     <div id="AJAX_APP"/>
7   </body>
8 </html>
```

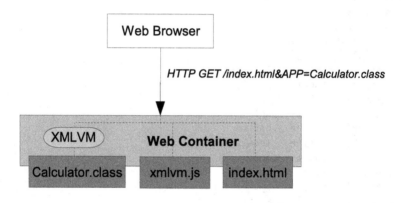

Fig. 3. Architecture

The header of this page includes a JavaScript file called xmlvm.js that contains a JavaScript version of the runtime library required by the application. Without this library, running the application would result in unresolved externals. The <body> tag will invoke function bootXMLVM() once index.html has been successfully loaded. This function, which is defined in xmlvm.js, will parse the URL and retrieve the APP parameter (Calculator.class in this example). bootXMLVM() will then issue an HTTP request containing the application to be loaded to the Web Container. Upon receiving this request, the Web Container uses XMLVM to create a JavaScript version of Calculator.class that is being returned to the browser where it will be executed. The application will render itself in a visual placeholder denoted by the <div> element with ID AJAX_APP in the index.html page shown above.

4   Prototype Implementation

We have implemented a prototype based on the ideas outlined in the previous section to show the feasibility of our approach. We have leveraged as many Open Source tools as possible. The Web Container is implemented using a light-weight HTTP engine called Simple (see [4]). We use the Byte Code Engineering Library (BCEL) from the Apache Foundation (see [2]) to inspect the contents of a Java class file. Using BCEL, it is relatively easy to translate a class-file to XMLVM. We have implemented an XSLT stylesheet to translate XMLVM to JavaScript. Furthermore we have implemented a rudimentary JavaScript library for certain Java-API that are used in the example explained below.

To test our framework, we have implemented a calculator using Sun's Abstract Windowing Toolkit (AWT). The calculator, which is shown on the left side of Figure 4, allows simple mathematical operations. The source code of the application is 322 lines of Java. The screenshot on the left-hand side of Figure 4 shows the desktop version of the calculator. Even this simple application makes use of several external classes such as widgets (e.g., Buttons, Labels), Layout Managers, and utility classes (e.g., String and Float).

The class file of this Java application results in 1920 lines of XMLVM. After applying the stylesheet, the resulting JavaScript is 1693 lines of code. The xmlvm.js library, which implements all the API that is needed by the calculator, adds up to another 1210 lines of JavaScript code. The right side of Figure 4 shows the calculator as an AJAX application running inside Firefox. The buttons shown on the right side are HTML-buttons created by the AJAX application.

The xmlvm.js library contains implementation for all external references of our calculator application. These external dependencies include JavaScript implementations for java.awt.Button, java.awt.Panel, java.awt.BagLayout, java.lang.String, java.lang.Float, and several other classes. The JavaScript version of these classes is semantically equivalent to their Java counterparts. The JavaScript version of java.awt.Button for example has the same API as its Java counterpart, but will draw an HTML button inside the browser at the appropriate location using CSS.

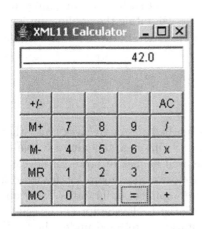

Fig. 4. Calculator as an AWT and AJAX application

Ideally, `xmlvm.js` should contain JavaScript implementations for the complete Java Runtime Library. Currently, `xmlvm.js` is hand-coded, specifically for the needs of our calculator application. Since the majority of the Java Runtime Library is itself written in Java, it is possible to automatically convert those class files via XMLVM to JavaScript. The only portions of the Java Runtime Library that would need to be hand-coded are JNI (Java Native Interface) calls. It is to be noted that while we believe that the majority of the Java Runtime Library can thus be automatically translated to JavaScript, this will not be possible for certain features. For example, threads cannot be supported in JavaScript since none of the JavaScript interpreters allow multithreaded applications.

5   Related Work

Several projects – commercial and Open Source – exist that aim at providing an easy migration path for legacy Java applications to web applications. Web-Cream is a commercial product by a company called CreamTec (see [1]). They have specialized in providing AWT and Swing replacements that render the interface of the Java application inside of a web browser. WebCream makes use of proprietary features of Microsoft's Internet Explorer and therefore only runs inside this browser.

Two Open Source projects, both hosted at SourceForge, follow the same idea of exposing Java desktop applications as web applications. The first one is called WebOnSwing (see [8]). Unlike WebCream, this project is not tailored for a particular browser. One feature offered by WebOnSwing are templates that allow to change the look-and-feel of the application that is rendered inside the browser. Another project with similar features, but not quite as mature, is SwingWeb (see [7]).

The major difference between these approaches and the one introduced in this paper is that none of them supports code migration. While the user interface rendered inside the browser looks similar, every event such as pushing a button, requires an HTTP request to the remote server. Migrating the application logic to the browser dramatically increases the responsiveness of the application while reducing the load on the remote server.

6   Conclusion and Outlook

AJAX applications have gained prominence as their interactiveness rivals that of desktop applications. Writing portable JavaScript is a difficult task due to the fact of cross-browser incompatibilities as well as lack of powerful development tools for JavaScript. In this paper we propose a code migration framework that would allow a programmer to write a web application in Java. Using our framework, the Java application can be translated to JavaScript and executed inside any browser. The prototype implementation is released under the GNU GPL and is available at `www.xml11.org`. This web site also hosts the calculator demo discussed earlier.

As for the next step, we will investigate the dynamic translation of the Java Runtime Library in order to avoid hand-coding this complex library. We also plan to investigate the restriction of self-contained applications. Fixed resources such as databases can obviously not be migrated. We therefore need to investigate a way to keep part of the application on the server side and use proxies to communicate between the migrated and the stationary portions of the application.

References

1. CreamTec, LLC. *WebCream*. http://www.creamtec.com/webcream/.
2. Markus Dahm. Byte code engineering. Java Informations Tage, pages 267–277, 1999.
3. European Computer Manufacturers Association. *ECMAScript Language Specification*. http://www.ecma-international.org/publications/standards/Ecma-262.htm.
4. Niall Gallagher. *Simple - A Java HTTP engine*. http://sourceforge.net/projects/simpleweb/.
5. Jesse Garrett. *Ajax: A New Approach to Web Applications*.
   http://www. adaptivepath.com/publications/essays/archives/000385.php.
6. Peter-Paul Koch. *Writing Portable JavaScript*. http://www.quirksmode.org/.
7. Tiong Hiang Lee. *SwingWeb*. http://swingweb.sourceforge.net/swingweb/.
8. Fernando Petrola. *WebOnSwing*. http://webonswing.sourceforge.net/xoops/.
9. WebSideStory. *U.S. Browser Usage Share*. http://www.websidestory.com/.

High Performance SOAP Processing Driven by Data Mapping Template

Wei Jun, Hua Lei, Niu Chunlei, and Zheng Haoran

Technology Center of Software Engineering, Institute of Software
Chinese Academy of Sciences, Beijing 100080, China
wj@otcaix.iscas.ac.cn

Abstract. Web Services, with loosely-coupled, high-interoperable and platform-independent characteristics, is gaining popularity in distributed computing. However, web services suffers performance penalty because its protocol stack is based on XML. SOAP is used to specify wire message format in web services, and SOAP processing largely affects the performance of web services. In this paper, we firstly analyze the performance of web services on Java platform, and identify that data model mapping between XML data and Java data is the main impact factor on performance. Therefore, we propose a new scheme of data model mapping - "Dynamic Early Binding" which enables to improve SOAP processing by avoiding Java reflection operations and proactively generating processing codes. This dynamic early binding is realized by Data Mapping Template (DMT), which is specified by extended context free grammar and implemented by pushdown automaton with output. We introduce the technique into our developed SOAP engine – SOAPExpress. The effectiveness is illustrated by yielding over 100% speedups compared to Apache Axis 1.2 in our benchmark.

1 Introduction

Recently, with the development and standardization of web services protocols such as XML, SOAP and WSDL, a new distributed computing paradigm based on web services is gaining momentum. Web services supplies the XML-based service description, service registry and service invocation mechanisms, and solves the interoperability problems between heterogeneous platforms.

Web services are platform-independent, high interoperable compared to other distributed computing component models such as EJB, CORBA and DCOM. However, web services suffers performance penalty which prevents it from widely using in high performance computing. The performance of distributed system is strongly determined by their wire format [1]. The traditional client-server communication paradigms such as RPC offer high performance, but these systems rely on the assumption that communicating parities strictly abide certain protocol which causes highly coupling; the distributed communication paradigm such as Java-RMI adopts serialized object which lessens system coupling, but brings additional marshalling costs; web services uses XML as the message format which realizes high interoperability between heterogeneous platforms. However XML parsing and marshalling dramatically decrease the system performance.

F. Eliassen and A. Montresor (Eds.): DAIS 2006, LNCS 4025, pp. 152–168, 2006.

SOAP protocol defines the message format of web services, which serves as the basis of loosely-coupled, high interoperable web services. The core function component of web services is SOAP Engine, which parses the XML-based SOAP message and carries on the data model mapping between XML data and platform dependent application data, so on. SOAP engine determines the performance of web services. This paper will focus on how to speedup the data mapping between XML data and Java data to improve the performance of SOAP engine.

We first analyze the performance of web services based on widely used SOAP engine Apache Axis 1.2[2], and identify that data model mapping between XML data and Java data is the main impact factor on performance.

Based on experiments, we propose a new data model mapping paradigm "Dynamic Early Binding". Dynamic Early Binding avoids the use of Java reflection by keeping record of the mapping information and actions in dynamically generated template. The template will be specified based on context-free grammar (CFG), and implemented by pushdown automaton with output actions. We apply the Dynamic Early Binding technique into a high performance SOAP Engine - SOAPExpress we developed. The average SOAP processing performance of SOAPExpress is heavily improved compared with Apache Axis 1.2.

This paper is structured as follows: First, we survey related works in section 2. Section 3 analyzes the performance impact points in SOAP message processing, introduces the performance-related techniques, and proposes the Dynamic Early Binding technique. In section 4, we present the realization of Dynamic Early Binding technique – Data Mapping Template (DMT) in detail. Section 5 introduces the application of DMT in SOAPExpress, and illustrates that the DMT improves the performance of SOAPExpress heavily on experiments. We conclude the paper and discuss our future works in section 6.

2   Related Works

There have been several studies on the performance of the SOAP processing [3],[4],[5],[6],[7]. These studies all agreed that XML based SOAP protocol incurred a substantial performance penalty compared with binary protocols.

Davis conducted an experimental evaluation on the latency performance of various SOAP implementations, comparing with other protocols such as Java RMI and CORBA/IIOP [3]. A conclusion was drawn that two reasons may cause the inefficiency of SOAP. One is about the multiple system calls to realize one logical message sending. Another is about the XML parsing and formatting. The similar conclusion was drawn in [4] by comparison with CORBA. Chiu et al. pointed put that the most critical bottleneck in using SOAP for scientific computing is the conversion between floating point numbers and their ASCII representations [5]. And Kohlhoff indicated that optimizing the SOAP encoding and decoding will improve the performance of business application in the context of web services [6]. Studies in [3],[4],[5],[6] all considered that besides XML parsing, the transformations between XML data and application data are key impact factor on SOAP performance. Ng et al. confirmed this conclusion by undertaking benchmarks on commercial SOAP implementations [7].

Bidirectional data mappings between XML data and Java data are also called deserialization and serialization. They greatly affect the overall performance of SOAP processing. In recent research, various mechanisms are utilized to optimize the deserialization [8] and serialization [9]. In [8], rather than re-serializing each message from scratch, a serialized XML message copy is saved in the sender's stub, changes for the next same type of message will be tracked, and saved copy is reused as a template for the next sending. The serialization usually includes two processes, first getting structured field value of application object, and then mapping field value into XML data. In [8], several means were introduced to optimize the latter process, but not mention the former. The approach in [9] reuses matching regions from the previously deserialized application objects, and only performs deserialization for a new region that has not been processed before. However, for large SOAP message, especially for SOAP message whose data always changed with different sending, the performance improvement of [9] will be decreased. Also, Java reflection is adopted by [9] as a means to set and get new values, for large object, especially deeply nested object, this will increase performance penalty.

3   Background on Web Services Performance

This section will first analyze the SOAP message processing on the server side, and find the performance bottlenecks. Then we will introduce some basic techniques in SOAP processing, which are the basis of our research work.

3.1   Analysis of Web Services Performance

We use Apache Axis 1.2, one of the most popular web services middleware systems as our testing environment. Apache Axis works as a web application that is located in a web container, so the web container carries on the work of receiving SOAP request message and sending response message through HTTP protocol. Though the HTTP protocol is a possible bottleneck for web services, we will not discuss the point in this paper.

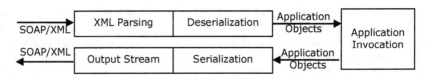

Fig. 1. SOAP processing flow

We divide SOAP message processing into five stages which are shown in Fig. 1.

1. XML Parsing Stage. The XML request message will be parsed by XML parser. In this stage, AXIS1.2 uses the SAX parser as XML parser; it reads the ASCII format data and records the SAX event in the buffer.
2. Deserialization Stage. The parsed XML data will be deserialized to application objects that will be presented to the web services as application object parameters.

At this stage, Axis1.2 replays the recorded SAX event and notifies the deserializers of SAX events to do the deserialization work.

3. Application Invocation Stage. This stage contains the business logic, which calls the application of targeting web service and gets the result of the application. The time spent in this stage is closely related with the complexity of application, no matter whether the business logic is wrapped as a web service or as an EJB.

4. Serialization Stage. This stage is the reverse process of deserialization stage; the application object result will be serialized to XML content. In AXIS1.2 implementation, the XML content is written into a memory buffer.

5. Output Stream Stage. In this stage, the buffered response XML data is written into the output stream. After that, the output stream will be written to the HTTP response object, and the web container will send the response XML data back to client through HTTP connection.

This section surveys the time cost on each stage, and analyzes the bottlenecks of SOAP message processing. As shown in Figure 1, the XML Parsing stage and deserialization stage carry on the mapping from XML data model to Java data model, and serialization stage and output stream stage carry on mapping from Java data model to XML data model.

We choose the WS Test 1.0[10] to test the time spent on different stages in the SOAP message process and to analyze the performance bottleneck. WS Test is a web services test developed by Sun Microsystems. Because we focus on SOAP message process, the web service methods perform no business logic but simply return the parameters that were passed in. It is designed to measure the performance of various types of web services calls, which are described below:

1. echoVoid: Sends and receives an empty message. This tests the performance of the web services infrastructure.

2. echoStruct: Sends and receives an array of size 20, the element of the array is a complex type composed of three elements, each of which is an integer, float and string data type respectively. This method is to test the SOAP engine's ability to process array of complex flat objects

3. echoList: Sends and receives a linked list of size 20, each element of the list is a Struct defined in echoStruct. This method is to test SOAP engine's ability to process deeply nested object.

The experimental environment is set as follows. CPU: Pentinm-4.1 2.80 GHz, Memory: 512 MB, OS: Windows XP Professional SP2, JVM: J2SK 1.4.2, Web services middleware: Apache AXIS 1.2, Web container: Tomcat 5.0, XML Parser: Apache Xerces-J 2.6.2. The web service client performs 10,000 iterations for each web service, and the client load is 5 hits per second.

Fig. 2 shows the average time spent on SOAP message process stages, the XML payload is 4 KB, and here the XML payload refers to size of XML data which is to be deserialized to object data. From the experiments, we can see that there are three performance components in the SOAP message process: XML Parsing, deserialization, and serialization. In the XML Parsing stage, the time required for XML parsing of the whole process time is about 80%, 39%, 38% for echoVoid, echoStruct, echoList respectively. In deserialization stage, the time percentages are 33% for

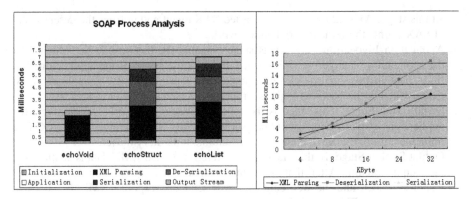

Fig. 2. Processing time on stages   Fig. 3. Processing time on XML payload

echoStruct and 32% for echoList. In serialization stage, the time percentages are 19% for echoStruct and 18% for echoList. In the paper, we call these three stages "Data Model Mapping" which includes the data mapping between XML data and Java data.

In summary, the time spent on these three components is above 90% of the whole time, and deserialization and serialization occupy more than 50%. We increase the XML payload of echoList and record the time spent on these three stages.

Fig. 3 shows the time of method echoList spent on XML parsing, deserialization and serialization stages on different XML payload. As input XML payload increases in size, the time spent on XML parsing and deserialization is also increased, so is the time spent on serialization stage. However, the time spent on deserialization and serialization stages grows dramatically faster than that of XML parsing. As shown by the statistics, the deserialization becomes the biggest part when the size of XML payload exceeds 8KB. So we can conclude that for small XML payload, the XML parsing will be the biggest performance component, but for median and large XML payload, deserialization and serialization will account for the performance latency.

In the deserialization stage and serialization stage of Apache Axis1.2, data mappings between XML data and java object are implemented by java reflection technique. However, java reflection technology is generally considered to be inefficient, according to our experiments, for complex java object, especially nested java object such as linked list in echoList, most of the time is spent on java reflection operations.

3.2 XML Pull Parsing

The SOAP message is based on XML format, so XML parsing is an important component in SOAP message processing. However, XML parsing is normally considered to be time-consuming. In section 3.1, results further point out that XML parsing accounts for more than 35% of the whole SOAP message processing time. So the high performance of XML parsing will lead to the improvement of SOAP message processing. Now the most popular XML parsing paradigms is DOM[11] and

SAX[12]. The DOM builds a complete object representation of the XML document in memory, and then the application visits the built XML model. This can be memory intensive for large documents. SAX parses the whole XML document into a series of SAX event, and informs the application through callbacks. Apache Axis adopts SAX to parse the XML document, compared to DOM, the SAX needn't read the whole document into memory. However, writing the callback methods to deal with XML document adds complexity to application. Meanwhile, both the SAX and DOM require two passes through XML data, firstly, they build the XML representation of the whole XML document; secondly, the application visits the built representation. The extra pass through XML document reduces the SOAP message processing.

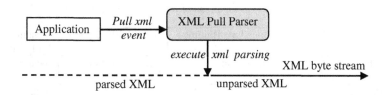

Fig. 4. XML Pull Parsing

As shown in Fig.4, XML Pull Parsing is an application-driven XML parsing paradigm. The application pulls the XML event from XML Pull Parsing, and gets the event of XML elements sequentially. XML Pull Parsing needn't read the whole XML data into memory like DOM, or to write callback method like SAX. Also, it goes through XML data at one pass to avoid extra performance penalty. Because of above advantages, XML Pull Parsing is adopted by us as the XML parsing mechanism, and works as the basis of dynamic template-driven data model mapping technique.

3.3 Dynamic Early Binding

The SOAP processing of web services in client and server side is actually the data model mapping between SOAP message and platform-dependent data. The indispensable elements of data model mapping include XML data definition in XML schema, data definition in specific platform and the mapping rule between them.

Section 3.1 shows that the data model mappings between XML data and Java data heavily impact the performance of SOAP engine in Java platform. We will firstly introduce the widely used binding techniques - early binding and late binding in Data Model Mapping, then present a new data binding paradigm "dynamic early binding" which combines the advantages of early binding and late binding. In this subsection, we will use *data binding* and *Data Model Mapping* alternatively.

SOAP message mainly consists of Body and Head which are wrapped in the Envelope. The Head contains the QoS information such as security and reliability; and the Body consists of the business logic information such as operations, parameters or returned results all in XML format. Fig.5 shows the XML and Java data type included in SOAP request message of a web service. It represents the data model mapping between XML data and Java data.

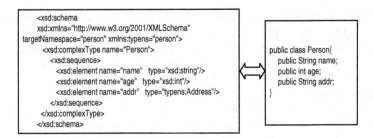

Fig. 5. XML schema vs. Java type

Table 1. Comparison of binding techniques

	Dynamic Late Binding	Static Early Binding	Dynamic Early Binding
Key techniques	Java reflection	code generation	dynamic code generation
Performance	Low	high	high
Flexibility	high	low	high
Binding-Info Getting	run time	compile time	Run time
Representative	Apache Axis, Castor	XMLBeans	DMT

Here we firstly explain two pairs of concepts:

- Late binding vs. Early binding

  The difference between these two binding paradigms is the time to get binding information, and here the binding information refers to the mapping information between XML data and Java data. Late binding gets the binding information at run time, and the getting and using of binding information are carried out in parallel; early binding gets the binding information at compilation time, and then uses binding information at run time

- Dynamic binding vs. Static binding

  Here the dynamic binding refers to the binding mechanism which can add new mapping XML-Java type pair at run time. In contrast, static binding can only add new mapping pairs at compile time.

According to the above definition, the existed data binding implementations can be classified to two categories: **Dynamic Late Binding** and **Static Early Binding**.

- The Dynamic Late Binding gets the binding information by Java Reflection technique at run time, and getting and using of binding information are carried in parallel, such as Apache Axis and Castor.

- In contrast, the Static Late Binding generates the Java template files which record the binding information before runtime, and then carries on the binding between XML data and Java data at runtime. The static late binding such as XMLBeans improves the performance by avoiding the frequent use of Java reflection; however, it couldn't add new binding XML-Java pair at runtime, which lessens the flexibility compared to dynamic early binding.

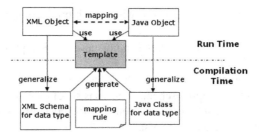

Fig. 6. Dynamic early binding

As illustrated in Fig. 6, **Dynamic Early Binding** generates the Java template class which we call **Data Mapping Template-DMT** at runtime by dynamic code generation techniques, and then the DMT will drives the data mapping process. The dynamic early binding avoids the Java reflections which improve the model mapping performance; meanwhile, the DMT files can be generated and managed at run time which makes dynamic early binding the similarly flexible as dynamic late binding. The dynamic early binding combines the advantages of static early binding and dynamic late binding, and is the key technique of high performance SOAP processing.

4   DMT Driven Data Model Mapping

We analyze the features of dynamic early binding, and point out that it will be one of key techniques to improve SOAP engine performance. In this section, we present our solution for the realization of dynamic late binding – Data Mapping Template (DMT), its description model and implementation model.

4.1   Specifying DMT by Extended Context-Free Grammar

Figure 5 describes the XML data type defined by XML Schema and Java data type defined by Java language. Here we use extended context-free grammar to depict XML data model and Java data model, and use mapping scheme of grammar production to describe the mapping relationship of two data models.

Definition 1. Data Mapping Template – DMT. For a data type T, the data mapping template DMT = (G^X, G^J) , G^X and G^J are context-free grammars for XML data model and Java data model.

Definition 2. Context-Free Grammar for DMT. G= (V, T, P, S, M)

- V is a set of non-terminals, $\forall A \in V$, A is called non-terminal. For G^X, V is the set of data type T which is defined by XML schema, including simple type, composite type and array type. For G^J, V is the set of data type T which is defined by Java language, including primitive types, user-defined Java class, and array types.
- T is a set of terminals, $\forall \alpha \in T$, α is called terminal. For G^X, T is the set of XML tag names; for G^J, T is the set of Java field names.

- P is the set of grammar productions, where each production p is like A→α, A∈ V, α∈ V ∪ T, |A|≤|α|.
- S is one of non-terminals as start symbol, and the S represents the data model defined by this grammar.
- M is set of mapping schemes, which defines actions in the reduction process. ∀m∈ M, m is called mapping scheme, and consists of a group of atomic operations. The mapping scheme m and production p correspond to each other one by one, ∀m∈ M, ∃p∈ P, p↔m, and vice versa.

In the definition of Grammar G, each grammar production corresponds to one or a group of atomic operations, Table 2 shows the atomic operations for the XML data model and Java data model. XML data is organized as tree-structured format, the element value of which is parsed and approached by XML parser. The atomic operations of XML model include the creating of XML element, setting and getting operations of child element, setting and getting operations of element value.

Table 2. Atomic operation set of XML and Java data model

Operation set A^X for XML data model	Operation set A^J for Java data model
creatElement(eleName)	creatJavaType(typeName)
getElementValue(eleName)	setSimpleValue()
setElementValue(eleValue)	setFieldValue(fieldName, fieldValue)
addChildElement(ele)	getFieldName()
getNextChildElement()	getFieldValue(fieldName)
returnElement()	setIndexValue(index, indexValue)
	getIndexValue(index)
	returnTypeValue()

Java is an object-oriented language, the data types of which include primitive types, array types and user-defined classes. The primitive types include primitive types supported by Java platform such as int and primitive wrapper classes such as Integer. The Java class describes user-defined date type, the field of which can be accessed directly as a public class variable or indirectly as a variable via some accessing methods (setters and getters). The element of array types can be accessed and assigned at specific index. The atomic operations of Java data model include the creating and getting value operations for different Java data types, the field value setting and getting operations for user-defined Java classes, the index value setting and getting operations for array types, and the setting operation for primitive types.

Table 3 shows the grammar G and mapping scheme M for XML data model and Java data model. G^X describes the XML data model defined by XML Schema. In grammar production P^X, **S** is the start symbol, **tag** represents the name of start element, **tag'** represents the name of end element; T^X represents the XML data type, which can be classified into XML Schema's built-in simple type T^{XS}, array type T^{XA}, and composite type T^{XC}. G^X depicts the XML data model into a structured tree which is composed of tag names. T^X has two attributes T^X.**ele** and T^X.**value**. T^X.**ele** represents the XML data of XML type, and T^X.**value** represents the corresponding Java data.

Table 3. Mapping Schemes of G^X, G^J

G^X's mapping scheme M^X	− **S → tag** {T^X.ele = S.ele} **T^X tag'** { S.value = T^X.value} − **T^X →** {T^{XC}_0.value = createJavaType(),T^X.ele = T^{XC}_0.ele }**T^{XC}_0**{T^X.value = T^{XC}_0.value} − **T^{XC}_i → tag** {$T^{X'}$.ele = T^{XC}_i.getNextChildElement() }**$T^{X'}$** {T^{XC}_i.setFieldValue($T^{X'}$.value)} **tag'** {T^{XC}_{i+1}.value=T^{XC}_i.value, T^{XC}_{i+1}.ele=T^{XC}_i.ele } **T^{XC}_{i+1}** − **T^{XC}_{i+1} →ε, i = 0,1,2,...** − **T^X →** {T^X.value = createJavaType(), T^{XS}.ele = T^X.ele}**T^{XS}** {T^{XS}.value = T^X.value} − **T^X →** {T^{XA}.value = createJavaType(),T^{XA}.ele = T^X.ele }**T^{XA}** {T^X.value = T^{XA}.value} − **T^{XS}→ε**{T^{XS}.setSimpleValue(T^{XS}.getElementValue())} − **T^{XA} → tag** {T^X.ele = T^{XA}.getNextChildElement()} **T^X** {T^{XA}.setIndexValue(T^X.value)} **tag' T^{XA}** − **T^{XA} → ε**
G^J's mapping scheme M^J	− **S →** {S.createElement(), T^J.value = S.value, T^J.ele=S.ele} **T^J** { S.addChildElement(T^J.ele)} − **T^J →** {T^{JC}_0.ele = T^J.ele, T^{JC}_0.value = T^J.value} **T^{JC}_0** − **T^{JC}_i → field** {$T^{J'}$.value = T^{JC}_i.getFieldValue(field)}, $T^{J'}$.createElement()} **$T^{J'}$** {T^{JC}_i.addChildElement($T^{J'}$.ele), T^{JC}_{i+1}.value=T^{JC}_i.value,T^{JC}_{i+1}.ele=T^{JC}_i.ele} **T^{JC}_{i+1}** − **T^{JC}_{i+1} → ε, , i = 0,1,2,...** − **T^J →** {T^{JS}.ele = T^J.ele, T^{JS}.value = T^J.value}**T^{JS}** − **T^{JS} →** {T^{JS}.setElementValue(T^{JS}.value)}**ε** − **T^J →** {T^{JA}.ele = T^J.ele , T^{JA}.value = T^J.value}**T^{JA}** − **T^{JA} →** {$T^{J'}$.createElement(), $T^{J'}$.value = T^{JA}.getIndexValue()} **T^J** − {T^{JA}.addChildElement(T^J.ele) } **T^{JA}** − **T^{JA} → ε**

G^J describes the Java data model defined by Java language. In grammar production P^J, T^J represents the XML data types, which can be classified into primitive type T^{JS}, array type T^{JA}, and Java class T^{JC}; **field** is the field name in user-defined Java class. T^J has two attributes T^J**.value** and T^J**.ele**. T^J**.value** represents the Java data value of Java type, and T^J**.ele** represents the corresponding XML data value. In G^J, the Java data type is seen as a structured-tree, the primitive type tree has only a root node, the array type tree has the root node with same-structured children nodes, and the children nodes of the class type tree represent its field types. The Java data type can be described in tree-structured manner as XML data in Table 3.

Section 3.3 mentioned that the XML data types defined by XML schema have certain mapping rules to data types of different platforms, and JAX-RPC [13] defines the mapping rules between Java data type and XML data type. So grammar G^J and grammar G^X can be generated by analyzing Java data type and it's mapping rules to XML schema. Fig.7 shows the generation algorithm of G^X and G^J, the input of algorithm is a Java data type, and the output is G^X and G^J by analyzing the hierarchy of Java data type using Java reflection in a depth first traverse. To be simple, the algorithm in Fig 7 omits the recursive analytic logic for user-defined classes and array type. The G^X and G^J of data type in Fig 5 are shown below:

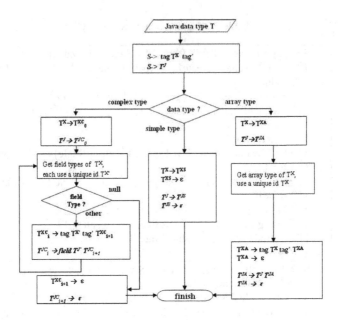

Fig. 7. Algorithm for generation of G^X and G^J

G^X	$S \rightarrow p$ {T^x.ele = S.ele} $T^x p'$ {S.value = T^x. value}
	$T^x \rightarrow$ {T^{xc}_0.value = new Person(),T^{xc}_0.ele = T^x.ele} T^{xc}_0 {T^x.value = T^{xc}_0.value }
	$T^{xc}_0 \rightarrow$ **name** {T^{xn}.ele = T^{xc}_0.getNextChildElement()} T^{xn} {T^{xc}_0.value.name =
	T^{xn}.value} **name'** {T^{xc}_1.value = T^{xc}_0.value, T^{xc}_1.ele = T^{xc}_0.ele }T^{xc}_1
	$T^{xn} \rightarrow$ {N.ele = T^{xn}.ele, N.value = new String()}**N** { T^{xn}.value = N.value}
	$N \rightarrow \varepsilon${N.value = N.getElementValue()}
	$T^{xc}_1 \rightarrow$ **age** {T^{xa}.ele = T^{xc}_1.getNextChildElement()}T^{xa} {T^{xc}_1.value.age = T^{xa}.value}
	age' {T^{xc}_2.value = T^{xc}_1.value, T^{xc}_2.ele = T^{xc}_1.ele }T^{xc}_2
	$T^{xa} \rightarrow$ {A.ele = T^{xa}.ele, A.value = (int)0} **A** { T^{xa}.value = A.value}
	$A \rightarrow \varepsilon${A.value = Integer.parseInt(A.getElementValue())}
	$T^{xc}_2 \rightarrow$ **addr** {T^{xad}.ele = T^{xc}_2.getNextChildElement()} T^{xad} {T^{xc}_2.value.addr =
	T^{xad}.value } **addr'** {T^{xc}_3.value = T^{xc}_2.value, T^{xc}_3.ele = T^{xc}_2.ele }T^{xc}_3
	$T^{xc}_3 \rightarrow \varepsilon$
	$T^{xad} \rightarrow$ {ADDR.ele = T^{xad}.ele, ADDR.value = new String()} **ADDR** { T^{xad}.value =
	ADDR.value}
	ADDR $\rightarrow \varepsilon${ADDR.value = ADDR.getElementValue()}
G^J	$S \rightarrow$ {S.createElement("p"), T^j.value = S.value, T^j.ele = S.ele } T^j
	{S.addChildElement(T^j.ele)}
	$T^j \rightarrow$ {T^{jc}.ele = T.ele, T^{jc}.value = T^j.value}T^{jc}
	$T^{jc}_0 \rightarrow$ **name** { T^{jn}.value = T^{jc}_0.value.name, T^{jn}.createElement("name")} T^{jn}
	{T^{jc}_0.addChildElement(T^{jn}.ele), T^{jc}_1.value = T^{jc}_0.value, T^{jc}_1.ele = T^{jc}_0.ele} T^{jc}_1
	$T^{jn} \rightarrow$ {N.ele = T^{xn}.ele, N.value = T^{xn}.value} **N**
	$N \rightarrow$ {N.setElementValue(N.value)}ε
	$T^{jc}_1 \rightarrow$ **age** { T^{ja}.value = T^{jc}_1.value.name, T^{ja}.createElement("age")} T^{ja}

$\{ T^{jc}_1.\text{addChildElement}(T^{ja}.\text{ele}), T^{jc}_2.\text{value} = T^{jc}_1.\text{value}, T^{jc}_2.\text{ele} = T^{jc}_1.\text{ele} \}\ \mathbf{T^{jc}_2}$

$\mathbf{T^{ja}} \rightarrow \{ A.\text{ele} = T^{ja}.\text{ele}, A.\text{value} = T^{ja}.\text{value} \}\ \mathbf{A}$

$\mathbf{A} \rightarrow \{ A.\text{setElementValue}(A.\text{value})\}\varepsilon$

$\mathbf{T^{jc}_2} \rightarrow \mathbf{address}\ \{ T^{jad}.\text{value} = T^{jc}_2.\text{value.addr}, T^{jad}.\text{creatElement}(\text{"address"})\}\ \mathbf{T^{jad}}$

$\{ T^{jc}_2.\text{addChildElement}(T^{jad}.\text{ele}), T^{jc}_3.\text{value} = T^{jc}_2.\text{value}, T^{jc}_3.\text{ele} = T^{jc}_2.\text{ele} \}\ \mathbf{T^{jc}_3}$

$\mathbf{T^{jc}_3} \rightarrow \varepsilon$

$\mathbf{T^{jad}} \rightarrow \{ \text{ADDR.ele} = T^{jad}.\text{ele}, \text{ADDR.value} = T^{jad}.\text{value}\}\ \mathbf{ADDR}$

$\mathbf{ADDR} \rightarrow \{ \text{ADDR.setElementValue}(\text{ADDR.value})\}\varepsilon$

4.2 Implementing DMT by Pushdown Automaton with Output

Last Section introduced the DMT's conceptual model by extended Context-Free Grammar, and this section will give out the implementation model by pushdown automaton with output. For any data type T, the implementation model of DMT is a pair of pushdown automata which is used to recognize grammar (G^X, G^J), and we call this kind of pushdown automation with output **Data Mapping Automaton**. The execution of data mapping automaton is the execution of grammar's mapping schema, and also the mapping process from one data model to another.

Definition 3. Data Mapping Automaton DMA= $(Q, \Sigma, \Gamma, Z_0, q_0, F, O, \delta)$

- Q is a set of states, $\forall q \in Q$, q is the state of DMA;
- Σ is the set of input symbols;
- Γ is a set of stack symbol, $\forall A \in \Gamma$ is a stack symbol;
- $Z_0 \in \Gamma$ is the start stack symbol;
- $q_0 \in Q$ is the start state of DMA ;
- F is the set of final states, $\forall f \in F$, f is the final state;
- O is a set of output actions;
- δ is the state transition function and governs the behaviors of the automaton. δ $(q, a, Z) = \{ (p_1, \gamma_1, o_1) , (p_2, \gamma_2, o_2) , ..., (p_m, \gamma_m, o_m) \}$, represents that When read input symbol is a, the top stack element is Z and the state is q, DMA can transit the state to p_i and pop the top stack element Z, then push the stack symbol γ_i into the stack, and carry on the output action o_i, for $i = 1, 2, 3, ..., m$.

The Data Mapping Automaton DMA= $(Q, \Sigma, \Gamma, Z_0, q_0, F, O, \delta)$ can be generated by an extended context-free grammar G= (V, T, P, S, M). The transformation and equivalence proof between context-free grammar and pushdown automaton can be found in [14].

Fig 8 shows the data mapping automata DMA^X and DMA^J for grammar G^X and G^J, both of which are comprised of input object, input transformer, stack, state controller (SC) and state table (ST). The input transformer will first transfer the input object into what can be recognized by DMA; state table is a two-dimensional array P[A, a], A is indexed by non-terminal and a by terminal, array element P[A,a] records the state transition and output action; state controller controls the state transition and executes the output actions.

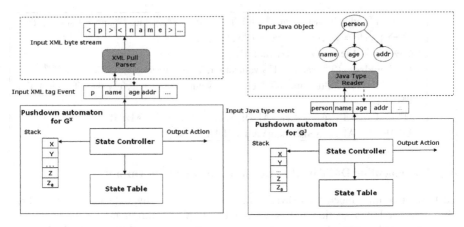

Fig. 8(a). DMA^X for grammar G^X **Fig. 8(b).** DMA^J for grammar G^J

The input object of DMA^X is XML byte stream, and the input transformer is XML Pull Parser. When DMA^X starts, its state controller drives XML Pull Parser to read the XML byte stream and get the XML tag events. State controller looks up state table by the XML tag event and the top stack symbol, and then makes the state transition and executes the mapping actions in the state table such as creating new Java object, setting value of Java object, etc. When DMA^X stops, a Java object will be constructed and returned.

The input object of DMA^J is Java object, and the input transformer is Java Type reader. The Java data types can be viewed as a structural-tree. For a specified Java data type, a virtual data type tree can be generated and kept in memory. The Java type reader traverses the virtual data type tree in a depth-first manner, and returns Java type event to state controller. DMA^J 's state controllers looks up state table by Java type event and top stack symbol, and makes the state transition and executes the mapping actions such as initializing XML output stream, writing the Java object into the XML output stream in a structural manner, etc. When DMA^J stops, a XML output stream will be generated and returned.

For the mapping from XML data to Java data, DMA^X is utilized to traverse input XML stream and construct a Java object by DMA^X's output actions. In contrast, DMA^J is used to visit the fields of Java object in a structural manner and build the XML output stream.

The DMT driven mechanism makes the best of XML Pull Parser to complete the mapping from XML data to Java data in one traversal of XML data. Also DMT uses Java Type Reader to read structural data type information, and completes the generation of XML output stream when DMA^J traverses the Java object once.

5   Application and Evaluation of DMT in SOAPExpress

SOAPExpress is the high performance SOAP engine using XML Pull Parsing and dynamic early binding techniques. The dynamic early binding improves the performance of data model mapping in SOAP message processing, and also keeps the flexibility by adding new mapping type at run time. The dynamic early binding is realized by DMT-driven data model mapping introduced in Section 4.

5.1 Application of DMT in SOAPExpress

SOAPExpress is hosted as a web application by Tomcat. As shown in Fig 9, when SOAPExpress receives a request message, Service-In Handler undertakes to get the name of targeting web service by XML Pull Parser. For RPC-encoded and literal-wrapped style, SOAP body contains the operation information of a service. Through DMT Manager, Service-In Handler can get all the DMTs corresponding to an operation's input parameters, the DMT instances will take charge of the data model mapping from XML data to Java data. After that, Service Invoker invokes the service and returns the Java object result. Then, Service-Out Handler gets the DMT instances of output parameters from DMT Manager, and the DMT instances drive the mapping from Java object to XML output stream.

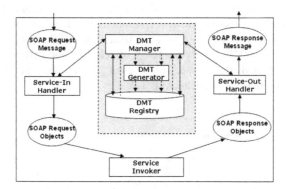

Fig. 9. SOAP processing in SOAPExpress

There are three components in SOAPExpress to support the DMT driven data mapping. The DMT Manager supplies APIs for search, generation and record of DMTs. DMT Generator creates the DMTs from Java data type definitions. DMT instances are recorded and placed in DMT Registry, which to be used to quickly locate some DMT.

Service-In/Out Handlers look up DMT instances firstly through DMT Manager. The DMT Manager will check the existence of DMT instances. If existed, DMT instances will be returned directly; if not, DMT Manager will call the DMT Generator to generate the DMT instances for corresponding input and output parameters, then return them and put them into DMT Registry.

DMT Registry is in charge of recording and holding DMT instances. DMT Registry is indexed by service name which is bound by DMT instances with its input and output parameters. The main function of DMT Registry is to maintain the mapping relationship from service name to DMT instances.

The DMT Generator composes of Type Analyzer, Model Builder and Byte Code Generator. Firstly, Type Analyzer uses Java reflection to obtain the hierarchy of some

Java type, and then Model Builder builds the java object data and XML data from obtained information by the generation algorithm depicted in figure 7. After that, Byte Code Generator generates the bytecode of DMT using Javassist [15] at runtime. The DMT instance for a java type is generated only once at the first time, can be reused as long as the service has no changes.

5.2 Experiments and Results Analysis

This subsection will test the performance of SOAP message processing by SOAPExpress, and compare the result with Apache Axis 1.2. The test suite and environment are the same as the setting in section 3.1.

Figure 10 illustrates the performance comparison between Apache Axis 1.2 and SOAPExpress for WS Test 1.0, the XML payload is 4KB for *echoStruct* and *echoList*. The measure is on SOAP processing time, which begins from the point SOAPExpress receives a HTTP request and ends at the point SOAPExpress returns the HTTP response. The statistics shows that times about method *echoVoid* are very close for these two SOAP engines, since method *echoVoid* has no business logic and just returns empty SOAP message. However, about method *echoStruct*, the processing time of SOAPExpress is only about 46% of Apache Axis 1.2; about method *echoList*, the proportion is about 44%. The parameters of echoList and echoStruct are complex array type and nested data type. The result shows that the performance of SOAPExpress is higher than Apache Axis 1.2.

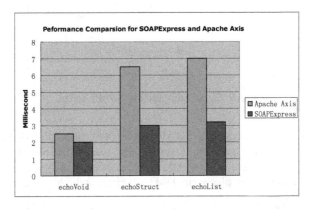

Fig. 10. Performance Comparison of Apache Axis 1.2 and SOAPExpress

We increase the XML payload, and analyze the impact of XML payload on SOAP message processing performance. Fig 11 shows that when the XML payload increases, the time of SOAPExpress increases much slower than that of Apache Axis 1.2. The Section 3.2 points out the frequent use of Java reflections cause performance penalty for large XML data. The DMT-driven data model mapping avoids the use of Java reflection, and keeps the processing time increases slowly with XML payload.

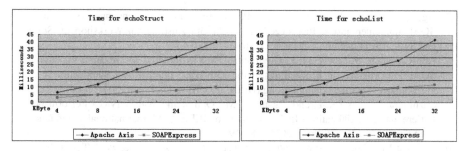

Fig. 11. Comparison of Apache Axis 1.2 and SOAPExpress on XML payload

6   Conclusion and Future Work

This paper proposes a new data model mapping paradigm "Dynamic Early Binding", and presents its realization - Data Mapping Template (DMT), which is specified by extended context free grammar and implemented by pushdown automaton with output actions. The DMT-driven data mapping technique realizes quick mappings between XML data and Java data by dynamically generating templates at runtime. The DMT technique has been utilized in the implementation of a high performance SOAP engine – SOAPExpress. The testing results show that the performance of SOAPExpress is better than Apache Axis 1.2. For medium and large size of SOAP message, the performance advantage of SOAPExpress is much more obvious.

The dynamic early binding technique –DMT proposed in the paper doesn't support the complete XML infoset yet. Such as *namespace* and *attribute*, they will be considered to add into the DMT definition and implementation. Also, exception handling will be treated in the implementation of DMT - pushdown automaton in our future work.

References

1. Bustamante, F. E., Eisenhauer, G., Schwan, K., and Widener, P.: Efficient wire formats for high performance computing. In Proceedings of Supercomputing 2000(SC 2000), IEEE CS Press(2000) 64-64.
2. The Apache Software Foundation, Apache Axis 1.2. http://ws.apache.org/axis/.
3. Davis, D. and Parashar, M.: Latency performance of SOAP implementations. In Proceedings of the 2nd IEEE/ACM International Symposium on Cluster Computing and the Grid, IEEE CS Press(2000) 407-412.
4. Elfwing,R., Paulsson, U., Lundberg, L.: Performance of SOAP in Web Service Environment Compared to CORBA. Proceedings of the Ninth Asia-Pacific Software Engineering Conference (APSEC'02). IEEE CS Press(2002) 84-96.
5. Chiu, K., Govindaraju, M., Bramley, R.: Investigating the limits of SOAP performance for scientific computing. In Proceedings of the 11th IEEE International Symposium on High Performance Distributed Computing (HPDC-11), IEEE CS Press(2002) 246-254.
6. Kohlhoff, C. and Steele, R.: Evaluating SOAP for high performance business applications: Real-time trading systems. In Alternate Proceedings of the Twelfth International World. Wide Web Conference, (2003) 262-270.

7. Ng, A., Chen, S. P. and Greenfield, P.: An Evaluation of Contemporary Commercial SOAP Implementations. In Proceedings of the 5th Australasian Workshop on Software and System Architecture, Adelaide, Australia (2003) 64-71.
8. Abu-Ghazaleh, N. Lewis, M. J., Govindaraju, M.: Differential Serialization for Optimized SOAP Performance. In Proceedings of the 13th IEEE International Symposium on High Performance. Distributed Computing (HPDC-13), IEEE CS Press(2004) 55-64.
9. Suzumura, T., Takase, T. and Tatsubori, M.: Optimizing Web Services Performance by Differential Deserialization. In Proceedings of IEEE/ACM International Conference on Web Services, IEEE CS Press(2005) 185-192.
10. WS Test 1.0, http://java.sun.com/performance/reference/whitepapers/WS_Test-1_0.pdf.
11. Document Object Model, http://www.w3.org/DOM/.
12. Simple API for XML, David Brownell, SAX2, O'Reilly & Associates, Inc.(2002.)
13. Java API for XML-Based RPC, http://java.sun.com/webservices/jaxrpc/docs.html.
14. Linz, P.: An Introduction to Formal Languages and Automata, third edition, Jones & Bartlett Publishers (2001).
15. The JBoss Community, Javassist, http://www.jboss.com/products/javassist.

An Approach for Fine-Grained Web Service Performance Monitoring

Jan Schaefer

Fachhochschule Wiesbaden - University of Applied Sciences
Distributed Systems Lab
Kurt-Schumacher-Ring 18, D-65197 Wiesbaden, Germany
jan.schaefer@informatik.fh-wiesbaden.de

Abstract. Especially for the creation of *Service-Oriented Architectures* (SOA), Web service technologies are often *the* technology of choice. In this context, solutions for the management of Web services are becoming more and more important. This paper describes an approach to performance monitoring of Web services, which is based on the *Application Response Measurement* (ARM) standard. This approach enables generic (application source code-independent) and customizable instrumentation of synchronous, asynchronous and one-way Web service messages by attaching meta-data to messages.

1 Motivation

Integrating a company's existing software assets into a *Service-Oriented Architecture* (SOA) is gaining enormous popularity. This is caused by the promise of service unification and increased software reusability on the one hand and the evolution of Web service technologies, which are the most common SOA building elements, on the other hand. Companies have discovered the possibility of modernizing their legacy systems without necessarily having to modify their existing applications. To accomplish this, Web services are often created as wrappers for existing applications. Companies can benefit from a SOA in many ways. For example, they can use orchestration languages like the *Business Process Execution Language* (BPEL) to create new services by combining their existing (Web) services (called *service composition*). Although Web service technologies are a relatively easy way of integrating existing and newly developed applications, their interfaces also add another layer of complexity to applications. This adds to the importance of being able to monitor distributed systems in a homogeneous way. On one hand, developers might be interested in testing the effect of their changes on throughput and performance (e.g. response time) of system components. This includes, for example, the total processing times of single requests, the processing times in client and Web service or the transport times. On the other hand, administrators might primarily be interested in generic monitoring or tracking of failed or delayed transactions or performance bottlenecks. They could also use the detailed runtime information (e.g. execution times, states,

F. Eliassen and A. Montresor (Eds.): DAIS 2006, LNCS 4025, pp. 169–180, 2006.

values) to check *Service Level Agreements* (SLA). In recent years, birth has been given to several Web services-supporting platforms (e.g. Apache Axis [1], IONA Artix [2] and Microsoft .NET [3]). The vendors all claim full interoperability with each other's platforms, which is a major argument for using Web service technologies in the first place.

Web services management is still a relatively young discipline. Some *Enterprise Management Systems* (EMS) support managing Web services-based software and hardware (e.g. IBM TCAM [4] and CA Unicenter WSDM [5]). However, management capabilities for single and composed Web service transactions are still rare. Existing solutions for this are custom-tailored to specific Web services products and thus not easily deployed in heterogeneous environments. None of the existing Web services management specifications covers the monitoring or analysis of single Web services transactions. Instead, they confine themselves to monitoring deployed Web service applications and hardware devices (called *resource management*). The two specifications in this area are *Web Services for Management* (WS-Management [6]) and *Web Services Distributed Management* (WSDM [7]) with partially overlapping aims. This situation was additional motivation for the work presented in this paper (complete report in [8]).

The approach presented in this paper offers an instrumentation solution for Web services based on the *Application Response Measurement* (ARM) standard. In order to keep the approach as generic as possible, it does not require specific management agents or modification of the application to be instrumented. It relies on standardized specifications that multiple vendors incorporated into their products. It focuses on the timing of synchronous and asynchronous Web service invocations to gather performance-related measurement data. In this context, it has to be considered that multi-threaded processing and asynchronous messaging introduce additional requirements (e.g. for request and response message matching) in comparison to classical RPC-style interaction.

2   Application Response Measurement

The ARM standard, whose development is overseen by The Open Group, provides an API for instrumenting applications at the source code level [9]. The API supports execution time measurements of work units termed *ARM transactions* within distributed applications. ARM allows correlating nested measurements, even across host boundaries. For this purpose, the standard defines *ARM correlators*, which are unique tokens assigned to each ARM transaction. Correlators can be supplied when creating a nested transaction for relating this to the enclosing transaction. Passing correlators between application components, which might prove difficult especially in distributed systems, is the task of the application developer. ARM allows for the integration of applications directly with enterprise management systems. This creates a comprehensive end-to-end management capability, including the measurement of application performance, availability, usage and end-to-end transaction response time. To effect this integration, developers have to add ARM calls to their application code, which

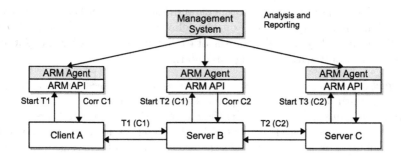

Fig. 1. Transaction Correlation using ARM API

are processed by an ARM agent during application execution. The process of finding relevant measurement points and inserting measurement code is called *instrumentation*.

The management agent collects status, response time and – optionally – additional measurement quantities associated with the transaction (see figure 1). Together with the agent, the instrumented application may also provide information to correlate parent and child transactions. For example, a transaction that is invoked on a client may drive transactions on an application server, which in turn drives other transactions on other application and/or database servers. This allows the construction of a calling hierarchy that illustrates which transactions are *nested* into or dependent on others in subsequent transactions. The example in figure 1 leads to the following ARM transaction hierarchy: server C uses the correlator received from server B, which uses the correlator received from client A. Thus, the ARM transaction C depends on B and B depends on A.

ARM measurement results and correlations have to be evaluated by ARM implementations (agents), which are available, for instance, from BMC, CA, HP, IBM (Tivoli) and tang-IT. Their implementations and analysis tools are often integrated with their respective management solutions and quite different from each other. However, The Open Group also provides a free SDK, which contains implementations of the standardized interfaces and can be used for testing and validating instrumented applications.

The ARM standard is developed by members of The Open Group, namely IBM, HP and tang-IT. With the release of ARM 4.0, the available C and Java bindings provide equivalent functionality for the first time. The approach presented here uses the Java binding of ARM 4.0 [10], which contains new features such as asynchronous reporting of transaction information.

3   Web Services and ARM

3.1   Message Exchange Patterns

The *Web Services Description Language* (WSDL [11]) defines four transmission primitives: one-way (client to service), request-response (client to service and back), solicit-response (service to client and back) and notification (service to client). This paper concentrates on the following *Message Exchange Patterns* (MEP), because they describe the set of exchanged messages for the primitives (in-out and in-only with changing direction):

- *Synchronous request-response*: the client sends a request to the service and blocks until it receives the response from the service.
- *Asynchronous request-response*: the client sends a request to the service and continues processing. The client either has to check for response arrival (e.g. by polling), or it has to enable the service to invoke it (e.g. by offering a callback method).
- *One-way*: the client sends a request to the service and continues processing without blocking or expecting a response.

3.2   SOAP Message Handlers and Contexts

SOAP [12] *Message Handlers* and *Message Contexts* are both defined in the *Java API for XML-based RPC* (JAX-RPC [13]) specification, which supports building Web services that use *Remote Procedure Calls* (RPC) and XML. The JAX-RPC API hides the complexity of SOAP messages from the developer, and the runtime system converts the API calls to and from SOAP messages. JAX-RPC supports stateless message handlers (also known as *interceptors*), which allow the modification of messages before and after they have been dispatched to a service or client implementation (e.g. to add security or management information). To use handlers, no application level code has to be modified. Instead, handlers are added through deployment configuration. There are two types of message handlers: client- and server-side handlers. They are invoked depending on their associated Web service's or client's role in the message exchange (see figure 2), and their order is determined by their deployment configuration. Message handlers implement the *Chain of Responsibility* design pattern, which means that a message is processed by all handlers (in a handler chain), before it is dispatched to the targeted service. JAX-RPC also supports one-way messaging in addition to the request-response messaging style normally done with RPC. JAX-RPC is supported by most Web service platforms.

Message contexts are used to store meta-data about messages (e.g. security or management information) or to exchange state information between application

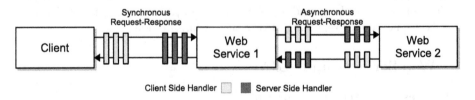

Fig. 2. Message Handler Chains

level and message handling chain. Generally, this meta-data does not cross host boundaries, but some platforms allow attaching it to messages. This enables a meta-data exchange between clients and services.

3.3 Instrumentation Challenges

This paper presents a solution for generic ARM-based instrumentation of Web service platforms. For this, the subsequently introduced problems had to be solved.

1. *Isolation of instrumentation code*: Often, instrumentation is a static process. Instrumentation calls are inserted into source code, which means that every application has to be instrumented explicitly (hard coded). If the application code is modified, the instrumentation code may have to be modified as well. This process is error-prone and slows down development speed. In addition, developers must know the ARM API. For Web services, this means that every Web service – depending on the scope of instrumentation – would have to be instrumented manually by experienced ARM users.

2. *Support for different message exchange patterns*: In an asynchronous message exchange (messaging scenario), both the request and response messages are defined as a one-way message in the WSDL contract. Thus, they are only semantically related, and only the application logic "knows" the meaning of received response messages. If a client receives a related response directly from a previously invoked service, the response is received *directly*. If a client receives a response from a different service, the response is received *indirectly*. As a result, a mechanism for relating request and response messages has to be created, which allows starting and stopping ARM transactions (measurements) correctly.

3. *Transport of ARM data and correlators*: Another problem arises when thinking about how ARM data has to be exchanged between services. Of course, it must be meta-data rather than an invocation parameter. To correlate ARM transactions, correlators must be propagated, because whenever a client or service receives a message (even if it is a response message!), the correlator might be required for starting a new (dependent) ARM transaction.

4 Architecture

4.1 Design Decisions

This paper presents a solution for generic rather than manual instrumentation as described in section 3.3.1. Therefore, the JAX-RPC message handler and message context mechanisms were selected as hooks for the ARM-based instrumentation. More specifically, message handlers encapsulating the ARM-related code were created for intercepting and augmenting messages, and message contexts were defined for storing the ARM-related meta-data required during the instrumentation process.

For in-out MEPs, the ARM handlers are used to measure the total processing time of business transactions, from the moment a request is sent, until its related response is received (a client-side measurement). It is also possible to use ARM handlers for measuring the service's response time per invocation only (a server-side measurement). By using both client- and server-side ARM handlers, it is possible to calculate message transfer times as well. The instrumentation by configuration allows inexperienced ARM users to instrument services; no knowledge of the ARM API is required and existing service implementations do not have to be modified. In addition, experienced ARM users can manually instrument services to gain more fine-grained performance data. Using configurable ARM handlers for instrumentation is defined as *system-level instrumentation*, manually instrumenting services is defined as *user-level instrumentation*. The developed instrumentation solution presented here allows using both system- and user-level instrumentation simultaneously. In addition, nested ARM transactions can use ARM correlators created by the enclosing ARM transaction for correlation: correlators are propagated to succeeding services, even across host boundaries (see section 3.3.3). ARM handlers and service implementations can access propagated correlators via the ARM context.

Even in a synchronous message exchange, handlers process messages asynchronously. Otherwise, a synchronous (blocking) call would prevent the Web service from processing multiple requests in parallel. Thus, the instrumentation model does not differentiate between synchronous, asynchronous and one-way communication. Furthermore, request and response are not even processed by the same message handler in asynchronous exchanges: the request is processed by a client-side handler, the response is processed by a server-side handler (see figure 2). Because of this, matching of request and response messages is provided by inserting unique ARM transaction IDs into the ARM message context of related messages, which enables ARM handlers to recognize relationships between messages (see section 3.3.2). Transaction IDs are also used for identifying ARM transactions: if an ARM handler is configured to stop a running ARM transaction, it uses the transaction ID inside the ARM context for the look-up. If the ARM context should be removed or missing, no messages can be matched and no ARM transactions can be stopped anymore.

Depending on its configuration, an ARM handler might have to store a received ARM context, which has to be returned in the response message, and a reference to a started ARM transaction. This information is stored in the ARM registry. If required (respectively configured), the registry information is used to restore a parent context and to stop an ARM transaction. This is required, because the processing of related request and response messages in message handlers can be interrupted due to multiple concurrent threads. However, each Web service (respectively its ARM handlers) only has to store the first received ARM context in each business transaction. All sub-requests that are created by this service have to use this context. Of course, ARM transaction references have to be stored for every started transaction.

Once the Web service finishes processing the business transaction (and a service's ARM handler is invoked for the last time), the parent ARM context is returned to the client inside the response message. Should the current Web service be only an intermediary in the business transaction, the parent ARM context is propagated to the next service. In in-only MEPs, the context of instrumented messages contains a time stamp, which denotes the start time of the associated ARM transaction, and an ARM correlator. One-way messages do not contain ARM transaction IDs in their message context, because they will not return to the invoking client. Thus, no request-response matching is required.

4.2   Overall Structure

Figure 3 shows the component interaction of the generic instrumentation model, which solves the problems presented in section 3.3.

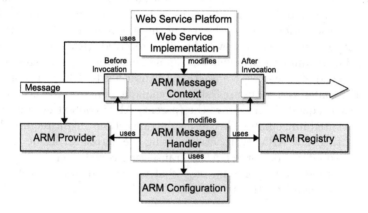

Fig. 3. Architectural Components

The *ARM Message Handler* component is responsible for intercepting and processing messages, before and after the invocation of the handler's associated Web service. It represents the main component of the instrumentation solution and provides client- and server-side message handlers that can be configured to instrument Web service message exchanges. The purpose of the handlers is to provide ARM operations that can be specified using the ARM configuration, based on handler type (client- or server-side), Web service name and operation name (see figure 4).

The *ARM Message Context* component represents a container for transferring ARM information that is exchanged between Web services in instrumented transactions. The context contains one section for use by ARM message handlers (system-level) and one for use by Web service implementations (user-level). Service code may read the system-level section of the context (e.g. for using the ARM correlator within as a parent correlator in user-level ARM transactions), but it must write to the user-level section only. For supporting one-way message exchanges and ARM transaction reporting, the context also contains a field that can hold a time-stamp (the start time of a reported transaction). Finally, the context contains a context ID. The context referenced by this ID is used by sub-transactions for retrieving the parent ARM context. Each of the available elements of the context is optional, so that they are only put on the wire if required.

The *ARM Provider* component encapsulates access to the ARM API, which for this approach was the official ARM 4.0 SDK (available from [9]). The provider also executes a base ARM application, which can be used for user- and system-level instrumentation. This avoids the overhead of creating an additional ARM environment, if there is no specific need for it.

The *ARM Configuration* component is queried for the action to be executed, whenever an ARM handler intercepts a message. A handler might have to start a new ARM transaction, stop a previously started ARM transaction or stay idle (context forwarding only). This allows users to keep the impact of the instrumentation on the performance of the rest of the system at a minimum. However, a handler alone cannot decide how to handle a received ARM context: it cannot be specified programmatically, which incoming and outgoing messages represent the start and end of a business transaction; the user has to define the appropriate action in the configuration (figure 6 shows a configuration example). When a service receives a request, it must save the (parent) ARM context even if no ARM action is executed immediately, because sub-transactions might require the context for starting new ARM transactions; using the correlator inside the parent context is mandatory for correct ARM transaction correlation. In the end, the handler processing the response message that is returned to the invoking client restores (and unregisters) the parent context.

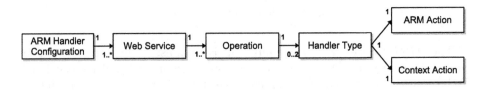

Fig. 4. ARM Configuration Structure

The configuration contains the following handler configuration for every operation a Web service provides or interacts with (see figure 4):

- The *ARM Action* attribute controls which instrumentation-related action an ARM handler must take: *idle* (handler stays passive and only forwards an existing ARM context), *start* (an ARM transaction) or *stop* (an ARM transaction).
- The *Context Action* attribute controls how an ARM handler treats the current ARM context: *idle* (use current context), *use* (the parent context), *save*

(register current context in ARM registry) or *restore* (the parent context and destroy the local copy in the ARM registry).

The *ARM Registry* component stores copies of ARM contexts and ARM transactions and serves as shared memory for all associated ARM handlers. It handles three types of records: One that contains active ARM transactions with associated ARM contexts, one that contains ARM contexts only and a third that contains currently inactive ARM transactions. The registry checks the stored records cyclically for timed-out ARM transactions and ARM contexts. For time-out checking, the stored items contain a time-stamp that is updated when a record is created or used. If an ARM transaction exceeds the maximum processing time (which is configurable), it is aborted and returned into the pool for inactive ARM transactions.

The ability to store ARM contexts is required to be able to undo changes to message contexts caused by new ARM transactions and is only required for instrumentation in ARM handlers, not for manual instrumentation. The active ARM transactions stored in the ARM registry are required for stopping them, once they are finished. The registry uses unique identifiers as keys for retrieving stored records. These keys are put into the ARM context as references to the records.

5   Prototypical Implementation

Initially, the instrumentation prototype was intended to be used to instrument Web services using both Apache Axis 1.2 and IONA Artix 3.0 as platform. However, it turned out that Axis lacks support for asynchronous WSDL operations. Thus, the prototype currently supports Artix only, but it could easily be ported to different Web service platforms implementing JAX-RPC, respectively platforms incorporating the message handler concept.

Artix is IONA's commercial Web services-based solution for *Enterprise Application Integration* (EAI). Artix supports multiple transports and message formats natively. It connects applications at the middleware transport level and translates messages only once using direct on-the-wire transformation instead of a canonical format. An open source offspring of Artix – called *Celtix* – is hosted by ObjectWeb [14].

Artix supplies the generic classes (*GenericHandler* and *GenericHandlerFactory*) implementing the JAX-RPC interfaces (*Handler* and *HandlerFactory*), which can be extended by developers to implement custom handlers. The handler implementation has to be wrapped in a plug-in, which can then be loaded by Artix clients and servers. The handler mechanism allows intercepting and modifying messages at four points of a message exchange. Both request and reply message can be handled at the client request-level, the client message-level, the server message-level, and the server request-level. Handlers at the request-level have access to the application's message context and the message's SOAP header respectively it's security properties. Handlers at the message-level have access to the raw message stream that is being written out on the wire and the application's message context only. For Artix, the instrumentation model presented in section 4 was implemented as a request-level handler, which can be configured using an XML configuration file.

The prototype was evaluated using a lab-level travel agency scenario featuring five interacting Web services: *Customer, Travel Agency, Airline, Car Rental* and *Hotel* (see figure 5). In this scenario, a customer sends booking orders to the travel agency, which then books flight, car and hotel room for him. Once the agency received all required information, it returns a booking confirmation to the customer. The services basically react on received requests by sending appropriate responses (containing dummy data), which means that they do not execute complex algorithms. The purpose of this scenario is to prove the applicability of the approach for asynchronous communication. Thus, all communication in this scenario takes places asynchronously, and all Web service operations are defined as WSDL one-way operations. The performance measurements were executed using one Artix client (providing the Customer callback service) and one Artix server (hosting the remaining Web services). Both applications were executed on different hosts.

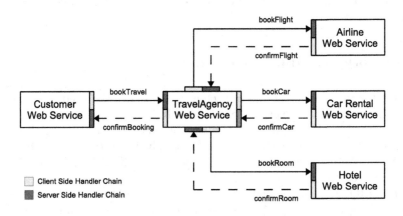

Fig. 5. Travel Agency Scenario (Messaging)

Figure 6 presents an extract of the travel agency scenario shown in figure 5 and the associated configuration. In this example, the communication between the travel agency and the airline Web services is fully instrumented: each invoked ARM handler either starts or stops an ARM transaction.

The tests for the prototype focused on correct message handling and measurements rather than on processing complex algorithms. When using passive ARM handlers, the processing time for one booking increased by 3.3% in comparison to a run without ARM handlers. Full instrumentation (start or stop of an ARM transaction in every handler, which results in eight measurements per customer request) introduced an overhead of 48.7%; using dummy ARM data in the message's SOAP header in combination with passive ARM handlers increased the

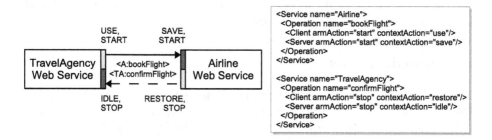

Fig. 6. Configuration Example

response time by 24.7% already. These results show that half of the overhead was caused by message meta-data. For otherwise short SOAP messages, this information increased the message size in a way that response times increased remarkably. However, idle ARM message handlers did not add remarkable overhead to the response time. Of course, the gathered measurement data shows correct dependencies between the executed transactions.

The performance penalty measured in this travel agency scenario is so grave, because the services themselves do not contain complex business logic (which would require more processing time). In addition, the messages exchanged between the Web service partners are rather short. For the presented approach, these circumstances represent the worst-case scenario. In a real-life application with more complex applications and messages, the percentage of the overhead would be lower.

6   Conclusion and Future Work

This paper presented a generic approach for performance instrumentation of synchronous, asynchronous and one-way Web services for end-to-end performance measurements. The approach allows a very fine-grained view upon deployed Web services and allows a user to configure the scope of instrumentation. The runtime information gathered shows the dependencies between Web service invocations and lists the durations of service invocations and instrumentation processing results. The instrumentation approach renders manual source code instrumentation and adaption to specific services unnecessary; the only remaining task is to define (configure) the required measurement points.

The approach relies on standardized JAX-RPC message handlers and message contexts for modifying SOAP messages and adding instrumentation information. It is based on ARM, an instrumentation approach broadly accepted by the industry and supported by large management platforms.

The prototype proves the usability of the approach, although the implementation needs to be optimized. Further steps will be optimization of the prototypical implementation, adaption to additional Web service platforms and instrumentation of a real world Web services-based application environment. In the future, this approach may provide an easy means for integrating Web services-based applications with management platforms.

Acknowledgements

The author would like to thank Prof. Dr. Reinhold Kroeger from Wiesbaden University of Applied Sciences and Damian McGrath, M.Sc. from IONA Technologies for supervising the work on his diploma thesis, on which this paper is based. He would also like to thank the people at IONA Technologies for the great support during his internship, in which he wrote this thesis.

References

1. The Apache Software Foundation: Apache Axis (Java). (2005) http://ws.apache.org/axis/.
2. IONA Technologies: IONA Artix. (2005) http://www.iona.com/products/artix/.
3. Microsoft Corporation: .NET Framework Developer Center. (2005) http://www.msdn.microsoft.com/netframework/.
4. IBM Tivoli: IBM Tivoli Composite Application Manager for SOA. (2005) http://www.ibm.com/software/tivoli/products/composite-application-mgr-soa/.
5. Computer Associates: Unicenter Web Services Distributed Management. (2005) http://www3.ca.com/solutions/Product.aspx?ID=4714.
6. AMD, Dell, Intel, Microsoft, Sun: Web Services for Management (WS-Management). (2004) http://msdn.microsoft.com/ws/2004/10/ws-management/.
7. Organization for the Advancement of Structured Information Standards (OASIS): OASIS Web Services Distributed Management (WSDM) TC. (2005) http://www.oasis-open.org/committees/wsdm.
8. Schaefer, J.: Methods and Tools for ARM-based Performance Instrumentation of Web Services. Diploma Thesis, Wiesbaden University of Applied Sciences (2005)
9. The Open Group: Application Response Measurement - ARM. (2005) http://www.opengroup.org/arm/.
10. The Open Group: ARM 4.0 Java Language Binding Technical Standard 4.0. (2003) http://www.opengroup.org/arm/uploads/40/3945/C037.pdf.
11. World Wide Web Consortium: Web Service Definition Language (WSDL) 1.1. (2001) http://www.w3.org/TR/2001/NOTE-wsdl-20010315.
12. World Wide Web Consortium: Simple Object Access Protocol (SOAP) 1.1. (2000) http://www.w3.org/TR/2000/NOTE-SOAP-20000508/.
13. Sun Microsystems: Java API for XML-Based RPC Specification 1.1. (2003) http://java.sun.com/xml/downloads/jaxrpc.html.
14. ObjectWeb: Celtix. (2006) http://celtix.objectweb.org/.

WSInterConnect: Dynamic Composition of Web Services Through Web Services

Josef Spillner, Iris Braun, and Alexander Schill

Dresden University of Technology, Dept. of Computer Science, Chair for Computer
Networks, 01062 Dresden, Germany
js177634@inf.tu-dresden.de, {iris.braun, alexander.schill}@tu-dresden.de

Abstract. In this paper, a model is presented which allows the composition of web services by means of a special web service, named WSInter-
Connect. Such a service might be used in a portal environment to allow
interactive services lookup and creation of permanent composed services
in the design stage, and for efficiently resolving missing parameters during the runtime of a process. The portal integration relies on augmented
service description files based on WSGUI concepts [1], and provides a
usable infrastructure for BPEL4People [4] concepts.

1 Introduction

The design of processes relying on web services has recently gained some attention in the area of human involvement. Specifically, several papers acknowledge
escalation hooks for decisions which cannot be drawn autonomously. Likewise,
the interaction with humans happens during design time, requiring facilities to
compose and reuse web services dynamically. Somewhere in between, services
attached to a process might have to be replaced at runtime.

WSInterConnect is a web service by itself which handles such simple composition models. It produces output information which is suitable for the actual
execution of the composite service, for example, in a BPEL (*Business Process
Execution Language*) engine. The way the service works is that it lets users create a sequence of operations based on WSDL files (*Web Services Description
Language*), taking into account structural differences of the input and output
messages of the service's operations.

It is however known that WSDL alone is not sufficient for describing web
services for direct usage by humans and processes alike. This led to augmented
service description efforts, namely WSGUI (*Web Services Graphical User Interface*) [2] for human interaction, WSDL-S (*Web Service Semantics*) to enable
autonomous discovery and matching of web service operations, and others. The
former will be referenced throughout this paper.

An example, which is modelled closely to existing BPEL4People ideas, is
presented to demonstrate service composition, human intervention and inference
of GUI elements by means of WSGUI. Integration into a portal environment,
including a user database and a task management portlet, fulfils the requirements
of the lifecycle of such a process as outlined in the BPEL4People draft.

F. Eliassen and A. Montresor (Eds.): DAIS 2006, LNCS 4025, pp. 181–186, 2006.

2   Web Service Composition

Traditional composition of web services happens either by creating the process descriptions by hand, or by using a graphical design tool. Often, these tools are easy to use but have severe limitations. In many cases, the message types of operations chained to each remain unchecked, resulting in type mismatch faults only at runtime. Additionally, a lot of overhead is generated by including such checks into the tool software, and compatibility is lowered by only supporting a restricted set of output formats. These shortcomings can be overcome by using a web service to handle the creation of process description files in various formats. The proposed service, WSInterConnect, will be described in detail in the next sections, beginning with a look on message comparison details.

Each web service operation takes one or more input parameters, and returns one or more output parameters, all possibly being of complex types, such that additional value restrictions, union types and lists can be represented. It is valid to assume a single parameter for input and output each, if both are considered to be complex on their own, forming a product type. In WSDL terms, a message might contain several message parts, but might also contain just one part which in turn consists of a sequence of elements.

Since WSDL data types are specified using XML Schema, a prerequisite for composing services interactively is to check for the compatibility of the output message of one operation with the input message of the other operation, with three possible outcomes for each check:

All-or-nothing compatibility: The messages are either fully compatible, or not at all. This can be trivially checked when only simple types are used, and recursively for complex types by parallel message comparison. An important note is that variable names might differ, only the type structure is important.

Subset compatibility: A sub-set relation can be specified, that is, one message is a subset of the other message. This includes list ranges as well as omissions of parameters on one side only. If the input of the second operation is a subset of the output of the first one, some variables will have to be discarded, otherwise some values will have to be injected, for instance by the user.

Arbitrary compatibility: Whenever none of the two cases above applies, the operations are considered to be incompatible. In such a case, WSInterConnect could reject to link them together in any form. An advanced implementation would however allow to both drop variables and let the user fill in missing values, as long as at least a certain percentage of compatibility is present.

Having identified the cases, the relevance of partial compatibility can be evaluated more easily.

In a fully automated services composition, only full operation compatibility can be allowed, while in an interactive environment such as a portal, the user can be the input source who determines the missing values of the input parameters of the second web service, in addition to the output of the first one. Likewise, if parameters occur in the output but do not have any matching counterpart in the following input, the user should allow to have them be dropped.

3   WSInterConnect

A web service which implements the concepts introduced above is called WSInterConnect. Its first functionality can be described as follows: For each pair of services, an operation is selected to serve as output of the first service and input of the second one, respectively. WSInterConnect will then create a composed *virtual* service, which requests from the user only those input variables which cannot already be filled out by the first service.

For more complex scenarios, rather than reinventing the wheel, existing process engines can be used to refer to WSInterConnect in order to request missing values. This is accomplished by the second functionality, resolving issues of missing parameters at run-time.

The first set of operations includes compare() and store(). The invokation and result of one WSInterConnect operation, compare(), which takes a number of WSDL URLs as its input, looks like about the following message conversation if the same WSDL is used for both input and output, effectively leading to a cartesian product of all operations offered by said WSDL:

```
<ConnectRequest>
 <wsout>http://localhost/mail.wsdl</wsout>
 <wsin>http://localhost/mail.wsdl</wsin>
</ConnectRequest>
<ConnectResponse>
 <comparisons>
  <comparison>
   <operation-output>signMail</operation-output>
   <operation-input>sendMail</operation-input>
   <status>compatible</status>
  </comparison>
  ...
 </comparisons>
</ConnectResponse>
```

The store() operation takes one of these matches and stores it as a composition for later use with a process engine.

Augmenting the WSDL for the WSInterConnect service, and the ConnectRequest operation in particular, with WSGUI information, makes it possible to generate a GUI which lets the user select the operations which are to be used for the composition. In addition, if *partial compatibility* is implemented, more detailed type mismatch information could be sent as to allow the structural alignment of input and output operation message format.

The basic WSGUI concepts shall be presented now briefly.

Pure WSDL files do not contain enough information to use web services as generic processes. Rather, specialised frontends have to exist to facilitate the navigation, data input, error handling and presentation of the results.

With WSGUI, it was shown to be possible to augment the WSDL files with user-centric visual hints, based on the XForms standard and some additional information like description texts and mime-type specifications.

WSGUI is an essential component in the realisation of interactively composed web services. To date there exist tools which attempt to handle this task without

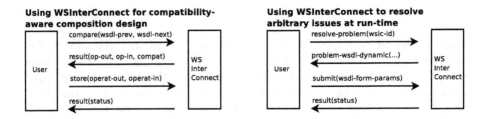

Fig. 1. Sequences describing usage patterns with WSInterConnect

WSGUI, but they are not up to current usability and internationalisation standards. Existing approaches like WSRP [5] are not able to adapt to fully arbitrary underlying data formats. Using the features of WSGUI, inferring GUI information from WSInterConnect is possible as follows.

There are two potential areas of WSGUI usage in combination with the service. First, the WSInterConnect service itself, by way of its `compare()` and `store()` operations, can be invoked dynamically by the user. This works like any other generic web service call in that its messages are rendered to a web page or client application. Second, the process as composed by WSInterConnect and executed by a process manager might call back so that extended WSGUI features such as marking certain fields (those which are already assigned a value within the process) as read-only, while permitting the user to fill out the remaining fields. Operations include `resolve-problem()` to retrieve the dynamically generated WSDL for a certain identifier, which has been added to WSInterConnect by the process, and `submit()` to submit the form which is based on the WSDL data, and rendered with WSGUI as described above. All major operations are shown together in figure 1.

4   Application Scenario

Following the often cited example of a travel agency, a public web service might exist which permits booking a flight, taking the four parameters name, destination, and suggested dates of flight and of return. A second service for booking the hotel rooms can reuse all of the data, but since the final destination city might not have an airport, the destination parameter is dropped and two new ones, for final destination and hotel category, are added instead, and it reuses the exact dates as returned by the first service.

This is a scenario where *partial compatibility* is involved. If for whatever reason the hotel booking service is not available, the user might on the fly substitute it with a compatible service. The substitute might however have a use for the flight destination city, for instance to provide a hotel room offer combined with airport shuttle service.

While this application scenario already suggests a possible use of WSInterconnect, the full power can be experienced when considering the following BPEL4People deployment scenario.

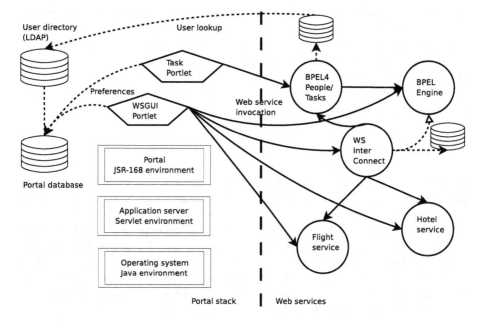

Fig. 2. WSInterConnect in a typical deployment of web services and a portal stack

Using web services in portals is a well-known concept for implementation of flexible service-oriented applications, for instance in telework scenarios [3]. The portal environment provides two necessary parts of the infrastructure: A user database, and a portlet container hosting various portlets. According to BPEL4People, web service escalation points are best suited for inclusion into a task tracker, which in this case runs as a service and is displayed in a dedicated portlet.

The architecture is outlined in the figure 2, distinguishing between the on-site portal stack and the web services.

The custom tracker portlet displays tasks with their priorities and deadlines, and contains hyperlinks to the WSGUI engine, parametrised with calls to the web services referenced by the BPEL4People engine so that clicking on the task presents an option list for resolving the task, which is automatically inferenced from the available options. This feature is using the `resolve-problem()` and `submit()` operations already introduced earlier.

When resolving a problem requires more results from other web services, the user could create new compositions on the fly from within the portal.

5   Related Work

There are a few tools which already handle the creation of processes based on web service composition, like X Workflow Composer [6] for direct process code generation, or commercial BPEL editors. They do however lack design-time parameter comparison and methods to retrieve missing parameters from the user of the service at run-time. Graphical editors like Triana PSE [7] often focus on ease of use, an aspect not in the centre of WSInterConnect development, so that leveraging its advantages into the graphical editors at a later date seems to be an important proof of the concepts presented in this paper.

Until now, no effort which combines concepts similar to WSGUI and service composition is known to the authors.

6   Conclusion

It has been shown how to let users interact with web services in an interactive and dynamic environment, without the need to pre-define the operations or the visual appearance thereof.

WSInterConnect has been finished in parts. It is not expected that this service will lead to a standalone deployment. Rather, advanced web services concepts can be combined with WSInterConnect in a useful and still explorative manner.

Current WSGUI research hints at generating the needed GUIs automatically for even more usage scenarios, thus projects like WSInterConnect will be less of a novelty and more common technology in the near future.

References

1. WSGUI concept project, J. Spillner, January 2006, `http://wsgui.berlios.de/`
2. *Creating GUIs for Web Services*, M. Kassoff, D. Kato and W. Mohsin, IEEE Internet Computing, September/October 2003, Vol 7, No. 4, 66-73, `http://logic.stanford.edu/~{}mkassoff/papers/wsgui.pdf`
3. *A service-oriented Architecture for Teleworking Applications*, I. Braun, A. Schill, Proceedings of IASTED International Conference on Internet and Multimedia Systems and Applications, Honolulu, August 2005, Acta Press, Calgary, p. 105-110
4. BPEL4People white paper, M. Kloppmann et. al., August 2005, ftp://www6. software.ibm.com/software/developer/library/ws-bpel4people.pdf
5. OASIS Standard: Web Services for Remote Portlets, Specification Version 1.0, (OASIS, 2003) `http://www.oasis-open.org/committees/wsrp`
6. X Workflow Composer, software project, S. Shirasuna, January 2006, `http://www.extreme.indiana.edu/xgws/xwf/`
7. *Triana as a Graphical Web Services Composition Toolkit*, S. Majithia et. al., Proceedings of UK e-Science All Hands Meeting, September 2003, EPSRC, p. 494-500 `http://www.trianacode.org/`

Bounding Recovery Time in Rollback-Recovery Protocol for Mobile Systems Preserving Session Guarantees

Jerzy Brzeziński, Anna Kobusińska, and Jacek Kobusiński

Institute of Computing Science
Poznań University of Technology, Poland
{Jerzy.Brzezinski, Anna.Kobusinska, Jacek.Kobusinski}@cs.put.poznan.pl

Abstract. This paper addresses a problem of integrating the consistency management of session guarantees with recovery mechanisms in distributed mobile systems. To solve such a problem, rollback-recovery protocol rVsSG, preserving session guarantees is proposed. The protocol employs known rollback-recovery techniques, however, while applying them, the semantics of session guarantees is taken into account. Consequently, rVsSG protocol is optimized with respect to session guarantees requirements. The paper includes the proof of safety property of the presented protocol.

Keywords: fault tolerance, rollback-recovery, mobile systems, session guarantees.

1   Introduction

Mobile computing brings about a new paradigm of distributed computing in which communication may be achieved through wireless or intermittently connected networks. In this paradigm, users can compute even if they relocate from one distributed resource to another, using different links at different locations. By enabling motion and location independence, mobility gives the opportunity to provide new services and allows supplementary information access that may occur any time and any place. Although being a relatively new area, mobile computing has attracted a lot of research efforts, motivated by both a great market potential and by many challenging research problems.

The impact of mobile computing on systems design goes beyond the networking level and directly effects data access and management. A key concept in providing high performance and availability in such an access is replication. Unfortunately, replication brings up a problem of replica consistency. Moreover, due to switching of clients, this problem gains a new dimension of complexity and thus, it should be tackled from new, client's perspective. For that reason, *session guarantees* [TDP+94], also called *client-centric* consistency models, have been proposed to define required properties of the system observed from client's point of view. Four session guarantees have been defined: *Read Your Writes* (RYW), *Monotonic Writes* (MW), *Monotonic Reads* (MR) and *Writes*

F. Eliassen and A. Montresor (Eds.): DAIS 2006, LNCS 4025, pp. 187–198, 2006.

Follow Reads (WFR) and protocols implementing them have been introduced [TDP⁺94, BSW05, Sob05]. Unfortunately these protocols assume that clients and servers are reliable and they do not crash. In practice, failures do happen, therefore, the existing consistency protocols should be provided with the fault–tolerant techniques, which allow servers to provide required session-guarantees despite their failures.

Thus, this paper addresses a problem of integrating the consistency management of session guarantees in systems with mobile clients, with recovery mechanisms. To solve such a problem, we propose rVsSG protocol, integrating logging and checkpointing techniques with coherence operations of VsSG consistency protocol [TDP⁺94, BSW05, Sob05]. Consequently, the proposed protocol offers the ability to overcome servers' failures transparently to the client, and preserves session guarantees at the same time. The rVsSG protocol is optimized in terms of checkpointing overhead, taking into account the specific requirements of required session guarantees. Moreover, correctness analysis of the protocol is carried out and its safety property is formally proved.

2   Session Guarantees

2.1   Basic Assumptions and Definitions

Throughout this paper, a replicated distributed storage system is considered. The system consists of a number of *servers* holding a full copy of *shared objects* and *clients* running applications that access these objects (see Fig. 1). Although all system components (mobile clients, servers, communication links) can be a subject of failures, in this paper we focus only on failures of servers. We assume *crash-recovery* model of failures, i.e. servers may crash and recover after crashing a finite number of times [GR04]. Servers can fail at arbitrary moments and we require any such failure to be eventually detected, for example by failure detectors [SDS99].

Clients are separated from servers, i.e. a client application may run on a separate computer than the server. A client may access a shared object after selecting a single server and sending a direct request to the server. Clients are mobile,

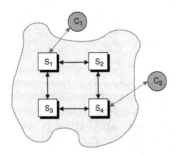

Fig. 1. Replication servers and client accessing them

i.e. they can switch from one server to another during application execution. Session guarantees are expected to take care of data consistency observed by a migrating client. The set of shared objects replicated by servers does not imply any particular data model or organization. Operations performed on shared objects are divided into *reads* and *writes*, denoted respectively by r and w. A read does not change states of the shared objects, while a write does. A write may cause an update of an object, it may create a new object, or delete an existing one. A write may also atomically update states of several objects.

Clients can concurrently submit conflicting writes at different servers, e.g. writes that modify the overlapping parts of data storage. Operations on shared objects issued by client C_i are ordered by a relation $\xrightarrow{C_i}$ called *client issue order*. Server S_j performs operations in an order represented by relation $\xmapsto{S_j}$. An operation performed by a server S_j will be denoted by $w|_{S_j}$ or $r|_{S_j}$. Relevant writes $RW(r)$ of a read operation r is a set of writes that has influenced the current state of objects observed by the read r.

A set of basic consistency conditions for sessions of mobile clients has been introduced in Bayou project [TDP+94]. Informally, RYW expresses the user expectation not to miss his own modifications performed in the past, MW ensures that order of writes issued by a single client is preserved, MR ensures that the client's observations of the data storage are monotonic and WFR keeps the track of causal dependencies resulting from operations issued by a client. The following formal definitions, brought in [Sob05], are based on those descriptional concepts.

Definition 1. *Read Your Writes (RYW) session guarantee is defined as follows:*

$$\forall C_i \forall S_j \left[w \xrightarrow{C_i} r|_{S_j} \implies w \xmapsto{S_j} r \right]$$

To illustrate RYW session guarantee, let us consider a user writing a TODO list to a file. After travelling to another location, the user wants to recall the most urgent tasks, and reads TODO list. Without RYW session guarantee the read may return any previous (possibly empty) version of the document.

Definition 2. *Monotonic Writes (MW) session guarantee is defined as follows:*

$$\forall C_i \forall S_j \left[w_1 \xrightarrow{C_i} w_2|_{S_j} \implies w_1 \xmapsto{S_j} w_2 \right]$$

Let us consider a counter object with two methods for updating its state: `increment()`, and `set()`, which increment value of the counter, and set its new value, respectively. A user of the counter issues the `set()` function, and then updates the counter by calling `increment()` function. Without MW session guarantee the final result would be unpredictable, because it depends on the order of the execution of these two functions.

Definition 3. *Monotonic Reads (MR) session guarantee is defined as follows:*

$$\forall C_i \forall S_j \left[r_1 \xrightarrow{C_i} r_2|_{S_j} \implies \forall w_k \in RW(r_1) : w_k \xmapsto{S_j} r_2 \right]$$

In case of MR, let us consider a mailbox of a traveling user. The user opens the mailbox at one location, and reads emails. Afterwards he opens the same mailbox at different location, and expects to see at least all the messages he has read previously. The new state may not reflect the true current state, but must be at least as new as the previously observed version.

Definition 4. *Writes Follow Reads (WFR) session guarantee is defined as follows:*

$$\forall C_i \, \forall S_j \left[r \overset{C_i}{\hookrightarrow} w |_{S_j} \implies \forall w_k \in RW(r) : w_k \overset{S_j}{\rightarrowtail} w \right]$$

To present the usage of WFR, let us consider a user that reads a file with some information. Afterwards this user prepares some notes he wants to add to the document. Because, he was on journey, his computer switched in the meantime to another server. When the user finally wanted to perform the operation the new server was properly updated and user could append his note.

Besides Bayou, there are other systems that implement consistency conditions based on session guarantees: CASCADE — a caching service for distributed CORBA objects [CFV00], Pastis — a highly scable, multi-user, peer-to-peer file system [PBS05], or OceanStore — a global persistent data storage system [KBC+00].

2.2   The VsSG Consistency Protocol

Data consistency in rVsSG is managed by VsSG *consistency protocol* [BSW05], which uses a concept of server-based version vectors, having the following form: $V_{S_j} = \left[v_1 \, v_2 \, ... \, v_{N_S} \right]$, where N_S is a total number of servers in the system and single position v_i is the number of writes performed by server S_j. Every write in VsSG protocol is labeled with a *vector timestamp*, set to the current value of vector clock V_{S_j} of server S_j, performing the write for the first time. The vector timestamp of write w is returned by function $T : \mathcal{O} \mapsto V$. All writes performed by the server in the past are kept in set $\mathcal{O}_{S_j}$. On the client's side, vectors W_{C_i} and R_{C_i} are maintained, representing writes issued by client C_i and writes relevant to reads issued by this client, respectively. The sequence of past writes is called *history*. A formal definition of history is given below:

Definition 5. *A history H_{S_j} at time moment t, is a linearly ordered set* $\left(\mathcal{O}_{S_j}, \overset{S_j}{\rightarrowtail} \right)$, *where $\mathcal{O}_{S_j}$ is a set of writes performed by server S_j, till the time t and relation $\overset{S_j}{\rightarrowtail}$ represents an execution order of writes.*

In order to satisfy the client's requirements concerning data consistency, the system intercepts client requests, and extends the standard communication. The request sent from a client C_i to a server S_j carries the operation that is to be performed and vector W, calculated according to the operation type and set SG of session guarantees required for the operation. W is set either to W_{C_i} or R_{C_i}.

On receipt of request sent by a client, server S_j checks whether for vectors V_{S_j} and W the following condition is fulfilled, $\forall i : V_{S_j}[i] \geq W[i]$, which is expected to be sufficient for providing appropriate session guarantee. If the state of the server is not sufficiently up to date, the request is postponed and will be resumed after synchronization with another server.

During writes performed by server S_j, its version vector V_{S_j} is incremented at position j and a timestamped operation is recorded in history H_{S_j}. The current value of the server vector clock is returned to the client and causes the update of the client's vector W_{C_i}.

VsSG protocol eventually propagates all writes to all servers. During synchronization of servers, their histories are *concatenated*. The concatenation of histories H_{S_j} and H_{S_k}, denoted by $H_{S_j} \oplus H_{S_k}$, consists in adding new operations from H_{S_k} at the end of H_{S_j}, preserving at the same time the appropriate relations [BSW05].

2.3   Checkpoint and Log Definitions

Below, we propose formal definitions of fault-tolerance mechanisms used by rVsSG protocol:

Definition 6. *Log Log_{S_j} is a set of triples:*

$$\{ \langle i_1, o_1, T(o_1) \rangle \, \langle i_2, o_2, T(o_2) \rangle \, ... \, \langle i_n, o_n, T(o_n) \rangle \},$$

where i_n represents the identifier of the client issuing a write operation $o_n \in \mathcal{O}_{S_j}$ and $T(o_n)$ is timestamp of o_n.

During a rollback-recovery procedure, operations from the log are executed according to their timestamps, from the earliest to the latest one.

Definition 7. *Checkpoint $Ckpt_{S_j}$ is a couple $\langle V_{S_j}, H_{S_j} \rangle$, of version vector V_{S_j} and history H_{S_j} maintained by server S_j at time t, where t is a moment of taking a checkpoint.*

In this paper we assume, that log and checkpoint are saved by the server in the stable storage, able to survive all failures [EEL$^+$02]. Additionally, we assume that the newly taken checkpoint replaces the previous one, so just one checkpoint for each server is kept in the stable storage.

3   The rVsSG Protocol

3.1   General Idea

To preserve required session guarantee, the rollback-recovery protocol must ensure that writes issued by client and essential to preserve this guarantee are not lost after the server failure and its recovery. Checkpointing every single write operation fulfills this requirement, but results in frequent saving of server state in the stable storage, which is time–consuming. Logging procedure overcomes this disadvantage and takes less time than checkpointing. On the other hand, the log size may grow infinitely and may turn out to be too large. Thus, in the proposed protocol we use the known technique of combining logging and checkpointing. However, while applying these techniques, the semantics of operations, characteristic of session guarantees, is taken into account. Consequently, in rVsSG protocol, only operations essential to provide session guarantees are logged, so checkpoints are optimized with respect to required session guarantee requirements. Moreover, in rVsSG protocol, servers save only some of obtained operations, namely those received directly from clients. Operations obtained during synchronization procedure, even if required by session guarantee, are just performed by the server, because they have already been saved in the stable storage (in the log or in the checkpoint) of other servers. Hence, even if writes obtained in the result of synchronization procedure are lost, the required session guarantee is not violated. This steams from the fact, that such writes will be obtained again during consecutive synchronizations.

3.2   Protocol Implementation

Every request issued by client C_i indicates client's requirements for the issued operation that are calculated based on the type of operation (checked by iswrite(o) function), and set SG of session guarantees (lines 1, 3 and 6).

The server, which obtains the write request directly from client C_i, checks whether the request can be performed accordingly to required session guarantees (line 9). If the state of server S_j is not sufficiently up to date, the obtained request is postponed (line 10), otherwise server's S_j data structures are updated: the value of version vector V_{S_j} is increased and operation o is timestamped, to give o a unique identifier (lines 13-14). Afterwards, o is logged to stable storage (line 15). It is important that logging of write takes place before performing this request. Such an order is crucial, as the operation that is performed but not logged, may be lost in the case of subsequent failures. After the operation is performed (line 16), it is added to the history H_{S_j} of performed writes (line 17). With every logged operation the size of the log is increased, and thus a recovery takes more time. Therefore, in order to bound a recovery time after the server failure, the server state is occasionally checkpointed (line 19). The rVsSG protocol assumes, that a checkpoint is taken every K logged operations (line 18). K is constant and its value depends on the system characteristics. After the checkpoint is taken, log Log_{S_j} is cleared (line 20). Essential is the fact, that firstly the checkpoint is taken, and only afterwards the content of log Log_{S_j} is cleared.

The read request from client C_i received by server S_j is performed (line 24), if the condition from line (line 9) is fulfilled for this operation.

The update message received from other servers changes the state of server S_j, only if the history H contains writes that has not been performed by S_j yet (line 37). Such update operations are performed (line 38) and processed by S_j(lines 39-40).

Upon sending a request $\langle o \rangle$
to server S_j at client C_i

1: $W \leftarrow 0$
2: **if** (iswrite(o) **and** MW $\in SG$)
    or (**not** iswrite(o) **and**
    RYW $\in SG$) **then**
3:    $W \leftarrow \max(W, W_{C_i})$
4: **end if**
5: **if** (iswrite(o) **and** WFR $\in SG$)
    or (**not** iswrite(o) **and**
    MR $\in SG$) **then**
6:    $W \leftarrow \max(W, R_{C_i})$
7: **end if**
8: send $\langle o, W, i \rangle$ to S_j

Upon receiving a request $\langle o, W, i \rangle$
from client C_i at server S_j

9: **while** $\left(V_{S_j} \not\geq W\right)$ **do**
10:    wait()
11: **end while**
12: **if** iswrite(o) **then**
13:    $V_{S_j}[j] \leftarrow V_{S_j}[j] + 1$
14:    timestamp o with V_{S_j}
15:    $Log_{S_j} \leftarrow Log_{S_j} \cup \langle o, T(o) \rangle$
16:    perform o and store results in res
17:    $H_{S_j} \leftarrow H_{S_j} \oplus \{o\}$
18:    **if** K operations is logged **then**
19:        $Ckpt_{S_j} \leftarrow \langle V_{S_j}, H_{S_j} \rangle$
20:        $Log_{S_j} \leftarrow \emptyset$
21:    **end if**
22: **end if**
23: **if** (**not** iswrite(o)) **then**
24:    perform o and store results in res
25: **end if**
26: send $\langle o, res, V_{S_j} \rangle$ to C_i

Upon receiving a reply $\langle o, res, W \rangle$
from server S_j at client C_i

27: **if** iswrite(o) **then**
28:    $W_{C_i} \leftarrow \max(W_{C_i}, W)$
29: **else**
30:    $R_{C_i} \leftarrow \max(R_{C_i}, W)$
31: **end if**
32: deliver $\langle res \rangle$

Every Δt at server S_j

33: **foreach** $S_k \neq S_j$ **do**
34:    send $\langle S_j, H_{S_j} \rangle$ to S_k
35: **end for**

Upon receiving an update $\langle S_k, H \rangle$
at server S_j

36: **foreach** $w_i \in H$ **do**
37:    **if** $V_{S_j} \not\geq T(w_i)$ **then**
38:        perform w_i
39:        $V_{S_j} \leftarrow \max(V_{S_j}, T(w_i))$
40:        $H_{S_j} \leftarrow H_{S_j} \oplus \{w_i\}$
41:    **end if**
42: **end for**
43: signal()

On rollback-recovery
44: $\langle V_{S_j}, H_{S_j} \rangle \leftarrow Ckpt_{S_j}$
45: $Log'_{S_j} \leftarrow Log_{S_j}$
46: $R_{S_j} \leftarrow 0$
47: **foreach** $o'_j \in Log'_{S_j}$ **do**
48:    **choose** $\langle o'_i, T(o'_i) \rangle$ **with minimal**
       $T(o'_j)$ **from** Log'_{S_j} **where** $T(o'_j) > V_{S_j}$
49:    $V_{S_j}[j] \leftarrow V_{S_j}[j] + 1$
50:    perform o'_j
51:    $H_{S_j} \leftarrow H_{S_j} \oplus \{o'_j\}$
52:    $R_{S_j} \leftarrow T(o'_i)$
53: **end for**

Fig. 2. Checkpointing and rollback-recovery rVsSG protocol

After the failure occurrence, the failed server restarts from the latest checkpoint (line 44) and replays operations from the log (lines 47-53) according to their timestamps, from the earliest to the latest one.

4   Safety of rVsSG Protocol

The safety property asserts that clients access object replicas maintained by servers according to required session guarantee, regardless of servers' failures.

Lemma 1. *Every write operation w issued by client C_i and performed by server S_j that received w directly from client C_i, is kept in checkpoint $Ckpt_{S_j}$ or in log Log_{S_j}.*

Proof. Let us consider a write operation w issued by client C_i and obtained by server S_j.

1. From the algorithm, server S_j before performing the request w, saves it in the stable storage by adding it to log Log_{S_j} (line 15). Because logging of w takes place before performing it (line 16), then even in the case of failure the operation w is not lost, but remains in the log.
2. Log Log_{S_j} is cleared (line 20) after taking by S_j the checkpoint (line 19). Therefore, the server failure that occurs after clearing the log does not affect safety of the algorithm, because writes from the log are already stored in the checkpoint.
3. After the checkpoint is taken, but before the log is cleared (between lines 19 and 20) writes issued by client C_i and performed by server S_j are stored in both the checkpoint $Ckpt_{S_j}$ and the log Log_{S_j}.

Lemma 2. *The rollback-recovery procedure recovers all write operations issued by clients, performed by server S_j and logged in log Log_{S_j} in the moment of failure occurrence.*

Proof. Let us assume that server S_j fails. After the failure, operations from the log are recovered (line 47), and cause the update of vector V_{S_j} (line 49). Afterwards they are performed by S_j (line 50) and added to history H_{S_j} (line 51). Assume now, that failures occur during recovery procedure. Due to such failures the results of operations that have already been recovered are lost again. However, since log Log_{S_j} is cleared (line 20) only after the checkpoint is taken (line 19) and it is not modified during the rollback-recovery procedure (line 45), log's content is not changed. Hence, the recovery procedure can be started from the beginning without loss of any operation issued by clients and performed by server S_j after the moment of taking checkpoint.

Lemma 3. *After the failure and recovery of server S_j, all write operations obtained during synchronization with other servers are performed by S_j again before applying new operations issued by a client and requiring results of lost operations to provide session guarantees.*

Proof. By contradiction, let us assume that server S_j has performed new operation o obtained from client C_i, before performing again operation w, received during a former synchronization with other servers and lost because of S_j failure. Due to underlying VsSG protocol [BSW05], the following condition must be fulfilled (line 9) to perform operation o: $V_{S_j} \geq W$. More precisely, when o is a read operation required with RYW session guarantee, or a write operation requiring MW, above condition is equivalent to $\forall l : V_{S_j}[l] \geq W_{C_i}[l]$. In case of requiring by a client C_i MR guarantee, while issuing read operation or WFR, while issuing a write, the considered condition is $\forall l : V_{S_j}[l] \geq R_{C_i}[l]$.

Suppose that write operation w issued by client C_i has been performed by server S_k. After obtaining the reply from S_k, client C_i modifies its version vector W_{C_i} at least in position k: $W_{C_i} \leftarrow max(W_{C_i}, V_{S_k})$ (line 28). Server S_j, in the result of synchronization with S_k, performs w and updates its version vector V_{S_j}, modifying V_{S_j} at least in position k (line 39). Without loosing the generality, we assume that after performing operation w, server S_j has performed read operation r issued by C_i, which has read results of w. In the result, after obtaining results of r, client C_i has modified its version vector R_{C_i} at least in position k: $R_{C_i} \leftarrow max(R_{C_i}, V_{S_j})$ (line 30).

If the failure of S_j happens, the state of S_j is recovered accordingly to values stored in $Ckpt_{S_j}$ (line 44) and in $Logs_{S_j}$ (lines 47-53). During recovering operations from the log, vector V_{S_j} is updated only in position j. Thus, the recovered value of $V_{S_j}[k]$ does not reflect the information on w. Hence, until the next update message is obtained, $V_{S_j}[k] < W_{C_i}[k]$ and $V_{S_j}[k] < R_{C_i}[k]$, which contradicts the assumption.

Lemma 4. *The server performs new operation issued by a client C_i only after all writes issued by this client and performed before the failure are recovered.*

Proof. By contradiction, let us assume that server S_j has performed new operation o issued by client C_i, before recovering and performing again write operation w received directly from C_i and lost in the result of S_j failure. According to the underlying VsSG protocol, for server S_j performing new operation o the following condition must be fulfilled (lines 9-10): $V_{S_j} \geq W$, where W represents one of vectors: W_{C_i} or R_{C_i}, depending on the type of operation o and required session guarantee.

By assumption, after obtaining by server S_j write operation w, vector V_{S_j} is modified: $V_{S_j}[j] \leftarrow V_{S_j}[j] + 1$ and results of performed operation, together with vector V_{S_j} are sent to the client. At the client's side, after the reply is received, vector W_{C_i} is updated at least in position j : $W_{C_i} \leftarrow max\left(W_{C_i}, V_{S_j}\right)$ (line 28).

Without loosing the generality, let us assume that after performing operation w, server S_j has performed read operation r issued by C_i, which has read results of w. In the result, after obtaining results of r, client C_i has modified its version vector R_{C_i} at least in position j: $R_{C_i} \leftarrow max(R_{C_i}, V_{S_j})$ (line 30).

Thus, when operation w is not recovered after the server failure and its recovery, then either $V_{S_j}[j] < W_{C_i}[j]$ or $V_{S_j}[j] < R_{C_i}[j]$, which contradicts the assumption.

Theorem 1. *RYW, MW, WFR and MR session guarantees are preserved by rVsSG protocol for clients requesting them, even in the presence of server failures.*

Proof. According to Lemma 1, every write operation performed by server S_j is saved in the checkpoint or in the log. After the server failure, all operations from the checkpoint are recovered. Further, all operations performed before the failure occurred, but after the checkpoint was taken, are also recovered (following Lemma 2). As stated by Lemma 4, all recovered write operations are applied before new operation obtained from a client is performed. Hence, for any client C_i and any server S_j, required session guarantee is preserved by the rollback–recovery and checkpointing rVsSG protocol.

Full versions of presented theorems and proofs, and the proof of liveness property of proposed protocol can be found in [BKKS05].

5   Determining Desirable Moments of Taking Checkpoints

In general, checkpoints may be taken according to the following scenarios: periodically, every K operations issued by clients, or on the basis of semantics analysis.

In rVsSG protocol, described in section 3, server S_j takes a checkpoint after logging K operations. The value of constant K depends on system characteristics, among which are the frequency of requests issued by clients, or the complexity of issued operations. By adequate determining K, the checkpoint overhead, and thus total execution time of application may be minimized. The semantics analysis of session guarantees further minimizes the number of taken checkpoints, because it allows to avoid taking checkpoints that include operations not required by considered session guarantees.

To indicate sets of above operations, let us discuss the following four situations. When considering RYW, write operations issued by client C_i and not followed by read request issued by the same client, are not required to preserve this guarantee. Thus, when client C_i issues only writes and does not want to see their results, then checkpointing such writes is unnecessary. In case of MW, when write operation issued by client C_i is not followed by another write request, then results of first write are not essential to preserving MW from client's C_i point of view. Hence, the first write does not need not to be checkpointed. For MR session guarantee, set of writes, which results influenced read request issued by client C_i, does not need to be taken into account while taking a checkpoint, when such a read is not followed by a new one issued by the same client. Finally, when read request issued by a client C_i is not followed by write issued by the same client, then the results of writes that modified the state of server observed by read need not to be checkpointed if WFR is required by C_i.

Following above analysis, for each session guarantee, sets of operations essential to preserve this guarantee can be distinguished, and desirable moment of taking a checkpoint, denoted by DMTC, can be defined. DMTC indicates such a moment, before which there is no need to take a checkpoint, because the server has not performed any operation required by given session guarantee. For each session guarantee, we indicate operations that determine DMTC. In the case of RYW, it is a read request obtained from a client. For MR it is also a read request, however the one that follows in the server execution order another read issued by the same client. With reference to MW session guarantee, DMTC is determined by obtaining a write request following in the server execution order all writes issued by the same client. Finally, for WFR session guarantee, it is a write request, following in the server execution order the read request issued by the same client.

Thus, the checkpointing and rollback-recovery protocol rVsSG, may be optimized, by taking checkpoints according to consecutive DMTC.

Below, we present an example of taking a checkpoint according to DMTC (Fig. ??). In the considered example, a system consists of two servers and two clients. Client C_1, issues operations which should be performed according to MR session guarantee. Server S_1 takes a checkpoint according to idea of DMTC, i.e. when it obtains the second read request issued by C_i. Of course, depending on system characteristics, in general checkpoints can be taken every n-th DMTC. But, there is no need to take checkpoitns between two following DMTC.

6   Conclusions

This paper has dealt with a problem of integrating the consistency management of distributed systems with mobile clients with the recovery mechanisms. To solve such a problem, the rollback-recovery protocol rVsSG, preserving session guarantees has been proposed and its correctness in terms of safety has been formally proved.

The proposed protocol takes advantage of the known rollback-recovery techniques like logging and checkpointing, however, while applying these techniques, the semantics of operations is taken into account. Consequently, in rVsSG protocol, only the operations essential to provide required session guarantees are logged. Moreover, in the paper, we determine, how to take checkpoints in the most desirable moments for each session guarantee.

Our future work encompasses the development of rollback-recovery protocols, which are integrated with other consistency protocols. Moreover, appropriate simulation experiments to quantitatively evaluate overhead of rVsSG protocol are being carried out.

References

[BKKS05] J. Brzeziński, A. Kobusińska, J. Kobusiński, and M. Szychowiak. rvswfr recovery protocol for mobile systems. Technical Report RA-017/05, Institute of Computing Science, Poznań University of Technology, November 2005.

[BSW05]   J. Brzeziński, C. Sobaniec, and D. Wawrzyniak. Safety of a server-based version vector protocol implementing session guarantees. In *Proc. of Int. Conf. on Computational Science (ICCS2005), LNCS 3516*, pages 423–430, Atlanta, USA, May 2005.

[CFV00]   G. Chockler, R. Friedman, and R. Vitenberg. Consistency conditions for a CORBA caching service. In *Proc. of the 14th Int. Conf. on Distributed Computing (DISC'2000), LNCS 1914*, pages 374–388, October 2000.

[EEL⁺02]   N. Elmootazbellah, Elnozahy, A. Lorenzo, Yi-Min Wang, and D.B. Johnson. A survey of rollback-recovery protocols in message-passing systems. *ACM Computing Surveys*, 34(3):375–408, September 2002.

[GR04]   Rachid Guerraoui and Luis Rodrigues. *Introduction to distributed algorithms*. Springer-Verlag, 2004.

[KBC⁺00]   J. Kubiatowicz, D. Bindel, Y. Chen, S. Czerwinski, P. Eaton, D. Geels, R. Gummadi, S. Rhea, H. Weatherspoon, W. Weimer, C. Wells, and B. Zhao. Oceanstore: An architecture for global-scale persistent storage. *Proceedings of the 9th International Conference on Architectural Support for Programming Languages and Operating Systems (ASPLOS 2000)*, 2000.

[PBS05]   F. Picconi, J-M. Busca, and P. Sens. Pastis: a highly-scalable multi-user peer-to-peer file system. *EuroPar 2005*, pages 1173–1182, 2005.

[SDS99]   N. Sergent, X. Défago, and A. Schiper. Failure detectors: Implementation issues and impact on consensus performance. Technical Report SSC/1999/019, École Polytechnique Fédérale de Lausanne, Switzerland, May 1999.

[Sob05]   C. Sobaniec. *Consistency Protocols of Session Guarantees in Distributed Mobile Systems*. PhD thesis, Institute of Computing Science, Poznan University of Technology, September 2005.

[TDP⁺94]   Douglas B. Terry, Alan J. Demers, Karin Petersen, Mike Spreitzer, Marvin Theimer, and Brent W. Welch. Session guarantees for weakly consistent replicated data. In *Proc. of the Third Int. Conf. on Parallel and Distributed Information Systems (PDIS 94)*, pages 140–149, Austin, USA, September 1994. IEEE Computer Society.

Intelligent Dependability Services for Overlay Networks

Barry Porter, Geoff Coulson, and Daniel Hughes

Computing Department, Lancaster University, Lancaster, UK
{barry.porter, geoff, hughesdr}@comp.lancs.ac.uk

Abstract. Application-level overlays have emerged as a useful means of offering network services that are not supported by the underlying physical network. Most overlays employ proprietary dependability mechanisms to render them more resilient to node failure; but the use of proprietary approaches leads to duplication of effort during development and adds design complexity. In this paper we propose *generic* dependability services which simplify the design of overlays. Our services are fully decentralized and are configurable to take advantage of current network conditions, which can enable us to make better repairs following failures.

1 Introduction

Overlay networks are application-level distributed systems, architecturally situated between the network (e.g. the IP layer) and the end-user application. They typically provide specialised virtual network topologies (e.g. trees or rings), or application-specific services (e.g. application-level multicast or ad-hoc routing) which are outside the scope of the underlying network. Their use is increasingly common and the types of overlays in use is increasingly diverse [1, 2, 3, 4, 5, 6].

As overlays become more widely deployed, their *dependability* becomes an ever more critical issue. In current practice, every overlay implements its own dependability mechanisms. For example, Chord [7] employs backup links and data replication, and Overcast [8] uses a specialised tree-repair strategy, both of which are intended to provide resilience in a single environment consisting of end-user hosts. In our present work, we seek to add dependability to overlay networks as a *generic service* which can operate in multiple environments including that of 'overlay deployment environments', which are becoming more common [9, 10, 11]. Our primary goal is to address fault tolerance issues in a systematic and re-usable manner, and thus to both simplify and enhance the design and deployment of dependable overlays. An associated, more general goal is to explore autonomic dependability in large scale overlay-based distributed systems, where self-configuring services can make intelligent decisions at runtime.

This paper presents an approach to providing generic dependability services to overlay networks, which can benefit from multiple configurations to intelligently provide redundancy and enact repairs in an overlay, taking into account the current environmental conditions in which the overlay is operating. In doing so,

F. Eliassen and A. Montresor (Eds.): DAIS 2006, LNCS 4025, pp. 199–212, 2006.

we argue that our services can improve the quality of repairs made to an overlay following failures, and present preliminary results in support of this.

The rest of this paper is organized as follows: In section 2 we examine several overlays and their proprietary fault-tolerance mechanisms. In section 3 we introduce our general approach to building dependability services, and in section 4 we present our initial results from evaluating our approach in an overlay deployment environment. Finally, section 5 discusses related work, and section 6 presents concluding remarks and aspirations for future work.

2   Analysis of Dependability in Overlay Networks

Our general observation is that while most overlays provide resilience in the face of node failure, the mechanisms used are targeted at a single environment, where each overlay node resides on an end-user host in an Internet-like environment. As a result, the approach taken by many overlays to repair themselves is to remove the failed nodes from the overlay and to attempt to continue to provide the same service without them. This causes a cumulative degradation of the overlay's functioning over repeated failures, as more nodes are lost. We also observe that the physical capabilities of an overlay's hosting nodes are typically not taken into account, which can further tend to degrade the functioning of the overlay. A final observation is that as overlays become more widely deployed and used in more demanding application areas, dependability becomes an increasingly pressing concern. For example, overlay dependability is crucial in Grid environments due to the large volumes of data that are typically handled [12].

To demonstrate that these limitations pervade a wide range of overlay types we now look in more detail at DHT overlays (in section 2.1), content dissemination overlays (in section 2.2) and flooding overlays (in section 2.3).

2.1   DHT Overlays

The general purpose of this class of overlay is to provide an efficient and scalable "key-based routing" facility in which a message can be routed in O(log N) hops (where N is the total number of nodes in the overlay) to a target node that is designated by a given key. In Chord [7], for example, all the nodes are organised as a logical ring. Chord nodes each maintain a so-called *finger list*—a list of increasingly distant nodes around the ring. This is used for O(log N) routing towards a target node. Chord nodes also store the IDs of their immediate "successor" and "predecessor" nodes in the ring so they can still make O(N) progress at times when the finger list is incomplete. One use of Chord is as a distributed data repository. In such an application, a data item which is submitted for storage in the repository is stored at the node whose ID is closest to a hash of the data. Pastry [1] works in a similar way to Chord, as does Tapestry [3], although the latter is organised as a mesh rather than a ring. Another popular DHT overlay, CAN [13], is organised such that nodes have zones of responsibility in a distributed coordinate space.

Despite their differences, all the above-mentioned overlays have a similar approach to dependability. In particular, when used as a data repository, they increase availability of the data by replicating data items on the n nodes whose ID is "closest" to the hash of a stored piece of data. The response to a node failure is to update the links in the routing tables of the affected nodes to reflect the change, and also to restore the number of replicants of data items stored at the failed node by copying them to further nodes.

The general disadvantage of this approach is that the self-repair algorithm permanently increases the load on the surviving nodes and reduces the total amount of redundancy in the overlay, as the same volume of data is redundantly stored at less hosts. We also observe that the physical resources of a node are generally not taken into account in DHT overlays; a node is given an ID and is expected to be able to store all data hashed to that ID. This expectation may be not be workable in a highly heterogeneous system that includes a significant number of poorly-resourced hosts.

2.2   Content Dissemination Overlays

Content dissemination overlays [14, 15, 4] deliver streaming content to multiple users in a scalable manner. They are typically organised as a tree with the sender at the root. Each non-root node receives data from its parent, and forwards it to each of its children using a point-to-point link.

TBCP [14] is a good representative of this class of overlay. TBCP builds a single rooted tree, and new nodes join the tree by first contacting the root node on a published or well-known address. The root node decides if it wants to accommodate the joining node as one of its direct children; if not, it forwards the join request to its most suitable child. This process recurses until the joining node finds a place in the tree. For performance reasons, TBCP attempts to build a tree that reflects the structure of the underlying IP network—i.e. the nodes contained in each sub-tree should tend to share IP-level locality. Decisions about whether to accept a node as a direct child or to pass it on are made on this basis. Another approach to maintaining a close correspondence between an overlay multicast tree and the underlying IP topology is to employ a network metric such as round trip time between nodes [4].

In terms of dependability, if a node fails, the default response in many such overlays is for all the nodes below the failure point to re-join via the root of the tree. The drawback of this is that the resultant bottleneck can cause traffic to be significantly disrupted during the (possibly extensive) re-building phase. One possible optimisation is to have each node record a "backup parent" [15]; but this also has complications: if the child of a failed node re-locates to a backup parent, it brings the entire sub-tree below it, which can result in a poorly balanced tree. Another approach is to simply assign the grandparent as the backup parent [8]. This keeps the tree balanced, but can increase the out-degree of the new parent, which may in the future place additional strain on that node potentially beyond its capacity [15]. The key points are that in each approach there is additional stress on some parts of the rest of the tree as a result of the failure, and that this is *cumulative* over multiple repairs.

In addition, when attaching a new node to an overlay, current schemes tend not to take into account the characteristics (e.g. in terms of processing power and link speed) of the underlying host machine: if a tree is built on top of hosts with greatly differing capabilities, it may not perform with adequate quality of service (QoS). In an extreme case, for example, if a low power PDA, or a PC with a dialup connection, is given many children it would have difficulty sending data out to all of these at a sufficient rate.

2.3   Flooding Overlays

This simple type of overlay is typically used to locate and acquire resources in a distributed environment. Messages are flooded to a (subset of a) node's neighbours, and the neighbours pass these messages onto *their* neighbours etc. This continues until either the target resource is located, the edge of the overlay is reached, or a maximum hop-count that messages are permitted to travel is reached. Unlike DHTs, queries in flooding overlays typically only reach a subset of the overlay's nodes (termed the "search horizon"), which means that there are no guarantees about locating resources that exist in the overlay.

Early flooding overlays such as Gnutella v0.4 [16] made no provision at all for dependability because it was assumed that resources would naturally be replicated over multiple nodes, and that flooding would likely locate a suitable copy. Version 0.6 of Gnutella, however, adds the notion of "super-peers" to the architecture in an attempt to enhance scalability. In v0.6, end-user computers are viewed as "leaf-peers" that do not directly engage in flooding. Instead, each leaf-peer attaches to a super-peer which manages a number of leaf-peers and maintains a list of resources held by these. This architecture reduces the number of nodes that engage in flooding and therefore increases the search horizon. As a side effect, however, it impacts dependability [17] in that the failure of a super-peer requires the leaf-peers it was supporting to locate another active super-peer. Furthermore, as the number of super-peers drops, the load on the remaining ones clearly increases, which tends toward the emergence of bottlenecks in the overlay.

3   Approach

3.1   Overview

Architecturally, we use a "Dependability Service" component, which can load and configure sub-services which address an area of dependability. An instance of the dependability service component and its sub-services resides alongside each overlay node, as shown in figure 1. Each service internally uses only 'soft state' (i.e. state that can be re-built from instantiation simply by existing in the environment), so that services are inherently self-repairing. Currently, our design uses three major sub-services: i) a *backup* service, ii) a *failure detection* service and iii) a *recovery* service.

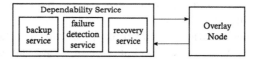

Fig. 1. The dependability services, horizontally composed with an overlay node

Before discussing each of these services, we first introduce the concept of `accessinfo` and `nodestate` records. In order to externally manage an overlay, we first elected to create a specification of what constitutes an overlay. Rather than providing fully transparent services, we are interested in taking the application-specific needs of each overlay into account, and in order to do this we needed to create a certain 'model' to which an overlay must conform.

Our overlay model has two basic 'types': `Accessinfo` records and `nodestate` records. An `accessinfo` record represents an overlay node's ID, or a neighbour link to another node in the overlay. Each overlay node will therefore have one `accessinfo` record giving its logical node ID, and a collection of records providing its list of neighbours. `Accessinfos` are expected to have 'context' (such as 'NodeID', 'child' or 'successor') included in them, though the internal structure of accessinfo records *is unknown to the services*, and entirely the decision of the overlay. They are named as such because they represent not only a way to store the structure of the overlay on a per-node basis, but they also allow service instances on neighbouring nodes to communicate with each other by passing to their overlay node an `accessinfo` record and a message to deliver to the service at the target node, thus exposing the structure of the overlay to the services.

`Nodestate` records represent any other state that is required by the overlay to be persistent across failures, such as resources in Chord or resource indices at Gnutella super-peers[1]. Again, their constitution is the choice of the overlay; our services simply know that they represent 'extra state' of a node that is not directly related to the overlay's core structure. We use both of these typed, 'black-box' objects to generalize overlays sufficiently for what we need to achieve, while still allowing significant room for specialization by overlays of their needs by filling in the black boxes in ways uniquely appropriate to them.

Our general approach to dependability centres on *decentralization, configurability* and *intelligent self-configuration*. We now discuss the three services mentioned above, outlining available configuration options in each.

3.2   Backup Service

The backup service is used to redundantly store `accessinfo` and `nodestate` records belonging to an overlay node in case that node fails. This data is stored on one or more appropriate backup hosts in the overlay (other than the host of

---

[1] Note overlays are not required to have `nodestate`; some overlays like simple multicast trees have only structural data, which is captured in full by `accessinfo` records.

the origin overlay node), and constitutes everything about a node that is needed to make repairs should it fail.

Our current implementation uses a simple 'push' variant where overlay nodes notify the backup service when neighbours or other overlay state is added or removed at that node. The local backup service at a node then transmits the collection of `accessinfo` and `nodestate` records to other nodes. In terms of configurability, the backup service can store more or less complete backup copies of each node on different hosts, providing a simple way to increase or decrease the amount of redundancy in the overlay.

In future work, we intend to make the backup service self-configuring, so that it can increase or reduce the amount of redundancy in the overlay according to observed regional stability of networks and hosts. Additionally, backups should ideally be stored at the most stable hosts in the overlay with the most free resources. We also seek to take advantage of the way our overlay model allows individual handling of `accessinfo` and `nodestate` records, such that we only alter existing backups to add new 'fragments' of data about a node instead of re-saving the full collection of these each time a change is made.

3.3   Failure Detection Service

The failure detection service is used to detect node failures in a decentralised manner. The service is currently implemented in the form of an overlay that is used to monitor the nodes of one or more "target" overlays that require dependability. Having detected a failed node, an instance of the failure detection service informs the recovery service instance(s) on the neighbour(s) of that failed node. A number of overlay types could be used for failure detection, with various protocols, but our current implementation makes use of gossip protocols [18].

Because distributed failure detection is already a well-researched area in its own right, we do not pursue this aspect of the dependability service in this paper.

3.4   Recovery Service

The general behaviour of a recovery service component is, on learning of the failure of a neighbouring node from the failure detection service, to create a strategy to repair the overlay. We currently use two different methods to achieve this; i) recovering failed nodes on alternative hosts, and ii) adapting the overlay to perform the same duties without the failed nodes.

When recovering failed nodes on alternative hosts, the service first discovers suitable hosts (i.e. with sufficient free resources), then instantiates new overlay nodes on those hosts, and injects backed up data into each, essentially re-creating each failed node. At nodes that neighboured these failed nodes, `accessinfo` records are manipulated by the service so that they point to the newly restored node(s). This is the most transparent method of repair, as the overlay structure does not change, but clearly requires the availability of suitable alternative hosts and the ability to locate them. We return to this issue in section 4.1.

When adapting the structure of the overlay to operate without the failed nodes, the service needs to know how to perform the adaptation; that is, what the structural and behavioural rules of the overlay are. We can use various levels of interaction with the overlay in order to acquire such information when a repair needs to be made, but we present the most generic approach here which requires least interaction with the overlay. It uses the observation that several types of overlay can be structurally repaired using the same procedure, by adding all outward-pointing 'perimeter' connections from the failed section of overlay (i.e. neighbour links from failed nodes to neighbouring live ones) to one selected live neighbour of the failed section, and adjusting connections at all other live neighbours of the failed section to point to that same selected neighbour. Any recovered `nodestate` is also inserted into the selected node.

Using either of the above repair 'styles', or a combination of both, it is necessary to select a *coordinator* to actually carry out the repair. To do this, the nodes neighbouring (or 'bordering') a failed node or failed section of overlay discover each other by locating the backup of a failed neighbour, extracting its neighbours, and testing each for failure, then recursing the procedure, until each link terminates (transitively) in a node reported to be alive. These nodes then communicate with each other, using an agreement algorithm to select one of them as the repair coordinator. We do not have space to present the algorithm in detail here, but interested readers are referred to [19]. Briefly, its properties include that only the nodes bordering a failed section (or single failed node) of overlay are involved in its repair, limiting the effort of repair to the affected area of overlay. This is because recovery service instances are initially only concerned with the failure of their direct neighbours, expanding their area of concern as they discover additional connected failed nodes. The algorithm is resilient to further node failures while repairs are taking place, and is also able to select the repair coordinator based on dynamically-acquired data at the time of the failure, such as free resources on each border node and their network latencies.

4   Evaluation

4.1   Gridkit: Overlays as Part of Middleware Services

The environment on which we focus for our evaluation is an overlay deployment environment called Gridkit [10], which is a middleware service supporting communication-based Grid systems in diverse networks. Gridkit and its overlay networks are constructed from software *components*, and overlay networks are used as a substrate for 'interaction types' requested by an application (e.g. multicast, publish-subscribe), operating in a heterogeneous Grid-like environment. The architecture of overlay nodes is specified into a *control*, *state* and *forwarder* component, allowing overlays to be composed in a 'stack' to provide advanced services (a typical example is using Scribe [2] atop Pastry for publish-subscribe style communication), where messages travel up and down the stack (e.g. between forwarder components). More details on Gridkit are available in the literature [10].

For our dependability services, we are particularly interested in two aspects of the environment that Gridkit operates in; its *heterogeneity*, where hosts of massively variable capabilities are connected together in a suitable overlay, and its *altruistic* nature. This latter aspect can be harnessed by Gridkit's *resource discovery* framework, a service capable of discovering Gridkit-enabled hosts in the network with specified types and levels of resources.

When our recovery service is used in such an environment, it can *switch* between the structural adaptation and node restoration repair styles as available Gridkit hosts and resources dictate. This is a powerful ability, meaning that the overlay may not need to 'degrade' at all following a failure, as failed nodes can be restored on alternative Gridkit hosts, maintaining (if possible) a constant node (and host) population through failures. If suitable hosts are *not* available, the recovery service can simply employ structural adaptation to repair the overlay as normal.

We now present results from a Gridkit-like environment which show how this kind of intelligent, configurable repair can be beneficial in practice. We employ the following criteria in evaluating the dependability service:

- *ongoing memory use* refers to the average ongoing memory load on the hosts used by the overlay;
- *average request handling load* refers to the average number of user requests handled by a host per second;
- *average recovery time* refers to the time taken to recover failed node from the time of detection of the failure;
- *messaging overhead* refers to the total amount of maintenance-related overlay traffic per unit time.

In the following, we first, in section 4.2 present a detailed quantitative analysis of the dependability service in comparison to the proprietary dependability mechanisms supported by the Chord DHT. Then, in section 4.3, we offer a more general qualitative analysis.

4.2   Comparison with Chord's Dependability Mechanisms

To perform this evaluation, we developed Java software that emulates a set of hosts as operating system processes and inter-host links as IPC calls. We then ported the backup and recovery services (using only the node restoration repair style) to this environment. Failures are simulated in terms of a script and notified to overlay nodes running on the simulated hosts as if by the failure detection service. On top of this, we developed two Chord implementations: one is standard Chord [7], and the other is a modified Chord that replaces Chord's proprietary dependability mechanisms with our dependability APIs.

Our experimental Chord configurations employed a successor list size of 2, and an identifier space size of 8. We used ring sizes of 12 nodes, but included 17 'Gridkit' hosts, each of which was capable of hosting an arbitrary number of nodes; initially 12 hosts supported a single node each, and the others were idle[2]. The rings were used to store a set of 60 different data files. Each of these, which were of identical size, was hashed to a key and stored on the node closest to that key. Although the assignment of files to nodes was 'random', the same assignment was used for each experimental run. Each node duplicated its state on one additional node—in the standard Chord case, through replication; in the modified Chord case, via the backup service. In each run of the experiment, we observed the effects of failing 7 hosts, one every 10 seconds. This resulted in the standard Chord version being left with 5 nodes at the end of the run, and the modified version being left with 12 (as the 7 failed nodes were recovered by the dependability service). The file data was injected into the ring at time T+20, and the first failure occurred at T+42. All the results presented below are averaged over all hosts used by the overlay in question (n.b. obviously by the end of the standard Chord runs there were only 5 hosts in use; whereas there were 10 by the end of the modified Chord runs).

In terms of *ongoing memory use*, figure 2 (a) shows the average memory load on the overlay's hosts. It can be seen that, in the case of standard Chord, the load increases steadily from the time of the first host failure (at time T+42). However, in the case of modified Chord, because the total load is spread over more available hosts, the average load is much smaller. Note that the slight increases at times 68 and 91 are due to the fact that a host is from that point supporting 2 nodes (as mentioned, there are 12 nodes but only 10 hosts in use at the end of the run). Note also that between times 26 and 42 (which is a failure free period) modified Chord consumes slightly *more* memory than standard Chord. This is due to the overhead of storing backups in a generic fashion. In conclusion, this experiment confirms that modified Chord in the face of node failure can spread the load over a wider range of hosts than standard Chord and thus reduces host memory overload and consequent service degradation.

We evaluated *average request handling load* by counting the number of requests arriving in each second at each host. A single designated node generated requests for a random selection of 15 of the 60 files stored in the ring at a rate of 15 requests per second. Figure 2 (b) shows that the average request handling load is similar for the two cases until T+42, when the first host failure occurs. From this point onward, in the case of standard Chord, a constant number of requests is being handled by a shrinking number of hosts—therefore the request handling load steadily climbs. In the case of modified Chord, however, the number of hosts stays around the same so that the request handling load is roughly constant (again the slight increase is due to two hosts supporting two nodes). In conclusion, this experiment confirms that our approach can maintain the request handling patterns of the original ring topology across node failures, and therefore reduce bottlenecks. Note, incidentally, that request handling load does *not* translate directly to average request latency, because network latency must also be taken into account in this. In fact, standard Chord will tend to a *lower* average network latency as failures occur, simply because there are fewer nodes

---

[2] The nature of our criteria is independent of the size of the Chord ring involved, so there is no loss of generality in using such a "small" ring.

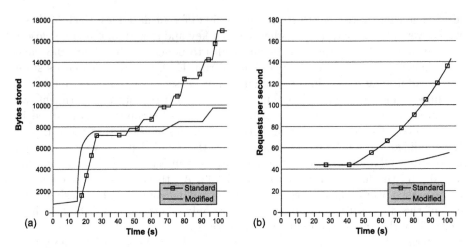

Fig. 2. Average memory load (a) and requests per second (b) at hosts used by the overlay

left in the ring. However, our approach will increasingly "win" as the ring becomes more loaded with data—as this happens, the per-host request handling load will progressively overshadow the effects of network latency.

We evaluated *average recovery time* in modified Chord simply by measuring the average latency between failure detection and recovery completion. This was measured as 179ms. In standard Chord, of course, nodes are not recovered: instead the predecessor of the failed node simply re-designates the failed node's successor as its successor; therefore recovery time is negligible. Thus the standard Chord time is close to 0ms. Essentially, we are paying "up front" for later payoffs in terms of improved memory use and reduced request handling load. This tradeoff is increasingly in our favour as more failures occur—recovery time in our approach is constant (and quite small) for each failure, while the degradation caused by compensating for the loss of a node in standard Chord is cumulative as failures increase.

Finally, we measured overlay *messaging overhead* in terms of the numbers of overlay maintenance-related messages. More specifically, we totalled the byte count of these per second and divided by the number of hosts involved. The results are shown in figure 3. It can be seen that there is a small start-up cost incurred by modified Chord between time 0 and the time of the data injection (at T+20). This is due to backups being taken as the ring is built; it tails off as the ring stabilises. Following data injection, both cases suffer a spike; this is larger in the case of modified Chord, again due to the overhead of creating generic backups. Subsequently, however, modified Chord fares slightly better than standard Chord—except transiently when failures occur. The reason for the higher ambient overhead of standard Chord is the need to continuously maintain the successor list; modified Chord does not have this requirement, although it does need to

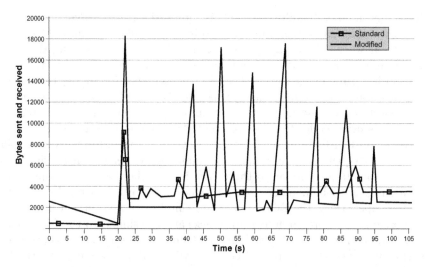

Fig. 3. Average number of overlay maintenance-related bytes per second per host

maintain the Chord finger table as this is an inherent part of the operation of the overlay. In conclusion, the recovery "spikes" are traded off for a generally improved level of service in terms of messaging overhead. As above, the overhead is transient while the adverse effects of *not* restoring nodes is permanent and cumulative.

To summarise, repeated failures in Chord using its proprietary dependability approach lead to reduced overall redundancy in the overlay, and more stress being put on other nodes in the long term to compensate for the failures. By restoring failed nodes in Gridkit where possible, we maintain the structure and integrity of the overlay across failures, and the benefit of this grows progressively with the amount of data stored in the ring and number of node failures.

4.3 Qualitative Evaluation

We now extrapolate from the DHT-specific arguments above to the other overlay classes mentioned in section 2.

First, consider content dissemination overlays such as TBCP. In such overlays, the ongoing memory use and request handling load criteria are not applicable as the purpose of the overlay is simply to forward "live" data. The main difference relates to the average recovery time criterion. There are basically two cases depending on the tree repair strategy used. First, consider the "rejoin at root" strategy (see section 2.2). Here, the node restoration approach avoids two pathologies: i) overloading of the (bottleneck) root node; and ii) long outages in cases where the failed node has many descendents. Second, consider the "backup parent" strategy. Here, our approach can avoid the pathology of structural degradation. In particular, it avoids stressing the backup parent which might have to deal with a larger number of children than it is equipped for; and it avoids situations in which the tree may become unbalanced if a large subtree is moved from one branch to another. These pathologies can be avoided by recovering the failed node on an alternative host and re-integrating it into the overlay in the same logical position, removing the need for any re-configuration of the tree. There is a trade-off involved in all of these situations. For simple cases (e.g. where the failed node has few descendents), the proprietary methods may be faster; the benefit of restoring nodes becomes particularly apparent in large trees.

Second, consider flooding overlays such as Gnutella v0.6. In terms of ongoing memory use, request handling load, and maintenance-related messaging overhead, the benefits are similar to those seen in the Chord case—as super-peers fail, rather than their memory use and request handling load burdening other surviving super-peers, the failed nodes are simply restored on alternate hosts when possible. The corresponding drawbacks are also similar to the Chord case. The main difference between the Chord and Gnutella cases is in terms of recovery time (for super-peers). In standard Gnutella v0.6, leaf nodes that were attached to a failed super-peer must locate an alternative super-peer, which may in some cases require the intervention of the user. In a dependability service enhanced Gnutella, however, leaf nodes would be automatically informed of the location of the recovered super-peer.

5   Related Work

Classic work on fault-tolerance services for distributed applications has focused on management 'frameworks' [20, 21]; these often have hierarchical arrangements with various dedicated 'managers' (usually replicated for fault-tolerance) to recover from failures. In contrast, we seek to develop entirely *decentralized* services which are horizontally composed with the application, affording us scalability and enhanced service resilience, and removing reliance on administrated infrastructure to host our services.

The Resilient Overlay Network project [22] highlights the usefulness of overlays to improve levels of service beyond those of the physical network, but RON is aimed at providing dependable communications over the Internet using an overlay and does not address the failure of overlay nodes themselves. While our approach can also be used to provide dependable communications by introducing dependability to a target overlay network, it is more general and focuses not only on the overlay surviving, but also on any data in the overlay being persistent.

There are some overlays such as Narada [23], and some simple flooding overlays (e.g. Gnutella v0.4), that employ dependability mechanisms which do not degrade over multiple recovery operations, and which do take account of host resources. However, the number of such overlays is sufficiently small that our approach is still very widely applicable; moreover the overlay-specific dependability techniques of these overlays are generally not suitable for overlays of different types. We are not aware of any work except ours that is aimed specifically at making overlays themselves dependable in a generic way.

Finally, our work is related to general trends in autonomic computing research [24] in that it is decentralized, using relatively lightweight components distributed throughout an overlay to monitor and manage it, and our services are self-configuring.

6 Conclusions

The heart of our proposal is to offer dependability to overlays in the form of generic services, which intelligently configure as appropriate to an overlay's environment. We have presented an example using an overlay deployment environment, where intelligent selection of a repair strategy can improve the performance of an overlay following multiple failures. The generalization and extension of existing overlay dependability mechanisms as external services allows commonly applicable standards of fault-tolerance across a wide range of overlays, and we have shown that the price of such genericity is not prohibitively high.

We currently have implemented both node restoration and structural adaptation repair styles in our recovery service, and have basic implementations of our failure detection and backup services.

In our future work, we intend to bring similar intelligence to our backup service, taking advantage of our overlay model to store only changes to an overlay node's `accessinfo` or `nodestate` records, and storing backups at the most suitable (i.e. highly resourced and stable) nodes, as well as varying the amount of redundancy used depending on the relative stability of the overlay.

We are also interested in helping to deal with network heterogeneity; as we discussed in section 2, many of today's overlays are not good at distributing load according to the resources of their members' hosts, and we believe that an additional service can address this issue by re-distributing load appropriately.

References

1. Rowstron, A., Druschel, P.: Pastry: Scalable, decentralized object location, and routing for large-scale peer-to-peer systems. Lecture Notes in Computer Science **2218** (2001) 329
2. Castro, M., Druschel, P., Kermarrec, A.M., Rowstron, A.: SCRIBE: A large-scale and decentralized application-level multicast infrastructure. IEEE Journal on Selected Areas in communications (JSAC) (2002)
3. Zhao, B.Y., Kubiatowicz, J.D., Joseph, A.D.: Tapestry: An infrastructure for fault-tolerant wide-area location and routing. Technical Report UCB/CSD-01-1141, UC Berkeley (2001)
4. Pendarakis, D., Shi, S., Verma, D., Waldvogel, M.: ALMI: An application level multicast infrastructure. In: 3rd USNIX Symposium on Internet Technologies and Systems (USITS '01), San Francisco, CA, USA (2001) 49–60
5. Chawathe, Y., McCanne, S., Brewer, E.A.: RMX: Reliable multicast for heterogeneous networks. In: INFOCOM, Tel Aviv, Israel, IEEE (2000) 795–804
6. Clarke, I., Sandberg, O., Wiley, B., Hong, T.W.: Freenet: A distributed anonymous information storage and retrieval system. Lecture Notes in Computer Science **2009** (2001) 46

B. Porter, G. Coulson, and D. Hughes

7. Stoica, I., Morris, R., Karger, D., Kaashoek, M.F., Balakrishnan, H.: Chord: A scalable peer-to-peer lookup service for internet applications. In: Proceedings of the 2001 conference on applications, technologies, architectures, and protocols for computer communications, ACM Press (2001) 149–160
8. Jannotti, J., Gifford, D.K., Johnson, K.L., Kaashoek, M.F., O'Toole, Jr., J.W.: Overcast: Reliable multicasting with an overlay network. In: Proceedings of the Fourth Symposium on Operating System Design and Implementation (OSDI). (2000) 197–212
9. Touch, J.: Dynamic internet overlay deployment and management using the x-bone. In: ICNP '00: Proceedings of the 2000 International Conference on Network Protocols, Washington, DC, USA, IEEE Computer Society (2000) 59
10. Grace, P., Coulson, G., Blair, G., Mathy, L., Yeung, W.K., Cai, W., Duce, D., Cooper, C.: GRIDKIT: Pluggable overlay networks for grid computing. In: DOA '04: Proceedings of Distributed Objects and Applications, Cyprus (2004)
11. Li, B., Guo, J., Wang, M.: iOverlay: A lightweight middleware infrastructure for overlay application implementations. In: Proceedings of IFIP/ACM/USENIX Middleware, Toronto, Canada (2004)
12. Pallickara, S., Fox, G.: NaradaBrokering: A distributed middleware framework and architecture for enabling durable peer-to-peer grids. In: Middleware. (2003) 41–61
13. Ratnasamy, S., Francis, P., Handley, M., Karp, R., Shenker, S.: A scalable content addressable network. Technical Report TR-00-010, UC Berkeley, Berkeley, CA (2000)
14. Mathy, L., Canonico, R., Hutchison, D.: An overlay tree building control protocol. Lecture Notes in Computer Science **2233** (2001) 76
15. Yang, M., Fei, Z.: A proactive approach to reconstructing overlay multicast trees. In: IEEE INFOCOM, Hong Kong (2004)
16. URL: http://rfc-gnutella.sourceforge.net/developer/stable/index.html (2000)
17. Yang, B., Garcia-Molina, H.: Designing a super-peer network. In: Proceedings of the 19th International Conference on Data Engineering, Bangalore, India (2003)
18. Renesse, R.V., Minsky, Y., Hayden, M.: A gossip-style failure detection service. Technical Report TR98-1687, Cornell University (1998)
19. Porter, B., Taïani, F., Coulson, G.: Generalizing repair for overlay networks. Technical Report PTC–06–01, Lancaster University (2006)
20. Marzullo, K., Cooper, R., Wood, M.D., Birman, K.P.: Tools for distributed application management. IEEE Computer **24:8** (1991) 42–51
21. Bagchi, S., Whisnant, K., Kalbarczyk, Z., Iyer, R.K.: The chameleon infrastructure for adaptive, software implemented fault tolerance. In: Symposium on Reliable Distributed Systems. (1998) 261–267
22. Andersen, D.G., Balakrishnan, H., Kaashoek, M.F., Morris, R.: Resilient overlay networks. In: Symposium on Operating Systems Principles. (2001) 131–145
23. Chu, Y.H., Rao, S.G., Zhang, H.: A case for end system multicast. In: Measurement and Modeling of Computer Systems. (2000) 1–12
24. Ganek, A., Corbi, T.: The dawning of the autonomic computing era. IBM Systems Journal **42:1** (2003) 5–19

Model-Driven Development of Context-Aware Services

João Paulo A. Almeida[1,2], Maria-Eugenia Iacob[1], Henk Jonkers[1], and Dick Quartel[2]

[1] Telematica Instituut, P.O. Box 589, 7500 AN Enschede, The Netherlands
{JoaoPaulo.Almeida, Maria-Eugenia.Iacob, Henk.Jonkers} @telin.nl
[2] Centre for Telematics and Information Technology, University of Twente,
P.O. Box 217, 7500 AE, Enschede, The Netherlands
quartel@cs.utwente.nl

Abstract. In this paper, we define a model-driven design trajectory for context-aware services consisting of three levels of models with different degrees of abstraction and platform independence. The models at the highest level of platform independence describe the behaviour of a context-aware service and its environment from an integrated perspective. The models at the intermediate level describe abstract components, which realize the context-aware service in terms of a service-oriented abstract platform. At the lowest level, the realization of a context-aware service is described in terms of specific target technologies, such as Web Services, BPEL and Parlay technologies. Our approach allows service designers to concentrate their efforts on the services they intend to create and offer, by facilitating the handling of context information and automating design steps through model transformation. In addition, our approach enables the reuse of platform-independent models for different target platforms.

1 Introduction

The last few decades have led to an explosion of different means of communication and the availability of ubiquitous (mobile) computing devices and sensors. This combination has enabled the creation of mobile context-aware services, which sense the users' environment to provide relevant functionality to their users. The design and provisioning of such mobile context-aware services is a challenging task, which has justified the development of novel methods, abstractions and infrastructures for the development of such services (e.g., [7, 8, 11, 20]). In addition, the complexity, diversity and fast-changing nature of enabling technology platforms require design approaches that shield designers and providers from platform-specific details allowing them to concentrate their efforts on the services they intend to create and offer. These factors have led us to propose the model-driven design trajectory addressed in this paper.

Our model-driven design approach has three main objectives: (1) to facilitate service design by providing abstractions for context-aware service specification; (2) to improve the reusability of service specifications and designs, by promoting independence from specific technology platforms; and (3) to improve the overall efficiency of the service design process, by promoting the automation of design steps

F. Eliassen and A. Montresor (Eds.): DAIS 2006, LNCS 4025, pp. 213–227, 2006.

by model transformations. The target platforms we consider include middleware platforms and a part of the mobile telecommunications infrastructure, which is used to send messages to mobile terminal users, to establish calls, and to determine the current location and availability (or presence) of mobile terminal users.

We define three levels of models with different degrees of abstraction and platform independence. The models at the highest level of platform independence describe the behaviour of a context-aware service and its environment from an integrated perspective. This level abstracts from the way context information is obtained, focusing on context-aware behaviour. The models at the intermediate level describe abstract components, which realize the context-aware service in terms of a service-oriented abstract platform. This abstract platform is denoted as the A-MUSE Service Platform (in the Freeband A-MUSE project [12]). The A-MUSE Service Platform provides an abstraction of middleware and service discovery platforms and includes context and action services that are provided by telecom platforms such as Parlay [29]. In addition, this abstract platform supports service discovery with dynamic service properties, which allows one to discover services based on context information. At the platform-specific level, the realization of a context-aware service is described in terms of specific target technologies, such as Web Services, BPEL and Parlay technologies.

The paper is organised as follows. Section 2 sets the theoretical background for our method. A number of concepts such as platform independence and abstract platform are discussed here. Section 3 presents an overview of the different levels of models, abstract platforms and model transformations that play an essential role in the design trajectory. Section 4 discusses the specification of services at the highest level of platform independence in further detail. Section 5 discusses the design of services at the intermediate level of platform independence, and defines the A-MUSE Service Platform. Section 6 describes a model transformation that derives a platform-independent service design from a service specification. Finally, Section 7 summarises our results and indicate future research. The approach is illustrated in this paper with a running example: the Telemonitoring service.

2 Model-Driven Development

In most traditional development practices, the ultimate product of the design process is "the realization", deployed on available realization platforms. In several model-driven approaches, however, intermediate models are reusable and are considered final products of the design process. These models are carefully defined so as to abstract from details in platform technologies, and are therefore called *platform-independent models* (PIMs), in line with OMG's Model-Driven Architecture (MDA) [18, 22, 28]. PIMs can be defined with different degrees of platform independence, with respect to the extent to which these models constrain the selection of a target platform. For this reason, we organize the various models of an application into different *levels of platform independence* [3].

The concept of *abstract platform* [3, 4] is an important architectural concept of our approach to model-driven design. An abstract platform is an abstraction of infrastructure characteristics assumed to exist in the construction of platform-independent models of an application at some point in the design process.

An abstract platform defines an acceptable or, to some extent, ideal platform from an application developer's point of view. The characteristics of an abstract platform must have proper mappings onto the set of (concrete) target platforms that are considered for a design. In this way, the notion of abstract platform allows a designer to explicitly define levels of platform independence.

We follow a design process [5, 13] that covers two main phases: the *preparation phase* and the *service creation phase*, both briefly described below.

In the *preparation phase*, experts identify (and, when necessary, define) the required levels of models, their abstract platforms and the modelling language(s) to be used. In addition, during the preparation phase an expert may identify or define (automated) transformations between related levels of models. Since the design trajectory is effectively defined in this phase, it requires careful consideration of application domain requirements, target platform characteristics and design goals.

The results of the preparation phase are used in the service creation phase, as illustrated schematically in Fig. 1.

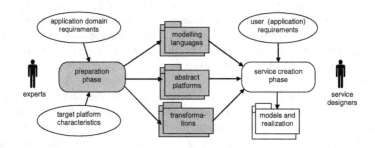

Fig. 1. The preparation phase and its results

The design process described in [5, 13] is neutral with respect to specific application domains and target platforms. In this paper, however, we consider the specific case of context-aware services, which are ultimately deployed on top of a (telecommunications) services infrastructure and middleware platforms. In this case, our objective in the preparation phase is to capture design knowledge that is applicable to a large number of different context-aware services and that can be later reused in the service creation phase in the design of a specific service, which addresses specific service requirements. This includes knowledge on how to cope with distribution in the middleware platforms targeted, but also includes knowledge on how context information is handled in the target context-aware services infrastructure.

The *service creation phase* entails the creation of models of a specific service using specific modelling languages and abstract platforms and applying (manual and automated) transformations to models. The service creation phase leads ultimately to a realization (or alternative realizations) of the service that satisfies user requirements, while capturing reusable platform-independent models of the service design. This phase also entails analysis, testing and validation of models and realizations. For an extensive presentation of the methodological support for both the preparation and service creation phase we refer to [5].

3 Design Trajectory Overview

This section explores the main activities and deliverables of the preparation phase in the design trajectory for context-aware services. We first consider a generic decomposition (architecture) of a context service. Based on this decomposition, we identify the characteristics of the A-MUSE Service Platform, and derive the necessary levels of models to be used in the service creation phase.

3.1 Context-Aware Services and the A-MUSE Service Platform

Context-awareness refers to the capabilities of applications to provide relevant services to their users by sensing and exploring the users' context [7, 11, 20]. *Context* is defined as a "collection of interrelated conditions in which something exists or occurs" [11]. The users' context often consists of a collection of conditions, such as, e.g., the users' location, environmental aspects (temperature, light intensity, etc.) and activities [8]. The users' context may change dynamically, and, therefore, a basic requirement for a context-aware system is its ability to sense context and to react to context changes (without intervention of the user). Changes in context can be considered external stimuli, namely *events*, which require a (re)*action* from the context-aware system.

A decomposition of a context-aware service reveals the architecture shown in Fig. 2. This architecture consists of *context sources*, which are able to sense context and represent it as context information in the scope of the system. The service provided by context sources is used by a *coordination component*, which requests actions to be executed by *action providers* depending on situations that can be inferred from context information. For example, two users may require a service to establish a call between them when they are located within a certain range of each other. An example of an action provider suitable for this service is a Parlay gateway [29], which can be requested to establish a telephone call between two users. Each user accesses the service through a user component, which provides the user interface and interacts with the *coordination component*.

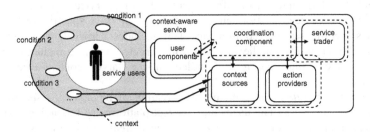

Fig. 2. Decomposition of a context-aware service

The user components and the coordination component exhibit service-specific behaviour, and are called service components. In contrast, context sources and action providers are general-purpose and, therefore, can be reused in several different context-aware services. For this reason, we consider context sources and action providers as part of the *A-MUSE Service Platform* (see elements encircled with dashed lines in Fig. 2). This platform also supports the interaction between the *user components* and the *coordination component* and the interactions between the coordination component and context sources and action providers. The service provided by context sources and action providers to the coordination component is registered in a *service trader*. This allows the coordination component to select context sources and action providers dynamically according to service offers that are registered in the service trader. Service offers have properties that can be used to select a particular service offer. For example, an action provider can be selected according to its geographical proximity to a user.

3.2 Levels of Models for Context-Aware Services Development

We define the scope of the design trajectory to include the design activities from the specification of a service at a high-level of abstraction to the realization of this service. Given this scope, one extreme approach to organizing the design trajectory would be to have one level of service specification and one level of service realization and one transformation that relates these two levels. However, the gap between these two levels of models may be very large. This means that a lot of effort should be invested in defining the transformation. This effort is rendered useless when changes in the target platform invalidate the transformation. Therefore, the opportunities for reuse can be increased if an intermediate level of models is introduced. This level of models uses an abstract platform to achieve platform independence, and, hence, models at this level can be reused for different target platforms. The organization of the design trajectory is depicted in Fig. 3. The three levels of models we have identified are:

Service specification level. This level of models describes the behaviour of a context-aware service from an external perspective. At this level, we do not distinguish the environment (including service users) and the service provider. The concept of action is used to model both the occurrence of events originated from context sources and the execution of actions. This allows modelling context-aware behaviour at a high-level of abstraction. At this level of abstraction, the service specifier ignores how context information is obtained from context sources. Services are described in a domain-specific language called Events-Conditions-Actions Domain Language (ECA-DL).

Platform-independent service design level. This level of models describes the behaviour of a context-aware service from an internal perspective, revealing a service-specific coordination component and the A-MUSE Service Platform. The A-MUSE Service Platform is the result of the composition of: a Service-Oriented-Architecture (SOA) abstract platform, which uses abstract interactions [2] to support the communication of application parts in this design; a service discovery platform which consists of a service trader; and general-purpose context and action services. This level of models reveals how context and action services are registered, searched for, and used by coordination components. The transformation denoted with T_1 in Fig. 3 introduces the coordination component so that the behaviour of the composition of the coordination component and the A-MUSE Service Platform performs the service specified at the service specification level.

Platform-specific service design level. This level of models describes the realization of the service for particular platforms. The flexibility of the relation between the platform-independent service design level and the platform-specific service design level allows different middleware platforms to be used. Model transformations can be used to create models at this level. For example, one could use them to generate the BPEL specification of the context-aware service that orchestrates (using a BPEL engine and SOAP [30]) web services (e.g. Parlay-X services [29]) for which WSDL interfaces [31] are provided. This transformation is illustrated in Fig. 3 denoted by T_2. In this figure, T_3 denotes a transformation to CORBA and Parlay.

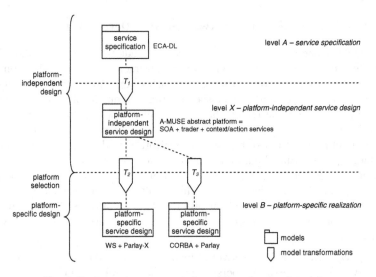

Fig. 3. Design trajectory consisting of three levels of models

4   Service Specification Level

At the level of service specification a context-aware service can be described in terms of *events*, which represent contextual changes, *queries* to context sources, and *actions*, which represent actions to be performed in order to provide the service to the user. We defined this level through a domain-specific language for the domain of context-aware services specification. We specialize elements of a general-purpose design language, namely the Interaction System Design Language (ISDL) [15, 26, 27], thus defining a dialect of it, which we call Events-Conditions-Actions Domain Language (ECA-DL). This language provides a means to specify behaviours in terms of actions and causality relations between these actions. The specialization consists of defining

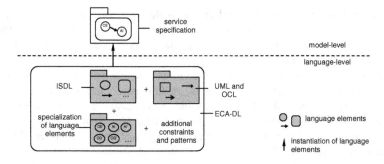

Fig. 4. Definition of the ECA-DL language for context-aware service specification

special types of actions, namely, context events (CE), context query requests (CQ), context query responses (CQ') and action invocation requests (AI) and action invocation responses (AI'). Context query requests and context query responses are always related by causality, forming a pattern. The definition of the ECA-DL is illustrated schematically in Fig. 4 (complete meta-models for ECA-DL in OMG's Meta-Object Facility (MOF) are described in [6]).

In order to illustrate the usage of the proposed language and approach, we consider the design of a "Telemonitoring service" for epilepsy patients [17]. The service assumes the availability of sensor technology that enables a wearable 24-hour seizure monitoring system. A couple of minutes before the onset of a seizure, the monitoring system detects its signs. The patient is warned of an imminent seizure and based on location information a voluntary aid person (e.g., spouse) or a health team can be dispatched for assistance.

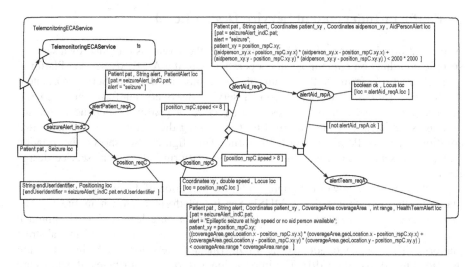

Fig. 5. The Telemonitoring service specification (exported from Grizzle [14] ISDL tool)

The Telemonitoring service specification is depicted in Fig. 5. Ovals represent specialized actions (with a naming convention with suffixes). Arrows indicate enabling relations between actions; white diamonds represent choice and white squares denote disjunction.

A simple naming convention has been used to indicate the type of action: suffix _indC denotes context events; suffixes _reqC and _rspC denote context query requests and context query responses; and suffixes _reqA and _rspA denote action invocation requests and action invocation responses. The event seizureAlert_indC represents that an (imminent) epileptic seizure has been detected in a patient being monitored. The action alertPatient_reqA requests the patient to be informed about the seizure. Following a seizure alert, the patient's current location and speed is requested (position_reqC followed by position_rspC). An aid person within range of the patient is informed of the seizure and the current location of the patient (alertAid_reqA). When no aid persons are available or the speed of the patient exceeds a certain value (which could indicate a hazardous situation) a health team capable of handling epileptic seizures is dispatched to the location of the patient. The Grizzle ISDL tool [14] is used for model editing and simulation of service specifications.

ISDL allows designers to use a modelling language of their choice to define the attributes of actions and constraints on these attributes. For ECA-DL, we have chosen to use UML class diagrams [25] for the (context) information attributes. Further, we use a subset of the Object Constraint Language (OCL) [24] to express constraints on information attributes. Constraints on information attributes serve to specify context-dependent conditions and action results, and can also be used to specify required *properties* of action services. This is illustrated in the constraints of action alertAid_reqA in Fig. 5: only an aid person within range of the patient is informed of the seizure.

5 Platform-Independent Service Design Level

At the platform-independent service design level, the service is provided by a service-specific coordination component in cooperation with the A-MUSE Service Platform. This abstract platform is the result of the composition of: a Service-Oriented-Architecture (SOA) abstract platform; a service discovery platform; and general-purpose context and action services. The structure of platform-independent service designs is depicted schematically in Fig. 6, revealing the hierarchy of elements that constitute the A-MUSE Abstract Platform. This figure also shows the relation between the service specification level and the platform-independent service design level.

A schematic overview of the approach for the definition of the hierarchy of abstract platforms that constitutes the A-MUSE Service Platform is shown in Fig. 7. The *service-oriented abstract platform* is defined using a pure language-level approach [4], i.e., the modelling language used defines the characteristics of the abstract platform. The language adopted is ISDL (meta-models for ISDL in MOF are described in [6], based on [9]). The information and location attributes of actions are described with UML. Constraints on these attributes are described with OCL. Since

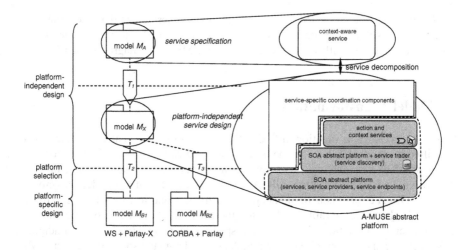

Fig. 6. Abstract platforms at the platform-independent service design level

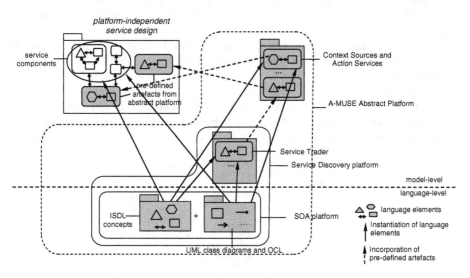

Fig. 7. Defining the hierarchy of abstract platforms definition

this level defines a composition of various (potentially distributed) components, which operates through services, it is necessary to describe the interactions between components. This is done with abstract interactions, which can be represented in ISDL ([2] discusses how these abstract interactions can be realized on different middleware platforms). The *service discovery abstract platform* is built on top of the underlying service-oriented abstract platform and is defined with a model-level approach, i.e., with the definition of reusable modelling artefacts. This abstract platform consists of a service trader component, defined in ISDL. On top of that, context and action services are defined, completing the A-MUSE Service Platform.

We omit any detailed ISDL descriptions of the service trader and context and action services due to space limitations. We refer the reader to [6] for the complete ISDL specifications with OCL constraints and UML class diagrams for information attributes.

6 Model Transformation

Given a service specification in ECA-DL, a platform-independent service design, specified in standard ISDL, can be derived automatically using model transformation. As a proof of concept, we have implemented this transformation using the Graph Rewriting And Transformation (GReAT) software developed at Vanderbilt University [1, 18]. GReAT has been implemented within the Generic Modelling Environment (GME) [19], a configurable toolset for the creation of domain-specific modelling environments. An editor for a domain-specific language (called a 'paradigm' in GME) can be created based on a metamodel of the language specified in MetaGME, a graphical UML-like metamodelling language (which in itself has been defined as a GME paradigm) [18]. One of the main drawbacks of the GME is its use of proprietary formats for metamodelling and model exchange, rather than conforming to standards such as MOF and XMI.

In GReAT, model transformations are specified using a graphical graph transformation language called UML Model Transformer (UMT), which has also been defined as a GME paradigm. The transformation specification makes use of metamodels of the source and destination languages defined in MetaGME. For our example, we have defined metamodels for ECA-DL (source) and ISDL (target), and a UMT specification to derive a platform-independent service design from a service specification. Fig. 8 illustrates this.

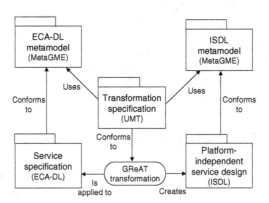

Fig. 8. Overview of the transformation approach

One of the central concepts of the GReAT model transformation approach is the substitution of graph patterns, which provides an intuitive way to express the types of transformations that we want to perform here. Fig. 9 shows an example of a UMT

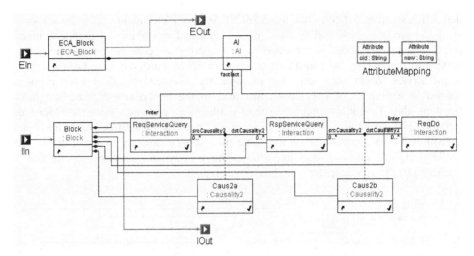

Fig. 9. Example of a UMT transformation rule

transformation rule, which for each ECA-DL action of type AI (action invocation request), creates a sequence of three interactions in the ISDL design. These are interactions between the coordination service component and the A-MUSE abstract platform.

The interactions realize the abstract action, involving a request to the service trader, a response from the service trader and the invocation of the appropriate action service according to the response issued by the service trader. Similarly, rules have been defined for the other ECA-DL action types, as well as rules to derive the relations between actions and rules concerning the action attributes. Fig. 10 shows the effect of this rule in an informal way.

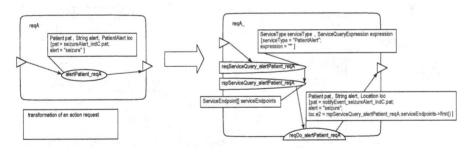

Fig. 10. Informal illustration of the AI transformation rule

The platform-independent service design is the result of the application of all the transformation rules to the service specification. Fig. 11 shows the generated coordination component. The dashed lines represent causality relations already present in the service specifications.

The TelemonitoringECAServiceCoordination enforces the behaviour defined at the service specification level (shown in Fig. 5). The coordination component uses context and action services that constitute the A-MUSE Service Platform, including the ability to send and receive SMSs and to check the position and availability of mobile terminal users. The service trader is consulted to find appropriate context sources and action services depending on the constraints on information attributes that have been specified at the service specification level. For example, the seizureAlert_indC context event is refined in a number of interactions that lead to the notifyEvent_SeizureAlert_indC between the TelemonitoringECAServiceCoordination and the EventBasedSeizure-Service. The constraint on the location of aid persons in alertAid_reqA has been transformed into a constraint on the value of a service property in the query of the reqServiceQuery_alertAid_reqA interaction. This is a dynamic service property that is evaluated by the service trader after the query is issued.

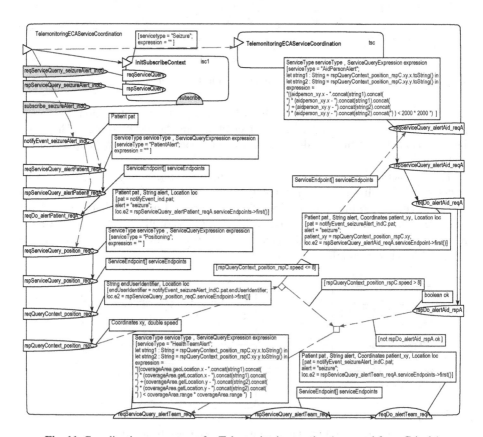

Fig. 11. Coordination component for Telemonitoring service (exported from Grizzle)

7   Conclusions

In this paper we have proposed a model-driven design trajectory for context-aware and mobile services, in which a number of concepts such as platform independence, abstract platform, context-awareness and service orientation play an important role.

We have presented the design trajectory by discussing the necessary levels of models, the choice of modelling languages, and the definition of platforms and transformations. Further, we have illustrated the application of our approach by means of an example (i.e., the Telemonitoring service). The Telemonitoring design exercise helped us to emphasize the role of model transformations, but also to understand to what extent the whole design process can be automated.

The service specification level emphasizes ease of use for the service specifier and platform independence for service specifications. A context-aware service is defined from its integrated perspective abstracting from any components that may support the execution of the service in terms of technology platforms such as Parlay or Parlay-X (which provide context and action services in the telecommunications domain) and Web Services or CORBA (which provide service-oriented middleware architectures, including some service discovery functionality).

The abstract platform at the platform-independent service design level has been chosen based on the pattern of service discovery found in a number of middleware platforms (e.g., OMG CORBA trader [23] and the UDDI registry [21]) and in the ODP trader [16]. The trader service in the A-MUSE Service Platform is capable of supporting a simple constraint language and is capable of supporting dynamic service properties, which allows contextual information to be used to trade for services, as we have shown in the Telemonitoring example. These capabilities of the service trader do not have to be implemented in the coordination component, therefore simplifying the design of transformations that use the A-MUSE platform as target. For a discussion on the realization of the service trader in UDDI and CORBA trader we refer the reader to [6]. We believe the service discovery abstract platform described in this paper is domain neutral and can be used where a service-oriented architecture is needed, without dependence on a particular technology platform such as Web Services.

We have used ISDL (and ECA-DL as a specialization thereof) to model the behavioural aspects of services for three main reasons. Firstly, ISDL supports a broad spectrum of abstraction levels which allows us to cover from service specification to service design seamlessly. Secondly, the concept of abstract interaction enables us to capture service designs in a middleware-platform-independent manner (as shown in [2]). And, finally, conformance rules have been defined [26] which can be used to verify whether service designs respect service specifications.

We have used UML class definitions and OCL constraints to model context information. In the context of the A-MUSE project, we are investigating the use of semantic models expressed in OWL. The latter may allow the designer to automatically reason whether, for example, two services are semantically connectible. We are also working on the further development of the ECA-DL and the A-MUSE abstract platform. Tool support for the various levels of models in this design trajectory will be incorporated in an integrated environment for model-driven service engineering.

Acknowledgements

This work is part of the Freeband A-MUSE project (http://a-muse.freeband.nl), which is sponsored by the Dutch government under contract BSIK 03025. Marten van

Sinderen, Luís Ferreira Pires and Remco Dijkman are acknowledged for their suggestions and remarks on the model-driven approach reported in Sections 2 and 3.

References

1. Agrawal, A., Karsai, G., Ledeczi, A.: An end-to-end domain-driven software development framework. In: Companion of the 18th Annual ACM SIGPLAN Conf. on Object-Oriented Programming, Systems, Languages, and Applications (OOPSLA), ACM Press (2003) 8–15
2. Almeida, J.P.A., Dijkman, R., Ferreira Pires, L., Quartel, D., van Sinderen, M.: Abstract Interactions and Interaction Refinement in Model-Driven Design. In: Proc. 9th IEEE EDOC Conference (EDOC 2005), IEEE Computer Society Press (2005) 273–286
3. Almeida, J.P.A., van Sinderen, M., Ferreira Pires, L., Quartel, D.: A systematic approach to platform-independent design based on the service concept. In: Proc. 7th IEEE Int'l Conf. on Enterprise Distributed Object Computing (EDOC 2003). IEEE Computer Society Press (2003) 112–123
4. Almeida, J.P.A. Dijkman, R. van Sinderen, M., Ferreira Pires, L.: On the Notion of Abstract Platform in MDA Development, In: Proc. 8th IEEE Int'l Conf. on Enterprise Distributed Object Computing (EDOC 2004), IEEE Computer Society Press (2004) 253–263
5. Almeida, J.P.A., Iacob, M.E., Iacob, S.: Methodological Framework for Freeband Services Development, Freeband A-MUSE/D2.3a, TI/RS/2004/092, Telematica Instituut, Enschede, The Netherlands (2004); https://doc.telin.nl/dscgi/ds.py/Get/File-47390
6. Almeida, J.P.A., Iacob, M.E., Jonkers, H., Quartel, D.: Platform-Independent Modelling of Service Infrastructure Components, Freeband A-MUSE/D1.6, TI/RS/2005/078, Telematica Instituut, Enschede, The Netherlands (2005); https://doc.telin.nl/dscgi/ds.py/Get/File-59319
7. Dey, A. K., Salber, D., and Abowd, G. D.: A Conceptual Framework and a Toolkit for Supporting the Rapid Prototyping of Context-Aware Applications. Human-Computer Interaction, 16(2-4) (2001) 97–166
8. Chen, H. Finin, T., Joshi, A.: An ontology for context-aware pervasive computing environments, Knowledge Engineering Review, Special Issue on Ontologies for Distributed Systems, Vol. 18, No. 3. Cambridge University Press (2003) 197–207
9. Dijkman, R.M.: Consistency in Multi-Viewpoint Architectural Design, Ph.D. thesis, University of Twente, The Netherlands (2006)
10. Dirgahayu, T.: Model-Driven Engineering of Web Service Compositions: A Transformation from ISDL to BPEL, M.Sc. thesis, University of Twente, The Netherlands (2005)
11. Dockhorn Costa, P. Ferreira Pires, L., van Sinderen, M.: Designing a Configurable Services Platform for Mobile Context-Aware Applications, International Journal of Pervasive Computing and Communications (JPCC), Vol. 1, No. 1. Troubador Publishing (2005)
12. Freeband A-MUSE Project; http://a-muse.freeband.nl
13. Gavras, A., Belaunde, M., Ferreira Pires, L., Almeida, J.P.A.: Towards an MDA-based Development Methodology for Distributed Applications. In: Software Architecture: First European Workshop (EWSA2004), LNCS 3047, Springer (2004) 230–240
14. Grizzle; http://isdl.ctit.utwente.nl/tools/grizzle
15. ISDL home; http://isdl.ctit.utwente.nl/

16. ITU-T / ISO: ODP Trading Function: Specification, ITU-T Recommendation X.950 I IS 13235-1 (1997)

17. Jonkers, H., Iacob, M.E., Lankhorst, M., Strating, P.: Integration and Analysis of Functional and Non-Functional Aspects in Model-Driven E-Service Development. In: Proc. 9th IEEE EDOC Conference (EDOC 2005), IEEE Computer Society Press (2005) 229–238

18. Karsai, G., Agrawal, A.: Graph transformations in OMG's Model Driven Architecture. In: Applications of Graph Transformations with Industrial Relevance, Second International Workshop (AGTIVE2003), Charlottesville, VA, USA (2003) 243–259

19. Ledeczi, A. et al.: The Generic Modeling Environment. In: Proc. Workshop on Intelligent Signal Processing, Budapest, Hungary (2001)

20. McFadden, T., Henricksen, K., Indulska, J., Mascaro, P.: Applying a Disciplined Approach to the Development of a Context-Aware Communication Application. In: 3rd IEEE Int'l Conf. on Pervasive Computing and Communications (PerCom), IEEE Computer Society Press (2005) 300–306

21. OASIS: OASIS - Committees - OASIS UDDI Specifications TC; http://oasis-open.org/committees/uddi-spec/doc/tcspecs.htm

22. Object Management Group: MDA-Guide, Version 1.0.1, omg/03-06-01 (2003)

23. Object Management Group: Trading Object Service Specification, Version 1.0, formal/00-06-27 (2000)

24. Object Management Group: Unified Modelling Language: Object Constraint Language version 2.0, ptc/03-10-04 (2003)

25. Object Management Group: UML 2.0 Superstructure, ptc/03-08-02 (2003)

26. Quartel, D.: Action relations Basic design concepts for behaviour modelling and refinement, Ph.D. thesis, University of Twente, Enschede, The Netherlands (1998)

27. Quartel, D. Ferreira Pires, L., van Sinderen, M.: On Architectural Support for Behaviour Refinement. In: Journal of Integrated Design and Process Science, Vol. 6, No. 1. IOS (2002)

28. Selic, B.: The Pragmatics of Model-Driven Development. IEEE Software, Vol. 20, No. 5, IEEE Computer Society Press (2003) 19–25

29. The Parlay Group: "The Parlay Group – Specifications"; http://www.parlay.org

30. World Wide Web Consortium: SOAP Version 1.2 Part 1: Messaging Framework, W3C Proposed Recommendation (2003); http://www.w3.org/TR/soap12-part1

31. World Wide Web Consortium: Web Services Description Language (WSDL) 1.1, W3C Note (2001); http://www.w3.org/TR/wsdl

Utilising Alternative Application Configurations in Context- and QoS-Aware Mobile Middleware

Sten A. Lundesgaard, Ketil Lund, and Frank Eliassen

Simula Research Laboratory, Network and Distributed Systems,
P.O. Box 134, N-1325 Lysaker, Norway
{stena, ketillu, frank}@simula.no
http://www.simula.no/departments/networks

Abstract. State-of-the-art dynamic middleware uses information about the environment in order to evaluate alternative configurations of an application and select one according to some criteria. In the context of applications sensitive to Quality of Service, we have identified the need for a platform independent description of configurations that includes non-functional behaviour, and that allows handling of a large number of application configurations. In this paper, we present a modelling principle and a service plan concept, which together represents such a description. The modelling principle and plan concept extend state-of-the-art with i) a model of the alternative configurations that ensure a minimum of reconfiguration steps; ii) a specification that contains information elements of the configuration, dependencies to the environment, and QoS characteristics; and iii) a platform independent specification. In the paper, we also perform a qualitative assessment of our approach, and we describe a proof-of-concept implementation.

1 Introduction

The mobile domain represents a dynamic heterogeneous environment that constitutes a considerable challenge to application developers. Dynamic middleware for component-based applications is one answer to this challenge. These middleware platforms provide a traditional run-time environment, and, in addition, employ late-binding and reflection principles for dynamic (re)configuration of applications (e.g., OpenORB [1] and UIC [2]). However, today's state-of-the-art solutions within this field have some important shortcomings that need to be solved.

First, existing approaches force the application developer to explicitly specify all alternative application architectures. With many different combinations of hardware and software in heterogeneous environments, this gives a large number of different configurations and computationally intensive reconfiguration steps.

Second, dynamic middleware solutions for components mainly combine context-awareness with reconfiguration mechanisms, ignoring the Quality of Service (QoS) characteristics of the different application configurations. As a consequence they fail to support applications where QoS characteristics are critical, such as applications for streaming and conferencing.

F. Eliassen and A. Montresor (Eds.): DAIS 2006, LNCS 4025, pp. 228–241, 2006.
© IFIP International Federation for Information Processing 2006

Third, in current state-of-art solutions, the specifications of the application configurations are defined for a particular middleware. Thus, the specification and its information elements are specialised for a specific set of tasks and platforms, making reuse difficult.

In this paper, we present a service modelling principle and a service plan concept that together provide a solution for these shortcomings. To briefly illustrate the principle and concept, we use the life-cycle of an application (see Figure 1). At design time, the service modelling principle is utilised for de-composition of the application into service compositions, atomic services, and alternatives thereof. The service plan concept provides the artefacts needed to deploy specifications of the alternative application configurations. We refer to the process of identifying and choosing an application configuration as *planning*. Service plans enable the middleware to perform planning, by providing information about the alternative application configurations, any dependencies to context elements (runtime environment, communication technology, storage facilities, etc.) and the resulting QoS characteristics for resources available (processing load, data rate, memory usage, etc.). For configuration of the application service plans provide the composition and parameter configurations of the components. When reconfiguration is needed, service plans provide meta-data about the running application and holds references to both composition and single components.

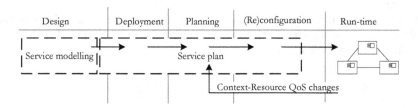

Fig. 1. Life-Cycle

The remainder of this paper is structured as follows. In Sect. 2 we present the service modelling principle, the service plan concept, and how to apply these in the different life-cycle phases. Sect. 3 assesses the principle and concept using qualitative criteria. In Sect. 4 we describe the implementation of our context- and QoS-aware mobile middleware and the proof-of-concept work related to this paper. Sect. 5 discusses related work. Finally, Sect. 6 presents our conclusions and future research.

2 Enabling Alternative Application Configurations

We start by presenting the service modelling principle and the service plan concept, before describing how these two make it possible to utilise alternative application configurations in a context- and QoS-aware middleware.

2.1 Service Modelling Principle

In Service Oriented Computing (SOC) an application is viewed in terms of service levels of abstraction [3], with resource services at the lowest level up to aggregated services at the highest level. This view is also the foundation of our service modelling principle, where we order the service levels by introducing a service model. At the highest level, denoted the *service level*, the service is offered to the user (or client software). This service is divided into a composition of sub-services of a finer granularity, at the *sub-service level* in the service model. These sub-services may again be divided into service compositions. When a service can not be decomposed any further it is considered an atomic service. At the *atomic service level* the implementation of a service is a self-contained software component.

In SOC, semantic representations of components are used to make the software suitable for late-binding [3], i.e., components are bound together during (re)configuration. This is also one of the reasons why semantic descriptions, referred to as *service types*, are included in our service modelling principle. Another reason is the separation this establishes between the design of the application behaviour and the alternative application configurations. Each service in the service model therefore has a type, and all alternative implementations of a service must conform to the same service type. This enables us to model alternatives at all service levels in one single service model. Thus, we avoid one architecture model for each application configuration. The variations between these alternatives are not constrained by the service modelling principle, but by the deployable artefacts and the middleware. In our work we have three types of variations: service compositions, parameter configurations, and components.

Figure 2 exemplifies both the decomposition of an application and the alternative implementations of the service types. In the figure, the service types *j1* and *jl2* have two alternative implementations each.

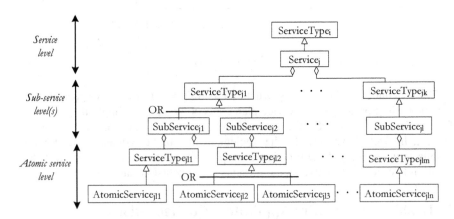

Fig. 2. Service Model

2.2 Service Plan Concept

As described above, the service model allows for alternative implementations of services at all abstraction levels. The dynamic mobile middleware use run-time information about the environment choose the most suitable among these application configurations. Therefore, we need to be able to specify dependencies to context elements in the environment and the QoS characteristics of the application configuration, in addition to the software architecture and behaviour [4].

The semantics of a service is represented as a *service type*. We introduce the *service plan* as the association between a service type and one implementation of that type, and, if applicable, with a particular parameter configuration. Thus, the service plan concept effectively bridges the gap between the layered service model of an application and the corresponding running application. By specifying application configurations and providing information about the alternatives, the service plans enable the dynamic middleware to identify and choose between configurations. While existing approaches use specifications defined for particular middleware and therefore are specialised for a specific task, the service plan is defined at a conceptual level to ensure that the result is middleware independent.

As can be seen from the conceptual model in Figure 3, a service plan contains five information elements: i) *Service* is the name of the service type of which the plan specifies the implementation, ii) *Implementation* specifies either a component or a composition of service types, iii) *Dependencies* to context elements in the environment and their properties, iv) *ParameterConfiguration* lists values for configuration of the implementation, and v) *QoSCharacteristics* of the specified implementation. An important attribute of our service plan concept is the support for compositions of service types. A service composition can in turn be part of another service composition, enabling the specification of the application as a recursive structure of service types.

Together, these elements provide a complete specification of a service implementation, separated from the implementation itself, and independent of any middleware. There are, however, some challenges associated with a platform independent specification of dependencies and QoS characteristics. In particular context and resource models that define the semantics and classifications of context elements and resources are needed. These models are applied when modelling the properties and QoS characteristics of context elements and resources in the environment and designing the context and resource managers for the middleware. However, this is a separate challenge that we discuss in [5].

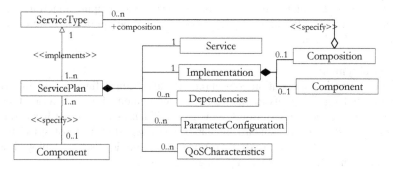

Fig. 3. Conceptual Model

2.3 Application Life-Cycle

In the following sections we outline how to utilise the service model and service plans in the different phases of the application life-cycle (illustrated in Figure 4), from design to (re)configuration. Where appropriate, we make recommendations regarding design and technologies considered useful for a mobile middleware.

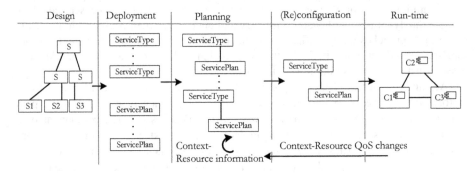

Fig. 4. Life-Cycle

2.3.1 Design

In the design phase, alternative configurations with context dependencies and QoS characteristics are identified. There are two approaches. Decompose the application, starting at the service level, into a hierarchy of services with alternatives (top-down approach). Alternatively, start at the bottom with atomic services and compose these into sub-services, which again may be combined to other services (bottom-up-approach). Both approaches result in one service model with the abstraction levels of the application, semantic representations of all services that form the application, and the alternative implementations that constitute the application configurations.

For each implementation, any dependencies to context elements must be identified. A context model is recommended to ensure that the middleware interprets the specified dependencies correctly. Furthermore, suitable descriptions of the QoS characteristics are required, which typically involves specifying mapping functions between different QoS levels. QoS and resource models should be applied to ensure a correct interpretation by the middleware.

2.3.2 Deployment

After the alternative application configurations have been defined in one model, service types and service plans are prepared for deployment. For the service type, one may use Web-Service Description Language (WSDL), as this format has certain desired properties: an open standard, readable, and supported by most software engineering tools. For the same reasons, service plans should also be deployed as text files, such as the eXtensible Mark-up Language (XML).

In the text file, information elements that constitute the service plan should be presented as an ordered tree, in order to make it easy for the middleware to read the data and move up and down inside the file. An example of a tree structure for service plans is shown in Figure 5. Below the root there are child nodes that divide the tree into five branches, one for each of the information elements specified in the conceptual model (see Figure 3). Out of these five branches, only *ServiceType* and *Implementation* are mandatory, since these are required when publishing the service. The *QoSCharacteristic* node has four children, which reflect the QoS modelling method that we apply to define the QoS characteristics of a service (exemplified in [17]). Another QoS modelling principles may result in other nodes. The *Implementation* node is somewhat different from the others, as it is the only parent with two alternative children, *composition* or *component*. Composition is used when the implementation is a service composition, while component specifies a single component.

During deployment, service types and plans are loaded and interpreted. This functionality can be implemented in the middleware in different ways. For instance, the loader can be activated from an operations and management console and only upload service types and plans in certain catalogues. Alternatively one may choose to confine loading to a predetermined set of alternative service configurations, by using a configuration file for the loader.

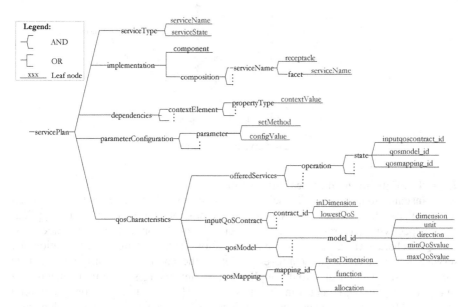

Fig. 5. Ordered Tree Structure for Service Plans

2.3.3 Planning
When a user requests access to an application, the context- and QoS-aware middleware uses the deployed service types and plans to identify the alternative configurations suitable for the current environment, and to choose the one that provides satisfactory QoS. For synthesising the alternative configurations from the information inside the service plans, we suggest the *service configuration* pattern (see Figure 6). The service configuration is asked to resolve itself, using the type of the requested service, together with a plan for that type, as input. This is done for each alternative

plan, resulting in one service configuration object for each alternative configuration of the application. In case of a service composition, the service configuration analyses the connections between the receptacle and facet ports of the service *implementation*. From this the service configuration creates the *next level* of service types and service plans, shown in Figure 6.

Service configurations that can not execute in the current environment are filtered, by checking the specified *dependencies* against context information. Next, the service configurations are compared by using the *QoS mapping* functions at each level inside the service configurations. There are different methods available, such as comparing predicted end-to-end QoS for similar dimensions or applying utility functions. Furthermore, in case of several possible configurations with satisfactory QoS, the middleware can either maximise utility/QoS or minimise the resource load.

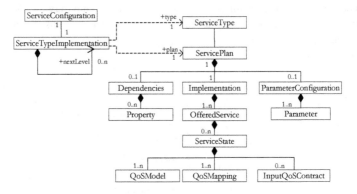

Fig. 6. Service Configuration

2.3.4 Configuration and Reconfiguration

After instantiation, the selected service configuration, together with the associated service plans, change roles from specifying one possible configuration of the application to specifying the architecture, behaviour, parameter configuration, dependencies, and QoS characteristics of a running application. Thus, during reconfiguration the service plan concept is a meta-level model of the application configuration. This model is casually connected to the application, so any changes made to the meta-level causes corresponding changes in the application. The causal connection is enforced by the middleware. For reconfiguration this is useful, since it makes the implementation open for inspection without having to involve the components.

If context dependencies or QoS requirements are violated, the middleware will re-plan the service, and if another service configuration meets the QoS requirements, the middleware reconfigures the application. Within the middleware, a reconfiguration manager, or equivalent, handles the reconfiguration. There are many ways to design the reconfiguration manager and the causal connection between a service plan and the corresponding base level composition/component, but this is a separate challenge not discussed here.

3 Qualitative Assessment

In Sect. 1, we presented three major issues that need to be addressed when using dynamic component middleware as platform for QoS-sensitive applications. In this section, we go through each of these issues, and describe how they are met by our service modelling principle and service plan concept.

Configuration manageability. There are two facets of this issue. First, to be able to achieve and maintain both functional properties and QoS in a dynamic heterogeneous environment, a large number of alternative application configurations must be designed and deployed. Second, the required changes should be as few as possible when reconfiguring, i.e., avoid solutions that require that the entire application has to be replaced. The service modelling principle and service plan concept address the manageability issue by combining service layers and three (re)configuration methods (composition, parameter configuration, and component implementation) into one service model. Service layers make it easy for application developers to design the alternatives at a suitable abstraction level, from which, when deployed, a range of different alternative application configurations can be derived. For instance, a sub-service with three alternative implementations, which again consist of sub-services that have nine alternative implementations, a total of 27 alternative compositions can be derived. All these alternatives are represented in one single service model, so we avoid individual architecture models for each configuration. The three (re)configuration methods address the manageability issue, by giving the application developers full control of the composition, parameter configurations, and component implementations. Together with the service layers, these reconfiguration methods ensure that the dynamic middleware only reconfigures the parts of the application that is required, and without always having to perform computational intensive reconfiguration steps associated with changing the entire component composition.

QoS-awareness. Existing dynamic middleware platforms for component based applications do not combine context- and QoS-awareness. Hence, we require a specification with information elements that puts the middleware in a position to identify application configurations that can execute in a particular context and to choose one of these based upon the end-to-end QoS characteristics (assuming the middleware has context information about the environment and information about the resource QoS characteristics). The service plan has information elements for specifying both dependencies to context elements in the environment and QoS characteristics of the implementation. When applied to the implementations, service plans can specify context dependencies and QoS characteristics at all levels in the service model. The service plan concept is technology independent, but we recommend XML for deployable files and a design pattern for synthesising the application configurations (explained in Sect. 2). Both are extensible, which makes it easy to combine the service plan concept with any context model, QoS model, or mapping functions between QoS level.

Platform Independence. To be able to deploy the application and the alternative configuration on different context- and QoS-aware middleware solutions, the specification must be platform (i.e., middleware, network, and operating system) independent. This requires that one adhere to the fundamental principle of separation of concern. In particular, specifications of application configurations and their QoS characteristics must be independent of the functional code, and the transitions between the phases in the life-cycle, e.g., design to deployment, deployment to planning, and planning to (re)configuration, use technologies that are independent of middleware and programming language. The service modelling principle gives the required separation between the semantic representation of the service and the specification of the alternative implementations. Furthermore, the service plan provides the specification of the implementation at a conceptual level, making it easy to implement and utilise throughout the application life-cycle.

4   Implementation

In order to show that the service modelling principle can be used together with existing software modelling principles, we have applied it to a component-based video streaming application. It was important to make the modelling realistic, and not merely an exercise. Thus, a scenario of the complete system including the environment, user mobility, and different terminal types was prepared (refer to [17] for a complete description). In the scenario, video is pre-encoded in different combinations of frame rate, resolution, and colour scheme. Figure 7 shows the service model (simplified) of the video streaming application, which has alternative implementations at both sub-service and atomic service levels (i.e., it utilise the three configuration methods).

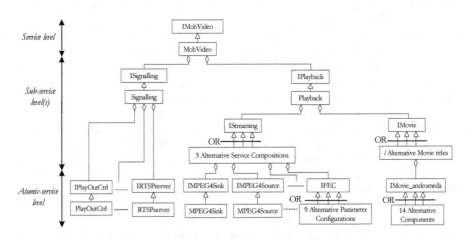

Fig. 7. Service Model of a Video Streaming Application

Even though our implementation has only one video title, the service model specifies a total of 266 alternative application configurations. After converting the service model into deployable artefacts, 39 service plans are derived. Compared to solutions which employ one architecture model for each configuration, our service model principle reduces the number of specifications by a factor of six. Furthermore, the combination of service levels and service plans divides the complex task of modelling context dependencies and QoS characteristics into small, manageable pieces. Thus, we avoid the explicit specification of all configurations, whether it is as one large or multiple individual specifications. A task that proved to be difficult was defining the QoS mapping functions. We found that this requires benchmark test results of components running on different classes of hardware, operating system, run-time environment, and network.

Both service type and service plan are included in the architecture of our context- and QoS-aware middleware; QuAMobile (QUality of service-Aware component Architecture for MOBILE computing) [6][7]. The core of the architecture, depicted in Figure 8, has hooks for domain specific plug-ins *service planner, context manager, resource manager, configuration manager,* and *reconfiguration manager.* To test the ability of the dynamic middleware to choose an application configuration suitable for a particular environment, we have designed a graphical test tool where the characteristics of the environment are defined. For entering user QoS requirements, a Web- based interface is hooked up to QuAMobile through an Applet and a façade to the *service context.* In our implementation, service types are deployed as WSDL-files and service plans as XML-files. During loading service plan XML-files are interpreted, and information from the tree (illustrated previously in Figure 5) is extracted using the Java Document Object Model open-source software, rel. 10 beta. Created components are placed in the *repository,* while types and plans are published in the *broker.*

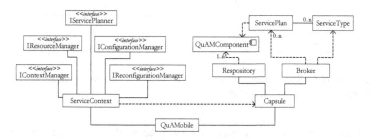

Fig. 8. QuAMobile Core

During planning the deployed service plans and the abstraction levels of the service model come into practical use. The planning phase commences when a service re- quest with the name of the service type and the user's QoS requirements are sent from the presentation layer (Web-pages and Java applets) to the business layer (where QuAMobile resides), and to the service planner. The implementation uses the service configuration pattern illustrated in Figure 6. An instance of the service configuration class synthesises the alternatives by resolving the application from the top. At any point where it detects alternative service plans for the same service type, it clones itself and asks each new service configuration object to continue resolving from the level that has been resolved till now. Synthesized service configurations that can not execute in the current environment are filtered, by checking the specified context dependencies against information from a shared context and resource data model [5].

Next, the QoS characteristics are calculated by using mapping functions, which map between different QoS levels (resource-application, application-application, and application-user). The QoS mapping functions have variables, such as resource QoS, context properties, and other QoS mapping functions. Together with the mapping function, these are processed by our QoS calculation software, which is based on the Java Expression Parser, rel. 2.3. Figure 9 shows examples of QoS mapping functions. In the implementation, QoS prediction starts at the atomic service level (bottom-up calculation). Predicted QoS is stored inside the service configuration object. After predicting the end-to-end QoS characteristics, the service planner removes service configurations that have service implementations that do not meet the specified *min-QoSValue* and *maxQoSValue* (see Figure 5). The last task of the planning process is to check the predicted QoS against the user QoS requirements, which in QuAMobile are expressed in dimensional utility functions.

```
<mapping_id>startUpTimeplay
    <funcDimension>startUpTime</funcDimension>
    <function>(((tmpeg4 SMALLEREQUAL 1000) = 5);
                 .    .    .
                ((tmpeg4 SMALLEREQUAL 10000) = 2);
                ((tmpeg4 SMALLEREQUAL 31840) = 1))</function></mapping id>
```

a)

```
<mapping_id>tmpeg4
    <funcDimension>startUpTime</funcDimension>
    <function>tmpeg4source+trtpTrans+2*tfec+tprefetchStart+12*tmpeg4sinkEmptyB</function>
</mapping id>
```

b)

```
<mapping_id>trtpTrans
    <funcDimension>delay</funcDimension>
    <function>vbitRate/(20*RrtpTrans)</function></mapping_id>
```

c)

Fig. 9. Example of QoS mapping functions: a) user QoS to utility, b) application to user QoS, c) context-resource to application QoS

The chosen service configuration is forwarded to the *configuration manager*. If/ when the resource monitors or context sensors detect changes in the environment, the planning phase is restarted, and if successful, a list of components to delete, create, and new bindings, are forward to the *reconfiguration manager*.

5   Related Work

When developing applications for dynamic middleware, Architecture Description Languages (ADLs) can be used for specifying the functional aspects of the application configuration. A number of ADLs are available; see the discussion of ADLs provided by Medvidovic et al [8]. Some of these ADLs, such as ACME [9] and Darwin [10], support hierarchical composition, but they need to be extended with support for alternative configurations at different abstraction levels. Furthermore, ADLs are, in general, a design-time artefact, and not intended for managing run-time adaptation.

There are ADLs that have been extended with reconfiguration steps, e.g., Plastik [11] and Rainbow [19]. Both use an extension of ACME which enables the application developer to specify (one) application configuration and a set of conditions under which reconfiguration shall take place. A compiler converts the ACME specification to platform specific, executable files. Compared to Plastik and Rainbow, the service plan concept provides more information, e.g., parameter configurations and dependencies to context elements. Furthermore, the service plan concept assumes that the middleware has logic for deciding which part to reconfigure. In Plastik and Rainbow, this is decided prior to run-time using action policies/strategies.

To ensure that the application behaviour is maintained during reconfiguration, specifications of the reconfiguration steps have been developed (see survey by Bradbury et al [4]). These specifications assume that one particular application configuration is running, ignoring the need to find an initial configuration that can execute in an arbitrary environment. The service modelling principle and service plan concept address this weakness by providing specifications of alternative application configurations that can be used for both initial configuration and reconfiguration.

The QoS of an application is strongly dependent on the characteristics of the available resources. Thus, a specification must include the QoS requirements at resource level. However, users do not relate to resources; their perception of quality is subjective, e.g., sound quality, video contrast, or cost. Therefore, QoS requirements to an application are often specified at the user level and mapped down to resources. Such specifications are commonly referred to as QoS specification languages (see survey by Jin et al [12]). The XML-based Hierarchical QoS Mark-up Language (HQML) [13] and the Component Quality Modelling Language (CQML) [14] are two examples of QoS specification languages. HQML was designed for distributed Web-based multimedia applications, and uses XML-tags for the partitioning and for information elements. The XML file is associated with the Web application, and accessed by a Web-client with a plug-in that interprets the information elements inside the XML file. CQML, in addition to specifying user and application QoS requirements, can be utilised in UML-based analysis models of the application, enabling both model-driven QoS-awareness and run-time QoS interpretation and mapping. A principle difference between QoS specification languages and our service plan is that the service plan is developed as a concept for the application life-cycle. If considering only deployment, there are similarities between a service plan and HQML or CQML specifications, because they both relate resources to the user level. With respect to information elements, the service plan has support for specifying context dependencies, a feature that is generally lacking from QoS specification languages [12].

There are examples of research projects that address all phases of the application life-cycle and QoS-awareness, e.g., $2K^{Q+}$ [15] and Quality Object (QuO) [16]. $2K^{Q+}$ provides a QoS software engineering environment for specifying alternative component compositions and their QoS characteristics, which are then compiled for running on the $2K^Q$ middleware. Part of this environment is the QoSTalk [13] graphical programming and consistency checking tool, which uses the HQML QoS specification language. This engineering environment employs a platform dependent compiler, i.e., it produces executable code for (re)configuring of the application. Furthermore, it requires that the middleware has probing facilities that can measure QoS and resource usage for a test-run of the application configuration. Results from the QoS probing are fed into the compiler and, thus, set the conditions for reconfiguring the application. The QuO framework relies on a suite of description languages for specifying QoS. Specifications are compiled to executable code, which is used for monitoring QoS and controlling the interaction between distributed objects across a CORBA middleware. Our service plan concept and QuO specifications serve the same purpose, but a service plan has more information, is platform independent, and thus represents a more flexible solution.

Most existing approaches assume that the target environment is known at design time. One example of a middleware that is not based on this assumption is the Context-Aware Reflective mIddleware System for Mobile Applications (CARISMA) [18]. It uses application profiles to (re)configure the middleware. If a mobile device is used in an unforeseen environment, the application can adapt to the profile, and thereby change the behaviour of the middleware. Thus, the application profile is a dynamic specification, while the service plan is static in order to enable predictable (re)configurations. The service plan concept supports unforeseen environments, by allowing alternative service plans of the same application.

6   Conclusions

This paper focuses on how dynamic middleware for the mobile domain can utilise alternative application configurations. We have identified three issues that are important to address in order to achieve such platform-based configuration, and that current state-of-the-art solutions fail to target: first, the heterogeneity of both hardware and software within this domain means that the developer must be provided with means to manager a large number of alternative configurations; second, QoS characteristics of the different configurations must be specified, to enable the middleware to select among the alternative configurations; and third, to enable separation of concerns, and thereby reuse, the specifications must be platform independent.

Our approach for handling these three issues is based on a service modelling principle for designing a large number of variants, and a service plan concept used to connect service types to implementations of the types. Service plans also specify the QoS characteristics and context dependencies of the implementations. Using the life-cycle of an application we have presented a qualitative assessment of our approach, and demonstrated how the service model and the service plans, together, cover all phases of the life-cycle. Finally, we have described our implementation of the principle and the concept in our dynamic mobile middleware called QuAMobile, which serves to demonstrate the feasibility of our approach.

Currently our work is on the design of the causal connections from the service configuration object and the service plans, down to the running component instances, and we are studying the integration of the service plan into a software engineering tool.

References

1. Coulson, G., Blair, G., Clarke, M., and Parlavanzas, N.: The design of a configurable and reconfigurable middleware platform. Distr. Computing Journal, Vol. 15 (2002), 109-126
2. Roman, M., Kon, F., and Campbell, R.: Reflective Middleware, From Your Desk to Your Hand. IEEE Distributed Systems Online, Vol. 2, No. 5 (2001)
3. Huhns, M.N., and Singh, M.P.: Service-Oriented Computing: Key Concepts and Principles. IEEE Internet Computing, Vol. 9, Issue 1 (2005), 75-81

4. Bradbury, J., Cordy, J., Dingel, J., and Wermelinger, M.: A Survey of Self-Management in Dynamic Software Architecture Specification. Proc. of the ACM SIGSOFT International Workshop on Self-Managed Systems (2004), 28-33
5. Amundsen, S., and Eliassen, F.: Combined Resource and Context Model for QoS-aware Mobile Middleware. Accepted for the 19th International Conference on Architecture of Computing Systems, (2006)
6. Amundsen, S. Lund, K., Eliassen, F., and Staehli, R.: QuA: Platform-Managed QoS for Component Architecture. Proc. of the Norwegian Informatics Conference (2004), 55-66
7. Solberg, A., Amundsen, S., Aagedal, J., and Eliassen, F.: A Framework for QoS-aware Service Composition. Proc. of ACM International Conference on Service Oriented Computing, ACM Press (2004).
8. Medvidovic, N., and Taylor, R.N.: A Framework for Classifying and Comparing Architecture Description Languages. Proc. of the 6th European Software Engineering Conference (1997), 60-76
9. Garlan, D., Monroe, R., Wile, D.: ACME: Architectural Description of Component-based Systems. Foundations of Component-based Systems, Cambridge University Press (2000), 47-68
10. Magee, J., and Kramer, J.: Dynamic Structure in Software Architectures. Proc. of ACM SIGSOFT'96: 4th Symposium on the Foundations of Software Engineering (1996), 3-14
11. Batista, T., Joolia, A., and Coulson, G.: Managing Dynamic Reconfiguration in Component-based Systems. Lecture Notes in Computer Science, Proc. of the 2nd European Workshop on Software Architecture, Vol. 3527 (2005), 1-17
12. Jin, J., and Nahrstedt, K.: QoS Specification Languages for Distributed Multimedia Applications: A Survey and Taxonomy, IEEE Multimedia Magazine, Vol. 11, No.3 (2004), 74-87
13. Xiaohui, G., Nahrstedet, K., Yuan, W., Wichadakul, D.: An XML-based Quality of Service Enabling Language for the Web. Journal of Visual Language and Computing, Special issue on Multimedia Languages for the Web, Academic Press, Vol. 13, No. 1 (2002)
14. Aagedal, J.: Quality of service support in development of distributed systems. Ph.D. thesis, University of Oslo (2001)
15. Wichadal, D., Nahrstedt, K., Gu, X., and Xu, D.: 2K^{Q+}: An Integrated Approach of QoS Compilation and Reconfigurable, Component-Based Run-Time Middleware for the Unified QoS Management Framework. Lecture Notes in Computer Science, Proc. of the ACM International Conference on Distributed Systems Platforms, Vol. 2218 (2001), 373-394
16. Loyall, J., Bakken, D., Schantz, R., Zinky, J., Karr, D., Vanegas, R., and Anderson, K.: QoS Aspect Languages and Their Runtime Integration. Lecture Notes in Computer Science, Proceeding of the 4th International Workshop on Languages, Compilers, and Runtime Systems for Scalable Computers, Vol. 1511 (1998), 303-318
17. Amundsen, S., Lund, K., Griwodz, C., and Halvorsen, P.: Scenario Description –Video Streaming in the Mobile Domain, Technical report (2005), http://www.simula.no/~stena/techReports/ScenarioDescription/ScenDesc_MobVideo_B1.pdf
18. Capra, L., Emmerich, W., and Mascolo, C.: CARISMA: Context-Aware Reflective mIddleware System for Mobile Applications. IEEE Transactions on Software Engineering, Vol. 29, No. 10 (2003), 929-945
19. Garland, D., Cheng, S-W., Huang, A-C., Schmerl, B., Steenkiste, P.: Rainbow: Architecture-Based Self-Adaptation with Reusable Infrastructure. IEEE Computer, Vol. 37, No. 10 (2004), 46-54

Timing Driven Architectural Adaptation

Andrew Wils, Yolande Berbers, Tom Holvoet, and Karel De Vlaminck

K.U.Leuven DistriNet
Department of computer science
Celestijnenlaan 200 A, 3001 Leuven
{andrew.wils, yolande.berbers,
tom.holvoet, karel.devlaminck}@ cs.kuleuven.be

Abstract. Self-adaptation is currently addressed in general frameworks and reference architectures but not in the application architecture. This paper defines concrete concepts to specify timing driven self-adaptation in the software architecture. This self-adaptation is aimed at high-end embedded component based applications. We create an architectural view of a music application describing this kind of adaptation and discuss its implementation. The novelty of our approach is the definition of separate constructs for the monitoring, the adaptation decision logic and the adaptation itself. This allows independent specification of policy and mechanisms and the possibility to adapt other applications in order to satisfy important constraints. The implementation itself consists of reusable run-time counterparts of the constructs. These counterparts are managed by the component middleware and configured by the architectural specification. This way one does not need to write additional self-adaptation code.

1 Introduction

The increasing diversity and interconnection of applications leaves much of their configuration to be dealt with at run-time. The vision of autonomic computing acknowledges this as a problem leading to new levels of complexity [1]. The autonomic computing solution is that computing systems should manage themselves given high-level objectives. One of these objectives is to maintain a satisfactory performance regardless of the available resources. This paper addresses self-adaptation to uphold timing constraints. We focus on applications with CPU intensive tasks for which the user has performance expectations. An example of such an application is the music community application presented in Figure 1. This application enables the user to browse, play and share music as well as chat about it. These tasks are CPU intensive, yet we want an acceptable Quality-of-Service (QoS) for all of them, even in situations with widely varying resources. The self-adaptation will change the resource consumption by means of coarse-grained adaptations to uphold a satisfactory QoS. To master the complexity of this kind of self-adaptation, we need mechanisms and policies that specify and control the adaptation process.

F. Eliassen and A. Montresor (Eds.): DAIS 2006, LNCS 4025, pp. 242–255, 2006.

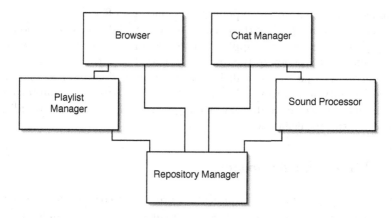

Fig. 1. High level component diagram of a music community application

The ideal solution relies on the perfect prediction of an application's resource behavior based on resource profiling, but this is not an option for unknown platforms and interactive behavior. A more realistic approach is the use of general feedback based frameworks and architectures with reusable adaptation mechanisms (e.g. [2], [3]). This approach usually employs a general "observe – process – adapt" cycle. Although this cycle provides a good starting point for application adaptation, there is still a gap to fill to enable the actual implementation of such applications.

In particular, the frameworks advocate reusable mechanisms but do not define a high-level approach to specify the use of the mechanisms. Timing constraints are non-functional requirements and pertain to large portions of the application. Likewise, coarse-grained application adaptation should also be specified at a level that is close to the functional requirements. To illustrate this, let us reconsider the music community application. The basic functionality of the application is built around distributed music repositories. Using these repositories, users can browse, play and share each other's music. Although the diagram in Figure 1 only shows a coarse architectural view, much of the timing driven adaptation can already be defined at this level. Obvious constraints are that the music must not stutter (a constraint on the Sound Processor), and that the GUI control widgets are responsive enough. Appropriate adaptation actions could be: omitting certain components (such as the optional chat service), switching components (one could use an alternative codec component in the Sound Processor) and "tuning" the resource behavior of a component (e.g. by setting a codec's compression rate).

We propose a feedback-based solution to uphold timing performance that is twofold. First, we introduce two architectural constructs to specify independently the monitoring of timing constraints and the execution of architectural configuration changes. Such coarse grained adaptations have a large influence on resource use, are easy to specify on a high level and do not require changing the application's functional components. Second, we offer an explicit architectural construct to encapsulate the decision logic that links constraint monitoring and adaptation. This way, the application developer can specify a coarse-grained run-time adaptation policy in the architecture at design-time.

Throughout the paper, we will illustrate the introduced concepts with the music community application. We show that reified run-time counterparts of our constructs reduce the addition of timing driven adaptation to providing the right architectural specifications.

2 Architectural Approach

The software architecture of an application provides a coarse-grained decomposition in components and connectors. It abstracts away the complexity of the low level design and enables reuse of functionality. Also, a reified implementation of components allows to adapt the application while it is running [4]. Apart from the user requirements, software architecture should also cover important non-functional requirements and show how it can uphold these requirements.

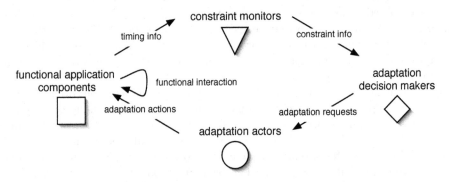

Fig. 2. Architectural constructs and the "observe - process - adapt" cycle

Figure 2 shows how we achieved this. In particular, we concretized the "observe - process - adapt" cycle [4] for timing based application adaptation using special architectural constructs. Figure 2 introduces three new constructs to complement application components:

constraint monitors specifying timing constraints on message flows between application components and how these constraints must be checked at run-time;

adaptation actors specifying how application components and component compositions may be altered at run-time;

decision makers detailing an adaptation policy to connect monitor evaluations with the appropriate adaptation actors.

We call the architectural view that describes this monitoring-based adaptation the *run-time adaptation view*. This view is based on a component instance diagram but defines a run-time adaptation process with reified versions of the above constructs as follows. Decision makers encapsulate QoS levels for a component group. Constraint evaluations determine this QoS and the decision maker maps QoS levels to adaptation actions that are to be executed to uphold the QoS.

The next sections further detail the syntax and semantics of constraint monitors, adaptation actors and decision makers. Following this, we present and evaluate a reusable run-time implementation to carry out the architectural monitoring and adaptation specification.

3   Case Study

As an illustration of a diverse and interconnected distributed application, we chose to implement a prototype version of the mentioned music community application. This application, called Dale, was designed to use timing driven self-adaptation so that it could run on a variety of platforms. Adding constraints and adaptation in the implementation or even the object oriented design is not an easy task: the application consists of over 50 classes, whereas the architectural component view is much simpler and closer to the user requirements. Figure 3 shows a part of the Dale component instance diagram focusing on playlists. It is this diagram for which we will create a run-time adaptation view.

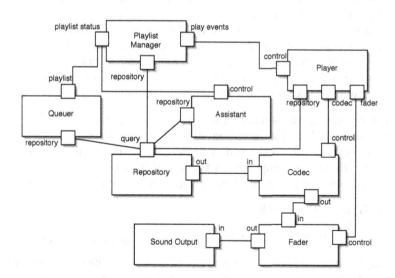

Fig. 3. Playlist component instance diagram

The diagrams in the paper use a component model with asynchronous message based communication. Messages can only be sent out and received through ports. Connectors relay messages from one port to one or more others.

The `Repository` component forms the heart of the Dale application: it contains songs and their meta-data. The `Playlist Manager` defines this playlist and dictates songs to play to the `Player` component. The latter is responsible for setting up the right `Codec` component and getting the audio through a `Fader` component to a `Sound Output` component. Finally, the `Queuer` component keeps the playlist automatically filled and the optional `Assistant` offers advice on related songs to queue.

4   Architectural Constructs

4.1   Constraint Monitors

At the software architecture level, ports declare the messages that are processed and passed around between components. We introduce *constraint monitors* to encapsulate declarative timing constraints on a number of events pertaining this processing and passing around of messages. Architecturally, we link constraints to ports rather than to connectors in order not to limit a constraint to events involving two directly connected components. For example, in Figure 3, one could specify a deadline involving ports from the `Playlist Manager` and `Sound Output`, although these are not directly connected to each other. The constraint monitor construct is depicted as a triangle and is attached to all ports that are involved in the timing constraints.

Constraint monitors do not only encapsulate constraint information, they also state that the constraints should be monitored at run-time. For this reason, we define time as it is handled at the target platforms: a series of discrete time events (monotonously increasing) generated by a system clock. To express the message related events, we adopt an event model defining three types of events:

send corresponds to the sending of a message through a port;
receive corresponds to the reception of a message on a port;
processed corresponds to the end of processing in the component. When this event is reached, a component without a thread of its own will no longer send outgoing messages (send events) until it receives a new message.

The BNF syntax is as follows:

$$\langle\text{message event}\rangle \longrightarrow \langle\text{port}\rangle{:}\langle\text{message}\rangle_{\text{send}|\ \text{receive}|\ \text{processed}}$$

For example, for an audio decoding component, $\text{mp3{:}packet}_{receive}$ signifies the arrival of the message `packet` on the port `mp3`. Similarly, $\text{mp3{:}packet}_{processed}$ means that the component to which the port belongs has processed the given packet and sent out the decoded audio, if any.

To model deadlines, we chose a modified language based on RTL ([5], [6]), although our approach can be used with other formalisms. The RTL syntax uses the @ function to denote the occurence time of a particular event. To give an example involving the mp3 port, here is a constraint limiting the processing time of the request to 20 ms:

$$@(\text{mp3}: \text{packet}_{processed}) \leq @(\text{mp3}: \text{packet}_{receive}) + 20\text{ms}$$

This particular form applies to all instances of mp3:packet. Another use of the @ function has more fine-grained control. For example, the following function indicates that the time between two successive instances of mp3:packet should be equal or less than 20 ms:

$$@(\text{mp3}: \text{packet}_{receive}, \; i + 1) \leq @(\text{mp3}: \text{packet}_{receive}, \; i) + 20\text{ms}$$

Figure 4 shows the constraint monitors that were defined in the earlier presented playlist related instance diagram. Curved connections distinguish the interaction from software connector-based interaction: monitors do not influence (functional) behavior, they merely observe. Of course, the act of observation always influences non-functional aspects, such as performance. Section 5 shows that the involved run-time overhead is limited.

The fill queue constraint monitor in Figure 4 places an upper-bound on the time between the playlist reporting it needs a new song, and the queuer providing the song. The responsiveness constraint monitor checks that song changes are timely processed by the player (eventually resulting in a fader command). Finally, the no stutter constraint monitor checks for audio buffer under-runs.

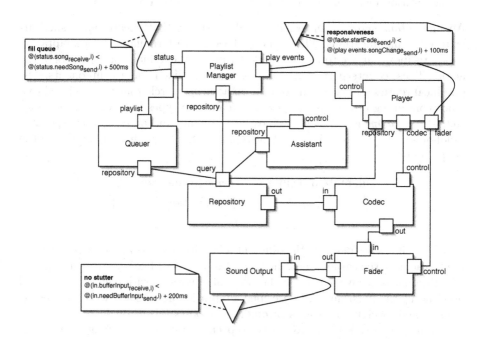

Fig. 4. Constraint monitors for the Dale playlist diagram

4.2   Adaptation Actors

As mentioned in the introduction, we want to specify and support coarse-grained changes in resource consumption for component based applications. We define constructs to describe the manipulation of messages and components for the following adaptation actions:

Component configuration: a component's resource consumption is changed by configuring its settings. This is the equivalent of changing variability parameters [7];

Run-time component optionality and variability: resource use is changed by omitting components or by choosing alternative components. A static approach for this has already been investigated in [8].

We put forward two major objectives for our constructs:

Adaptations are fully determined by the specification. No extra application code is necessary to enable the adaptations at run-time. The adaptation code can be automatically generated or the middleware coordinates the adaptations. This reduces the developer's burden and speeds up development time;

Adaptations are carried out efficiently. The user of the system should only notice the effects of an adaptation, not the adaptation action itself. The described adaptations should therefore be easily translatable to an efficient adaptation mechanism, to keep user distraction to a minimum.

An *adaptation actor* is an architectural construct that encapsulates such architectural modifications. These manipulations are formulated into adaptation action recipes that are to be executed at run-time by reified counterparts of the actors. These counterparts can send messages just like regular components. The graphical representation of an adaptation actor is a circle that is associated to a block containing the action recipes. We define two types of actors: the *message router* and *component tuner*. Recipes have a name and body and are specified as follows (curly brackets in fixed font represent the beginning and ending of the recipe body):

$$\langle\text{adaptation recipe}\rangle \longrightarrow recipe\ \langle\text{recipe name}\rangle\ \texttt{\{}$$
$$\texttt{\{}\langle\text{adaptation action}\rangle\ \texttt{;\}}$$
$$\texttt{\}}$$

In what follows, we describe the different adaptation actors and how they can be used to achieve the earlier mentioned adaptations. Just like regular components, adaptation actors have ports, but they are not annotated with rectangles to avoid overloading the diagrams. All described adaptation actions are accomplished by sending and receiving messages through these ports.

The purpose of a message router is to specify run-time "switching" of message flows. This is done by a reified run-time counterpart that relays messages across its ports. To specify this, we define the link and unlink actions:

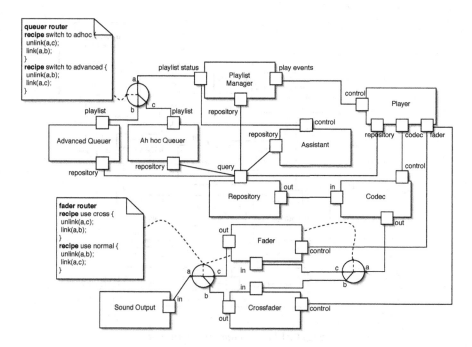

Fig. 5. Dale message routers

$$\langle\text{link action}\rangle \longrightarrow \mathit{link}\ (\langle\text{port}\rangle,\langle\text{port}\rangle)$$
$$\langle\text{unlink action}\rangle \longrightarrow \mathit{unlink}\ (\langle\text{port}\rangle,\langle\text{port}\rangle)$$

When a link action is executed, all messages that are received through the first stated port must be relayed to the second. Using this, one can enable "multicast" or "router" like message flows. Figure 5 shows the message routers we have defined for the music application. The `queuer router` switches requests for new songs from an ad-hoc based queue algorithm to a more CPU intensive one that takes into account user preferences. The other two routers switch between a normal fader and one that cross-fades between songs. These two have been paired by a dotted line, meaning that the recipe declaration applies to both. The `Crossfader` component needs 2 decoded streams at a time and is more CPU intensive. Note that we make some assumptions about component state and message synchronization. First, switching of message flows should only be used when the components that receive messages directly or indirectly from a message router do not require reception of all messages. Second, a component receiving messages via different "switched" paths must not rely on the order of received messages, as we are using an asynchronous component model.

A component tuner configures one or more components. The actor achieves this by sending configuration messages to regular component ports.

The action for sending a message is as follows:

$$\langle\text{send action}\rangle \longrightarrow \langle\text{port}\rangle...\langle\text{message}\rangle\ (\ [\ \{\langle\text{key}\rangle:\langle\text{val}\rangle\}\ ]\ )$$

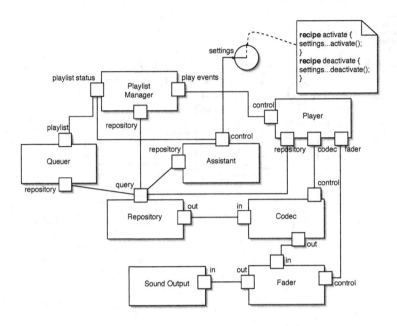

Fig. 6. Playlist component tuners

The triple-dot notation denotes the sending of the message with the supplied key-value parameters.

The semantics of a component tuner are straightforward: when a recipe contains one or more of these send actions and the former is executed, the described messages are sent out through the denoted port, optionally containing the specified key-value parameter pairs. Figure 6 shows a component tuner in the Dale music application that deactivates the assistant, freeing up CPU resources.

4.3   Decision Makers

Now that we have adaptation actors and timing monitors, we need to link them. We base the logic on levels of perceived QoS that are defined in another architectural construct called a *adaptation decision maker*. Decision makers encapsulate how the timing constraints and adaptation actions relate to the perceived quality at run-time. A level's quality is defined by one or more constraint monitor conditions. When the conditions are met, the level is entered. Adaptation recipes can be linked to be executed upon entering the level. For our purposes we defined three monitor conditions that provide an abstract representation of the constraint state, but the constraint state can be divided otherwise. The red level indicates that the involved constraint is violated and adaptation is necessary. The yellow level indicates that there are few or no constraint violations. Green indicates that the constraints are easily respected and that there may be room for inverse adaptations.

The syntax for this is as follows:

⟨decision level⟩ ⟶ *on* ⟨monitor clause⟩ [{, ⟨monitor clause⟩}] {

   { ⟨recipe name⟩ ; }

   }

⟨monitor clause⟩ ⟶ ⟨monitor name⟩ . ⟨monitor condition⟩

⟨monitor condition⟩ ⟶ *red* | *yellow* | *green*

The exact interpretation of monitor conditions is done by the run-time infrastructure. The latter should also avoid so-called "yo-yo" effects. An example mapping for switching to the green level could be that there are no deadline violations and there is a CPU margin for which the linked recipes did not already cause violations. A complete run-time mapping algorithm is outside the scope of this paper.

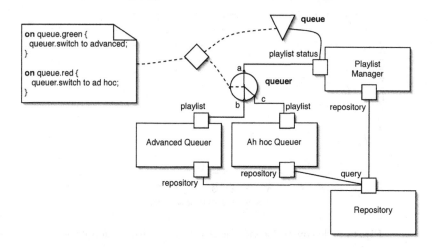

Fig. 7. Dale queue decision maker

Figure 7 shows one of the three decision makers we have defined in the Dale application. The decision maker links the `fill queue` constraint with the queue adaptation actors. The other decision makers are created similarly. The second one links the responsiveness of the `Playlist Manager` controls to the components that access the repository frequently: the `Assistant` and `Queuer`. The third one links the `no stutter` constraint to the fader actors to control the decoding load.

5   Evaluation

The first aspect of evaluation is expressiveness. Timing monitors only monitor events that can be made visible in the software architecture, e.g. that involve the

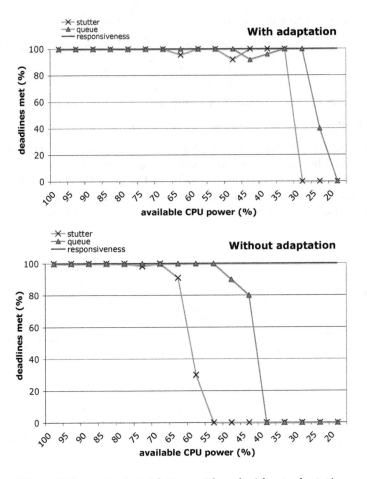

Fig. 8. Dale constraint violations with and without adaptation

handling of messages. This is deliberate: if an event is important enough that it needs a constraint, it should be visible at this level. However, next to message events, there may be extra events that could be useful, such as the initialization of a component or redeployment. These events may be added to the event model of the timing constraints.

Although adaptation actors do not require any additional code, components may need to be rewritten to support the assumptions made in Section 4.2.

Second, we tested the run-time aspects. We have implemented our Dale case, the run-time monitors and adaptation logic in DRACO [9], a Java based component run-time platform. In terms of code overhead, the monitors and actors can be kept quite small (each less than 20 KB), as DRACO allows interception and injection of messages in an application.

To test the effectiveness of the adaptations, we ran the application with and without the adaptation activated to see in which circumstances it performed adequately. Figure 8 shows the run-time behavior of the earlier discussed component setup. We ran the tests on a 1.5 GHz PowerPC computer with Sun's Java 1.4.2 SDK. We simulated different CPU conditions (slower CPU's and different CPU loads) by slowly increasing the time to process the calls of the music repository and codec. We recorded the number of deadline violations with and without adaptation. Noticeable difference between adapted and non-adapted scenario's can be seen when the available CPU power decreases below 65 % and the adaptation actors for the fading algorithm execute the adaptation recipe `normal`. Also, starting from 45 % and less, the advanced queue algorithm cannot keep up with the requests of the `Playlist Manager` and the `queuer` message router switches to the ad-hoc queue algorithm. As can be seen, the adaptations keep the deadline violations at an acceptable level until the CPU power drops below 30 %, when the audio stream cannot be decoded fast enough anymore. Also note that the responsiveness constraint is not affected by the less powerful CPU.

As for efficiency of the mechanisms, the additional overhead is limited for CPU intensive tasks. We measured the message throughput of a connector with messages that took 5 ms to process. Adding a timing monitor decreased the throughput with less than 2 %. Similarly, the decrease in throughput of a message router is less than 5 %. A component tuner imposes no additional overhead. The decision makers are periodically activated and do not influence message throughput.

6   Related Work

Traditional real-time software typically resides on a dedicated system. The timing constraints involved have been extensively tested or proven and there is little need to ensure those constraints at run-time (apart from the addition of some exceptional counter-measures). That is why the many formalisms to specify timing constraints (e.g. UML [10] and extensions [11] [12]) lack support for added run-time behavior and adaptation logic. However, timing constraints tend to be re-adopted in the larger context of Quality of Service (QoS) and resource awareness. QoS management frameworks try to integrate resource management and adaptive behavior. The Quality Object's Contract Description Language (CDL) and CQML specify changes using callback functions. Rainbow also uses low-level adaptation mechanisms but aims for reusability of abstract adaptation strategies and operators [3].

The $2K^Q$ methodology [13] offers middleware-supported adaptation by specifying component dependencies in functional graphs. From these graphs, all possible component configurations are translated. QoS adaptation is then defined and associated with transitions between component configurations. The adaptation behavior is thus somewhat hidden in the set of component configurations. $2K^Q$ suggests the use of middleware entities to recreate a new configuration.

The Quality Objects framework is perhaps the best known example of adaptive middleware. QuO specifies an architecture for implementing distributed adaptive applications; the adaptation itself however is worked out at a low level. Also, efforts have been made to package the QuO monitoring and adaptation into reusable entities called Qoskets [14]. Qoskets offer pre-defined but reusable adaptation code that can be added to CORBA objects, provided that the right wrapper code is written.

In order to tackle the development of adaptive applications, some research efforts explored the concept of QoS developer. They claim that the application developer needs help specifying and implementing adaptive QoS and propose that this work must be done by another person. The people behind the Quality Objects framework call this person a qoskateer [14]. If such a person would be necessary in a project, specifying the adaptation architecturally reduces the responsibilities of the qoskateer to a minimum.

7   Conclusions and Future Work

The handling of non-functional constraints such as timing is an important requirement for upcoming pervasive distributed applications. Defining constraints late in the development process may lead to the discovery of structural flaws in the architecture and entanglement of the adaptation in the functional design. We defined simple architectural constructs that have a clear goal: monitor timing constraints for component based applications and uphold them by carrying out architectural adaptations. These concepts do not offer a general replacement for domain specific adaptation solutions such as bandwidth control or grid application management, but can be used in most distributed resource-intensive or time-critical applications.

Throughout the paper we worked out an architectural run-time adaptation view of a music application we implemented. Although the architecture may need to be tailored to clearly define timing constraints and adaptation opportunities, the tailoring itself adds clarity to the architectural design. If the state and synchronization assumptions are respected, no extra code is needed to enable the adaptation actors at run-time. Although the overhead of the run-time mechanisms is limited, it is best to only define adaptations that have a significant influence on resource consumption.

The separation of constraints, decision logic and adaptation opens up possibilities to execute adaptations to uphold constraints that belong to other applications. This will be a topic for future research. Finally, it would be interesting to define adaptation actors that handle distribution. This way, resource intensive components could be migrated to uphold constraints.

References

1. Kephart, J.O., Chess, D.M.: The vision of autonomic computing. IEEE Computer (2003)
2. Cheng, S.W., Garlan, D., Schmerl, B., Sousa, J.P., Spitznagel, B., Steenkiste, P., Hu, N.: Software architecture-based adaptation for pervasive systems. In: International Conference on Architecture of Computing Systems (ARCS'02): Trends in Network and Pervasive Computing, LNCS (2002)

3. Garlan, D., Cheng, S.W., Huang, A.C., Schmerl, B., Steenkiste, P.: Rainbow: Architecture-based self-adaptation with reusable infrastructure. Computer **37** (2004) 46–54

4. Oreizy, P., Gorlick, M.M., Taylor, R.N., Heimbigner, D., Johnson, G., Medvidovic, N., Quilici, A., Rosenblum, D.S., Wolf, A.L.: An architecture-based approach to self-adaptive software. IEEE Intelligent Systems **14** (1999) 54–62

5. Mok, A.K., Liu, G.: Efficient run-time monitoring of timing constraints. In: RTAS '97: Proceedings of the 3rd IEEE Real-Time Technology and Applications Symposium (RTAS '97), Washington, DC, USA, IEEE Computer Society (1997) 252

6. SEESCOA Consortium: Software engineering for embedded systems using a component-oriented approach, (SEESCOA). http://www.cs.kuleuven. be/~distrinet/projects/SEESCOA (2002)

7. van Ommering, R.: Building product populations with software components. In: ICSE '02: Proceedings of the 24th International Conference on Software Engineering, New York, NY, USA, ACM Press (2002) 255–265

8. Meijler, T.D., Schoenmaker, S., de Ruijter, E.: Modeling in an architectural variability description language. In: Proceedings of the Workshop "Planen, Scheduling und Konfigurieren, Entwerfen" (PUK2003). (2003)

9. Vandewoude, Y., Rigole, P., Urting, D.: Draco: an adaptive runtime environment for components. Appendix of the EMPRESS deliverable for Run-time Evolution and Dynamic (Re)configuration of Components (2003)

10. Berkenkötter, K.: Using UML 2.0 in real-time development: a critical review. In: Proceedings of the workshop on Specification and Validation of UML models for Real Time and Embedded Systems (SVERTS). (2003)

11. Graf, S., Ober, I., Ober, I.: Timed annotations in UML. STTT, Int. Journal on Software Tools for Technology Transfer (2005) under press.

12. Gu, Z., Shin, K.G.: Synthesis of real-time implementation from UML-RT models. In: Proceedings of the 2nd RTAS Workshop on Model-Driven Embedded Systems. (2004)

13. Nahrstedt, K., Wichadakul, D., Xu, D.: Distributed qos compilation and runtime instantiation. In: Proceedings of IEEE/IFIP International Workshop on QoS 2000(IWQoS2000). (2000)

14. Schantz, R., Loyall, J., Atighetchi, M., Pal, P.: Packaging quality of service control behaviors for reuse. In: ISORC '02: Proceedings of the Fifth IEEE International Symposium on Object-Oriented Real-Time Distributed Computing, Washington, DC, USA, IEEE Computer Society (2002)

Fault-Tolerant Replication
Based on Fragmented Objects

Hans P. Reiser[1], Rüdiger Kapitza[2], Jörg Domaschka[1], and Franz J. Hauck[1]

[1] Distributed Systems Lab, University of Ulm, Germany
{hans.reiser, joerg.domaschka, franz.hauck}@uni-ulm.de
[2] Department of Distributed Systems and Operating Systems,
University of Erlangen-Nürnberg, Germany
kapitza@informatik.uni-erlangen.de

Abstract. This paper describes a novel approach to fault-tolerance in distributed object-based systems. It uses the fragmented-object model to integrate replication mechanisms into distributed applications. This approach enables the use of customised code on a per-object basis to access replica groups and to manage consistency. The addition of fault tolerance to the infrastructure has only little overhead, is fully transparent for clients, and does not require internal modifications to the existing middleware. Semantic annotations at the interface level allow the developer to customise the provision of fault tolerance. Operations can be marked as read-only to allow an execution with weaker ordering semantics or as parallelisable to allow true multithreaded execution. A code-generation tool is provided to automatically produce object-specific fragment code for client access and for replica consistency management, taking into account the annotations, the interface specification, and the non-replicated implementation. A further contribution of our code-generation approach is the support of deterministic multithreading in replicated objects.

1 Introduction

The development of fault-tolerant applications in distributed systems is a complex task. It can be simplified for the developer by providing support for fault-tolerance at the middleware level. Replication support has previously been added to middleware systems like CORBA in various ways, for example using the interception approach [13], the integration approach [3], or the service approach [4]. The approaches differ in their properties regarding transparency, efficiency, and portability; each approach has its specific advantages, but also disadvantages.

Recent publications (e.g., [2, 5]) indicate that the current support for replication in general-purpose distributed object middleware is not yet sufficient in several regards. One of the limitations is the lack of interoperability between multiple middleware infrastructures. For example, typical fault-tolerant CORBA systems require all replicas to run on the same ORB implementation. Often, clients must use the same manufacturer's ORB to benefit from the fault-tolerance mechanisms. Consequently, heterogeneity in terms of middleware platform or programming language—an important feature and one of the main objectives of CORBA—lacks support.

F. Eliassen and A. Montresor (Eds.): DAIS 2006, LNCS 4025, pp. 256–271, 2006.

Replica nondeterminism is a source of problems, both in passive replication in case of replica faults and in active replication [23]. If potentially nondeterministic actions are not simply prohibited in replica implementations (a popular approach), they have to be intercepted and coordinated by the infrastructure. One problematic source of nondeterminism is multithreaded execution of object operations. Many fault-tolerant infrastructures solve this problem by forcing a strictly sequential execution of all client requests in total order. This solution has serious limitations, as it not only lacks performance, but is also inherently deadlock-prone. Only few systems (e.g, [15, 8, 23]) offer a multithreaded solution with an adequate deterministic thread scheduling strategy. Such approaches require that the service uses specific locking methods that can be intercepted by the fault-tolerance infrastructure.

Furthermore, most existing fault-tolerant object middleware systems provide no mechanism to use semantic knowledge about the replicated object. Often, this is not the most efficient solution: If, for example, it is known that some methods are read-only or parallelisable, weaker ordering semantics than total order can be employed to improve efficiency. A replication infrastructure can provide such optimisations automatically only if it has access to semantic information explicitly expressed by the object developer.

The contribution of this paper are approaches to handle several of these problematic issues in fault-tolerant middleware systems. Our implementation provides an infrastructure for fault-tolerant distributed applications in the AspectIX middleware based on fragmented objects. The fragmented-object model [12, 7, 21] is a versatile approach to design complex distributed services that do not strictly adhere to a simple client-server structure. It supports dynamic loading of object-specific fragment code at the client side and at replica locations. This flexibility of a fragmented-object middleware enables the integration of fault-tolerance support without requiring internal middleware modifications. The access to replica groups remains fully transparent for clients. At the same time, the directly loaded object-specific fragment code avoids the overhead of interception strategies or other delegation approaches.

At the core of our architecture, we provide a code-generation tool that automatically creates client-side access fragments and server-side replica fragments based on the non-replicated object implementation, the interface definition, and semantic annotations. This way, the transition from an existing implementation to a replicated one is automated as much as possible, with only minimal developer intervention required. Annotations can be provided to specify if an object operation interacts with the replica and modifies its state, if it is a read-only operation, if it is parallelisable with other methods, or if it is a method that can be computed locally at the client side without interacting with the replica group.

Our replication system allows multithreading inside actively replicated objects. A deterministic thread scheduler supports an arbitrary number of reentrant mutex locks, condition variables that allow threads to block and be woken up by other threads, and timeouts on blocking synchronisation operations. Language-specific synchronisation statements need to be mapped to the synchronisation interface of the scheduler. Our Java-based prototype provides a code-generation tool that automatically transforms native Java synchronisation statements. This allows application developers to use

Java-specific constructs (e.g., synchronized statements) to express the required coordination, as they would do in non-replicated code. The multithreading issues of replication remain fully transparent for the application developer. Semantic annotations can be used to further improve the thread-scheduling mechanism. For example, multiple methods that are marked as parallelisable can all be executed in parallel without coordinating their lock acquisitions.

This paper is structured as follows: Section 2 discusses established approaches to fault tolerance in traditional middleware and surveys in more detail the fragmented-object model. Section 3 presents the realisation of fault-tolerant replication in the AspectIX middleware based on fragmented objects. It describes our code-generation process, which considers semantic annotations, and discusses the advantages of our approach regarding multithreading. Section 4 evaluates our system. Finally, Section 5 concludes.

2   Background

2.1   Approaches to Replication Support in Distributed Object Middleware

Replication adds redundancy to a system, which makes it possible to tolerate the failure of some of the nodes on which an object is located. Some strategy, like active or passive replication, is required to keep the replicas in a consistent state. In passive replication, only a single designated primary replica executes all operations; secondary replicas are able to take over the primary's functionality if it fails. In active replication, all replicas execute all operations. This causes more overhead than passive replication in failure-free executions, but allows faster reaction to failures (ideally, the failure of a single node remains fully unnoticed by clients). In addition, keeping all replicas constantly up-to-date allows using load-balancing for read-only requests, which are handled by only one replica.

Several research projects have investigated ways for adding fault-tolerance mechanisms to distributed object middleware. For fault-tolerance in CORBA systems, the OMG provides the FT-CORBA specifications [16, Chap. 23] as a general standard, without specifying exact implementation details. The implementation of this standard in existing CORBA middleware is usually based on the interception approach, the service approach, or the integration approach.

The interception approach initially was propagated by the Eternal system [13]. Eternal intercepts IIOP messages between the ORB and the operating system. This way, any off-the-shelf ORB can be used, and replication becomes fully transparent for clients and servers. However, such interception requires adequate support at the operating-system level. Fault-tolerance mechanisms are fully separated from the ORB core; information about remote invocations can only be obtained by parsing the marshalled invocation data.

A prominent example for the service approach is OpenDREAMS [4]. This system encapsulates fault-tolerance mechanisms inside a CORBA service. The only direct interaction of application objects is with a local Object Group Service (OGS), which in turn coordinates with other OGS instances and executes the requested operations at the replicas. This approach does not offer replication transparency, as clients are aware of the OGS, and adds an additional step of indirection, which increases latency. Its outstanding benefit is that no proprietary extensions to the ORB or the operating system are needed.

In the integration approach, the ORB is directly modified to provide the desired support for fault tolerance. In general, this provides the most efficient solution. However, this approach usually inhibits any interoperability with clients running on standard off-the-shelf CORBA platforms. Orbix+Isis [3] and Electra [11] are examples where the integration approach has successfully been used.

Replication may also be added to other non-CORBA middleware infrastructures. For example, the AROMA system [14] transparently enhances the Java RMI system with mechanisms for consistent object replication. It modifies the Java RMI infrastructure to intercept remote invocations and maps them to a reliable, totally ordered group communication protocol. As another example, the .NET remoting infrastructure provides the possibility to load custom stub code ("real proxy") instead of the default stub. This makes it possible to transparently add custom support for replication [19].

Our fault-tolerance infrastructure is based on the AspectIX middleware, which provides support for *fragmented objects*. This support is implemented as an extension to a standard CORBA ORB. With fragmented objects, custom fragment code can be loaded transparently at client side and replica side on a per-object basis. Our fault-tolerance architecture provides code-generation tools to create fragment code for fragmented objects. This code can be used on any middleware that supports our fragmented-object model; to this extent our approach is portable and not restricted to a specific vendor's ORB. Furthermore, it provides client-side transparency and has optimal efficiency, as the client directly invokes fragment methods without unnecessary indirection steps.

2.2   The Fragmented-Object Model

In a traditional client/server system based on remote method invocations, the functionality of an object completely resides on a single node. For transparently accessing the object, the client-side middleware instantiates a stub that handles remote invocations (Fig. 1a). Usually, the stub code is automatically generated from an interface specification. All objects with the same interface share the same stub code. The middleware runtime systems instantiates the stub as soon as the client binds to an object reference. The bind operation is either requested explicitly by the client, or it is performed implicitly when an object reference is passed to the client through the marshalling mechanisms of the ORB.

In the fragmented-object model, the distinction between client stubs and the server object is no longer present. From an abstract point of view, a fragmented object is a unit with unique identity, interface, behaviour, and state, as it is in classic object-oriented design. The implementation of these properties, however, is not bound to a certain location, but may be distributed arbitrarily on various fragments (Fig. 1b). Any client that wants to access the fragmented object needs a local fragment. In addition, there can be fragments that are deployed on nodes without a client. The client interface of a local fragment is identical to that of a traditional stub. However, the local fragment can be specific for exactly that object. Two objects with the same interface can lead

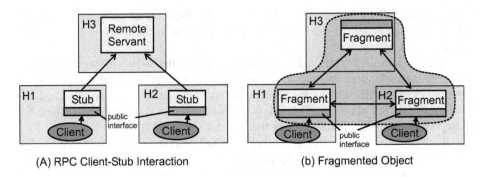

(A) RPC Client-Stub Interaction   (b) Fragmented Object

Fig. 1. Traditional Client/Stub Structure vs. Fragmented Object

to completely different local fragments. This internal structure allows a high degree of freedom on where the state and functionality of an object is provided, and how the interaction between fragments is done. The internal distribution and interaction is hidden from the outer interface. In addition, the distribution of functionality to fragments can even be changed dynamically at runtime.

The AspectIX middleware provides support for fragmented objects. Unlike other fragmented-object middleware infrastructures such as FOG [12] and Globe [7], it even supports implicit binding of fragmented objects upon the receipt of a marshalled object reference. All reference-related operations are handled by a generic reference manager and pluggable profile managers [6]. AspectIX uses CORBA IORs as references and also provides interoperability with standard CORBA applications. In addition to CORBA IIOP profiles, a custom IOR profile (called APX) for fragmented objects is supported. When binding to such a reference, fragment-specific code is transparently loaded; for this purpose, AspectIX provides a Dynamic Loading Service (DLS [9]) that enables the lookup, selection, and loading of platform-dependent code at run-time. From a client point of view, the interface of a local fragment is identical to that of a standard CORBA object.

3   The AspectIX Replication Architecture

3.1   Overview

On top of the basic infrastructure for fragmented objects, we provide support for fault-tolerant active replication of distributed objects. This chapter first outlines our architecture, which encapsulates replication inside a fragmented object. We discuss the internal implementation structure of the fragments, illustrate the use of the AspectIX profile in the IOR to reference replica groups, and describe the run-time infrastructure, which is used to create and administrate replica groups. Subsequently, we explain how semantic properties can be defined by developer annotations. Finally, we focus on the code-generation process that automatically produces fragment code from the interface definition, the semantical annotations, and the non-replicated implementation.

3.2   Fault-Tolerant Replication with Fragmented Objects

A fault-tolerant service in the fragmented-object model is represented by a single distributed object which is composed of replica fragments and access fragments (Fig. 2). The development process consists of defining the global object interface in CORBA IDL, implementing the functional parts of the service, and creating the fragment code. The creation of fragment code is done automatically by tools; these tools can make use of additional semantic annotations provided by the developer, as we will describe in Section 3.3. This enables the generation of a customised layer between the client and the core framework and also between the framework and the replica implementation.

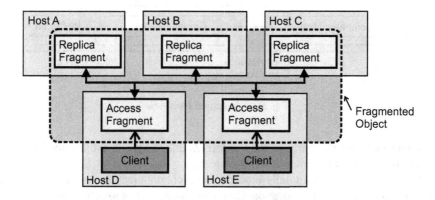

Fig. 2. Replication with Fragmented Objects

Details of the Fragment Architecture. The layered design of access and replica fragments in our architecture is shown in Fig. 3. Access fragments are used by client applications; the replica fragments contain the object state. Replica fragments do not support direct client access. Instead, an access fragment is instantiated at the same location as the replica fragment. For simplicity, this detail is not shown in Fig. 3.

Starting at the client side, the client application accesses the fault-tolerant fragmented object via its interface like any other CORBA object. The generated access fragment may contain optional developer code that is directly embedded (see Section 3.3). Furthermore, it contains a *Context Handler*, code for marshalling and unmarshalling of requests (equal to a standard client-side stub), and code for remote communication.

If client A invokes a method at a replicated object B, a node failure during the invocation can make it necessary to repeat the invocation. This happens if the client A communicates with a replica fragment that fails. The re-invocation contacts a different replica of B. Alternatively, A can be replicated itself. In this case, the access fragment provides client-side duplication suppression by selecting one replica of A to actually make the remote invocation. If this selected replica fails, another replica of A repeats the invocation. To preserve the at-most-once invocation semantics of CORBA, in both cases the repetition of the invocation needs to be detected and filtered out at the replica

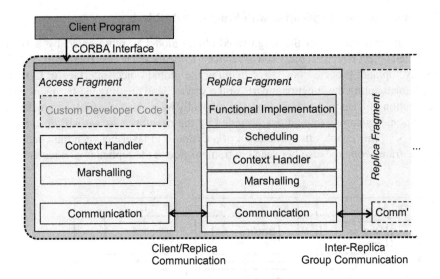

Fig. 3. Architectural Overview

fragments of *B*. For this purpose, the *Context Handler* adds context information with a consistent unique ID that identifies the request.

At the network level, a totally ordered group communication system provides the basis for consistent active replication. Currently, our prototype uses the JGroups system [1], which is based on the closed-group approach. This implies that group communication is only used between replicas; any replica can act as a gateway to communicate between an access fragment and the replica group. However, our implementation easily supports the exchange of the network layer, such that group communication systems with an open-group model—like our own group communication framework [18]—can be used. This potentially improves performance (e.g., the access fragment can directly multicast its request to all replicas). For tolerating Byzantine failures, an appropriate variant

With the gateway approach, the *Communication* element in the access replica is responsible for transmitting calls to one available replica. If this replica fails, the *Communication* transparently reconnects to another replica fragment and reissues the call. If the call has already been processed by the replicas, this is detected and the invocation result is returned from a cache. The *Communication* component in replica fragments is responsible for passing requests to group communication. All requests that are received from group communication are placed into a totally ordered queue for subsequent processing in the upper layer.

The upper layer consists of three different components: First, the *Marshalling* component deserialises requests and serialises replies. The replica side of the *Context Handler* component is used for the suppression of duplicated requests. The *Scheduling* component is responsible for the internal message management and for the deterministic multithreading support, which is explained in detail in Section 3.5. On the top end, requests are passed to the functional implementation that was provided by the developer; this implementation may partially get modified by the code generation process (see Section 3.4)

IOR References to Replica Groups. As described in Section 2.2, the AspectIX middleware uses CORBA IORs to reference fragmented objects via an APX profile. This profile contains a unique object ID, a specification of the initial fragment type to load, and contact information of other fragments. The initial fragment type can be specified in a language-independent way; equivalent fragment implementations may exist for various programming languages or execution platforms. The Dynamic Loading Service (DLS) of AspectIX loads the appropriate code based on the specification from the IOR profile [9].

The initially loaded fragment evaluates the contact information from the IOR profile. In the gateway approach, this information consists of a list of all replica gateway addresses of the group. In the open-group approach, address information for the group communication system (like a multicast address for group discovery or the addresses of gossip servers) can be stored in the contact information. The removal or addition of replicas triggers the creation of a new version of the replica group's IOR. The standard approach for updating the client's IORs, which is also used in FT-CORBA, is to include the client's current IOR version in each invocation request to the replica group. If this version is out-of-date, the replica will send the current version in the reply to the client.

This approach is practical in many situations; however, it does not provide any guarantees that all client-side IORs will get updated in time before they no longer provide valid contact information. To improve this situation, we additionally support the concept of a lifetime specified within the IOR references [10]. During the specified lifetime, the replica group guarantees that the IOR information can be used to contact the group; in the gateway approach, this means that at least one of the replica gateway addresses included in the IOR remains accessible. Optionally, the address of a location service can be specified in the IOR, which manages an up-to-date contact information for the replica group. This is useful if the distribution of a fragmented object changes frequently and the risk of stale references is high.

Run-Time Infrastructure. Similar to other fault-tolerant middleware infrastructures, AspectIX uses the factory pattern to create and set up replicas. Replication groups are implemented as self-managing entities; this reduces the complexity of the necessary infrastructure compared to other systems that require a dedicated replication manager. In addition, the management automatically benefits from the same fault-tolerance mechanisms as the replicated object itself.

Starting a new replicated service involves several steps. First, a factory must be acquired via a factory finder. A factory finder represents a search scope for possible places of execution, as defined by the CORBA Life Cycle Specification [17]. Currently, our factory finder is implemented straightforwardly in plain CORBA and well-known on every node within a domain. This way, a node can register its local factories and it can lookup factories from all other nodes. Multiple factory finders can be provided for fault tolerance.

Our generic factory for object creation offers two methods: one for setting up an initial replica of a replicated fragmented object and another one for setting up additional

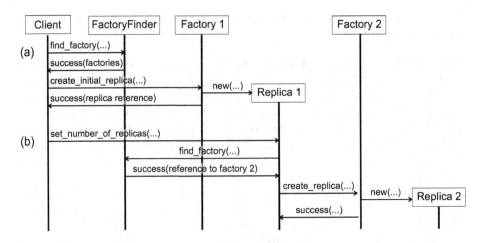

Fig. 4. Creation of first and additional replicas

replicas. After lookup of one or more factories via the factory finder, one of them is requested to instantiate the first replica via `create_initial_replica()` (see Fig. 4 (a)). The factory creates the initial replica and activates the fragment object. Afterwards, the object is returned to the calling client and, as it is a fragmented object, a local access fragment is dynamically instantiated. This results in a simple client/server structure with only one replica. The management code within this replica is able to control the creation of additional replicas.

A management interface of the fragmented object is used to adjust the desired number of replicas (see Fig. 4 (b)). If the client increases the number of replicas, the existing replica group is triggered to add the necessary number of additional replicas. The replica-side fragment contacts the factory finder to request additional factories. In the next step, a reference to the fragmented object is passed to a factory. At the factory side, the fragmented object is transparently bound by the middleware, which loads the initial fragment. Under control of the factory, the local fragment is reconfigured to be a replica fragment. The state of the existing replica group is transferred to the new replica similar to the CORBA Life Cycle Service. The addition of replicas is repeated until the desired replication level is reached or until no additional factories are found. The failure of a replica in the group is detected by a failure-detection mechanism at the group-communication level. After detecting a failure, the replica group automatically sets up a new replica in the same way, as long as another factory is available.

3.3   Semantic Information from Object Developers

A simple scheme for generating client-side and replica-side fragment code only uses IDL interface information, like a traditional CORBA IDL compiler does for stubs and skeletons. Additionally, our architecture allows the developer to express semantic knowledge in order to improve and customise the replication mechanisms. Currently, we support several annotations on a per-method basis:

```
1    interface  CC_processor {
2       transaction_id  charge(in  card_data  card ,  in  float  amount)
3            raises(CardNotValid ,   TransactionFailed );
4
5    #pragma  annotate(readonly)
6       boolean  validate_card(in  card_data  card)  raises(CardNotValid );
7
8    #pragma  annotate(local)
9       boolean  validate_card_checksum(in  card_data  card)
10           raises(CardNotValid );
11   };
```

Fig. 5. IDL with semantic annotations

- readonly: A method marked as read-only does not modify the relevant replica state. Instead of executing this method in total-order at all replicas, it is sufficient to invoke it on one available replica.
- parallelizable(methodlist): A method marked as parallelisable with respect to a set of other methods can be executed in parallel with the specified list of other methods. This allows true multithreading.
- local: The implementation of a method marked as local will be placed in the client-side fragment. This way, methods that need no access to the replica state can be executed locally at the client, while still being conceptionally part of the distributed object.
- intercepted: A method marked as intercepted will execute custom code at the client-side before and after invoking the remote method at the replica group. This mechanism can be used for local preprocessing, for caching, or for the accumulation of multiple client invocations into one remote invocation to the replica group.

Our current implementation uses annotations embedded as #pragma instructions within the IDL file, as the example in Fig. 5 illustrates. Our flexible IDL compiler IDLflex [22] allowed us to implement this solution easily.

3.4   Code Generation for Fragments

In our replication infrastructure, the creation of fragment implementations is automated by a code-generation tool. Two basic fragment types are required (see Section 3): A replica fragment for consistency management and a client-side access fragment. The current prototype of the code-generation tool is based on IDLflex [22], an IDL-compiler that generates customisable code. IDLflex parses CORBA IDL, evaluates an XML-based mapping specification, and uses this specification to create arbitrary output code. It includes two standard mapping specifications for the Java programming language, one for standard CORBA and one for AspectIX fragmented objects.

For replication support, the IDL-compiler was extended to support semantic annotations in IDL files, expressed as #pragma annotate statements. Within a custom

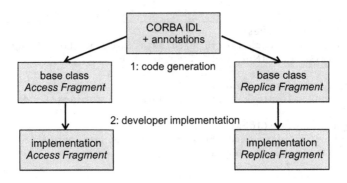

Fig. 6. Development Process of Fault-Tolerant Fragmented Object

mapping specification, these annotations are evaluated and used to control the code-generation process.

The development process of a fault-tolerant fragmented object is illustrated by Fig. 6. The annotated IDL is used to create a base class for the access fragment and the replica fragment. Additional developer code can be added to the access fragment if required by *local* or *intercepted* operations, as we describe below. The implementation of the replica fragment is similar to that of a non-replicated CORBA servant. The main differences are that (1) it has to inherit from the generated replica base class and (2) it has to implement methods for state transfer.

The generated code depends on the code annotations. If at least one *read-only* method is present, the generated code for the *Communication* component will examine all invocation requests. If the requested method is marked as read-only, it will be passed directly to the implementation of one replica, bypassing the totally ordered group communication.

The *Scheduling* component interacts with the deterministic thread-scheduling support of our replication infrastructure (see Section 3.5). The generated code of the component knows which methods are marked *read-only* and *parallelisable*. This information is made available to the thread scheduler in order to maximise the concurrency of request execution.

Specifying a method as *local* causes the method's implementation to be placed in the access fragment instead of the replica fragment. Such method implementation must not access replica state. This approach is useful for methods that, for example, validate client data in a state-independent way or that provide static information to the client.

For each method annotated as *intercepted*, an abstract method is created in the access fragment; the actual method implementation must be provided by the developer. A protected method is provided in the access fragment for accessing the real implementation at the remote replica group; this method can be used within the developer code in the access fragment. Applications for such interceptions are client-side caching strategies or the accumulation of multiple client method invocations with subsequent manipulation of the replicated object's state with only one invocation to the replica group. Our current prototype requires that the developer manually implements the additional client-side code.

Another aspect of the creation of replica fragment code is the ability to modify the functional object implementation. This approach is used to intercept native Java synchronisation code. Synchronisation operations need to be intercepted by our deterministic thread scheduler (see Sect 3.5). By replacing all relevant statements with custom code, such interceptions is possible without internal modification to JVM or operating system. The same approach could be used to intercept Java API calls to nondeterministic methods like the generation of time-stamps or random numbers.

3.5   Multithreading in Actively Replicated Services

Active replication requires a deterministic execution of all state-modifying actions. If multiple threads are allowed to access the replicated object in parallel, the order in which threads access shared data may vary between replicas; this can lead to an inconsistent object state.

The popular solution of using a single-threaded execution has several drawbacks. If a replica group issues a nested invocation, it has to idle until this invocation returns; if a second thread used this waiting time for computations, it would result in improved performance. The single-threaded approach is also deadlock prone: If such a nested invocation calls back a method on the first replica group, this call is blocked by the waiting thread, resulting in a deadlock. Similarly, with a single-threaded model, condition variables that suspend the current thread until woken up by another thread cannot be used.

To provide support for multithreading, we integrated our deterministic thread scheduler for active replication [20] into our AspectIX replication architecture. Our scheduler uses an algorithm similar to that by Zhao et al. [23], improved by support for condition variables and for native Java synchronisation mechanism. It provides a non-preemptive, deterministic mechanism for thread scheduling. A new thread is only created or an existing thread is only resumed, if all other existing threads have reached a safe state, i.e., have terminated or have blocked waiting for a mutex, for a condition variable notification, for a timeout, or for a nested invocation reply. All decisions are fully deterministic, and consequently remain consistent among all replicas. Lock requests, lock releases, and condition variable access need to be passed to our thread scheduling algorithm.

We do not want to modify the execution environment (i.e., the JVM), but still want to allow implementing synchronisation in the replicated object with native Java mechanisms (`synchronized` statements, etc). To intercept these statements, our code generation tool automatically transforms these statements into appropriate synchronisation calls to the deterministic scheduler in the replica fragment, as described above. This approach requires that the synchronisation of a replicated object is fully encapsulated within the replica fragment. That is, we assume that lock object instances used by the replica implementation are not used for synchronisation in code outside the replica fragment, but within the same JVM (Java virtual machine). Developer code within the access fragment has no direct access to the object state and thus does not require synchronisation.

Based on the semantic annotations, the scheduling algorithm can be further improved. A thread may be created or resumed not only if all other threads have reached a safe state, but also if it is marked as parallelisable with all other threads that have not terminated. Special care needs to be taken for read-only methods, which are only executed in one replica. These methods are not allowed to use wait/notify operations on condition variables, as this could lead to an inconsistent scheduling of other modifying methods.

4   Evaluation

Our semantic annotations at the interface level offer ample opportunities to tune and optimise the implementation of replicated objects. In many cases these are very application specific, e.g., if a resource intensive subtask is moved from server to client side. In this section, we present two general examples, which show the possible speed-up of our approach. All presented measurements were made on AMD Opteron 2.2 GHz Linux server machines connected via a switched 100Mbit/s ethernet, using our AspectIX ORB with JGroups 2.2.9.1 for group communication and Java SDK-1.5.0. The JGroups stack was configured to use TCP connections and TOTAL ordering.

In the first example, we measured the difference in invocation time between a read-only method and a modifying method. The read-only method invocation is not distributed via the group-communication framework but instead sent directly to one of the replicas. Fig. 7(a) shows the average time per invocation, obtained from at least ten runs with 5000 client invocations. A single client accesses a replica group with the number of replicas increasing from one to five nodes. The invocation cost for modifying methods is dominated by the cost of the totally ordered group communication. This underlines the benefit from using semantic knowledge about object methods for building an efficient fault-tolerant replication system.

The second example analyses our support for condition variables in the deterministic scheduler. We implemented a simple replicated counter that is increased by a producer and decreased by a variable number of consumers. Without condition variables, the consumers must use polling (for our measurements, a one ms delay between retries was used); with condition variables, a consumer call can block within the counter object at a condition variable until it is woken up by a producer call. We again show the

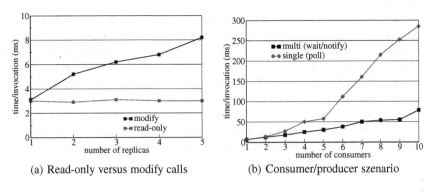

(a) Read-only versus modify calls   (b) Consumer/producer szenario

Fig. 7. Efficiency gains by read-only annotations and by multithreading

average time per consumer invocation, averaged over repeated experiments with 5000 calls per client. The time is expected to increase linearly with the number of consumers, as multiple consumers compete for values produced by a single producer. As shown in Fig. 7(b), the multithreaded approach with condition variables outperforms a single-threaded implementation; the benefit increases with a rising number of clients.

5 Conclusions

We have presented an architecture for fault-tolerant replication of objects in distributed systems based on the fragmented-object model. A fragmented-object middleware loads custom code at client side and server side on a per-object basis. This enables the implementation of generic fault-tolerance support fully transparent for clients, without internal modifications to the middleware, and without the overhead of indirections that take place in the interception or service approach to fault-tolerance support.

The core of our architecture is a code-generation process that automatically produces client-side access fragments and replica-side consistency management fragments, based on the interface specification, the functional implementation provided by the object developer, and semantic annotations. Our current prototype uses semantic annotations inside the IDL interface definitions, and supports the Java programming language.

We use the semantic annotations for selecting consistency mechanisms for method invocation, strategies for thread scheduling, and for supporting client-side computations. Methods can be marked as read-only, which allows their execution without strict total-order requirements. They can be marked as parallelisable, which enables parallel execution by our multithreading support for actively replicated objects. Furthermore, parts of the functional object implementation can be directly placed at the client side.

Code transformation is also used for removing nondeterministic behaviour in object implementations. We specifically use this to allow multithreading in actively replicated objects; native Java synchronisation mechanisms are replaced with code that allows interception by our deterministic thread scheduler.

Our prototype assumes that a fragmented object middleware is used, but our concept is not strictly limited to such a platform. Other platforms that provide means to load custom object-specific code at the client side, for example based on the smart-proxy principle, can similarly use our code-generation concept for supporting fault tolerance. One advantage of the fragmented-object approach is its flexibility that even supports dynamic reconfiguration at run-time.

References

1. Bela Ban. Design and implementation of a reliable group communication toolkit for Java. Technical report, Dept. of Computer Science, Cornell University, 1998.
2. Ken Birman. Can web services scale up? *Computer*, 38(10):107–110, 2005.
3. Kenneth P. Birman and Robbert Van Renesse. *Reliable Distributed Computing with the ISIS Toolkit*. IEEE Computer Society Press, Los Alamitos, CA, USA, 1993.
4. Pascal Felber. *The CORBA Object Group Service: A Service Approach to Object Groups in CORBA*. PhD thesis, École Polytechnique Fédérale de Lausanne, Switzerland, 1998. Number 1867.

5. Pascal Felber and Priya Narasimhan. Experiences, strategies, and challenges in building fault-tolerant CORBA systems. *IEEE Trans. Comput.*, 53(5):497–511, 2004.

6. Franz J. Hauck, Rüdiger Kapitza, Hans P. Reiser, and Andreas I. Schmied. A flexible and extensible object middleware: CORBA and beyond. In *Proc. of the Fifth Int. Workshop on Software Engineering and Middleware.* ACM Digital Library, 2005.

7. Philip Homburg, Leendert van Doorn, Maarten van Steen, Andrew S. Tanenbaum, and Wiebren de Jonge. An object model for flexible distributed systems. In *Proceedings of the 1st Annual ASCI Conference*, pages 69–78, 1995.

8. Ricardo Jiménez-Peris, Marta Patiño-Martínez, and Sergio Arévalo. Deterministic scheduling for transactional multithreaded replicas. In *SRDS '00: Proceedings of the 19th IEEE Symposium on Reliable Distributed Systems (SRDS'00)*, page 164, Washington, DC, USA, 2000. IEEE Computer Society.

9. Rüdiger Kapitza and Franz J. Hauck. DLS: a CORBA service for dynamic loading of code. In *Proc. of the OTM'03 Conferences (DOA, Sicily, Italy, Nov. 3-7, 2003)*, number 2888 in LNCS. Springer, 2003.

10. Rüdiger Kapitza, Hans P. Reiser, and Franz J. Hauck. Stable, time-bound references in context of dynamically changing environments. In *MDC'05: Proc. of the 25th IEEE Int. Conf. on Distributed Computing Systems - Workshops (ICDCS 2005 Workshops)*, 2005.

11. Silvano Maffeis. Adding group communication and fault-tolerance to CORBA. In *Proceedings of the Conference on Object-Oriented Technologies, (Monterey, CA), USENIX*, pages 135–146, 1995.

12. Mesaac Makpangou, Yvon Gourhant, Jean-Pierre Le Narzul, and Marc Shapiro. Fragmented objects for distributed abstractions. In T. L. Casavant and M. Singhal, editors, *Readings in distributed computing systems*, pages 170–186. IEEE Computer Society Press, 1994.

13. Luise E. Moser, P. M. Melliar-Smith, and Priya Narasimhan. Consistent object replication in the eternal system. *Theor. Pract. Object Syst.*, 4(2):81–92, 1998.

14. Nitya Narasimhan, Louise E. Moser, and P. M. Melliar-Smith. Transparent consistent replication of Java RMI objects. In *DOA*, pages 17–26, 2000.

15. Priya Narasimhan, Louise E. Moser, and P. M. Melliar-Smith. Enforcing determinism for the consistent replication of multithreaded CORBA applications. In *SRDS '99: Proceedings of the 18th IEEE Symposium on Reliable Distributed Systems*, page 263, Washington, DC, USA, 1999. IEEE Computer Society.

16. Object Management Group (OMG). Common object request broker architecture: Core specification, version 3.0.2. OMG document formal/02-12-02, 2002.

17. Object Management Group (OMG). Life cycle service specification, version 1.2. OMG document formal/02-09-01, 2002.

18. Hans P. Reiser, Udo Bartlang, and Franz J. Hauck. A reconfigurable system architecture for consensus-based group communication. In *Proc. of the 17th IASTED Int. Conf on Parallel and Distributed Systems (Phoenix, AZ, USA, Nov 14-16, 2005)*, 2005.

19. Hans P. Reiser, Michael J. Danel, and Franz J. Hauck. A flexible replication framework for scalable and reliable .NET services. In *Proc. of the IADIS Int. Conf. Applied Comuting 2005, Vol I, Algarve, P*, pages 161–169, 2005.

20. Hans P. Reiser, Franz J. Hauck, and Rüdiger Kapitza. Deterministic multithreading for replicated CORBA applications, 2006. submitted for publication.

21. Hans P. Reiser, Franz J. Hauck, Rüdiger Kapitza, and Andreas I. Schmied. Integrating fragmented objects into a CORBA environment. In *Proc. of the Net.ObjectDays (Erfurt, Germany)*, 2003.

22. Hans P. Reiser, Martin Steckermeier, and Franz J. Hauck. IDLflex: a flexible and generic compiler for CORBA IDL. In *Proc. of the Net.ObjectDays (Erfurt, Germany, Sep. 10-13, 2001)*, 2001.
23. Wenbing Zhao, Louise E. Moser, and P. M. Melliar-Smith. Deterministic scheduling for multithreaded replicas. In *WORDS '05: Proceedings of the 10th IEEE International Workshop on Object-Oriented Real-Time Dependable Systems*, pages 74–81, Washington, DC, USA, 2005. IEEE Computer Society.

Towards Context-Aware Transaction Services

Romain Rouvoy[1], Patricia Serrano-Alvarado[2], and Philippe Merle[1]

[1] INRIA Futurs - Jacquard Project,
LIFL - University of Lille 1,
59655 Villeneuve d'Ascq Cedex, France
{romain.rouvoy, philippe.merle}@inria.fr
[2] ATLAS-GDD Team,
LINA - University of Nantes,
44322 Nantes Cedex 03, France
patricia.serrano-alvarado@univ-nantes.fr

Abstract. For years, transactional protocols have been defined for particular application needs. Traditionally, when implementing a transaction service, a protocol is chosen and remains the same during the system execution. Nevertheless, the dynamic nature of nowadays application contexts (e.g., mobile, ad-hoc, peer-to-peer) and context variations (semantics-related aspects) motivates the need for transaction service adaptation. Next generation of transaction services should be adaptive or even better self-adaptive. This paper proposes CATE: (1) a component-based architecture of standard 2PC-based protocols and (2) a Context-Aware Transaction sErvice. Self-adaptation of CATE is obtained by context awareness and component-based reconfiguration. This allows CATE to select the most appropriate protocol with respect to the execution context. We show that using CATE performs better than using only one commit protocol in a variable system and that the reconfiguration cost is negligible.

1 Introduction

The dynamic nature of nowadays application contexts (e.g., mobile, ad-hoc, peer-to-peer) and context variations (semantics-related aspects) justifies the need for application adaptation [1]. Next generation of applications should automatically tune themselves and apply optimizations in order to maximize performances, to evolve, to face different contexts or to adapt the execution process according to context variations.

Component-based models are a good solution to make possible software adaptability [2] mainly because component-based architectures facilitate static and dynamic configuration. Implementing component-based adaptive applications is a very active and consolidated research/industrial issue [3, 4]. Nevertheless, there has been little work on adaptability of middleware services, such as persistence, replication, transaction, or communication [5, 6, 7].

In distributed transaction management, commit protocols ensure atomicity, which means that all transaction operations success (commit) or none of them

F. Eliassen and A. Montresor (Eds.): DAIS 2006, LNCS 4025, pp. 272–288, 2006.
© IFIP International Federation for Information Processing 2006

(abort). The most used commit protocol is Two-Phase Commit (2PC) [8]. There exists a number of 2PC optimizations and some of them are so widely used that, as 2PC, are part of transaction processing standards. 2PC variations are proposed to optimize transaction execution costs, to address particular transaction semantics (e.g., read-only), to execute on different network topologies, etc. For instance, the 2PC Presumed Commit protocol (2PC-PC) [9] is well suited for high transaction commit rates, whereas 2PC Presumed Abort (2PC-PA) [9] is more appropriate for high transaction abort rates.

Traditionally, transaction service implementations are tailored for a particular application context. A transactional protocol is chosen and remains the same even if the application context changes. This may lead to unexpected poor performances. To deal with context variations of transactional applications, the transaction management system should be adaptive or even better self-adaptive. We consider self-adaptation as the ability of being aware of the application context changes and the capacity of reacting to them. This paper proposes CATE, which is composed of (1) a component-based architecture of standard 2PC-based protocols and (2) a Context-Aware Transaction sErvice. Self-adaptation of CATE is obtained by a context-aware mechanism and component-based reconfiguration. This allows CATE to select the most appropriate protocol with respect to the execution context. The implementation performance results show that using CATE performs better than using only one commit protocol in a variable system and that the reconfiguration cost is negligible.

This paper is organized as follows. Section 2 briefly introduces the atomic commit protocols used in this work. Section 3 introduces the component-based implementation and the evaluation of the 2PC, 2PC-PA, and 2PC-PC protocols. Section 4 presents our Context-Aware Transaction Service, its implementation and some empirical measures obtained when using it. Finally, Section 5 presents some related work, and Section 6 concludes and gives future work.

2   Overview of Commit Protocols

In database systems, correct concurrent data access is ensured using transactions. Transactions are characterized by the well-known ACID (Atomicity, Consistency, Isolation and Durability) properties, which are guaranteed by transaction services. While we consider that consistency, isolation and durability properties are supported by the application resource managers (e.g., Database), this paper focuses on the atomicity property. In particular, our work focuses on the self-adaptability of the atomicity property. For the purposes of this paper, we concentrate on some standard 2PC-based protocols, which are the 2PC, 2PC-PA and 2PC-PC protocols.

To describe the behavior of these 2PC protocols, we use UML sequence diagrams (see Figures 1 to 3). It allows us to identify four actors: Application, Coordinator, Participants, and Log. Then, the sequences describe the behavior of the 2PC, 2PC-PA and 2PC-PC protocols in terms of communication schema and logging issues. Indeed, the resilience of commit protocols to system and communication failures is achieved by logging the progress of the protocol in the logs (stable storage) of the coordinator and the participants. There exist two types of log writes: *force* and *non-force*. The first one is immediately flushed into the log, generating a disk access. Non-force writes are eventually flushed into the log. Thus, there exists a window of vulnerability in using non-force writes until they are flushed.

Figures 1 to 3 introduces three commit protocol use cases. Two cases correspond to the situation where the Application orders the Coordinator to commit. In this case, the commit protocol can issue with a Commit (e.g., Figure 1(a)) or a Failure (e.g., Figure 1(b)) depending on the Participants votes. In the third case, the Application orders the Coordinator to abort and the commit protocol issues automatically with an Abort decision (e.g., Figure 1(c)).

2.1   Two-Phase Commit (2PC)

2PC, the most used commit protocol, consists of two phases (see Figure 1). During the *voting phase*, the coordinator sends a *prepare* message to all participants. At the *decision phase*, the coordinator decides to commit (if all the participants vote *yes*) or abort (if at least one participant votes *no*) the transaction and notifies the participants of its decision. When the participants receive the final decision, they send an *acknowledge* message to the coordinator and release all resources held by the transaction. When the coordinator has received all the acknowledgements from the participants that voted yes, it ends the protocol and forgets the transaction. In 2PC, the coordinator force writes a *decision* record and non-force writes an *end* record at the end of the protocol. Participants force write their votes and the coordinator's decision. Write operations are logged before sending the corresponding message.

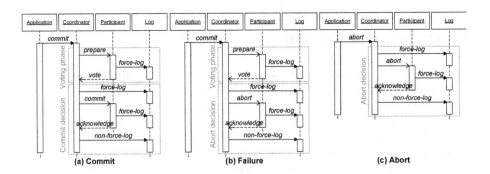

Fig. 1. The 2PC protocol

2.2   2PC Presumed Abort (2PC-PA)

2PC-PA reduces the cost associated to aborted transactions. When the coordinator decides to abort a transaction, it discards all information related to the

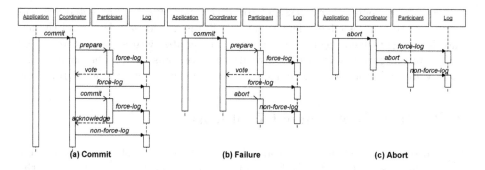

Fig. 2. The 2PC-PA protocol

transaction and sends an *abort* message to all the participants without logging the abort decision (see Figure 2(b) failure case). The participants non-force write the *abort* record and do not have to send an *acknowledge* message to the coordinator. In case of failures, the coordinator, not finding any information in the log regarding the transaction will deduce an abort decision. The commit case of 2PC-PA remains the same as in 2PC.

2.3   2PC Presumed Commit (2PC-PC)

2PC-PC, as opposed to 2PC-PA, reduces the cost of committed transactions. In 2PC-PC, the coordinator interprets missing information as a commit decision. To do so, the coordinator has to force write an *initiation* record for the transaction before sending *prepare* messages to participants (see Figure 3). When the coordinator decides to commit a transaction it force writes a *commit* record then it sends the commit decision. The participants non-force write the commit decision and release all the transaction resources without acknowledging the commit decision to the coordinator. Otherwise, when the coordinator decides to abort a

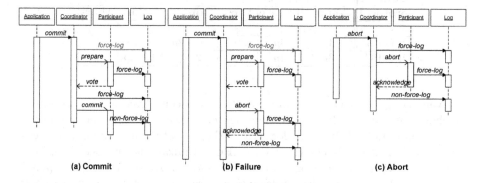

Fig. 3. The 2PC-PC protocol

transaction, it sends *abort* messages to all the participants that voted yes and waits for the acknowledges. The abort decision is not logged. When all the acknowledgements have been received, the coordinator writes a non-forced *end* record and discards all information related to the transaction. The participants force write the abort decision and send an acknowledgement to the coordinator.

3   Evaluation of Commit Protocols

Evaluation of commit protocols is often based on theoretic cost evaluation of message exchanges, and number and type of logs. This section aims at verifying the conformance of the theoretic costs to empirical measures obtained when implementing the protocols introduced in Section 2. The originality of this implementation lies in the definition of reusable components to implement various commit protocols. These components are reused in CATE to support self-adaptability of commit protocols as described in Section 4. The following sections analyse the theoretic costs of studied protocols, introduces details about the implementation of those protocols, and shows some empirical measures resulted from the execution of implemented protocols.

3.1   Theoretic Cost Measures

We show that these protocols differ in the number of messages sent and the number of forced log writes. Table 1 summarizes the three 2PC-based protocol costs. The differences between commit protocols lead to different completion time of the commit processing, communication and disk access costs. As in Section 2, the *Abort* use case considers transactions aborting unilaterally whereas the *Failure* use case depicts transaction aborting during the voting phase.

Table 1. The commit protocol theorical costs

Commit protocol	Messages			Forced log writes		
	Commit	Failure	Abort	Commit	Failure	Abort
2PC	$4p$		$2p$	$1 + 2p$		$1 + p$
2PC-PA	$4p$	$3p$	p	$1 + 2p$	$1 + p$	1
2PC-PC	$3p$	$4p$	$2p$	$2 + p$	$1 + 2p$	$1 + p$

Even though 2PC is widely implemented, it is considered as very expensive as shown in Table 1. It costs $4p$ message exchanges (p being the number of participants) and $1 + 2p$ forced log writes (the cost of non-forced log writes can be ignored). This highlights why several 2PC optimizations have been proposed.

Besides saving one force log write at the coordinator and at the participant's sites, 2PC-PA saves one *acknowledge* message from each participant in the abort case. Thus, when the commit process fails, 2PC-PA costs $3p$ messages and p forced log writes. If the transaction aborts unilaterally, 2PC-PA costs only 1 message and 1 forced log write, making it cheaper than 2PC and 2PC-PC. The cost to commit a transaction is the same as in 2PC.

Compared to 2PC, 2PC-PC saves one forced log write and one *acknowledge* message from each participant for the commit case at the expense of one extra *initiation* forced log write at the coordinator. Thus the cost of committing a transaction is $2 + p$ forced log writes and $3p$ messages. For the abort case, 2PC-PC has one extra forced log write at the coordinator, the *initiation* record. Thus, aborting a transaction costs the same as in 2PC ($1 + 2p$ forced log writes and $4p$ messages).

Thus, it is cheaper to use 2PC-PA in a system where transactions are most likely going to abort, whereas, it is cheaper to use 2PC-PC if transactions are most probably going to commit. In a system where transactions have the same probability of abort and commit, it is cheaper to use 2PC-PA.

3.2 Implementation Issues

This section introduces the implementation of commit protocols presented in Section 2. These commit protocols are implemented using component-based software engineering. Before getting into the architecture details, we extend the definition of component proposed in [10] with the concepts defined in the Fractal component model [2]. A component architecture (or *configuration*) is mainly composed of *components* and *bindings*. A component is a software entity, which exports functions through *server interfaces* and imports its dependencies via *client interfaces*. A binding connects a client interface to a server interface to resolve a component dependency.

The proposed architecture generalizes the commit protocols to reuse common functionalities. The objective is (1) to make a component-based implementation of the three commit protocols presented in Section 2 and (2) to express principal differences only through bindings. Therefore, each commit protocol reuses exactly the same components but assembled with different bindings (see Figure 4).

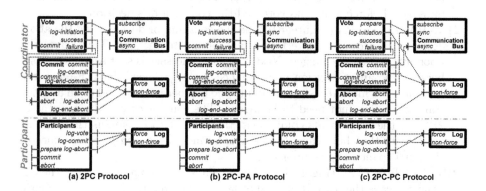

Fig. 4. Component-based architecture of 2PC-based protocols

To implement the commit protocols, we do not require to reify the Application object depicted in Figures 1 to 3. Thus, we define 3 components: Coordinator, Participants, and Log. To enforce the reuse of components, the Coordinator component is split into 3 components: Vote, Commit, and Abort. This separation means that a commit protocol encloses not only the 2PC protocol but also an abort protocol in case of failure. This abort protocol is reused to support aborting transactions unilaterally. Communication is supported by a Communication Bus component. The communication bus supports sending *synchronous* or *asynchronous* (using a callback approach) messages.

In Figures 1 to 3, the coordinator sends the prepare, commit and abort messages to all participants. Thus, the *prepare*, *commit* and *abort* client interfaces of the Coordinator are bound to the Communication Bus. In Figures 1 to 3, the coordinator and the participants require to journalize the steps of the commit protocol in a log. Thus, the Coordinator and the Participants component interfaces are bound to the *force* or *non-force* server interface of the Log component depending on the method call label declared in the sequence diagrams.

The coordinator part of this architecture is embedded in the transaction service whereas the participant part is implemented by resource managers (e.g., database managers) involved in the system. The implementation of the 3 commit protocols reuses these 6 components by changing only the bindings to provide the different semantics.

2PC. In 2PC (Figure 4(a)), the Coordinator sends a synchronous *prepare* message to all participants. Participants should attach their vote to the callback message returned to the coordinator. When a decision is taken, the Coordinator calls the *log-commit* (resp. *log-abort*) interface, which is bound to the *force* interface of the Log. The *commit* (resp. *abort*) message is sent synchronously to allow participants to *acknowledge* the decision. To terminate the protocol, the Coordinator non-force writes an *end* record calling the *log-end-commit* (resp. *log-end-abort*) interface. The Participants component receives (from the Communication Bus) the *prepare*, *commit*, and *abort* messages. It force writes its vote and the coordinator's decision.

2PC-PA. In 2PC-PA (Figure 4(b)), as the coordinator does not log the abort decision, the *log-abort* interface is not bound to the Log. This leaves the Coordinator code unchanged. Next, the *abort* message is sent asynchronously because the abort decision does not need to be acknowledged. Finally, the *log-end-abort* interface is not bound to the Log because the end of an aborted transaction does not need to be logged. The commit case is the same as in 2PC. In the Participants component, the commit case remains the same as in 2PC. In the abort case, *log-abort* is bound to the *non-force* interface of the participant's Log component.

2PC-PC. In 2PC-PC (Figure 4(c)), before sending the *prepare* message, the Coordinator calls the *log-initiation* interface. Compared to the other protocols, such an interface is bound to the *force* Log interface. In 2PC-PC, the commit decision is sent asynchronously because it is not necessary to acknowledge the commit decision. Since the end of a committed transaction does not need to be logged, the *log-end-commit* interface is not bound to the Log. The abort decision is not logged, nevertheless, the *abort* message is sent synchronously. The end of an aborted transaction is non-force written into the log. In the Participants component, the *log-commit* and *log-abort* interfaces are bound respectively to the *non-force* and *force* interfaces of the Log.

3.3 Empirical Evaluation

The objective of this section is to compare the theoretic cost evaluation with the empirical evaluation of the component-based implementation of 2PC, 2PC-PC, and 2PC-PA protocols. This comparison (1) validates our implementations of 2PC-based protocols regarding to their specification, and (2) confirms the theoritical cost evaluations of these 2PC-based protocols with an empirical evaluation. The scenario of Figures 5, 6 and 7 evaluates the average completion time of a number of transactions executed sequentially varying the number of participants (from 0 to 5). This scenario is applied to the 2PC, 2PC-PA and 2PC-PC protocols. Experiments have been done on a PC Pentium IV 2,4GHz with 1Gb of memory using the Ubuntu Linux distribution, the Sun J2SE Development Kit 5.0, and the AOKell implementation of the Fractal component model [11].

In Figure 5, all executed transactions are committed. In this case, 2PC-PC behaves better than 2PC and 2PC-PA. This is because 2PC-PC saves 1 forced log write and 1 acknowledge message from each participant. The initial overhead of 2PC-PC is due to the initiation record that is automatically force written. 2PC and 2PC-PA have similar performance because their commit case follows the same process.

In Figure 6, all executed transactions fail during the commit process. This shows that 2PC-PA, whose completion time is closed to 0, performs much better than 2PC and 2PC-PC. This is because 2PC-PA saves 1 acknowledge message from each participant in the abort case (see Section 2.2). 2PC and 2PC-PC have similar performance because they have similar costs even if 2PC-PC makes an extra force log write (see Section 2.3).

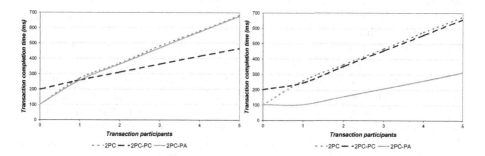

Fig. 5. High commit rate   **Fig. 6.** High failure rate

In Figure 7, all executed transactions are aborted unilaterally. In this case, 2PC-PA performs much better than 2PC and 2PC-PC. This is because 2PC-PA uses only 1 asynchronous message and 1 forced log write to abort the transaction. 2PC and 2PC-PC have similar performance because their abort case follows the same process. The abort protocol applies only one issue. This predictable issue is applied by several 2PC optimizations [12, 13, 14] to exploit the efficiency of transaction aborted unilaterally.

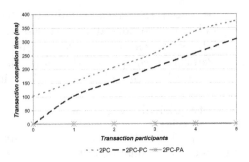

Fig. 7. High abort rate

4   CATE: A Context-Aware Transaction sErvice

In this section, we introduce the second part of our proposal, a Context-Aware Transaction sErvice (CATE), which supports application context variations. The objective of CATE is to apply the best fitting 2PC protocol in presence of unpredictable commit rates.

Section 4.1 shows the context aware mechanism used in our approach. Section 4.2 introduces the reconfiguration process. Section 4.3 presents the policy used to enable commit protocol reconfiguration. Section 4.4 presents some performance measures. Finally, Section 4.5 discusses several issues concerning CATE.

4.1   Context Awareness

In this paper, we consider the transaction abort and commit rate as the application context. Thus, to be able of changing at the right moment, the commit protocol, it is necessary to monitor the abort and commit rates of transactions. The commit rate represents the occurrence of the commit use case of a transaction service whereas the abort rate represents the occurrence of the failure and the abort use cases. This logic is named *adaptation policy*. An adaptation policy is defined by a kind of ECA rules (Event, Condition, Action). The Event is the commit/abort rate, the Condition specifies when it is necessary to change the active protocol and the Action is the protocol change.

Figure 8 shows a transaction manager (Tx Manager) and its relationship with some transaction components (Tx(2PC-PX)). The Context Awareness component implements the adaptation policy. It monitors the number of committed and aborted transactions. Besides, it decides when the active protocol should be changed. This is possible thanks to the predefined ECA rules. For instance a ECA rule may say: if (abort-rate < 10%) then use 2PC.

To count the number of committed and aborted transactions, the Context Awareness component uses the *subscribe* interface provided by the Communication

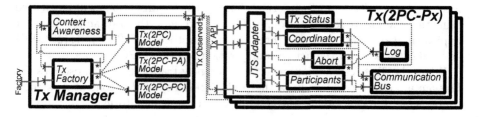

Fig. 8. CATE component-based architecture

Bus component of each transaction (see Figure 4). The *subscribe* interface allows subscribing to different kinds of events. Thus, the Communication Bus of active transactions notifies the Context Awareness component when each Coordinator sends *commit* or *abort* messages to the participants.

Figure 8 shows the general architecture of the CATE implementation, which supports JTS transactions [15]. The Tx(2PC-Px) component represents a JTS transaction implementing the 2PC-Px protocol. The JTS Adapter component is bound to components grouping the core functions provided by CATE. These core components include those presented in Figure 4 plus other general components such as the Tx Status. The Coordinator component reifies the commit protocol applied by the transaction. The Abort component reifies the abort protocol applied by the transaction when aborting unilaterally. This component reuses the Abort component defined in Figure 4 and it is configured with the 2PC-PA protocol. Thus, CATE provides the best completion time in case of predictable abort decisions. The Tx Manager component is in charge of managing the instance of active transactions. Figure 8 shows the Tx Manager component and its relation with the Tx(2PC-Px)'s Communication Bus component.

The commit protocol reconfiguration is done through a dedicated *configuration* attribute. This attribute is read by the Tx Factory component when new transactions are created. Depending on the value of this attribute, the Coordinator component implements the 2PC, 2PC-PA, or 2PC-PC protocol. Thus, the reconfiguration process consists of changing the value of this attribute depending on the predefined Conditions.

4.2   Reconfiguration Rules

To dynamically switch over another protocol, the Context Awareness component needs to *stop* the transaction factory, *unbind* the current protocol, *bind* the new one, and *restart* the transaction factory. In that way, newly created transactions use the appropriate commit protocol.

When the Context Awareness component decides to change a protocol (based on defined Conditions) it calls the *change-config* interface bound to the *configuration* interface of the Tx Factory component. Then the Tx Factory component connects the *active-config* interface to the appropriate configuration, which is listed by the *available-config* interface. Thus, future transactions will be created using this new active configuration. In Figure 8, we show the transaction manager implementation containing the three commit protocols (Tx(2PC), Tx(2PC-PC) and Tx(2PC-PA)) and the active configuration is Tx(2PC-PC).

When the Tx Factory component creates a new transaction, it subscribes the *listener* interfaces (retrieved via the *probe* interface) of the Context Awareness component to make possible the commit/abort event monitoring.

4.3   Adaptation Policy

Knowing the current commit/abort rate allows predicting the future transaction context. That is, if the abort rate is about 30%, we consider that this tendency will remain the same in a near future. This is why the abort/commit rate motivates the reconfiguration.

The Condition that specifies when to change of commit protocol in CATE (see Section 4.1) is based on the following equation:

$$\begin{cases} x + y = 100 \\ x \times C_{2PC-PC} + y \times A_{2PC-PC} < x \times C_{2PC-PA} + y \times A_{2PC-PA} \end{cases}$$

Where x (resp. y) represents the number of transaction committed (resp. aborted) and C_{2PC-PX} (resp. A_{2PC-PX}) represents the commit (resp. abort) cost of the 2PC-PX protocol (here 2PC-PA and 2PC-PC protocols).

The solution of this equation is:

$$\begin{cases} y = 100 - x \\ x > \dfrac{100 \times (A_{2PC-PA} - A_{2PC-PC})}{(C_{2PC-PC} - A_{2PC-PC} - C_{2PC-PA} + A_{2PC-PA})} \end{cases}$$

Figure 9 applies this solution to the measures of Figure 5 and 6. It appears that the limit between 2PC-PC and 2PC-PA depends on the number of transaction participants. For example, in the case of transactions involving 20 participants, 2PC-PC becomes more interesting than 2PC-PA when the commit rate is above 54%. This limit is used by CATE to switch between the 2PC-PC and the 2PC-PA configurations.

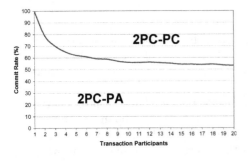

Fig. 9. 2PC-PA/2PC-PC border rate

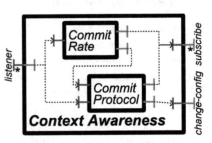

Fig. 10. Adaptation policy architecture

Figure 10 introduces the component-based architecture of the adaptation policy. This policy is composed of two parts. The Commit Rate component computes the appropriate commit rate depending on the average number of transaction participants. Thus, the component reconfigures the Commit Protocol component depending on the execution context variations. The Commit Protocol component reconfigures the transaction factory depending on the current commit rate. The computation of the commit rate is based on a configurable weighted moving average. It ensures that the commit protocol is adapted to important fluctuations in the commit rate without reconfiguring too often.

4.4   Empirical Performance Measures

CATE does not switch to 2PC because taking as context only the commit/abort rate, 2PC is more expensive than the other considered protocols. The scenario of Figures 11 and 12 evaluates the average completion time of 50 transactions executed sequentially with constant commit/abort rate variations (10 transactions commit, then 10 transactions abort, then 10 transactions commit, etc.). Transaction services using static configuration of 2PC, 2PC-PA and 2PC-PC protocols are executed and compared to CATE. Figures 12 depicts the average completion time since the transaction service has been started.

The measures of Figure 11 show the average completion time that varies depending on the transaction commit/abort rates. Performance of CATE is the best thanks to its capacity of self-adaptation. 2PC-PA and 2PC-PC suffer from the context variations. In CATE, when the commit rate is high, the active protocol is 2PC-PC. Otherwise, CATE uses 2PC-PA. Thus, CATE benefits of the best performance of 2PC-PC and 2PC-PA. In this experiment, 2PC is used as the initial protocol. Performances of Figure 12 show that the CATE reconfiguration does not introduce important overheads compared to the static configuration of the use cases protocols while providing better completion time. The cost of switching between commit protocols appears only when a new transaction is created. CATE computes the commit rate of terminated transactions to create

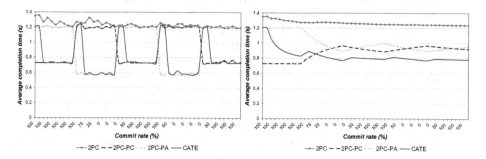

Fig. 11. Empirical performance measure   **Fig. 12.** History performance measure

a new transaction providing the best performing commit protocol. This mechanism coupled to a caching mechanism reduces the overhead of switching between the commit protocols.

4.5 Discussion

This section discusses various general aspects concerning CATE.

Reconfiguration of active transactions. Changing the protocol of active transactions compromises the recovery process in case of failures. That is why in CATE it is not possible to change the commit protocol once a transaction has begun. Different active transactions can use different commit protocols but each transaction begins and ends with the same commit protocol.

Using CATE. To be able of using CATE, for instance, in an application server, the following hypotheses should be guaranted. 1) The participant part is implemented by resource managers that are free to choose the way this implementation is done (Figure 8 suggests one implementation solution); 2) All considered protocols in CATE must be implemented by resource managers; finally, 3) Resource managers must be able to change the active protocol.

CATE extension. CATE may support other commit protocols that can be different to those used in this paper. We choose 2PC-based protocols as an experiment to show components reusability. Nevertheless, reusability is not necessary to the CATE operation. Thus, with CATE it is possible to switch to different commit protocol implementations, which makes it extensible. For example, 1PC and 3PC protocols can be considered because CATE monitors the commit rate of active transactions to find the best commit protocol. Besides, switching between 1PC or 3PC protocols requires the application to support 1PC or 3PC validation processes.

Predictable issues. Some commit protocols draw benefits from predicable issues of transactions [12, 13, 14]. Using piggybacking or callback mechanisms, they determine if the transaction is marked for read-only or abort before starting the commit protocol. Thus, depending on the known issue of the transaction, they can optimize the completion time of the transaction. This approach is complementary to our approach because CATE aims at optimizing transactions with unpredictable issues. However, CATE can also define transactions supporting several commit or abort protocols to improve the completion time of transaction with predictable issues.

Preserving the global semantics of the system. In software reconfiguration, it is necessary to preserve the semantics of the system. In our case, the transaction properties must be preserved. If an atomic commit protocol is replaced by another, which does not enforce the atomicity property (for instance, the semantic atomicity [16]), the transaction correctness is compromised. This is why in this paper, used protocols ensure the atomicity property. Thus, programmers must be careful about the choices they made when defining adaptive middleware systems.

5   Related Work

[5] proposes to dynamically adapt applications by composing at runtime (by weaving) functional (application-related) and non-functional concerns. Authors are interested in making the weaving process adaptive to runtime execution conditions. Their objective is to choose at runtime the appropriate non functional code. Thus, they propose to change the weaving of non-functional code according to context aware adaptation policies.

[6] proposes runtime application adaptability by assembling appropriate non-functional services thanks to service repositories. Repositories contain component-based non-functional services and meta-information describing such services. This approach requires the applications to be developed using the component-based approach. Our approach does not make any assumption about the application design and we choose to adapt the non-functional service itself rather than the instance of the used service.

Compared to our proposal, [5] and [6] consider non-functional services as the adaptation grain. Our approach proposes self-adaptability of non-functional services using components as adaptation granularity. Unlike [5] and [6], we made several experiments that underline the advantages of our proposal. Our proposal is validated with performance measures that show the self-adaptability advantages.

This paper improves [17] by providing a description of legacy 2PC-based protocols using UML Sequence diagrams. Descriptions of commit and abort protocols are supported and can be implemented as various configurations built with reusable components. This paper improves the adaptation policy presented in [17] to consider the commit rate variation depending on the number of transaction participants. The support of commit protocols for transactions with predictable issues has been introduced. The completion time of transactions with predictable issues, such as transaction aborting unilaterally, is improved compared to traditional commit protocols.

[12] proposes a new commit protocol for self-adaptive Web services, which supports both 2PC-PA and 2PC-PC participants. Such a protocol allows participants with different presumptions to be dynamically combined in one transaction. Compared to the work presented in this paper, [12] does not address evolution concerns. In our work, we use 2PC, 2PC-PA and 2PC-PC as use cases. Our approach can easily support new commit protocols to extend the application adaptive ability.

In general, works presented in [18, 19, 9] are simulation-based. Performance results focus on the semantics of transactions (e.g. read-only transactions, update transactions, transaction's length) and the presence of failures. Whereas, in this paper, besides addressing performance of each protocol based on commit and abort rates, we address the performance of changing the software configuration to migrate from a protocol to another. Our performance results, based on a prototype implementation, shows that the reconfiguration cost is negligible compared to gains obtained from the use of appropriate protocols depending on the application context.

6   Conclusions and Future Work

Self-adaptation is a current challenge in component-based software engineering. Several works have been devoted to adaptive applications, nevertheless, there has been little work on adaptability of non-functional services. This paper focused on transaction services, and more specifically on the commit process. On the one hand, it proposed a component-based architecture of standard 2PC-based protocols. Each protocol contains exactly the same components but assembled according to different configurations. On the other hand, it proposed a Context-Aware Transaction sErvice (CATE). CATE selects the most appropriate commit protocol with respect to the execution context. Performance measures show that changing the commit protocol depending on the context performs better that using only one commit protocol on a variable transactional system.

Our future work includes to study the component-based configuration of other 2PC-based protocols (e.g., [12]) but also 1PC and 3PC protocols. The idea is to extend CATE to support more commit protocols. The evaluation of runtime performances of these additional commit protocols will be useful to refine the CATE adaptation policies, e.g., adding new conditions and reconfiguration actions to switch between protocols.

Besides, we consider to investigate a model-driven approach to design commit protocols using UML sequence diagrams (see Figures 1 to 3) and to automatically generate the implementation of the `Coordinator` components and their bindings to the `Communication Bus` and the `Log` components. This model-driven approach, complementary to that we defined into [20, 21], will provide a dedicated high level language to define, study, compare commit protocols, and also an efficient way to implement them.

Availability. CATE is freely available under an LGPL licence at the following URL: http://gotm.objectweb.org.

Acknowledgments. This work is partially funded by INRIA, and the Region Nord - Pas-de-Calais.

References

1. Preuveneers, D., Berbers, Y.: Adaptive Context Management Using a Component-based Approach. In: 5th Int. Conf. on Distributed Applications and Interoperable Systems (DAIS). Volume 3543 of LNCS. Athens, Greece, Springer (2005) 14–26
2. Bruneton, E., Coupaye, T., Leclercq, M. *et al.*: An Open Component Model and its Support in Java. In: Int. Symp. on Component-Based Software Engineering (CBSE). Volume 3054 of LNCS. Edinburgh, UK, Springer (2004) 7–22 http://fractal.objectweb.org.

3. David, P., Ledoux, T.: Towards a Framework for Self-Adaptive Component-Based Applications. In: Int. Conf. on Distributed Applications and Interoperable Systems (DAIS). Volume 2893 of LNCS. Paris, France, Springer (2003) 1–14

4. Layaida, O., Hagimont, D.: Designing Self-Adaptive Multimedia Applications through Hierarchical Reconfiguration. In: 5th Int. Conf. on on Distributed Applications and Interoperable Systems (DAIS). Volume 3543 of LNCS. Athens, Greece, Springer (2005) 95–107

5. David, P., Ledoux, T.: Dynamic Adaptation of Non-Functional Concerns. In: ECOOP Workshop on Unanticipated Software Engineering. Malaga, Spain (2002)

6. Arntsen, A.B., Karlsen, R.: ReflecTS: a flexible transaction service framework. In: 4th Middleware Workshop on Adaptive and Reflective Middleware (ARM). Volume 116 of AICPS. Grenoble, France, ACM Press (2005) 1–6

7. Coulson, G., Blair, G., Grace, P. *et al.*: OpenCOM v2: A Component Model for Building Systems Software. In: IASTED Int. Conf. on Software Engineering and Applications (SEA). Cambridge, MA, ESA (2004) 1–6

8. Gray, J.: Notes on Database Operating Systems. In: Advanced Course: Operating Systems. Number 60 in LNCS, Springer (1978)

9. Mohan, C., Lindsay, B., Obermarck, R.: Transaction Management in the R* Distributed Database Management System. ACM Trans. on Database Systems (TODS) **11**(4) (1986)

10. Szyperski, C.: Component Software: Beyond Object-Oriented Programming. Addison-Wesley Longman Publishing Co., Inc. (2002)

11. Seinturier, L., Pessemier, N., Duchien, L. *et al.*: A Component Model Engineered with Components and Aspects. In: 9th Int. SIGSOFT Symp. on Component-Based Software Engineering (CBSE). LNCS Stockholm, Sweden, Springer (2006) To appear.

12. Yu, W., Wang, Y., Pu, C.: A Dynamic Two-Phase Commit Protocol for Self-Adapting Services. In: Int. Conf. on Services Computing (SCC). Shanghai, China, IEEE (2004) 7–15

13. Al-Houmaily, Y.J., Chrysanthis, P.K., Levitan, S.P.: Enhancing the performance of presumed commit protocol. In: Proc. of ACM Symp. on Applied computing (SAC). New York, NY, USA, ACM Press (1997) 131–133

14. Attaluri, G.K., Salem, K.: The Presumed-Either Two-Phase Commit Protocol. IEEE Transactions on Knowledge and Data Engineering **14**(5) (2002) 1190–1196

15. Cheung, S.: Java Transaction Service Specification. Sun Microsystems Inc., San Antonio Road, Palo Alto, CA. Version 1.0 edn. (1999)

16. Garcia-Molina, H.: Using Semantic Knowledge for Transaction Processing in a Distributed Database. ACM Trans. on Database Systems (TODS) **8**(2) (1983)

17. Serrano-Alvarado, P., Rouvoy, R., Merle, P.: Self-Adaptive Component-Based Transaction Commit Management. In: 4th Middleware Workshop on Adaptive and Reflective Middleware (ARM). Volume 116 of AICPS. Grenoble, France, ACM Press (2005) 1–6

18. Chrysanthis, P.C., Samaras, G., Al-Houmail, Y.: Recovery and Performance of Atomic Commit Protocols in Distributed and Database Systems. In: Recovery Mechanisms in Database Systems. Prentice Hall (1998)

19. Liu, M.L., Agrawal, D., Abbadi, A.E.: The Performance of Two Phase Commit Protocols in the Presence of Site Failures. Kluwer Academic Publishers Distributed and Parallel Databases (DAPD) **6**(2) (1998)

20. Rouvoy, R., Merle, P.: Towards a Model Driven Approach to Build Component-Based Adaptable Middleware. In: 3rd Middleware Workshop on Reflective and Adaptive Middleware (RAM). Volume 80 of AICPS. Toronto, Canada, ACM Press (2004) 195–200
21. Rouvoy, R., Merle, P.: Using Microcomponents and Design Patterns to Build Evolutionary Transaction Services. In: Int. ERCIM Workshop on Software Evolution. Lille, France (2006) To appear.

A Local Self-stabilizing Enumeration Algorithm

Brahim Hamid and Mohamed Mosbah

LaBRI- Université Bordeaux-1
351, cours de la libération
F-33405 Talence Cedex, France
{hamid, mosbah}@labri.fr

Abstract. We present a novel self-stabilizing version of Mazurkiewicz enumeration algorithm [1]. The initial version is based on local rules to enumerate nodes on an anonymous network. [2] presented the first self-stabilizing version of this algorithm which tolerates transient failures with an extension of messages complexity. Our version is based on local detection and correction of transient failures. Therefore, it ensures the fault-tolerance property without adding messages or reduces the messages' number of other version. In addition, we have developed an interface based on the Visidia platform to simulate faults through a graphical user interface. The implementation of the presented algorithm in this platform shows its dynamic execution and validates its correction.

1 Introduction

Distributed computing systems are becoming larger and larger, heterogeneous and complex. Since the applications running on these systems require the cooperation of many components, they are prone to failures and errors of many different types, leading to inconsistent executions. Hence, a desirable feature of a computation in a distributed system is fault-tolerance. A particularly suitable approach to deal with such a feature is to design self-stabilizing algorithms [3, 4].

The concept of self-stabilization [5] is introduced to design a system which tolerates transient failures. Informally, self-stabilizing algorithms ensure that after any failure, the system will automatically recover to reach a correct configuration in a finite time. In general, self-stabilizing algorithms are constructed in such a way that a given process will continue to function correctly in spite of intermittent faults.

An anonymous network is a network where all nodes execute the same algorithm without a unique identity for each node. In general, the task solved by an enumeration algorithm is the affectation of a different *name* to each node of an anonymous network. So, such algorithm may be used as a preprocessing task of many algorithms based on the identities. As well-known, many problems have no solutions in anonymous networks. The motivations of this work are in the first hand to design an enumeration protocol in anonymous networks using only local computations [1]. On the other hand, we show the adaptation of our developed framework [6] to enumeration algorithm in the presence of transient failures.

F. Eliassen and A. Montresor (Eds.): DAIS 2006, LNCS 4025, pp. 289–302, 2006.

We are interested on the study of the Mazurkiewicz enumeration algorithm [1] based on local computations. Mazurkiewicz's algorithm is a distributed algorithm to enumerate nodes in an anonymous minimal-covering graph when its size is known. A distributed enumeration algorithm on a graph G is a distributed algorithm such that the result of any computation is a labeling of the nodes that is a bijection from $V(G)$ to $1, 2, ..., |V(G)|$. [2] proposed a version of self-stabilizing enumeration algorithm with a final stage in which each node computes locally the set of final names from the final mailbox. Before this stage the node can choose a name which is greater than the size of the graph.

Many self-stabilizing algorithms have been already designed [7, 8]. However, most of these works propose global solutions which require to involve the entire system. As networks grow fast, detecting and correcting errors globally is no longer feasible. The solutions that deal locally with detection and correction are rather essential because they are scalable and can be deployed even for large and evolving networks. Moreover, it is useful to have the correct (non faulty) parts of the network operating normally while recovering locally the faulty components. Few general approaches providing local solutions to self-stabilization have been proposed in [9, 10, 11].

In [6], we consider the problem of designing algorithms encoded by local computations in a distributed system with transient failures. The developed formal framework allows to design and prove fault-tolerant distributed algorithms. We introduce correction rules which can be applied by faulty nodes or by their neighbors in order to self repair the incorrect states. Such rules have higher priorities than the main rules of the algorithm which ensure that the failures are repaired before continuing the computation. Of course, we deal only with predefined faulty local configurations. A tool called *Visidia* [12], validating the local computations model has been implemented. The distributed system of Visidia is based on asynchronous message passing model. However, it has been assumed that components of such a system do not fail. In this work, we show a simulation of fault-tolerant enumeration algorithm using this platform.

The paper is organized as follows. Models of distributed systems and graph relabeling systems and our framework are presented in Section 2. We give in Section 3 our solution to encode self-stabilizing enumeration algorithm. Section 4 gives its analysis and Section 5 shows an implementation of our protocol on Visidia platform. Finally Section 6 concludes the paper.

2 Preliminaries

2.1 The Model of Distributed System

A distributed system is modeled by a graph $G = (V, E)$, where $V(G)$ is the set of nodes and $E(G)$ is the set of edges. Nodes represent processes and edges represent bidirectional communication links. Two nodes are connected by an edge if the corresponding processes have a direct communication link. We denote by $N_G(v)$ the set of neighbors of v in the graph G, that is, $\forall\ u \in N_G(v),\ (v, u) \in E(G)$.

A ball center on u with radius 1 is the set $B(u) = \{u\} \cup N_G(u)$. The cardinality of set $V(G)$ (which is also the size of the corresponding network) is denoted by $\mid V(G) \mid$, and we assume that $\mid V(G) \mid = \mathcal{N}$. For any set A, we write 2^A (resp. A^n) to denote the set of all finite subsets of A (resp. the set of all n-tuples, for $n \in \mathcal{N}$ of element of A), where $\mathcal{N}$ is the set of all positives integers. In the considered networks, processes communicate and synchronize by sending and receiving messages through the links. There is no assumption about the relative speed of processes or message transfer delay, the networks are *asynchronous*. The topology is unknown and each node communicates only with its neighbors. The links are reliable and the process can fail and recover in a finite time. The failures that are tolerated in such a system are the transient failures of processes.

The set $N_G(v)$ (resp.$N_h(w)$) is composed of all the neighbors of v in the graph G (resp. the neighbors of w in the graph H). We say that a graph G is a *covering* of a graph H if there exists a surjective homomorphism φ from G onto H such that for every node v of $V(G)$ the restriction of φ to $N_G(v)$ is a bijection onto $N_H(\varphi(v))$. In particular, $(\varphi(v), \varphi(u)) \in E(H)$ implies $(v, u) \in E(G)$. The covering is *proper* if G and H are not isomorphic. It is called connected if G (and thus also H) is connected. A graph G is called *minimal-covering* if every covering from G to some H is a bijection.

The stabilizing algorithms are optimistic, they guarantee a return to a correct behavior within a finite time after all faulty behaviors cease. Self-stabilizing algorithms protect against transient failures, since they can automatically repair any fault in the system. The term *fault* refers to failure.

2.2 Graph Relabeling Systems (GRS) to Encode Distributed Algorithms

Local computations, and particularly graph relabeling systems [13] are a powerful model which provides general tools to encode distributed algorithms, to prove their correctness and to understand their power. In such a model we consider a network of processes with arbitrary topology represented as a connected, undirected graph where nodes denote processes, and edges denote communication links. Every time, each node and each edge is in some particular state and this state will be encoded by a node label or an edge label. According to its own state and to the states of its neighbors, each node may decide to realize an elementary *computation step*. After this step, the states of this node, of its neighbors and of the corresponding edges may have changed according to some specific *computation rules*. Let us recall that graph relabeling systems satisfy the following requirements:

(C1) they do not change the underlying graph but only the labeling of its components (edges and/or nodes), the final labeling being the result,

(C2) they are local, that is, each relabeling changes only a connected subgraph of a fixed size in the underlying graph,

(C3) they are locally generated, that is, the applicability condition of the relabeling only depends on the local context of the relabeled subgraph.

Let L be an alphabet and let G be a graph. We denote by (G, λ) a graph G with a relabeling function $\lambda : V(G) \cup E(G) \to L$. A labeling is said to be locally bijective if nodes with the same label have isomorphic labeled neighbors. Then, the graph G is said to be ambiguous if there exists a non bijective labeling of G which is locally bijective. For more examples the reader is referred to [1].

A graph relabeling system is a triple $\Re = (L, I, P)$ where L is a set of labels, I is a subset of L called the set of initial labels and P a finite set of relabeling rules. Consider an arbitrary system $\Re = (L, I, P)$ and a labeling function λ. A relabeling step will be denoted by $(G, \lambda) \xrightarrow[\mathcal{R}]{} (G, \lambda')$. The notion of computation then corresponds to the notion of relabeling sequence. A relabeling sequence with any steps will be denoted by $(G, \lambda) \xrightarrow[\mathcal{R}]{*} (G, \lambda')$. A relabeling sequence with k steps will be denoted by $(G, \lambda) \xrightarrow[\mathcal{R}]{k} (G, \lambda')$.

The program is encoded by a graph relabeling system $\Re = (L, I, P)$. The labels of each process represent the values of its variables. Each rule in set P is of the following form:

$$R1 : \mathbf{RuleN}\{Precondition\}\{Relabeling\}$$

$R1$ denotes the number of the rule and $\mathbf{RuleN}$ is the name of the rule. The *Precondition* part of a rule in the program of v_0 is a boolean expression (predicate) involving the labels of v_0 and the labels of its neighbors. The *Relabeling* part of a rule of v_0 updates one or more labels of v_0 and its neighbors. A rule can be executed only if its precondition is *true*. The rules are atomically executed, meaning that, the evaluation of a precondition and the execution of its corresponding relabeling, if the precondition is *true*, are done in one atomic step.

2.3   Self-stabilizing Graph Relabeling Systems

An algorithm is called self-stabilizing if it eventually starts to behave correct according to its specifications regardless of its initial configuration [5]. A *local configuration* of a process is composed by its state, the states of its neighbors and the states of its communication links. In this work we use the notion of local illegitimate configurations encoded by local computations [6]. For a labeled graph (G, λ), we say that a local configuration $f = (B_f, \lambda_f)$ is illegitimate for (G, λ), if there is no subgraph in (G, λ) which is isomorphic to f. In other words, there is no ball (neither sub-ball) of radius 1 in G which has the same labeling as f. Such labels are not used when the system runs in a correct manner.

Transient failures cause processes to change their states yielding illegitimate local configurations and therefore an illegitimate global configuration. A self-stabilizing system will be able to destroy such a fault by eventually stabilizing into a correct global configuration without restarting the system. A local stabilizing graph relabeling system is a triple $\Re = (L, \mathcal{P}, \mathcal{F})$ where L is a set of labels, $\mathcal{P}$ a finite set of relabeling rules and $\mathcal{F}$ is a set of illegitimate local configurations [6]. Let $\mathcal{G}_\mathcal{L}$ be the set of labeled graphs (G, λ) and $h : \mathcal{G}_\mathcal{L} \longrightarrow \mathbb{N}$ be an application associating to each labeled graph (G, λ), the number of its illegitimate configurations at this stage of the computation. Therefore, we denote by $h(G, \lambda, \mathcal{F})$ the current number of illegitimate configurations of the labeled graph (G, λ). A local stabilizing graph relabeling system must satisfy the two following properties:

- Closure : $\forall \ (G, \lambda) \in \mathcal{G_L}$ such that $h(G, \lambda, \mathcal{F}) = 0$,
  $\forall \ (G, \lambda') / (G, \lambda) \xrightarrow[\Re]{*} (G, \lambda') : h(G, \lambda', \mathcal{F}) = 0$.
- Convergence : $\forall \ (G, \lambda) \in \mathcal{G_L}, \exists$ an integer k, such that $(G, \lambda) \xrightarrow[\Re]{k} (G, \lambda')$ and $h(G, \lambda', \mathcal{F}) = 0$.

As for self-stabilizing algorithms, the closure property stipulates the correctness of the relabeling system. A computation beginning in a correct state remains correct until the terminal state. The convergence however provides the ability of the relabeling system to recover automatically within a finite time (finite sequence of relabeling steps).

In [6] we state the following result: if $\Re = (L, I, P, \mathcal{F})$ is a graph relabeling system with illegitimate configurations $\mathcal{F}$, then it can be transformed into an equivalent local stabilizing graph relabeling system $\Re_s = (L, P_s, \mathcal{F})$. The set P_s is composed of set P and some correction rules to detect and eliminate each illegitimate configuration of $\mathcal{F}$. The correction rules have higher priority than the rules in P.

3   The Local Stabilizing Enumeration Algorithm

3.1   The Mazurkiewicz's Enumeration Algorithm

An enumeration algorithm on a graph G is a distributed algorithm such that the result of any computation is a labeling of the nodes that is a bijection from $V(G)$ to $1, 2, ..., |V(G)|$. First, we give a description of the initial enumeration algorithm [1]. Every node attempts to get its own name, which shall be an integer between 1 and $|V(G)|$. A node chooses a name and broadcasts it with its neighbor-hood (i.e. the list of the name of its neighbors) all over the network. If a node u discovers the existence of another node v with the same name, then it compares its local view, i.e. the labeled ball of center u, with the local view of its rival v. If the local view v is "Stronger", then u chooses another name. Each new name is broadcast with the local view again over the network. At the end of the computation it is not guaranteed that every node has a unique name, unless the graph is non ambiguous. However, all nodes with the same name will have the same local view.

The crucial property of the algorithm is based on a total order on local views such that the "Strength" of the local view of any node cannot decrease during the computation. To describe this local view we use the following notation: if v has degree d and its neighbors have names $n_1, n_2, ...n_d$ with $n_1 \geq .... \geq n_d$, then $LV(v)$, the local view, is the d-uplet$(n_1, n_2, ...n_d)$. Let $\mathcal{LV}$ be the set of such ordered tuples. The alphabetic order defines a total order $\preceq$ on $\mathcal{LV}$. The nodes v are labeled by triples of the form (n, LV, GV) representing during the computation :

- $n(v) \in \mathbb{N}$ is the name of the node v,
- $LV(v) \in \mathcal{LV}$ is the latest view of v,
- $GV(v) \subset \mathbb{N} \times \mathcal{LV}$ is the mailbox of v and contains all the information received at this step of the computation. We call this set the global view of the v.

We define the list $sub(LV, n, n')$: the copy of LV where any occurrence of n is replaced by n' if n exists or adds n to LV otherwise. Let $LV \in \mathcal{LV}$ and $(n, n') \in \mathbb{N}^2$, if $n < n'$ then $LV \prec sub(LV, n, n')$. The initial labels of each node are $(0, \phi, \phi)$. Each node v has labels: $(n(v), LV(v), GV(v))$ and the labels obtained after applying a rule are $(n'(v), LV'(v), GV'(v))$. Let v_0 a node which is center of ball $B(v_0)$ and let $\{v_1, v_1 \cdots, v_d\}$ the set of its neighbors. Let $(n(v_i), LV(v_i), GV(v_i))$ the triple associated to the node v_i with $0 \le i \le d$. We call the ball of the center v and we write $B(v)$ the set composed of v and its neighbors. Now we present Mazurkiewicz's enumeration algorithm:

R1 : **Transmitting rule**
  Precondition :
  - $\exists\, v_i \in B(v_0), GV(v_i) \ne GV(v_0)$

  Relabeling :
  - $\forall\, v_i \in B(v_0), GV'(v_i) := \bigcup_{v_j \in B(v_0)} GV(v_j)$

R2 : **Renaming rule**
  Precondition :
  - $\forall\, v_i \in B(v_0), GV(v_i) = GV(v_0)$
  - $n(v_0) = 0$ or
    $n(v_0) > 0$ and $(\exists\, LV_1 | (n(v_0), LV_1) \in GV(v_0)$ and $LV(v_0) \prec LV_1)$

  Relabeling :
  - $n'(v_0) := 1 + max\{n \mid (n, LV) \in GV(v_0)\}$
  - $\forall\, v_i \in B(v_0) \backslash \{v_0\}, LV'(v_i) := sub(LV(v_i), n(v_0), n'(v_0))$
  - $\forall\, v_i \in B(v_0), GV'(v_i) := GV(v_i) \bigcup_{v_j \in B(v_0)} \{(n'(v_j), LV'(v_j))\}$

3.2   A Local Stabilizing Enumeration Algorithm

We present in the sequel a new enumeration algorithm encoded by local stabilizing relabeling systems. This protocol is optimal compared to that of [2]. In a correct behavior, when a name of v_0 is already chosen by another node v_i, v_0 (resp. v_i) will receive this information and change its name if the local view of v_0 (resp. v_i) contains the older modifications. In a corrupted behavior, when a name of v_0 is corrupted, v_0 detects this corruption, change its name to -1 and initialize its states, then one of its neighbors v_i detects this change, corrects some of the state of v_0. After that, v_0 chooses another number to rename itself.

Function $\delta_L(n)$ gives the number of occurrences of a name n in the list LV. We start by defining some illegitimate configurations to construct a set $\mathcal{F}$, then we improve the system by adding the correction rules to detect and to eliminate these configurations. The node v_0 is said to be corrupted or in the illegitimate configuration, if one of its components is changed using extra relabeling. This relabeling does not correspond to those of the previous rules. We can define the following predicates to denote theses behaviors.

1. Corruption of the name: $n(v_0) \neq 1 + max\{n \mid (n, LV) \in GV(v_0)\}$ or $n(v_0) > |V(G)|$.
2. Corruption of the local view: $\exists \, n_1 \in LV(v_0) \mid \neg \exists \, v_i \in B(v_0) \backslash \{v_0\} : n(v_i) = n_1$ or $n_1 > |V(G)|$.
3. Corruption of the global view: $\exists \, (n_1, LV_1) \in GV(v_0), \delta_{LV_1}(n(v_0)) \geq 2$ or $n_1 > |V(G)|$.

The function $choose\_unused(GV)$ chooses one unused name in the set of global view $GV \subset \mathbb{N} \times \mathcal{LV}$. We use the list $subset(GV, (n, LV), (n', LV'))$ to denote the copy of GV where any occurrence of (n, LV) is replaced by (n', LV') if $(n, LV) \in GV$ or adds (n', LV') to GV. For the present system, we deal with the following set $\mathcal{F} = \{f_1, f_2, f_3\}$ encoding the previous behaviors' predicates. Therefore, the correction rules are:

Rc1 : **Corruption of the name**
  Precondition :
  - $n(v_0) \neq 1 + max\{n \mid (n, LV) \in GV(v_0)\}$
    or $n(v_0) > |V(G)|$
  Relabeling :
  - $(n'(v_0), LV'(v_0), GV'(v_0)) := (-1, \phi, \phi)$
  - $\forall \, v_i \in B(v_0) \backslash \{v_0\}, LV'(v_i) := LV(v_i) \backslash \{n(v_0)\}$
  - $\forall \, v_i \in B(v_0), GV'(v_i) := GV(v_i) \backslash \{(n(v_0), LV(v_0))\}$

Rc2 : **Choose of the name**
  Precondition :
  - $n(v_0) = -1$
  Relabeling :
  - $n'(v_0) := choose\_unused(GV(v_0))$
  - $\forall \, v_i \in B(v_0) \backslash \{v_0\}, LV'(v_i) := sub(LV(v_i), n(v_0), n'(v_0))$
  - $\forall \, v_i \in B(v_0), GV'(v_i) := GV(v_i) \displaystyle\bigcup_{v_j \in B(v_0)} \{(n'(v_j), LV'(v_j))\}$

Rc3 : **Corruption of the local view**
  Precondition :
  - $\exists \, n_1 \in LV(v_0) \mid \neg \exists \, v_i \in B(v_0) \backslash \{v_0\} : n(v_i) = n_1$ or $n_1 > |V(G)|$
  Relabeling :
  - $LV'(v_0) := LV(V_0) \backslash \{n_1\}$
  - $GV'(v_i) := subset(GV(v_i), (n(v_0), LV(v_0)), (n(v_0), LV'(v_0)))$

Rc4 : **Corruption of the global view**
  Precondition :
   • $\exists\,(n_1, LV_1) \in GV(v_0),\ \delta_{LV_1}(n(v_0)) \geq 2$ or $n_1 >| V(G) |$
  Relabeling :
   • $GV'(v_0) := GV(v_0)\backslash\{(n_1, LV_1)\}$

4   Analysis

4.1   Properties

We define the relabeling system $\Re_s = (L, P_s, \mathcal{F})$, where $L = \{\{\mathcal{N} \cup \{0\}\} \times 2^{\mathcal{N}} \times 2^{\mathcal{N} \times 2^{\mathcal{N}}}\}$ and $P_s = \{R1, R2, Rc1, Rc2, Rc3, Rc4\}$ such that $Rc_j > R_i$. We now state the main results.

Lemma 1. *The system $\Re_s = (L, P_s, \mathcal{F})$ satisfies the closure property.*

Proof. We prove this Lemma by induction on the size of relabeling sequences. Let (G, λ) any labeled graph where $h(G, \lambda, \mathcal{F}) = 0$. Let (G, λ_k) a labeled graph obtained from (G, λ) by applying k rules only from the set $P = \{R1, R2\}$. From the definition of correction rules, they are applied when some illegitimate configurations are introduced. When $k = 0$ the Lemma is *true*. We suppose that the lemma remains *true* after applying k rules. Now we show that the lemma remains true after the application of $k+1$ rules. From the induction hypothesis, $h(G, \lambda_k, \mathcal{F}) = 0$. At this step, the only possible application rules are $R1$ and $R2$. By definition, such rules do not introduce illegitimate configurations, then $h(G, \lambda_{k+1}, \mathcal{F}) = 0$. Therefore, all the labeled graphs (G, λ') obtained from (G, λ) verify the property. Formally, if $h(G, \lambda, \mathcal{F}) = 0$ then $\forall\,(G, \lambda'),\ (G, \lambda) \xrightarrow{*}_{\Re} (G, \lambda')$:
$h(G, \lambda', \mathcal{F}) = 0$.   □

The proof of termination presented in [1] is based on the fact that no state can occur twice in the same run of the protocol. In the self-stabilization context when a system is subject to corruption, this fact is not automatically satisfied. Recall that [1] proposed an extension of its algorithm to deal with any graphs (including ambiguous graphs). Therefore, this extension may be used to treat the case of corruption [2]. Another way consists to treat locally the corruptions, then the corrections' actions are executed during the execution of the enumeration algorithm. Our solution satisfies the last way, its correction is shown in the following Lemma.

Lemma 2. *The system $\Re_s = (L, P_s, \mathcal{F})$ satisfies the convergence property.*

Proof. We study the case of each illegitimate configuration.

1. $\exists\,v_0 \in V(G)$ labeled such as:$n(v_0) \neq 1 + max\{n \mid (n, LV) \in GV(v_0)\}$ or $n(v_0) >| V(G) |$. The corrupted node v_0 applies rule $RC1$ to change its name to -1, then $RC2$ is executed by one of its neighbors v_i, after that v_0 executes $RC3$ to choose an unused number to rename itself. Let v_i one of its neighbors. The new state of v_i is such that the name (resp. the local view) of v_0 does not appear in the local view (resp. in the global view) of v_i. Then, the *Transmitting rule* allows to diffuse this novel state in all the graph.

2. $\exists \ v_0 \in V(G)$ labeled such as: $\exists \ n_1 \in LV(v_0) \mid \neg \exists \ v_i \in B(v_0) \backslash \{v_0\} : n(v_i) = n_1$ or $n_1 > \mid V(G) \mid$. Correction rule $RC2$ detects and eliminates such configuration.

3. $\exists \ v_0 \in V(G)$ labeled such as: $\exists \ (n_1, LV_1) \in GV(v_0)$, $\delta_{LV_1}(n(v_0)) \geq 2$ or $n_1 > \mid V(G) \mid$. Also, with the same reasoning, rule $RC4$ is applied to detect and eliminate this corrupted configuration.

The size of the relabeling sequence required, to eliminate all the illegitimate configurations and also to terminate the execution of the algorithm, is given in the section related to the complexity analysis. Formally, we have the following properties:

- The application of a correction rule decreases $h(G, \lambda, \mathcal{F})$ and induces the execution of the rule $R1$.
- The application of a rule in P does not increase $h(G, \lambda, \mathcal{F})$.
- $\forall \ (G, \lambda) \in \mathcal{G}_\mathcal{L}, \exists$ an integer k,

$$(G, \lambda) \xrightarrow[\Re]{k} (G, \lambda') : h(G, \lambda', \mathcal{F}) = 0 \qquad \square$$

Lemma 3. *The system $\Re_s = (L, P_s, \mathcal{F})$ encodes an enumeration algorithm.*

Proof. To show that the result is an enumeration, we use the same properties as those used in [1, 2]. Let G be a graph, to explain how this protocol denoted by $\mathcal{P}$ works, we introduce some notations. We denote by σ the state of the network which is composed of the local configurations of all the nodes. If $\sigma(v) = (n, LV, GV)$, then, n, LV, GV refer to the name, the local view and the mailbox of v at state σ. Thus, $\gamma(\sigma(v))$ is the name of the node v at state σ. Elements of mailbox are called messages; message m is sent by na if $m = (na, LV)$ for some LV. Name na is *known* to node v at state σ, if $\sigma(v) = (n, LV, GV)$ for some n, LV, GV and GV contains a message sent by na. We denote by $\sigma_k = (n_k(v), LV_k(v), GV_k(v))$ the label of each node $v \in V(G)$ after the kth step of the computation of $\mathcal{P}$. Protocol $\mathcal{P}$ satisfies the following properties whose proofs can follow the scheme of the one used in [1].

(I1) $\forall \ k \geq 0, v \in V(G)$: $LV_k(v) = LV_k(B(v)\backslash\{v\}) - \{0\}$,
(I2) $\forall \ k \geq 0, v \in V(G)$: $u, w \in B(v)$: $n_k(u) = n_k(w) \Rightarrow u = w$,
(I3) $\forall \ k \geq 0, v \in V(G)$: $n_k(v) \leq n_{k+1}(v)$ and $LV_k(v) \preceq LV_{k+1}(v)$ and $GV_k(v) \subseteq GV_{k+1}(v)$,
(I4) $\forall \ k \geq 0, v \in V(G), \forall \ (na, LV) \in GV_k(v)$: $\exists \ u \in V(G), n_k(u) = na$,
(I5) $\forall \ k \geq 0, v \in V(G), n_k(v) \neq 0$: $\forall \ na, na', na \leq na', v$ known $na' \Rightarrow v$ known na,
(I6) Protocol $\mathcal{P}$ is terminating for any graph,
(I7) The result of any run of $\mathcal{P}$ for any graph G is locally bijective,
(I8) $\mathcal{P}$ is an enumeration protocol for any unambiguous graph. $\qquad \square$

From the proofs of the three previous lemmas, we can state:

Corollary 1. *Starting from any labeled graphs, the system $\Re_s = (L, P_s, \mathcal{F})$ terminates.*

Corollary 2. *The relabeling system $\Re_s$ is local stabilizing. It encodes a self-stabilizing enumeration algorithm for any unambiguous graph.*

4.2   Complexity

In this section, we consider the model of distributed system described in Section 2.1 and we compute the complexity of our protocol in terms of relabeling rules or steps. The number of steps when the system does not contain any failure component is denoted by $\mathcal{M}$, the number of steps with failures is denoted by Σ. The complexity of the Mazurkiewicz enumeration algorithm is $\mathcal{M} = \theta(|V(G)|^3)$. The time of stabilization of the algorithm proposed in [2] is $\theta(t \times |V(G)|^2)$ steps, where t is the sum of the number of nodes and the highest name initially known. We use the following properties to give the stabilization time of our protocol:

1. Each node applies one rule in the set of correction rules to correct itself.
2. The application of the correction rules does not add illegitimate configurations. The application of the rule $RC1$ provokes the application of the rules $RC2$, $RC3$ and so $R1$.
3. In the worst case, for f_1 corruptions of names, f_2 corruptions of local view, f_3 corruptions of global view, the nodes apply $3f_1 + f_2 + f_3$ correction rules. Therefore, the stabilization time is $\theta(5 \times |V(G)|^3)$, when rule $R1$ is applied $|V(G)|^2$ times.

The worst case corresponds to the case of f_1. Let $f = 3f_1$, then the time of stabilization is $\theta(9f |V(G)|^2)$. So, the time for the enumeration algorithm subject to f corruptions is $\Sigma = \theta(9f |V(G)|^2 + (|V(G)| - f)^3)$. Starting from a configuration without corruptions, we obtain $\theta(|V(G)|^3)$. See that in [2], the parameter t is unbounded, and in our version f is bounded by $|V(G)|$.

5   An Implementation on the Visidia Tool

Visidia [12] is a tool to implement, to simulate, to test and to visualize distributed algorithms. It is motivated by the important theoretical results on the use of graph relabeling systems to encode distributed algorithms and to prove their correctness. Visidia provides a library together with an easy interface to implement distributed algorithms described by means of local computations. The distributed system of Visidia is based on asynchronous message passing model. However, it has been assumed that components of such a system do not fail. The threads representing the processes of the computation are created on the same machine.

A stage of computation [14] in Visidia is carried out after some synchronization, which can be achieved by using probabilistic procedures [15]. The processes are simulated by Java threads. The high level primitives including the synchronization procedures allows the user to implement local computations.

There are three types of local computations. To implement these local computations in an asynchronous message passing system, a randomized synchronization procedure is associated to each type, which are given in the following:

1. *Rendez-vous* (RV): In a computation step, the labels attached to nodes of K_2 (the complete graph with 2 nodes) are modified according to some rules depending on the labels appearing on K_2.

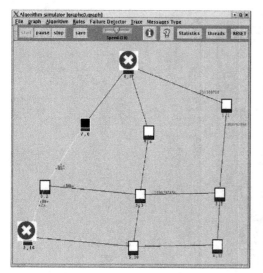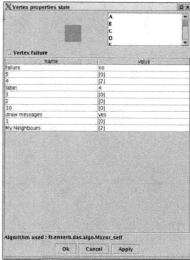

Fig. 1. The beginning of the simulation with transient failures

2. *Local Computation 1* (LC1): In a computation step, the label attached to the center of a ball is modified according to some rules depending on the labels of the ball, labels of the leaves are not modified.
3. *Local Computation 2* (LC2): In a computation step, the labels attached to the center and to the leaves of a ball may be modified according to some rules depending on the labels of the ball.

To simulate transient failures [16], the user can simulate the faulty of a process with the graphical user interface before the beginning of the simulation or during the simulation. For the enumeration algorithm, we show an execution by starting the algorithm with a randomized value of the name (labels). In the following figures, we present an execution of a local self-stabilizing enumeration algorithm on Visidia starting with faulty values as shown in the left part of Fig.1. For a graph of 10 nodes, each node is represented by two labels (*number, name*) where *number* is a number used to indicate and distinguish the nodes on the graphical interface and *name* is a value used by the enumeration algorithm. The maximum chosen value doesn't upper to 10, there are two nodes numbered 0 and 2 with incorrect names respectively 17 and 16. In the right part of Fig.1 we show the local view of the node 7, its number is 4 and has a neighbor 8 named 2. In the left part of Fig.2, the faulty node 2 (resp. 0) correct himself to 8 (resp. to 7). Then, the local view of the node 7 contains the correct named neighbor 0. Finally, Fig.3 shows the end of the execution of the enumeration algorithm. In the left part of this figure, the graph is totally named and in the right part we show the final local view of the node 7.

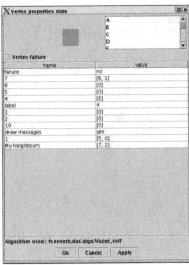
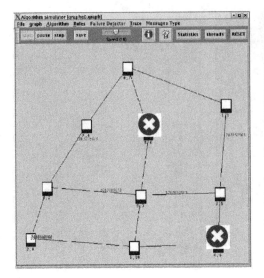

Fig. 2. Local correction of the transient failures

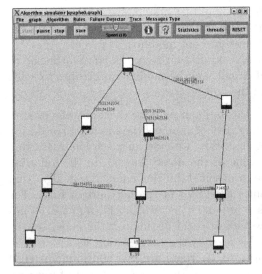

Fig. 3. The end of enumeration and the local views

6   Conclusion

In this paper, we have presented a method to encode self-stabilizing enumeration algorithm with local computations. We have adapted the method given in [6] to create an easy self-stabilizing Mazurkiewicz's enumeration algorithm. This kind of algorithm can be used to implement a system which tolerates transient failures. The method is based on defining a set of illegitimate configurations and adding correction rules to the initial graph rewriting systems. The resulting protocol encoded by local computations is able to detect and correct transient failures by applying correction rules.

This protocol is easy to understand and its translation from the initial algorithm requires little changes. The proof is decomposed into two steps. First the proof of self-stabilization which is based on our developed framework. Second the proof that this protocol does its expected task which is based on the same as [1]. For the complexity study, we show that our protocol is better than [2]. In this work, we had also shown that self-stabilization meets global detection of termination such as [17].

The simulation phase allows us to prove and to show the convergence of our protocol in the presence of transient failures. We show this by starting the execution of the algorithm with faulty labels. Therefore, the system detects and corrects these transient failures by applying correction rules.

References

1. A.W. Mazurkiewicz. Distributed enumeration. *Inf. Processing Letters*, 61(5):233–239, 1997.
2. E. Godard. A self-stabilizing enumeration algorithm. *Inf. Process. Lett.*, 82(6):299–305, 2002.
3. S. Dolev. *Self-stabilization*. MIT Press, 2000.
4. M. Schneider. Self-stabilization. *ACM Computing Surveys*, 25(1):45–67, 1993.
5. E.W. Dijkstra. Self stabilizing systems in spite of distributed control. *Communications of the ACM*, 17(11):643–644, 1974.
6. B. Hamid and M. Mosbah. An automatic approach to self-stabilization. In *6th ACIS International Conference on Software Engineering, Artificial Intelligence, Networking, and Parallel/Distributed Computing (SNPD2005), Baltimore, USA*, pages 129–132, May 2005.
7. A. Cournier, A.K. Datta, F. Petit, and V. Villain. Self-stabilizing pif algorithms in arbitrary network. *21th International Conference on Distributed Computing Systems (ICDCS 2001)*, pages 91–98, April 2001.
8. S. Ghosh, A. Gupta, T. Herman, and S. V. Pemmaraju. Fault-containing self-stabilizing algorithms. In *PODC '96: Proceedings of the fifteenth annual ACM symposium on Principles of distributed computing*, pages 45–54. ACM Press, 1996.
9. B. Awerbuch, B. Patt-Shamir, and G. Varghese. Self-stabilization by local checking and correction (extended abstract). In *Proceedings of the 32nd annual symposium on Foundations of computer science*, pages 268–277. IEEE Computer Society Press, 1991.
10. Y. Afek and S. Dolev. Local stabilizer. In *ISTCS '97: Proceedings of the Fifth Israel Symposium on the Theory of Computing Systems (ISTCS '97)*, page 74. IEEE Computer Society, 1997.
11. Y. Afek, S. Kutten, and M. Yung. The local detection paradigm and its applications to self-stabilization. *Theor. Comput. Sci.*, 186(1-2):199–229, 1997.
12. M. Mosbah and A. Sellami. Visidia: A tool for the VIsialization and SImulation of DIstributed Algorithms. http://www.labri.fr/visidia/.

13. I. Litovsky, Y. Métivier, and E. Sopena. Graph relabeling systems and distributed algorithms. In World Scientific Publishing, editor, *Handbook of graph grammars and computing by graph transformation*, volume Vol. III, Eds. H. Ehrig, H.J. Kreowski, U. Montanari and G. Rozenberg, pages 1–56, 1999.

14. M. Bauderon, Y. Métivier, M. Mosbah, and A. Sellami. Graph relabeling systems : A tool for encoding, proving, studying and visualizing distributed algorithms. *Electronic Notes in Theoretical Computer Science*, 51, 2001.

15. Y. Métivier, N. Saheb, and A. Zemmari. Randomized rendezvous. In Birkhauser, editor, *Colloquium on mathematics and computer science: algorithms, trees, combinatorics and probabilities*, Trends in mathematics, pages 183–194, 2000.

16. B. Hamid and M. Mosbah. Visualization of self-stabilizing distributed algorithms. In *9th International conference information visualization IV 2005, London, UK (to appear)*, page .. IEEE Computer Society, 2005.

17. A. Arora and M. Nesterenko. Unifying stabilization and termination in message-passing systems. In *ICDCS '01: Proceedings of the The 21st International Conference on Distributed Computing Systems*, page 99, Washington, DC, USA, 2001. IEEE Computer Society.

Adding Fault-Tolerance to a Hierarchical DRE System[*]

Paul Rubel, Joseph Loyall, Richard Schantz, and Matthew Gillen

BBN Technologies
Cambridge, MA
{prubel, jloyall, schantz, mgillen}@bbn.com

Abstract. Dynamic resource management is a crucial part of the infrastructure for emerging mission-critical distributed real-time embedded system. Because of this, the resource manager must be fault-tolerant, with nearly continuous operation. This paper describes an ongoing effort to develop a fault-tolerant multi-layer dynamic resource management capability and the challenges we have encountered, including multi-tiered structure, rapid recovery, the characteristics of component middleware, and the co-existence of replicated and non-replicated elements. While some of these have been investigated before, this work exhibits all of these characteristics simultaneously, presenting a significant fault-tolerance research challenge.

1 Introduction

Fault-tolerance (FT) is an important characteristic of many systems, especially mission critical applications that are prevalent in medical, industrial, military, and telecommunications domains. Many of these applications are distributed real-time and embedded (DRE), combining the challenges of networked systems (e.g., distribution, dynamic environments, and nondeterminism) with the challenges of embedded systems (e.g., constrained resources and real-time requirements). For these systems, failure of applications or infrastructure can lead to catastrophic consequences.

As part of the DARPA ARMS program, and in conjunction with a team of researchers from several organizations, we have been developing a *Multi-Layered dynamic Resource Management* (MLRM) capability supporting a new Total Ship Computing (TSC) paradigm for the next generation of Naval surface ship [2]. This MLRM system controls the allocation of computing and communication resources to applications (some critical and others non-critical) and reallocation of resources when failures occur and when missions change, while maximizing operational capability.

Because MLRM is a critical part of the TSC infrastructure, it is important that it survive failures and damage. However, MLRM has some characteristics, typical of similar DRE systems, that present challenges to making it fault-tolerant. In this paper, we describe our current efforts to make the MLRM fault-tolerant, concentrating on the following characteristics and challenges:

---

[*] This work was supported by the Defense Advanced Research Projects Agency (DARPA) under contract NBCHC030119.

F. Eliassen and A. Montresor (Eds.): DAIS 2006, LNCS 4025, pp. 303–308, 2006.

- *Hierarchical structure* – MLRM mirrors the hierarchical structure of the TSC infrastructure and must handle failures at each of the mission layer, resource pool and application layer, and resource layer.
- *Rapid recovery* – Because MLRM functionality is critical to keeping applications running and supporting ongoing missions, it is important that it be available continuously. Therefore, if MLRM fails it must recover as rapidly as possible, aiming for near zero recovery time.
- *Component middleware* – MLRM and TSC are being developed using emerging component middleware that offers many advantages, but exhibits different communication patterns than the traditional client-server model that many fault-tolerance techniques support.
- *Large numbers of elements with various degrees of fault-tolerance needs* – TSC and the MLRM subsystem itself are large distributed systems, with many interoperating elements, not all of which need to be fault-tolerant to the same degree. Traditional fault-tolerance solutions that require all elements to be part of a single approach fault-tolerance infrastructure are unsuitable.

We describe our current progress and findings in terms of each of these challenges and characteristics, and then describe our next steps toward achieving this work in progress.

2 Fitting Fault-Tolerance into a Layered DRE Structure

The MLRM architecture, illustrated in Figure 1, is hierarchical, with the following layers:

- The *Infrastructure Layer* deploys missions (consisting of application strings), assigns them to resource pools and security domains, and determines their relative priorities.
- The *Pool and Application String Layer* coordinates groups of related computing nodes (*pools*) and applications (*application strings*).
- The *Node* layer controls access to individual computing and communication resources.

The pool structure uses diversity in location and clustering to protect against large-scale damage or major system failures affecting a large portion of computing resources. With pools of computing hardware spread in different locations, the failure of one pool of resource still leaves sufficient computing capability for the critical operations.

To fit into this layered structure, we developed a top-down approach to fault-tolerance. We began developing fault-tolerance for MLRM to protect against the most catastrophic failures, so that the loss of a pool will not result in the loss of MLRM functionality. One of the functions of MLRM is to redeploy critical applications onto surviving nodes or pools in the face of a failure, but this is only possible if the MLRM functionality survives the failure. Therefore, we replicated the infrastructure layer MLRM elements across all the pools. If a pool fails, the infrastructure MLRM elements of the surviving pools take over to initiate the actions necessary to deploy critical functionality across the remaining pools. In this case, there is no need to replicate the pool level MLRM elements, since they will still exist in the surviving pools.

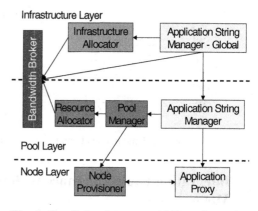

Fig. 1. Our fault-tolerance capability mirrors the layered structure of the MLRM architecture

3   Providing Rapid Recovery from Faults

Since MLRM has responsibility for recovering application functionality in the face of a node or pool failure, the infrastructure layer MLRM functionality must be constantly available. Therefore, the primary requirement for our MLRM fault-tolerance is *speed of recovery*. Because of the very short recovery requirements, and since our fault-model is concerned with node loss rather than misbehavior, we employ a tolerance strategy that *actively* replicates components. In this scheme, each replica of the infrastructure MLRM is processing incoming messages and sending out responses. As long as one replica out of n of the MLRM has not failed, that replica will be able to carry out the responsibilities of the MLRM immediately and failures of $n-1$ replicas can be tolerated.

We implemented active fault-tolerance for MLRM using MEAD [3] and Spread [1], both of which we customized, and in the case of MEAD, extended, and enhanced to support the features of the MLRM system. Spread provides a total order group communication system. We configured it for rapid recognition of the failure of group members. MEAD provides replication by intercepting CORBA calls and routing them through group communication, as well as code to suppress duplicate responses from replicas and recover from replica failures.

Figure 2 illustrates the results of experiments to evaluate the speed of our MLRM recovery. The experiments were conducted with three active replicas of MLRM infrastructure layer functionality[1] distributed over three pools. We failed one of the pools, by removing its network route, and measured the time for the remaining replicas, on hosts *alpha* and *hotel*, to recover from the failure.

The measured failover time includes the time needed for Spread to *detect* the failure of the group member. In all cases, the average detection+recovery time (hereafter called the *failover time*) was less than 200 ms. The mean failover time is 139 ms, with a standard deviation of 21 ms, to alpha and 128 ms, with a standard deviation of 6 ms, to hotel. The minimum failover time to both replicas is practically identical (119 and 118 ms, respectively), with a maximum of 185 ms for alpha and 135 ms for hotel.

---

[1] This first set of experiments only replicated the Infrastructure Allocator and Application String Manager-Global elements. We are in the process of replicating the Bandwidth Broker.

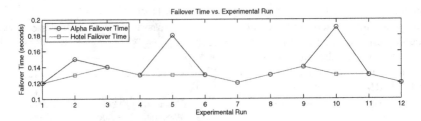

Fig. 2. Time to detect and recover from a failure of an MLRM replica

4 Integrating Fault-Tolerance with the CORBA Component Model

Many fault-tolerance concepts, and existing code bases (including MEAD), were designed to work with replicated servers in client-server architectures, such as CORBA 2. MLRM has been developed using the CORBA Component Model (CCM, or CORBA 3), which has many advantages including lifecycle support and availability of design tools. However, there are two main challenges associated with providing fault-tolerance in CCM.

The first challenge is that the MLRM, and CCM in general, exhibits a peer-to-peer structure, where components can play the role of both client and server simultaneously. Our initial software base only supported replicated servers with duplicate suppression of responses from replicated servers back to non-replicated clients. We extended this code base to support the replication of both clients and servers, and by monitoring and controlling the CORBA message request identifiers we were able to provide the suppression of duplicate requests (from replicated clients) and responses (from replicated servers).

The second challenge is that the deployment architecture of CCM is more complicated than most CORBA 2 solutions. Before a component can be deployed using CIAO [4], an open-source C++ CCM implementation, a *Node Daemon (ND)* starts up a *Node Application (NA)*, which acts as a container for new components. The ND makes CORBA calls on the NA, instructing it to start components, which are not present at NA start up time. Note that the components, when instantiated in the NA, need to be replicated, but the NDs should not be.

To illustrate this point, consider an existing FT component when a new replica is started. Since MEAD ensures that all messages to and from one replica are seen at every replica, the existing replicas will receive an extra set of bootstrap interactions each time a new replica is started. This will not only confuse the existing replicas, but the responses from the new replica will also confuse the existing NDs. We developed a way to allow direct point-to-point interactions during the bootstrapping process and then switch to using reliable, ordered, group communications once the replicas have started.

The CCM envisions components interacting within a large-scale assembly. Architecturally, the current MLRM is made up of multiple assemblies. This decision was a pragmatic one since the ability to dynamically redeploy applications was not supported at the time by CIAO. It also allows us to set the unit of FT, the process, to the unit of CCM deployment, simplifying the process of making the MLRM FT.

Finally, since CORBA and the MLRM are multi-language solutions, our FT infrastructure needs to support multiple languages and their interactions. Currently both C++ via CIAO and Java via JacORB are supported and co-exist in our MLRM solution.

5 Limiting the Effects of the Fault-Tolerance Infrastructure

In order to keep replicas consistent, MEAD ensures that messages are reliably delivered to each replica in the same consistent order. To enforce these constraints we used Spread. Any interactions with a replica, after the initial CCM bootstrapping, pass through Spread.

In the simple case of a client interacting with a replicated server, all interactions are necessarily over Spread. The situation becomes more complex in the MLRM case, because we are (currently) replicating only the Infrastructure layer. Elements in the Pool layer will necessarily interact with the Infrastructure layer using Spread. However, since the Pool and Node layers are not replicated, they do not need the same consistency guarantees. Furthermore, from a usability perspective, we do not want to force the Spread infrastructure on the node layer, which can include hundreds of components.

The necessity of containing the use of Spread becomes even more apparent as the interactions within the system increase and more objects and components are introduced and connected. One example of this, introduced in Section 4, occurs when replicas are bootstrapped. To provide acceptable performance for components that require Spread and to more efficiently use resources, we implemented functionality that limits the use of Spread to where it is strictly necessary.

Spread is strictly necessary in replicas and each replica is required to use Spread for all its communications. Every entity that does not interact with a replicated entity does not need to use Spread. For those components that interact with both replicated and non-replicated entities, we ensure that they respond to a request in the same manner they received the request. If a request is received over TCP it is responded to over TCP and similarly for Spread. When initiating a request, MEAD compares the destination port against a list of ports on which Spread should be used. If the destination port is on this list the message will go out over Spread, otherwise it will use TCP as if MEAD were not present.

This same mechanism is used to deploy new replicas. Until a replica has been started the ND and NA interact to without group communication as neither is replicated. Once the replicated component starts, no more ND/NA interactions are necessary. In the future we envision a more dynamic method for distinguishing replicas from non-replicated objects or components that does not require up-front configuration.

6 Conclusions and Future Work

As systems become more complex and mission-critical, fault-tolerance continues to be an important part of their design and deployment. While developing a solution for providing a fault-tolerant MLRM, we continue to solve problems related to the structure of the MLRM, its fault-tolerance requirements, its underlying structure and framework, and its size and scope. An immediate next step is the rigorous evaluation of the viability, efficiency and operability of the current approach to very rapid failover for these types of DRE components. Moving forward we are working on solutions for replicating components that cannot be actively replicated, some of which must interact with network hardware on which running Spread is not an option. As CCM implementations mature, we hope to be able to better integrate fault-tolerance with components, particularly during deployment and when determining if the use of group-communication is required for particular requests. As we gain more insights into commonalities between the different implementations of components and objects, higher-level abstractions should become more apparent, providing further opportunities for improvements.

Acknowledgments

We would like to thank our colleagues at CMU for their help with MEAD, particularly Aaron Paulos and Priya Narasimhan. Vanderbilt University's Distributed Object Computing (DOC) group has been invaluable in helping with CIAO and component deployment. Telcordia and SRC have also made valuable contributions to our work.

References

1. Yair Amir, Claudiu Danilov, Michal Miskin-Amir, John Schultz, and Jonathan Stanton. The Spread Toolkit: Architecture and Performance. Johns Hopkins University, Center for Networking and Distributed Systems (CNDS) Technical report CNDS-2004-1.
2. Roy Campbell, Rose Daley, B. Dasarathy, Patrick Lardieri, Brad Orner, Rick Schantz, Randy Coleburn, Lonnie R. Welch, and Paul Work. Toward an Approach for Specification of QoS and Resource Information for Dynamic Resource Management. Second RTAS Workshop on Model-Driven Embedded Systems (MoDES '04), Toronto, Canada, May 25-28, 2004.
3. P. Narasimhan, T. A. Dumitras, A. M. Paulos, S. M. Pertet, C. F. Reverte, J. G. Slember and D. Srivastava. MEAD: Support for Real-Time Fault-Tolerant CORBA. *Concurrency and Computation: Practice and Experience*, vol. 17, no. 12, 2005, pp. 1527-1545.
4. Nanbor Wang, Douglas C. Schmidt, Aniruddha Gokhale, Craig Rodrigues, Balachandran Natarajan, Joseph P. Loyall, Richard E. Schantz, and Christopher D. Gill. QoS-enabled Middleware, in Middleware for Communications, Qusay Mahmoud, Ed. Wiley and Sons, New York, 2003.

Using Speculative Push for Unnecessary Checkpoint Creation Avoidance

Arkadiusz Danilecki and Michał Szychowiak

Institute of Computing Science
Poznań University of Technology
Piotrowo 3a, 60-965 Poznań, Poland
{adanilecki, mszychowiak}@cs.put.poznan.pl

Abstract. This paper discusses a way of incorporating speculation techniques into Distributed Shared Memory (DSM) systems with checkpointing mechanism without creating unnecessary checkpoints. Speculation is a general technique involving prediction of the future of a computation, namely accesses to shared objects unavailable on the accessing node (*read faults*). Thanks to such predictions objects can be pushed to requesting nodes before the actual access operation is performed, resulting, at least potentially, in a considerable performance improvement. This mechanism is a foundation for the proposed SpecCkpt protocol based on independent checkpointing integrated with a coherence protocol for a given consistency model introducing little overhead. It ensures the consistency of checkpoints, at the same time allowing a fast recovery from failures.

1 Introduction

Modern Distributed Shared Memory (DSM) systems reveal increasing demands for efficiency, reliability and robustness. System developers tend to deliver fast systems which would allow to parallelize distributed processes efficiently. Unfortunately, failures of some system nodes can cause process crashes resulting in a loss of results of the processing and requiring to restart the computation from the beginning. One of the techniques used to prevent such restarts is *checkpointing*. Checkpointing consists in saving the processing state periodically (a *checkpoint*), in order to restore the saved state in case of further failure. Only checkpoints which represent a consistent global state of the system can be used when restarting computation (the state of a DSM system is usually identified with the content of the memory).

There are two major approaches to checkpointing: coordinated (synchronous) and independent (asynchronous). Coordinated checkpointing requires expensive synchronization between all (or a part of) the distributed processes, in order to ensure the consistency of the saved states. The significant overhead of this approach makes it impractical unless the checkpoint synchronization is correlated with synchronization operations of a coherence protocol ([7]). On the other hand, the independent checkpointing does not involve interprocess synchronization but, in general, does not guarantee the consistency. After a failure occurs, a

F. Eliassen and A. Montresor (Eds.): DAIS 2006, LNCS 4025, pp. 309–315, 2006.

consistent checkpoint must be found among all saved checkpoints, therefore the recovery takes much more time and may require more recomputation. A variant of the independent checkpoint – *communication induced checkpointing* (or *dependency induced checkpointing*) – offers simple creation of consistent checkpoints, by storing a new checkpoint each time a recovery dependency is created (e.g. interprocess communication). However, its overhead is too prohibitive for general distributed applications. Nevertheless, this approach has been successfully applied in DMS systems in strict correlation with memory coherence protocols. This correlation allows to reduce the number of the actual dependencies and to limit the checkpointing overhead significantly ([9]).

Speculation, on the other hand, is a technique which promises to increase the speed of DSM operations and to reduce the gap between DSM and message-passing systems. The speculation may involve speculative pushes of shared objects to processing nodes, before they actually demand access [10], prefetching of the shared objects with anticipation that the application process would need those objects ([1]) or self invalidation of shared objects to reduce the frequency of "3-hop-misses" ([8]) among other techniques.

This paper is organized as follows. In section 2, we present a formal definition of the system model and speculation operations. The previous work in this field, including the first variant of SpecCkpt protocol, is briefly described in Section 3. Section 4 discusses the ways of combining speculative pushes into DSM systems with checkpointing. Preliminary results are contained within Section 5 Concluding remarks and future work are proposed in Section 6.

2   DSM System Model

A DSM system is an asynchronous distributed system composed of a finite set of sequential processes P_1, P_2, ..., P_n that can access a finite set O of shared objects. Each P_i is executed on a DSM node n_i composed of a local processor and a volatile local memory used to store shared objects accessed by P_i. Each object consists of several values (*object members*) and *object methods* which read and modify object members (here, we adopt the object-oriented approach; however, our work is also applicable to variable-based or page-based shared memory). The concatenation of the values of all members of object $x \in O$ is referred to as *object value* of x. Here, we consider read-write objects, i.e. each method of x has been classified either as read-only (if it does not change the value of x and in the case of nested method invocation, all invoked methods are also read-only) or read-and-modify (otherwise). Read access $r_i(x)$ to object x is issued when process P_i invokes a read-only method of object x. Write access $w_i(x)$ to object x is issued when process P_i invokes any other method of x. Each write access results in a new object value of x.

To increase the efficiency of DSM, objects are replicated on distinct hosts, allowing concurrent access to the same data. A consistent state of DSM objects replicated on distinct nodes is maintained by a *coherence protocol* and depends on the assumed *consistency model*. Usually, one replica of every object is distinguished as a *master replica*. The set of all replicas of a given object is referred to as a *copyset*. The process holding master replica of object x is called x's *owner*. A common approach is to enable the owner an exclusive write access to the object. However, when no write access to x is performed, the object can have several replicas simultaneously accessible only for reading (shared replicas). The speculation introduces a special part of the system, called the *predictor*, which is responsible for predicting future actions of the processes (e.g. future read and write accesses) and proper reactions.

As a result of a read access issued to an object locally unavailable, the object is fetched from its owner and brought to the requester. Using speculation, however, the object may be fetched from its owner also before the actual read access (i.e. *prefetched*) or forwarded by the owner to potential object users (i.e. *pushed*), as a result of prediction. By $p_i(x)$ we will denote a prefetch operation of object x resulting from the prediction made at process P_i. By $f_{i,j}(x)$ we will denote a push operation of object x from owner P_i to potential object user P_j. The prediction is successful if the pushed or prefetched object is actually used, and the read fault is avoided. If the prefetched or pushed object is never used, the prediction was unsuccessful (and is referred to as *misprediction*).

Dependency of operations is a relation arising between $w_i(x)$ and any subsequent $r_j(x)$, $p_j(x)$ or $f_{i,j}(x)$ i.e. when process P_j uses (reads) a value previously written by P_i. *Local dependency* reflects the order of operations performed by a single process. To ensure system consistency in case of a failure, the system forces the object owner to make a checkpoint each time the dependency arises.

3   Previous Work

In the previous work on reliable speculative DSM systems ([4], [3]), it has been shown that a naive implementation of the speculation and, more specifically, prefetching may reduce DSM efficiency by introducing false dependencies, which in turn increase the number of unnecessary checkpoints. Since prefetches are seen by the object owner as read accesses, they create dependencies. However, because they are speculative operations, the object owner has no way to determine whether a prefetched object will actually be used (prediction was successful) or will be invalidated before using or never accessed by requesting node (on misprediction).

These problems are summarized as follows:

- An access to objects (fetches) may result from the speculation made by the predictor and therefore (in case of a false prediction), may not create a real dependency;
- Even when the access is explicitly marked as speculative, the process has no way of determining whether a true dependency between processes will ever be created, since it cannot determine whether the prediction is correct (otherwise, it wouldn't be a speculation).

To avoid the creation of unnecessary checkpoints, the changes to the underlying checkpointing protocol have been proposed. They consist in introducing a new replica state (PREFETCHED) and operation decoupling. In the proposed SpecCkpt protocol, prefetched objects are put into a special PREFETCHED state. The access to prefetch object would then require getting confirmation from the owner. This confirmation would be granted or not, depending on the underlying coherence protocol.

This protocol avoids unnecessary checkpoints at the cost of reducing positive speculation effects (even a successful prediction needs a confirmation message). We have verified our protocol using a simulated DSM system (see sec. 5) and we found our results somewhat dissatisfying. In some of the tested application our protocol behaved surprisingly bad, so we decided to search for another techniques.

4   Speculative Push

Another way of avoiding the creation of unnecessary checkpoints may be using a different speculation technique, namely speculative push. In prefetching, speculation is triggered by the node which has the object in the INVALID state; in the speculative push, it is the object's owner who triggers the speculation, pushing the object to potential requesters. It may be observed that in the prefetching, the requesting node has no way of determining whether the object owner has already checkpointed the object. So, it does not know whether the prefetch request would force the object owner to take a checkpoint, or not. In the latter technique however, the object's owner has obviously a full knowledge of its own local state and therefore is able to determine when the speculation results in making a checkpoint. Usually, the object's owner forwards the object to anticipated requesters after it finishes the object modifications. However, this may involve creating a checkpoint, which may be unnecessary (because the push may result from misprediction).

Our proposal is to trigger a speculative push of the object each time the object is checkpointed. Therefore, even if the push is unnecessary and creates a false dependency, it does not introduce additional costs (since the page is already checkpointed).

We have tested this proposal for sequential consistency model and MSI (Modified, Shared, Invalid) coherence protocol. The implemented algorithm is described as follows:

- Between the checkpoints, the object's owner records remote accesses to the objects in the SHARED state. Those will be potential candidates for data forwarding. Essentially, it is the object *copyset*.
- On local write access, the owner invalidates the copyset but keeps the list of the potential candidates (*possible copyset*).
- If the owner has the object in the MODIFIED state and receives a read request, it checkpoints the page before answering. The requester is removed from possible copyset list but added to the copyset list.

- After the owner has successfully checkpointed the object, it forwards the object to all potential requesters and clears the possible copyset list. Such new replicas are put into a special PUSHED state (and the respective nodes are put into the master replica copyset).
- Request from a node is ignored if the owner has already pushed the object to that node.
- The access to a replica in the PUSHED state is treated as the access to replica in the SHARED state, with the exception when a confirmation is sent to the owner. The only purpose of this confirmation is to provide feedback for the owner, so that it could add the node again to the possible copyset list.

5 Preliminary Results

The simulation was performed with the use of a backend [5] to Augmint simulator [2] and a set of applications from the SPLASH-2 suite [6]. The obtained results should be treated rather as indications of the trends, not the final results. Compared to the results found in literature, our simulation consequently tends to be too optimistic about the positive effects of prediction, probably because of the simplified simulator architecture (the impact of increased network traffic, costs of the owner searching, the cost of a single checkpoint is modelled as a constant).

Due to the space limits, we present only some of the results here. The following basic set of prefetch techniques was used for comparison: simple stride-based prefetch; prefetching pages which were recently invalidated; prefetching the same set of pages which were used before attempting a barrier; prefetching neighboring pages; and combination of all those techniques.

Table 1. The results of the simulation with standard application inputs and 8 processes, using the best prefetch technique

Application name	(a)	(b)	(c)	(d)	(e)	(f)	(g)
barnes	46	97	97	38	101	100	95
fft	11	98	97	54	103	101	100
lu	36	87	85	43	108	102	95
fmm	33	100	100	36	103	100	97

Different prefetching techniques prove to yield the best effects for different applications. We decided to choose those which were the most and the least efficient for every application and compare the reduction of execution time against the base checkpointing protocol without speculation. Relative reduction of execution time is shown in table 1. First, we evaluated the prefetching used without any modifications of the base MSI checkpointing protocol (column *b* and *e*). Then, we compared it to SpecCkpt protocol using the same techniques (column *c* and *f*). The misprediction ratio for those techniques can be found in columns

a and d. Finally, the g column represents the relative execution times achieved with SpecCkpt protocol using speculative pushes.

From the whole set of the obtained results, we concluded that the most influential factor is the misprediction ratio. If the misprediction ratio is low, then usually our SpeckCkpt protocol, using either prefetches or pushes, is outperformed by the base protocol. However, for different applications different techniques turned out to have a low misprediction ratio. It would be, in general, impossible for a DSM system to determine the best suited technique in advance. Therefore, in real systems, higher misprediction ratio is to be expected.

6   Conclusions

This paper proposed the use of speculative pushes instead of speculative prefetches in DSM systems with checkpointing. Since the object owner is able to determine whether the push will result in checkpoint or not, it may decide when the pushes do not introduce additional significant costs resulting from the checkpoints.

We intend to implement our protocols first in another simulator (to validate our results) and then in the real linux-based DSM system. We are in the process of validating and preparing tests of a few other ideas of improving our protocols, namely prefetch delaying and speculative checkpoints.

References

1. Bianchini, R., Pinto, R., Amorim, C. L.: Data Prefetching for Software DSMs. Proc. Int. Conference on Supercomputing, Melbourne, Australia (1998)
2. Carbajal, J., Michael, M., Nguyen, A-T., Torrellas, J., Sharma, A.: Augmint: A Multiprocessor Simulation Environment for Intel x86 Architectures. CSRD Technical Report 1463, March 1996
3. Danilecki A., Szychowiak M.: Checkpointing Speculative Distributed Shared Memory. To appear in Proc. 6th Int. Conference on Parallel Processing and Applied Mathematics PPAM'2005, Poznan 2005
4. Danilecki A., Szychowiak M.: Checkpointing Speculative DSM Systems, Research Report RA-021/05, Institute of Computing Science, Poznan University of Technology, 2005.
5. Danilecki A., Szychowiak M., Kobusinski J.: Simplified DSM simulation with the use of the Augmint backend, Research Report RA-04/06, Institute of Computing Science, Poznan University of Technology, 2006.
6. Gupta, A., Ohara, M., Singh, J., Torrie, E., Woo, S., The SPLASH2 Programs: Characterization and Methodological Considerations. Proc. 22nd Int. Symposium on Computer Architecture (ISCA 1995), May 1995
7. Kongmunvattana, A., Tanchatchawal, S., Tzeng, N.-F.: Coherence-Based Coordinated Checkpointing for Software Distributed Shared Memory Systems. Proc. 20th Conference on Distributed Computing Systems (2000) 556–563
8. Lai, A-C., Babak Falsafi, B.: Selective, Accurate, and Timely Self-Invalidation Using Last-Touch Prediction. Proc. 27th Int. Symposium on Computer Architecture (ISCA 27), Vancouver, BC, Canada (2000) 139–148

9. Park, T., Yeom, H. Y.: A Low Overhead Logging Scheme for Fast Recovery in Distributed Shared Memory Systems. Journal of Supercomputing Vo.15. No.3. (2002) 295–320
10. Rajwar, R., Kagi, A., Goodman, J. R.: Inferential Queueing and Speculative Push. International Journal of Parallel Programming (IJPP) Vo. 32. No. 3 (2004) 273–284

A Versatile Kernel for Distributed AOP

Éric Tanter and Rodolfo Toledo

University of Chile, Computer Science Dept.
Avenida Blanco Encalada 2120, Santiago, Chile
{etanter, rtoledo}@dcc.uchile.cl

Abstract. Aspect-Oriented Programming (AOP) promotes better separation of concerns in software systems by introducing aspects for the modular implementation of crosscutting concerns. As a result, modularity and adaptability of software systems are greatly enhanced. To date, very few AOP proposals take distribution into account. This paper considers the explicit introduction of distribution in AOP, by proposing support for distributed aspects: all dimensions of aspects are studied in the light of distribution. The result of this work is a versatile kernel for distributed AOP in Java: a flexible infrastructure that allows aspects to be defined and applied in a distributed manner, on top of which various distributed aspect languages and frameworks can be defined.

1 Introduction

Aspect-Oriented Programming (AOP) provides means for proper modularization of crosscutting concerns [8], *i.e.* concerns that cannot be cleanly modularized using traditional programming paradigms. Typical examples of such concerns are *non-functional* concerns such as monitoring, security, concurrency, etc., but also *functional* concerns such as observation relationships and, in general, coordination between different modules. Without AOP, the implementation of such concerns is scattered across several modules. The importance of AOP for practical software engineering is reflected in the growing interest manifested by industrial actors, in particular in application servers [10]. AOP also helps *adaptation* of software systems: for a given concern to be adaptable, it first has to be modularized.

The relation between AOP and distributed computing is interesting. Even though AOP is used in application servers, aspects are defined and applied locally to enhance the implementation of the application server; most AOP proposals to date do not support the remote definition and/or application of aspects. In other words, *AOP in distributed systems is NOT distributed AOP*. To our knowledge, only JAC [16], DJcutter [15], and AWED [4] address distributed AOP as such, by enhancing the language constructs of AOP to cover distribution. However, each proposal has its set of limitations, as will be discussed later. Among motivating examples of distributed AOP are distributed unit testing [15], sophisticated distributed cache policies and checking of architectural constraints in distributed systems [3].

F. Eliassen and A. Montresor (Eds.): DAIS 2006, LNCS 4025, pp. 316–331, 2006.

In this paper, we adopt a general approach to distributed AOP, by extending our previous work on *versatile kernels for AOP*: expressive and flexible infrastructures for AOP on top of which different AOP languages and frameworks can be developed [23, 24]. Our methodology consists in revising all the concepts of our AOP kernel for Java, Reflex [1], in the light of distribution. The result is a versatile AOP kernel for distributed AOP in Java, named ReflexD, which can be used to define and apply aspects in a distributed manner.

In Section 2, we discuss the notion of distributed AOP, analyzing the different elements of AOP and what it means to consider them in the light of distribution. Section 3 briefly introduces the notion of AOP kernels in general, since we follow this line of work here. Section 4 exposes the different elements of ReflexD, our versatile kernel for distributed AOP in Java. In Section 5 we explain how a distributed notion of control flow can be built with ReflexD, and apply it in Section 6. Section 8 discusses related work and Section 9 concludes.

2 Distributed AOP

We now briefly discuss the main elements of an aspect in AOP, in order to later analyze what *distributed AOP* means.

2.1 Elements of AOP

The anatomy of an aspect can be roughly described as follows:

- the **cut** of an aspect describes the execution points of a program to which the aspect applies, *e.g.* calls to state-changing methods on shape objects;
- the **action** of an aspect describes the effect of the aspect at its cut, *e.g.* tracing the underlying calls, or requesting a lock before proceeding;
- the **binding** between a cut and an action specifies issues such as when the action is executed (before, after or around the intercepted execution point), the context information to be exposed to the action, etc.

An aspect language typically extends a traditional programming language with language constructs for the above elements. For instance, the most-used Java AOP extension to date is AspectJ [11], which extends Java with constructs to define aspects, with pointcuts (the cut) and advices (the action). In AspectJ, the binding between a cut and an action is split between both: it is not a separate entity. Below is a simple tracing aspect in AspectJ:

```
aspect Trace {
  pointcut fooCalls(Object x): call(* A.foo(..)) && this(x);
  before(Object x): fooCalls(x) { // log call made by x }
}
```

A pointcut `fooCalls` is defined, matching all calls to method `foo` on objects of type A, and exposing a single parameter `x`, bound to the instance performing the call (using `this(x)`). Then an advice is associated to the pointcut: when the pointcut matches, the body of the advice is executed before the original call is performed. Variable `x` is available in the scope of the advice body.

[1] http://reflex.dcc.uchile.cl

2.2 Distributed AOP

Aspect-oriented programming enhances software modularity and adaptability by promoting better modularization of otherwise crosscutting concerns. The entailed benefits of using AOP are of interest for any kind of complex software systems, and in particular, distributed systems: for instance to express aspects covering crosscutting interactions between remote entities. However, as argued in [15], simply combining an existing AOP language such as AspectJ with an existing framework for distributed systems like Java RMI (Remote Method Invocation) [19] is not a solution.

As a matter of fact, a framework like RMI extends OOP to the world of distributed programming, but does not help for AOP. The fact that the very concepts of aspect languages are not extended to distribution forces programmers to define a distributed aspect as a collection of distributed entities realizing the whole aspect based on remote calls. It is not possible to define a distributed aspect as a simple, non-distributed entity [15]. Hence developing distributed aspects is made much more complex than it should be, and deployment issues are exacerbated. Leveraging AOP to distribution requires the very concepts of AOP to be revisited in the light of distribution:

- **distributed cut:** describing execution points of interest must possibly discriminate among execution *hosts* (*a.k.a. remote pointcuts* [15, 16]); a method call may be of interest only if called in a particular host.
- **distributed action:** the effect of an aspect should possibly be executed on a *remote* host, not necessarily where the cut is realized; *e.g.* the activity of a process in a production machine monitored on a separate machine.
- **distributed binding:** the specification of the binding between the cut and the action of an aspect may be done in any host, which may not be the host where the cut is realized or the action is executed.

This defines our approach to distributed AOP. Given the variability in each of the above elements, we target a flexible architecture covering these notions, focusing on the core semantics first; syntax is not considered in this work.

3   The Kernel Approach to AOP

This section briefly introduces the necessary background concepts on AOP kernels and our Java implementation, Reflex. More elements on Reflex will be introduced as necessary in the course of the paper.

3.1 Versatile Kernels for AOP

In previous work [23, 24], we have motivated the interest of being able to define and use different aspect languages, including domain-specific ones, to modularize the different concerns of a software system. We have proposed the architecture of a *versatile kernel* for multi-language AOP, and our current Java implementation, Reflex. An AOP kernel supports the core semantics of various AO languages

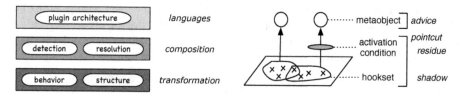

Fig. 1. Architecture of a versatile kernel for multi-language AOP

Fig. 2. The link model and correspondence to AOP concepts

through proper structural and behavioral models. Designers of aspect languages can experiment comfortably with an AOP kernel as a back-end, as it provides a higher abstraction level than low-level transformation toolkits. Furthermore, a crucial role of an AOP kernel is that of a *mediator* between different coexisting AO approaches: *detecting* interactions between aspects, possibly written in different languages, and providing expressive means for their *resolution* [21].

The architecture of an AOP kernel (Fig. 1) consists of: a *transformation* layer for basic weaving, supporting both structural and behavioral modifications of programs; a *composition* layer, for detection and resolution of aspect interactions; a *language* layer, for modular definition of aspect languages (as plugins).

3.2 Reflex in a Nutshell

Reflex is a portable library for structural and behavioral reflection in Java, operating as a `java.lang.instrument` agent on bytecode. This paper only deals with behavioral facilities, which follow the model of partial behavioral reflection of [25]: explicit *links* binding a set of program points (a *hookset*) to a *metaobject*. A hookset is defined as a condition over reifications of program elements: an `RPool` object gives access to `RClass` objects, which in turn give access to their members as `RMember` objects (either `RField`, `RMethod`, or `RConstructor`), which in turn give access to their bodies as `RExpr` objects (with a specific type for each kind of expression). These objects are causally-connected representations of code, offering a source-level abstraction over bytecode.

A link is characterized by a number of attributes, among which the *control* at which metaobjects act (before, after, around), their *scope* (per object, class, or global), and a dynamically-evaluated *activation condition*. Fig. 2 depicts two links, one of which is not subject to activation, along with the correspondence to the AOP concepts of the pointcut/advice model of AspectJ. In Reflex one can specify, on a *per-link* basis, the exact communication protocol (which method to call with which arguments) with the metaobject implementing the aspect action.

Links are a mid-level abstraction, in between high-level aspects and low-level code transformation. How aspect languages are defined and implemented over the kernel is out of the scope of this paper (see [24]); aspect composition in Reflex is treated in [21]; a detailed case study of supporting the dynamic crosscutting of

AspectJ in Reflex can be found in [17]. A simple AspectJ aspect, comprising of a single advice associated to a simple pointcut, is straightforwardly implemented in Reflex with a link (as in Fig. 2). Below is the implementation of the link equivalent to the `Trace` AspectJ aspect shown in the previous section[2]:

```
Hookset fooCalls = new Hookset(MsgSend.class, new NameCS("A"),
                               new NameOS("foo"));
Link trace = Links.get(fooCalls, new Tracer());
trace.setControl(Control.BEFORE);
trace.setCall("Tracer", "log", Parameter.THIS);
```

We first create a hookset selecting occurrences of the message sending operation, with a name-based class selector matching class `A` and a name-based operation selector matching occurrences of `foo` messages. Then a link is created, binding this cut to the action defined in a `Tracer` metaobject. The control of the link is set to before, and we specify that the `log` method of the tracer must be called, with the predefined parameter corresponding to the current instance (`THIS`).

Nevertheless, most practical AOP languages, like AspectJ, make it possible to define aspects as modular units comprising *more than one* cut-action pair. In Reflex this corresponds to different links, with one action bound to each cut. Furthermore, AspectJ supports higher-order pointcut designators, like `cflow`. In Reflex, the implementation of such an aspect requires an extra link to expose the control flow information. This is further discussed in Section 5.

4   A Kernel for Distributed AOP

We now go through the different features of our versatile kernel for distributed AOP in Java, ReflexD. ReflexD is an extension of Reflex, currently implemented using Reflex itself (for transparently handling remote communication and consistency between objects) and RMI as a base for remote invocation.

4.1   Distributed Cut

Reflective Model Extended. Cut definition in Reflex is based on a reflective model representing code as Java objects (`RClass`, `RMethod`, `RExpr`, etc.). To take distribution into account, the model is extended with the reification of a host:

```
public interface RHost {
  public String getName();
  public String getAddress();
  public Properties getProperties();
}
```

A `RHost` object reifies a running Reflex-enabled VM, identified by its name given at launch time; a `RHost` object can be obtained with `RHosts.get(address, name)` where `address` is the physical address (*server:port*) of the Reflex host named `name`. Apart from the name and address, the system properties of a host are also exposed. All other entities of the reflective model are augmented with the information of the host in which they are defined.

---

[2] Concrete syntax for Reflex is under development [22], but we do not use it here.

Hookset Extended. An aspect cut is expressed with a hookset, *i.e.* a condition over program elements from the reflective model. In addition to class and operation selectors, *host selectors* are used to express conditions over hosts:

```
public interface HostSelector {
    public boolean accept(RHost aHost);
}
```

The host selector discriminates the hosts of interest. A simple `NameHS` can do name-based selection, while more advanced selectors can use the host system properties. For instance, the following selector matches the group of *development hosts*, *i.e.* hosts that have a custom property `"type"` with value `"devel"`:

```
public class DevelopmentHosts implements HostSelector {
    public boolean accept(RHost aHost){
        return "devel".equals(aHost.getProperties().get("type"));
} }
```

It is therefore possible to define a link whose cut matches events in different hosts, providing the necessary support to handle distributed crosscutting.

Activation Extended. Dynamic activation of links in Reflex is done via either restrictions [17] or activation conditions (the main difference between both being the time at which they are bound, either weaving or runtime). These conditions, evaluated on the host where operations occur, can now take the current host into account (obtained with `Reflex.getThisHost()`) in order to condition links to *dynamic properties* of the hosts in which their cut is realized. Dynamic activation of links in Reflex has been used to provide *context-aware aspects* [21], which could also be of interest in the context of distributed AOP.

4.2   Distributed Action

Parameterization Extended. Passing parameters to metaobjects (*e.g.* `THIS` as in Sect. 3.2) makes it possible to define parameterized actions. A number of predefined parameters are provided beyond the `THIS`: method name, arguments, etc. Considering distribution, we add two predefined parameters: `HOST` and `HOSTNAME` to refer to the host (resp. its name) in which the cut is realized.

```
public class Tracer {
    public void log(Object aThis, RHost aHost){
        if("devel".equals(aHost.getProperties().get("type")))
            // do verbose logging
        else // do light logging
} }
```

Above is a tracer metaobject that accepts the current host as extra parameter, and performs verbose logging for development hosts, light logging otherwise.

Since a metaobject can execute remotely, the programmer needs control over *how* parameters are passed from the host where the operation occurrence is intercepted to the metaobject. The default Java RMI semantics is used (passing all objects by copy except remote ones), but in addition, Reflex makes it possible to explicitly state that a parameter must be passed by reference (a small Reflex library handles transparent remote invocations on any object). Below, we specify that the `THIS` must be passed *by reference* to the tracer:

```
Link trace = /* as before */;
trace.setCall("Tracer", "log", new ByRef(Parameter.THIS), Parameter.HOST);
```

Scope Extended. The scope attribute of a link specifies the association scheme of metaobjects *w.r.t.* base entities involved in the cut. If it is *per object*, then each object involved in the cut has its own metaobject reference (which may point to the same metaobject), while if it is *per class*, each class has one reference to it, and if it is global, the link itself holds the reference shared among all objects and classes involved. Considering distribution, the `Scope.GLOBAL` attribute is renamed `Scope.HOST` in order to make clear that there is one global instance *per host*. In order to obtain a globally-unique metaobject, one simply needs to use explicit (remote) creation of the metaobject, as discussed below.

Instantiation Extended. While the scope of a link determines the metaobject referencing scheme, instantiation addresses the bootstrapping of the metaobject reference. Reflex provides two alternatives for instantiation:

- explicit instantiation: the metaobject is manually instantiated before defining the link; the instance is shared among all entities involved in the cut.
- implicit instantiation: at link definition, the class of the metaobject is specified[3] so that, when first needed, a new metaobject instance is created and bound; subsequent invocations are performed on that metaobject instance.

For explicit instantiation, ReflexD provides a *remote object creation* service to create any object on any host, which returns a type-compatible reference to the remote object[4]. Below we remotely create a tracer on the `monitor` host, then interact with it (*e.g.* to configure it), before using it in the link definition:

```
RHost host = RHosts.get("178.1.2.3:4567", "monitor");
Tracer t = (Tracer) host.create("Tracer");
// ...interact with t...
Link trace = Links.get(fooCalls, t);
// ...configuration continued...
```

For implicit instantiation, the link definition must specify, in addition to the metaobject class to instantiate, the host on which the metaobject instance will reside. It can be either (Fig. 3):

- `ExecHost.THIS_HOST`: the current host, *i.e.* where the link is being defined;
- `ExecHost.APP_HOST`: the current application host, *i.e.* where the interception of operation occurrences occur;
- Any arbitrary host (with `new ExecHost(addr,name)`/`(aRHost)`).

For instance, using the following definition, if the link scope is *per object*, then any object involved in the cut of the link will have a dedicated tracer instance automatically created on the `monitor` host:

---

[3] Using an `MODefinition.Class` object. Reflex also supports metaobject factories to bootstrap metaobject references [25], but we do not discuss them in this paper.

[4] Further remote interaction with the object via RMI is handled transparently.

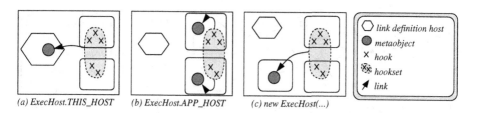

(a) ExecHost.THIS_HOST   (b) ExecHost.APP_HOST   (c) new ExecHost(...)

Fig. 3. Execution hosts

```
RHost host = /* as above */;
Link trace = Links.get(fooCalls,
          new MODefinition.Class("Tracer", new ExecHost(host)));
```

Conversely, using `ExecHost.APP_HOST` implies that each tracer instance will reside on the same host than the object in which the cut is realized.

4.3 Distributed Binding

The binding between a cut and an action in Reflex is an explicit entity: a link. So far, we have not explained how links are stored and applied.

Link Definition, Storage and Application. Link definition can be done at runtime, or prior to executing the main program, by specifying *link providers* to invoke on startup. Link providers can either be plugins of aspect languages, or plain Java classes (*a.k.a. configuration classes*) defining one or more links; a (set of) configuration class(es) can be given on the command line as arguments to the Java agent of Reflex:

```
% java "--javaagent:reflex.jar= -lp class:Config1,Config2" Main
```

The above launches the `Main` program using Reflex, first performing the configuration in classes `Config1` and `Config2`. Links are stored in a local *link repository*. Then, upon class loading, the Reflex agent queries the link repository to determine whether any link applies to the class being loaded. If it does, then code transformation is performed before the class is finally loaded in the VM.

Definition, Storage and Application Extended. In order to support a flexible distributed aspect infrastructure, ReflexD provides a *complete decoupling* of link definition, link storage, and link application. Hence the distributed architecture of ReflexD involves three types of hosts: *(1) Reflex hosts*, in which Reflex runs a program (possibly subject to links); *(2) aspect hosts* in which one or more link repositories are exposed, and to which Reflex hosts can connect; *(3)* any Java program running in any host can remotely populate link repositories. Such a decoupling is convenient to group links that can apply to a program according to some criteria, thereby raising the abstraction level of aspect configuration.

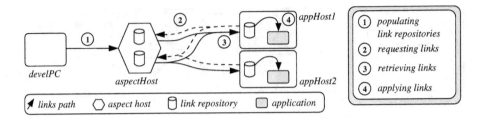

Fig. 4. Link repositories

Illustration. Consider four machines (Fig. 4): an aspect host machine `aspect-Host`, on which two link repositories are started, namely `debugLinks` and `prodLinks`, to hold debug links (*e.g.* logging) and production links (*e.g.* business observation relations), respectively; the developer's machine `develPC`, on which link definition is executed, populating both link repositories; and two Reflex hosts, `appHost1` and `appHost2` running the application.

First, on the `aspectHost` machine, the two repositories are started:

```
% java reflex.StartLinkRep debugLinks
% java reflex.StartLinkRep prodLinks
```

Then, on the `develPC` machine, two configuration classes `ConfDebug` and `ConfProd` are defined, and used to populate the corresponding repositories:

```
% java reflex.ExportToRep reflex://aspectHost/debugLinks ConfDebug
% java reflex.ExportToRep reflex://aspectHost/prodLinks ConfProd
```

Note that it is also possible to access a link repository programmatically, *e.g.*:

```
LinkRepository rep = LinkRepository.get("reflex://aspectHost/debugLinks");
rep.addLink(/* a link */);
rep.removeLink(/* a link */);
```

Finally, supposing the application in `appHost1` is deployed in a development environment, it is configured to use the links defined in both repositories:

```
% java "--javaagent:reflex.jar= -lp reflex://aspectHost/debugLinks,
                        reflex://aspectHost/prodLinks" Main
```

If `appHost2` is deployed in a production environment, it is enough to remove the reference to the `debugLinks` repository in the command line above. No other modification is needed, and only production links will apply.

Runtime Link Manipulation. A feature of Reflex that we have not mentioned until now is the possibility to manipulate links at runtime [25]: *e.g.* changing the metaobject associated to a base entity for a given link, or changing the activation condition of a link. Note that the latter makes it possible to dynamically deploy/undeploy aspects. Maintaining consistency between changes made to links in different hosts is done with a remote consistency framework developed with Reflex, which ReflexD makes great use of[5].

5   Distributed Control Flow

Control flow in aspect-oriented languages, as exemplified by AspectJ's `cflow` pointcut designator, is a very valuable feature that makes it possible to pick out execution points of interest provided they are in the control flow of others.

Control Flow. In Reflex, if a link depends on a control flow condition (*e.g.* log only top-level position changes on shape objects), it is subject to an activation condition, which checks the associated control flow condition. The control flow information has to explicitly exposed, by a dedicated link.

```
1 Hookset shapeMove = /* shape position changes */;
2 Link moveCflow = CFlow.get(shapeMove);
3 Link trace = Links.get(shapeMove, new Tracer());
4 trace.addActivation(new CFlow.IsNotBelow(moveCflow));  // dependency
```

The hookset corresponding to shape position changes is defined (1). This hookset is used in the two link definitions that follow. First, it is used to obtain a link that exposes control flow information (2). `CFlow.get` is a convenience method that returns a link matching the given hookset, to which a before-after meta-object called a `CFlowExposer` is bound. Such an exposer maintains a thread-local counter (or stack if context information must be kept) that keeps track of control flow. Overloaded versions of `CFlow.get` make it possible to explicitly pass the exposer instance to use, and to specify context information that must be collected by the exposer if any. The `trace` link also relies on the `shapeMove` hookset (3), and its activation depends on the control flow exposed by `moveCflow` (4): only calls that are *not below* that control flow will match (*i.e.* only top-level calls). Class `CFlow` offers other predefined activation conditions like `IsIn`, `IsOut`, and `IsBelow`.

Distributed Control Flow. Extending control flow to distributed systems is highly interesting, as it makes it possible to capture particular patterns of inter-host communications; *e.g.* trace all calls on a machine that are performed in the control flow of a call originating from another machine. There is an implementation challenge associated to distributed control flow: control flow information is intrinsically bound to a given thread, and thread identity is not preserved in a typical remote method invocation middleware like RMI. An alternative is to make use of a distributed call stack [1], however this raises other issues of efficiency. We rather adopt the same approach than in [15, 3]: custom socket implementations for RMI [20], which manage the propagation of thread-local information from one host to another in order to simulate the unicity of the caller thread. This solution works, but it is dependent on the RMI implementation.

---

[5] Due to space limitations, we do not discuss these issues in detail, nor do we present the remote consistency framework and other elements of the implementation. More information on the Reflex website (http://reflex.dcc.uchile.cl).

This being said, a distributed control flow library for Reflex is provided, illustrated in the next section. The underlying details are transparently handled by Reflex. Finally, note that control flow as discussed here is only a particular case of what event collectors can expose: it is possible to provide event collectors for matching event sequences for *stateful aspects* [6], or to support more advanced control flow properties as in [7].

6   Application: An Adaptive Image Server

We now consider an image server: an `ImgServer` is an RMI object that delivers images stored in a storage area. Clients can (in parallel) request images by calling `getImg(name)`; the `ImgServer` object translates the image name to a path, and requests an `ImgFinder` to retrieve the actual bytes of the image.

We consider an *image quality adaptation* aspect, which, based on the available bandwidth of *each client*, returns a possibly lower quality image. The design of this aspect relies on distributed control flow with context exposure: when `ImgFinder.findImg()` is called *in the control flow* of a client call to `ImgServer.getImg()`, the *actual* bandwidth value at the client site is used to determine the quality of the returned image. Link definition code is as follows:

```
1  RHost server = /* retrieve server host object */;
2  CFlowExposer exposer =
3         (CFlowExposer) server.create("CFlowExposer");
4  Hookset clientCalls = /* call to ImgServer.getImg() in any client */;
5  Link callCflow = DCFlow.get(clientCalls, exposer, new BWParam());
6
7  Hookset findCalls = /* calls to ImgFinder.findImg() in ImgServer */;
8  Link adapt =
9      Links.get(findCalls, new MODefinition.Class("QualityAdapter", exposer));
10 adapt.setControl(Control.AROUND);
11 adapt.setCall("QualityAdapter", "getImg", new Parameter.Arg(0));
12 adapt.addActivation(new DCFlow.IsInside(callCflow)); //dependency
```

First, a link to expose control flow information from client calls is defined (1–5). We explicitly create an exposer metaobject on the server host (1–3), which will store the bandwidth value for a client in a thread-local when `ImgServer.getImg()` is called (4). The corresponding link is obtained by passing both the hookset and the exposer to `DCFlow.get`, as well as a custom parameter object `BWParam` that encapsulates the know-how for extracting bandwidth value (5). Then the link matching calls to `ImgFinder.findImg()` in the server is defined (7–12). A `QualityAdapter` object will be created (on the server), passing it the exposer as constructor parameter (9). The link is set to act *around* such calls (10), by invoking the `getImg` method of `QualityAdapter` with the first argument as parameter (*i.e.* the path of the image to find) (11). Finally, the control flow dependency is set (12): the adaptation link only applies if `findImg` is called in the control flow of a client call.

Class `QualityAdapter` is straightforward:

```
class QualityAdapter {
    QualityAdapter(CFlowExposer exp){ this.exp = exp; }
    byte[] getImg(String path){
```

```
    int bw = exp.getValue(0);
    if(bw < threshold){
        // check existence of low-quality img, generate it otherwise
        // proceed with modified path
    } else // proceed as normal
} }
```

This example demonstrates how one can concisely define a distributed aspect in ReflexD. The example uses distributed hooksets (`clientCalls` matches on any client host), remote actions (the event collector operates on the server host), and distributed control flow. Without distributed AOP, coding such an aspect requires to manually handle the distributed nature of the aspect.

7 Discussion

Distribution is an inherently large and complex topic. Although it seems that distributed AOP can help in tackling some of the challenges faced in distributed computing, it would be simplistic to claim that distributed aspects can turn the development of distributed programs into an easy go. A number of challenging issues for distributed AOP need to be further explored.

Scalability. Our experiments with ReflexD are, as of now, pretty small. The exercise of Section 6 is a valid proof of concept, showing the interest of distributed AOP versus a manually-distributed implementation. Still, distributed AOP can only get to be a convincing approach for distributed programming if its scalability to larger and far more complex scenarios can be shown. As a first step in this direction, Benavides et al. report on a successful larger scale study with replicated caches [4]. Finally, it has to be expected that larger experiments will be developed if distributed AOP attracts attention from the distributed computing community, thereby helping in shaping the future of distributed AOP.

Failures. A distinctive characteristic of distributed programming is partial failures of the system. Introducing an infrastructure for distributed aspects therefore adds a new dimension of possible partial failures: for instance, in the communication between the cut of an aspect and its associated action (back and forth, once for the call, once for the return), or in the communication with link repositories. There are several approaches to this issue. At the very least, it should be possible to guarantee that the behavior of the original application is preserved when communication with an aspect action fails. We are currently exploring this solution and possible variants. It is important to note that this concern is different from that of *handling* partial failures in a given application using aspects.

Performance. The use of distributed aspects ought also to be evaluated in the light of performance. As of today, we have not performed significant benchmarks of ReflexD. Reflex as such is among the most efficient portable AOP implementations in Java [9]. Still, the ReflexD infrastructure introduces a number of possible overheads. A major source of potential overhead actually lies in the use of advanced control flow features in aspects: distributed control flow as presented previously, and most importantly aspects that rely on distributed event sequences [4], pose a challenge to efficient implementations. However, the recent achievements in optimizing (local) trace matching for aspects brings optimism in this regard [2].

8 Related Work

The issue of crosscutting concerns and code tangling related to distribution was first addressed in the literature by Lopes [14]: it is shown that dedicated aspect languages for handling concurrency and remote parameter passing strategies greatly improve understandability and maintainability of code. However no distributed aspects are considered. More recently, Soares *et al.* have reported on the use of AspectJ to encapsulate RMI code in aspects, showing that current AOP technologies (that do not support distributed AOP as such) require in-depth knowledge of the middleware (RMI) [18].

In the area of distributed AOP, three proposals relate to ours: JAC [16], DJcutter [15], and AWED [4][6] (previously known as Dhamaca [3]). DJcutter and JAC both introduced remote pointcuts, making it possible to specify on which hosts join points should be detected. Although JAC allows distributed aspect deployment to various containers with a consistency protocol between hosts, DJcutter adopts a centralized architecture with an aspect host where all aspects reside and advices are executed. This is in contrast with AWED and ReflexD, which make it possible to execute advices in (several) arbitrary host(s): multiple parallel advice execution in specific hosts is possible, and programmers can control where aspects are deployed. In this regard, ReflexD goes a step further than AWED by providing greater flexibility in the localization of advices (metaobjects), and by allowing to customize the remote parameter passing strategy for each parameter passed to a remote advice. Furthermore, compared to the centralized architecture of DJcutter, both AWED and ReflexD adopt a decentralized architecture. AWED only supports two deployment modes: local to the aspect definition host, or global to all hosts. Conversely, ReflexD is more flexible by supporting stand-alone link repositories to which a Reflex host can connect. JAC, AWED and ReflexD support dynamic deploy/undeploy of aspects with distributed effect.

Both DJcutter and AWED represent hosts as plain strings, whereas in ReflexD they are reified as RHost objects giving access to the system properties of the hosts. So groups of hosts, as provided in AWED, can be intensionally and dynamically defined in ReflexD. Since the fact that a host belongs to a group is just one kind of metadata that can be associated to it, the explicit representation of hosts as objects in ReflexD is more general and expressive.

---

[6] The implementation of the AWED language is called DJasCo. In the following we simply refer to both the language and the DJasCo implementation as AWED.

An interesting feature of AWED is the possibility to control whether advice execution is done synchronously or asynchronously. This is something we have not considered yet, but which is clearly possible to achieve. As of now, advice execution is synchronous in ReflexD.

With respect to control flow, DJcutter, AWED and ReflexD adopt the same implementation strategy. However in ReflexD the use of custom sockets is completely hidden from the programmer. Finally, AWED supports distributed sequences of events for stateful aspects [6]. However, the AWED implementation does not handle the challenging issue of distributed time, so inconsistencies can occur when matching event sequences. At present stateful aspects have not been implemented in Reflex, but they can be supported via event collectors. Their correct semantics in a distributed setting remains a challenge for future research.

Finally, work on distributed AOP can be useful for a new generation of reflective middleware [12] based on AOP. ReflexD can be seen as an open middleware for distributed AOP, which in turn can be used in the implementation of adaptable middleware.

9 Conclusion

We have presented the extension of our work on versatile kernels for AOP to distributed systems, yielding a flexible and expressive infrastructure for distributed aspect-oriented languages and frameworks in Java. All dimensions of aspects have been revisited in the light of distribution, including distributed cut based on an extended reflective model, distributed action with fine-grained customizable parameter passing and flexible instantiation, and complete decoupling of definition, storage and application of aspects. We have illustrated the expressiveness of ReflexD with the provision of abstractions for distributed control flow and their application in an adaptive image server. Compared to other distributed AOP proposals, ReflexD provides more flexibility. Furthermore, although this paper does not focus on this issue, the fact that ReflexD is based on our work on AOP kernels implies that it is able to automatically detect interactions between (distributed) aspects, and provide expressive means for their resolution.

As regards future work, apart from extending the concrete syntax developed for Reflex to ReflexD, we plan to study the support for stateful aspects, and experiment with different aspect languages useful in a distributed setting, both general purpose (such as AWED) and domain-specific (such as SOM [5] for scheduling of concurrent requests).

Acknowledgments. We thank Guillaume Pothier and Ángel Núñez for their work on ReflexD, and Leonardo Rodríguez for his comments on a draft of this paper, and the anonymous DAIS reviewers for their useful remarks.

É. Tanter is financed by the Milenium Nucleous Center for Web Research, Grant P01-029-F, Mideplan, Chile. Work partially-funded by the EU Network of Excellence CoreGRID and ITCC Chile-Korea.

References

1. Y. Aridor, M. Factor, and A. Teperman. cJVM: A single system image of a JVM on a cluster. In *International Conference on Parallel Processing*, pages 4–11, 1999.
2. P. Avgustinov, J. Tibble, E. Bodden, O. Lhoták, L. Hendren, O. de Moor, N. Ongkingco, and G. Sittampalam. Efficient trace monitoring. Technical Report abc-2006-1, abc Group, Mar. 2006.
3. L. D. Benavides Navarro. Dhamaca – an aspect-oriented language for explicit distributed programming. Master's thesis, Vrije Universiteit Brussel, Belgium, 2005.
4. L. D. Benavides Navarro, M. Südholt, W. Vanderperren, B. De Fraine, and D. Suvée. Explicitly distributed AOP using AWED. In *Proceedings of the 5th International Conference on Aspect-Oriented Software Development (AOSD 2006)*, pages 51–62, Bonn, Germany, Mar. 2006. ACM Press.
5. D. Caromel, L. Mateu, and É. Tanter. Sequential object monitors. In M. Odersky, editor, *Proceedings of the 18th European Conference on Object-Oriented Programming (ECOOP 2004)*, number 3086 in Lecture Notes in Computer Science, pages 316–340, Oslo, Norway, June 2004. Springer-Verlag.
6. R. Douence, P. Fradet, and M. Südholt. Composition, reuse and interaction analysis of stateful aspects. In Lieberherr [13], pages 141–150.
7. R. Douence and L. Teboul. A pointcut language for control-flow. In G. Karsai and E. Visser, editors, *Proceedings of the 3rd ACM SIGPLAN/SIGSOFT Conference on Generative Programming and Component Engineering (GPCE 2004)*, volume 3286 of *Lecture Notes in Computer Science*, pages 95–114, Vancouver, Canada, Oct. 2004. Springer-Verlag.
8. T. Elrad, R. E. Filman, and A. Bader. Aspect-oriented programming. *Communications of the ACM*, 44(10), Oct. 2001.
9. M. Haupt. *Virtual Machine Support for Aspect-Oriented Programming Languages*. PhD thesis, Technischen Universität Darmstadt, Germany, Dec. 2005.
10. JBoss AOP website, 2004. http://www.jboss.org/developers/projects/jboss/aop.
11. G. Kiczales, E. Hilsdale, J. Hugunin, M. Kersten, J. Palm, and W. Griswold. An overview of AspectJ. In J. L. Knudsen, editor, *Proceedings of the 15th European Conference on Object-Oriented Programming (ECOOP 2001)*, number 2072 in Lecture Notes in Computer Science, pages 327–353, Budapest, Hungary, June 2001. Springer-Verlag.
12. F. Kon, F. Costa, G. Blair, and R. H. Campbell. The case for distributed middleware. *Communications of the ACM*, 45(6):33–38, 2002.
13. K. Lieberherr, editor. *Proceedings of the 3rd International Conference on Aspect-Oriented Software Development (AOSD 2004)*, Lancaster, UK, Mar. 2004. ACM Press.
14. C. V. Lopes. *D: A Language Framework for Distributed Programming*. PhD thesis, College of Computer Science, Northeastern University, 1997.
15. M. Nishizawa, S. Chiba, and M. Tatsubori. Remote pointcut – a language construct for distributed AOP. In Lieberherr [13], pages 7–15.
16. R. Pawlak, L. Seinturier, L. Duchien, G. Florin, F. Legond-Aubry, and L. Martelli. JAC: an aspect-oriented distributed dynamic framework. *Software Practice and Experience*, 34(12):1119–1148, 2004.
17. L. Rodríguez, É. Tanter, and J. Noyé. Supporting dynamic crosscutting with partial behavioral reflection: a case study. In *Proceedings of the XXIV International Conference of the Chilean Computer Science Society (SCCC 2004)*, Arica, Chile, Nov. 2004. IEEE Computer Society Press.

18. S. Soares, E. Laureano, and P. Borba. Implementing distribution and persistence aspects with AspectJ. In *Proceedings of the 17th International Conference on Object-Oriented Programming Systems, Languages and Applications (OOPSLA 2002)*, pages 174–190, Seattle, Washington, USA, Nov. 2002. ACM Press. ACM SIGPLAN Notices, 37(11).

19. SUN Microsystems. *Remote Method Invocation*, 1998.

20. SUN Microsystems. *Using custom socket factories with Java RMI*, 2005.

21. É. Tanter. Aspects of composition in the Reflex AOP kernel. In *Proceedings of the 5th International Symposium on Software Composition (SC 2006)*, Lecture Notes in Computer Science, Vienna, Austria, Mar. 2006. Springer-Verlag. To appear.

22. É. Tanter. An extensible kernel language for AOP. In *Proceedings of AOSD Workshop on Open and Dynamic Aspect Languages*, Bonn, Germany, 2006.

23. É. Tanter and J. Noyé. Motivation and requirements for a versatile AOP kernel. In *1st European Interactive Workshop on Aspects in Software (EIWAS 2004)*, Berlin, Germany, Sept. 2004.

24. É. Tanter and J. Noyé. A versatile kernel for multi-language AOP. In R. Glück and M. Lowry, editors, *Proceedings of the 4th ACM SIGPLAN/SIGSOFT Conference on Generative Programming and Component Engineering (GPCE 2005)*, volume 3676 of *Lecture Notes in Computer Science*, pages 173–188, Tallinn, Estonia, Sept./Oct. 2005. Springer-Verlag.

25. É. Tanter, J. Noyé, D. Caromel, and P. Cointe. Partial behavioral reflection: Spatial and temporal selection of reification. In R. Crocker and G. L. Steele, Jr., editors, *Proceedings of the 18th ACM SIGPLAN Conference on Object-Oriented Programming Systems, Languages and Applications (OOPSLA 2003)*, pages 27–46, Anaheim, CA, USA, Oct. 2003. ACM Press. ACM SIGPLAN Notices, 38(11).

Transformation of Centralized Software Components into Distributed Ones by Code Refactoring

Abdelhak Seriai[1], Gautier Bastide[1], and Mourad Oussalah[2]

[1] Ecole de Mines de Douai, 941 rue Charles Bourseul,
59508 Douai, France
{seriai, bastide}@ensm-douai.fr
[2] LINA, université de Nantes, 2 rue de la Houssinière,
44322 Nantes, France
oussalah@lina.univ-nantes.fr

Abstract. Adapting software components to be used in a particular application is a crucial issue in software component based technology. In fact, software components can be used in contexts with characteristics different from those envisaged when designing the component. Centralized or distributed deployment infrastructure can be one of these assumptions. Thus, a component can be designed as a monolithic unit to be deployed on a centralized infrastructure, nevertheless the used infrastructure needs the component to be distributed. In this paper, we propose an approach allowing to transform a centralized software component into a distributed one. Our technique is based on refactoring and fragmentation of component source code.

Keywords: software component, adaptation, restructuration, distribution, refactoring.

1 Introduction

Component-based software engineering (CBSE) focuses on reducing application development costs by assembling reusable components like COTS (Commercial-Off-The-Shelf). However, in many cases, existing components can not be used in an ad-hoc way. In fact, using a software component in a different manner than for which it was designed is a challenge because the new use context may be inconsistent with assumptions made by the component. Deployment infrastructure may be one of these assumptions. For example, a software component may be designed as a monolithic unit to be deployed on a centralized infrastructure and, due to load balancing performance, security policy or other motivations, this component has to be distributed. The solution consists in adapting this component to its distributed use context.

Therefore, we propose in this paper, an approach aiming at transforming an object-oriented monolithic and centralized software component by integrating

F. Eliassen and A. Montresor (Eds.): DAIS 2006, LNCS 4025, pp. 332–346, 2006.

distribution facilities. Our approach is based on two transformations. The first one consists in refactoring component structure in order to create a composite-component (i.e. fragmented structure), while preserving component's behaviour. This transformation is achieved through a process composed of four stages. First, following the available infrastructure, the needed distribution configuration is expressed in a declarative style. Next, the monolithic component is fragmented to fulfil the distribution specification given during the first stage. After, components generated as fragmentation result are assembled. Finally, the component assembly is wrapped into a composite-component which is integrated into the application.

The second transformation makes the generated composite-component distributed. In fact, the refactoring process applied to a monolithic centralized component generates a composite one but still with centralized constituents. So, in order to create a distributed composite-component, we need to transform local composition links between its constituents into remote ones. Remote links reflect the distributed configuration specified for the adapted component services.

We discuss the proposed approach in the rest of this paper as follows. In section 2, we present an example of experimentation that illustrates our approach. Section 3 and 4 detail respectively, the refactoring process allowing to fragment a component and next the integration of the distribution mechanisms. Section 5 reviews related works. Conclusion and future works are provided in section 6.

2   Example of Illustration: A Shared-Diary Component

In order to illustrate our purpose, we use throughout this paper an example of a monolithic software component providing services of a shared-diary system accessible to multiple users. It allows to store and consult the personal diaries of each member of a group and it coordinates dependent events stored or generated by these diaries. The *shared-diary* component provides the following services:

1. Managing personal diary. This includes authentication, consulting events (e.g. meeting, activities, projects, etc.), querying the diary, etc. These services are provided through the *Diary* interface.
2. Organizing a meeting. This includes services permitting to confirm the possibility to organize a meeting where the date and the list of the concerned persons are given as parameters, services returning possible dates to organize a meeting, etc. These services are provided through the *Meeting* interface.
3. Managing absence. This includes services permitting to verify the possibility to add an absence event, to consult all the absence dates of one or some persons, etc. These services are provided through the *Absence* interface.
4. Right management. This includes services concerning absence right attribution, service related to diary initialisation, etc. These services are provided through the *Right* interface.
5. Updating the diary, the meeting dates, the absence dates and the absence rights of a person. These services are provided, respectively, through *DiaryUpdate*, *MeetingUpdate*, *AbsenceUpdate* and *RightUpdate* interfaces.

We consider that this component is a monolithic and centralized one. Also, we assume that, due to the considered load balancing policy, defined for the available deployment infrastructure, this component cannot be deployed on only one host. So, our goal is to transform this component for deploying it on a distributed infrastructure (Fig. 1). This result may be obtained by the fragmentation of the *shared-diary* component into four new components called *diary-manager*, *database-manager*, *absence-manager* and *meeting-manager* which may be deployed on distinguished hosts.

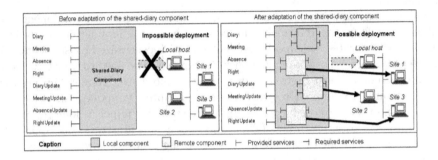

Fig. 1. Transformation of the *shared-diary* component into a distributed one

3   From a Monolithic Component to a Composite-Component

The first transformation to obtain a distributed component from a monolithic centralized one consists in refactoring component code through the fragmentation of its structure. As we have mentioned it previously, the component refactoring process (Fig. 2) is based on four stages which are detailed below.

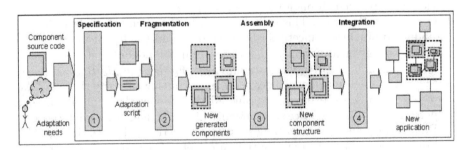

Fig. 2. Software component refactoring process

3.1   Specification of the Transformation Result

This first stage aims at indicating how services provided by the component to be transformed are to be deployed on the available distributed infrastructure. This is done by specifying for every provided service, its deployment host. This operation is realized using a script defining components to be generated and for each component, its provided interfaces. The script syntax[1] is given bellow.

```
StructuAdapt (CompToAdapt,
      {CompDef = <{PortDef={[||] InterfaceDef}+ }+?>,<host?> }*)
```

To illustrate this, let us reconsider our example of the shared-diary application, the goal of this component transformation is to reorganize services provided by this one in four new generated components (e.g. *Diary-Manager*, *DataBase-Manager*, *Absence-Manager*, *Meeting-Manager*). The *Diary-Manager* component (provided interfaces: *Diary* and *DiaryUpdate*) will be deployed on the local site whereas the *DataBase-Manager* component (provided interfaces: *Right* and *RightUpdate*), *Absence-Manager* component (provided interfaces: *Absence* and *AbsenceUpdate*) and *Meeting-Manager* component (provided interfaces: *Meeting* and *MeetingUpdate*) are deployed respectively on *site1*, *site2* and *site3*. The script allowing to obtain the needed structure is the following:

```
StructuAdapt (Shared-Diary,
 {Diary-Manager=<{P-Diary=Diary,DiaryUpdate}>}
 {DataBase-Manager=<{DB=Right, RightUpdate}>,<site1>}
 {Absence-Manager=<{P-Absence=Absence,AbsenceUpdate}>,<site2>}
 {Meeting-Manager=<{P-Meeting=Meeting,MeetingUpdate}>,<site3>}
)
```

3.2   Component Fragmentation

Specification done during the previous stage is used to refactor component structure. Component refactoring consists in fragmenting this component into a set of new generated components, while guaranteeing the component integrity and coherence. This stage is based on component code analysis.

Fragmentation Control: Component code refactoring must be realized without any change on this component's behaviour. Thus, two criteria must be checked: integrity of generated components and coherence of their respective states.

- *Generated component integrity.* The implementation of each component to be generated must be guaranteed to be sound. The soundness of this code[2]

---

[1] Symbols " + ", " * " indicate respectively one or more and zero or more elements. "{}" symbolizes a set of elements. When an interface is defined in several generated components, symbol "||" associated with the interface name indicates that this interface must be that which is used by the rest of the application.

[2] Proof of the satisfaction of these soundness criteria by the proposed refactoring approach is out of this paper scope.

implies that it must be syntactically and semantically correct (i.e. code must be conform to the corresponding object-oriented grammatical and semantic language rules), complete (i.e. dependent code elements must be accessible one to the others) and coherent (i.e. the behaviour corresponding to a generated component must be conform to the matching local behaviour in the monolithic component).

- *Generated component coherence.* The outside behaviour made by the generated components must be the same as the monolithic component's behaviour. That implies that local behaviours of generated components must be coherent, the ones compared to the others. This requires that local behaviours corresponding respectively to the generated components which are semantically related to other behaviours in other components must be identified to ensure their correlation.

Code Analysis and Fragmentation: The fragmentation which aims at generating new software components is realized by analysing the monolithic component source-code, determining for each new component to be generated its corresponding code, separating these codes, one from the others, and determining existing dependencies between them. These steps are mainly based on building, for each component to generate, its SBDG (i.e. Structural and Behavioural Dependency Graph). A SBDG is a graph where nodes are structural elements and arcs are the different forms of dependencies existing between these elements. Structural elements may be external (e.g. ports, interfaces, implementation class and methods matched with services provided by these interfaces) or internal (e.g. internal methods and inner classes) ones. Dependencies between structural elements are of two types: structural and behavioural dependencies. Structural dependencies correspond to composition relationships between structural elements. Thus, a software component is structurally dependent of its ports; a port is structurally dependent of its interfaces, etc. Behavioural dependencies represent method calls defined in a method code. It should be noted that the polymorphism property related to an object-oriented code does not allow to identify, by a static analysis and in a deterministic way, all existing behavioural links between methods. Thus, we insert in a SBDG all possible behavioural links existing between these structural elements (i.e. methods).

Once, the SBDG corresponding to a component to be generated is built, the code of each one of its structural elements is generated. These codes are connected between them in order to reflect the existing structural links between their corresponding structural elements. All the generated code represents the first version of a new component source-code. The next version of the generated component source-code transforms behavioural links existing between methods defined respectively by two different SBDG on composition links between the corresponding components (see Sect. 3.3).

For example, figure 3 shows a part of the SBDG corresponding to the *Meeting-Manager* and *Absence-Manager* components. As the *checking_meeting* method is linked to the *is_absent* method (i.e. the *checking_meeting* method of the *Meeting* interface calls the *is_absent* method of the *Absence* interface) which is contained

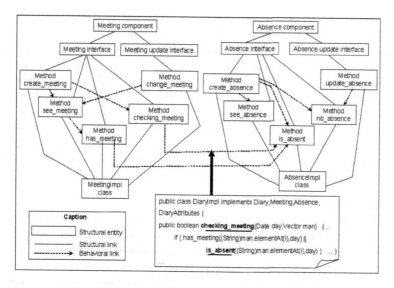

Fig. 3. A part of the *Shared-diary* component SBDG

in another interface, it is needed to create a behavioural link between the *Meeting* and *Absence* interfaces.

3.3 Assembly of the New Generated Components

The fragmentation stage generates unconnected components providing each one a sub-set from the initial component services. However, these services are not independents one from the others. In fact, they are linked through behavioural or resource sharing dependencies which are materialized through connections between generated components.

Connecting Components Via Behavioural-Dependency Interfaces: Components generated by fragmentation are connected using behavioural-dependency interfaces. These interfaces are used to materialize behavioural-dependencies between generated components according to the SBDG graph. Behavioural-dependency interfaces defined by a generated component are:

- Interfaces defining required behavioural-dependency services. These interfaces allow a component service to access all needed elements (i.e. methods) which are contained in other generated component implementations.
- Interfaces defining provided behavioural-dependency services. These services are those provided by this component and which are required by other components to assuring some of their services.

Connecting Components Via Resource-Sharing Dependency Interfaces: Components are also connected via interfaces used to manage resource sharing. We consider as resource every structural entity defined in the component code with an associate state. For example, instance and class attributes are considered as resources. Shared resources are those defined and used in two or more component implementations. So, we need to preserve a coherent state of these resources in all components sharing them (i.e. the same resource with the same state on all components). Coherence is ensured through two types of interfaces. The first one aims at permitting to communicate, between components, updates occurred on shared resources. The second interface type allows to guarantee a synchronized access to shared resources. The implementation of these communication interfaces is realized through the instrumentation of the object-oriented source-code corresponding to these services [2].

– Communication interfaces are:
  1. An interface defining required services permitting to notify shared-resource state updates. These services are defined as synchronous (i.e. every time when a shared resource is updated by a component, its execution can continue only after its state is updated by the other components sharing this resource). Component implementation is instrumented by adding notification code every time the shared resources updated.
  2. An interface defining provided services allowing to update shared resource states after this resource been updated by another component. Thus, component implementation is instrumented by adding code permitting to read new resource values and update the local resource copy.

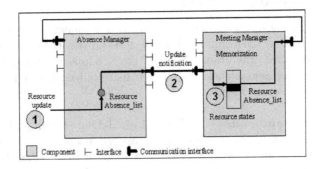

Fig. 4. Example of communication interfaces

Figure 4 shows an example of notification interfaces used to manage the *Absence_list* resource. This resource is an instance attribute whose value represents the absence days for a given person. It is shared by the *Absence-Manage* and *Meeting-Manager* components. When the *Absence_list* resource is updated by the *Absence-Manager* component (1), a notification is sent to the *Meeting-Manager* component (2). Then, this last one memorizes the new value (3).

- Synchronized access interfaces are:
  1. An interface defining required services permitting to acquire an authorisation to update shared resources, from components sharing these ones. These services are not called every time a shared resource is used in the component implementation code.
  2. An interface defining provided services allowing to release rights to update shared resources. These services are called by components sharing resources with the component providing this interface.

Figure 5 shows an example of synchronized access interfaces used to manage the *nb_day_free* resource. This resource is an instance attribute whose value represents the number of free days for a given person. It is shared by the *Absence-Manager*, *Database-Manager* and *Diary-Manager* components. First, *Absence-Manager* component which needs to update the *nb_day_free* resource (1) asks a right access to the other components which share this resource (e.g. *DataBase-Manager* and *Diary-Manager*) (2). Then, after it receives a notification from these components, *Absence-Manager* can update the *nb_day_free* resource (3).

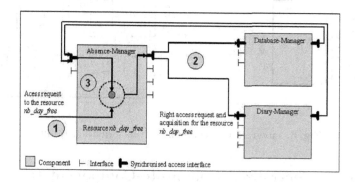

Fig. 5. Example of synchronized access interfaces

3.4   Integration of the Transformation Result

The last step of our process is the integration, in the subjacent application, of the component restructuring result obtained during the previous stages. It consists in connecting the new generated components with the other application components and to guarantee that the component transformation is achieved in a transparent way compared to the application components. In fact, the application must continue to be executed without any change compared to its initial configuration. So, integration requires to satisfy the following properties:

- Security condition: the application components should not be able to access, after the component transformation, to other services than those provided by the component before its transformation. In fact, all new interfaces (i.e. created by our process) must not be accessed by application components, except those created by transformation. For example, all components must not access to services allowing to modify a shared resource state (i.e. only components which share this resource can access to related services).

- Distribution feature: New generated components can be accessed and handled as separate entities. For example, it would be possible to specify a deployment configuration by a direct designation of the generated components (i.e. components generated by fragmentation).

Our solution to guarantee these properties consists in encapsulating components generated by fragmentation into a new composite-component. This new component allows to mask access to "non functional" services (i.e. it wraps all the generated components). Moreover, it provides interfaces allowing to manipulate the generated components. For example, these interfaces aim at permitting independent deployment of each sub-component.

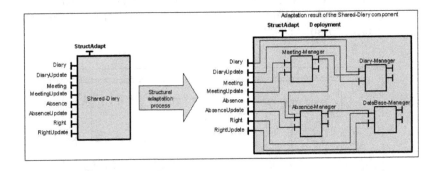

Fig. 6. Integration of component transformation result

4   From a Centralized Composite-Component to a Distributed Composite-Component

The fragmentation process realized during the first phase of our approach allows us to generate a new composite-component. However, this result cannot be distributed on several hosts because all sub-components use local binding. As many resources or services cannot be accessed using direct references because they are provided by remote components (i.e. sub-components are interconnected through bindings which can be local or remote references between provided and required interfaces), we need to ensure communications between local and remote components. In order to create distributed components, first, we need to specify the new component distribution (i.e. to specify sites for each component). This specification is realized through ADL generation (see Sect. 3.1). Then, the component structure is automatically updated (i.e. creation of new interfaces and components dedicated to the distribution management) and component code is instrumented in order to ensure coherence (i.e. a component may access to all resources or services needed during its execution).

In order to introduce distribution mechanisms into the composite-component generated during the first transformation process, we propose a distribution model for composite-components (Fig. 7). This model is composed of two parts. The first part is dedicated to the distribution management at the component content scale (i.e. new created interfaces and new added sub-components) and the other one defines all components needed at the controller scale (i.e. low-level services, network services, etc.).

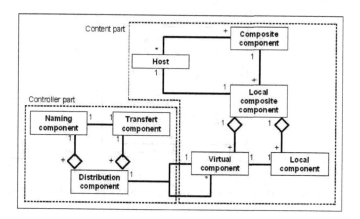

Fig. 7. Component distribution model

4.1   Distributed Composite-Component

A distributed component is a component whose sub-components may be deployed on different hosts. We distinguish three solutions which can be used to create a distributed component. The first one (see Fig. 8 Case B) consists in deploying sub-components on different hosts and the composite on only one. In this case, the composite-component instance contains only connectors which are used to transfer messages from provided composite ports (or interfaces) to sub-component ports (or interfaces) which may be provided by a local or a remote host (i.e. export binding). Moreover, sub-components are connected together through direct binding which may be local or remote ones. This strategy implies that sub-components may be accessible by a direct way. Moreover, the visibility of the internal composite structure is blurred. The second solution (see Fig. 8 Case C) consists in the use of virtual components within the composite. Virtual components are used in order to access a remote component (see below). This strategy allows to improve composite structure visibility. The last solution (see Fig. 8 Case A) consists in the creation of a composite-component into every host on which a part of the component is deployed. This solution allows to preserve a strong encapsulation of the created components. A composite-component instance is loaded on each host which contains a part of this component (i.e. at least one sub-component). Nevertheless, the entire composite-component is not instancied on each host. In fact, different copies of the composite-component are

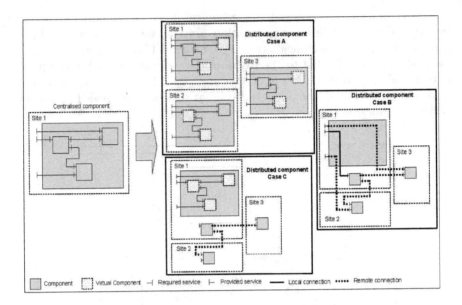

Fig. 8. Transformation from a centralized component to a distributed one

instancied. Each instance is composed of a set of local components and a set of virtual components.

Local Components: Local component means real component (i.e. sub-component) of the composite-component. They are generated during the fragmentation step of the first transformation. Each component is instancied in only one host (i.e. those which are specified by the administrator during the specification step).

Virtual Components

Virtual component structure: A virtual component provides the same interfaces than those of the remote component, however implementation (i.e. service code) is different. In fact, functional code is replaced by controller code which allows to invoke remote services. Two interfaces are added to this virtual component (Fig. 9): one is required and allows the component to send messages to the remote component and the other one is provided and allows the component to receive messages from the remote component. These two interfaces ensure remote communications. Bindings between virtual components are created using architecture description analysis (i.e. ADL analysis). For example, when a local component C1 deployed on site 1 is bound to a remote component C2 deployed on site 2 (i.e. a required interface of the component C1 is linked to a provided interface of the component C2), we create two links: one from the provided interface of the component C'2 (i.e. virtual component of C2 on site 1) to the required interface of the component C'1 (i.e. virtual component of C1 on site 2) and the other one from the provided interface of the component C'1 to the required interface of the component C'2. Communications between C'1 and C'2 components are realized through these two new interfaces whose services use the distribution components (see Sect. 4.2).

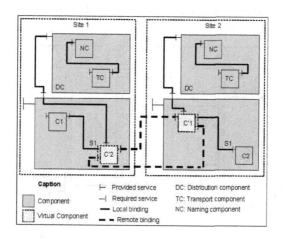

Fig. 9. Example of component distribution

Virtual component behaviour: A virtual component is a representation of a local component which is deployed on a remote host. In fact, it is used as connectors between local and remote components. Indeed, a local component service may invoke a remote service as if this one is provided by a local component (i.e. functional code of local components is not modified). Virtual components are used in order to transfer messages between local and remote components (i.e. delegation services). So, remote connections are realized only from a virtual component to another one because only these components are able to send and receive messages through network (Fig. 10). Thus, when a service of a component C1 calls a service provided by a remote component C2, the component C1 sends a message to the virtual component of C2. Then, this call is transformed into a call from the virtual component of C1 to the component C2. This transformation is realized through a remote connection between the virtual component of C2 and the virtual component of C1 (i.e. on the remote host).

4.2   Distribution Components

A new controller component called distribution component which allows to ensure remote communications is added to our model. It is composed of two subcomponents:

- A transport component: it allows virtual components to realize remote communications (i.e. services provided by the transport component allow to pack and unpack messages which are exchanged between local and remote components, and set up connections through network protocols).
- A naming component: it allows the transport component to find the host address on which local component services are instancied (i.e. services provided by the naming component allow to search and locate remote components).

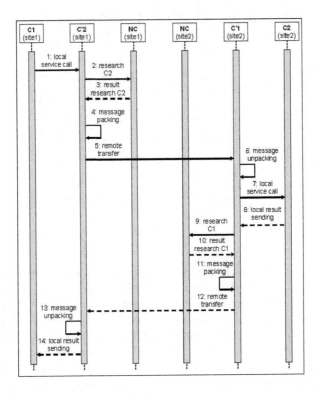

Fig. 10. UML2 Sequence Diagram of the distribution process between two components

As we explained previously, different component instances are loaded on deployment hosts. As a copy of the composite-component is created on each site, non-functional services (i.e. service allowing to manage component content, service allowing to manage bindings between components, service allowing to manage component life cycle, etc.) are duplicated. So, we need to ensure communication and coherence between component instances at the control scale in order to preserve software component integrity. For example, when the composite-component starts (i.e. call to the life cycle controller services), the other instances loaded on the remote hosts have to start their own component version. This operation can be realized using code instrumentation of controller services.

5 Related Works

We classify related works according to two criteria: the approach goal and the technique used to reach this goal. First, we present works related to software component adaptation. Next, we focus on works related to program transformation and restructuring and particularly those interested to object-oriented softwares.

Concerning the first criterion related to the adaptation goal, many adaptation approaches have been discussed in the literature [10]. Adaptation techniques can be categorized as either white-box or black-box. White-box techniques typically require understanding of the internal implementation of the reused component, whereas black-box techniques only require knowledge about the component's interface. A commonly discussed black-box technique is wrapping, also known as containment in COM literature. Superimposition [3] is an alternative technique. The idea behind is that the entire functionality of a component (i.e. rather than that of a single method) should be superimposed by certain behaviour.

To our knowledge no approach from those discussed in the literature, is interested in the adaptation of component structures. All are interested in service adaptation. This adaptation can be carried out in a static [11] or dynamic [12] way. Binary component adaptation (BCA) [11] is a mechanism to modify existing components (such as Java class files) to the specific needs of a programmer. It allows components to be adapted and evolved in binary form and on-the-fly (i.e. during program loading).

Concerning the second criterion related to restructuring approaches, we can quote refactoring techniques [13] that aim at restructuring an existing body of an object-oriented code, altering its internal structure without changing its external behaviour. Generally, refactoring is used to make the code simpler in order to include or understand it easier [8]. It also allows to find the potential bugs or errors more quickly. It makes it possible to eliminate the duplicated code. This technique aims at reorganizing classes, variables and methods in a new hierarchy in order to facilitate its future adaptation or extension [7].

Another technique of program analysis is slicing [14]. It is generally used for the code debugging and testing [1], for maintaining [9] or for transforming source code. The goal of this technique is to determine program behaviour but also that of all elements which it can contain (e.g. variables, methods, etc.). For example, slicing allows to detect all instructions which can affect a variable.

6 Conclusion and Future Works

We presented in this article an approach allowing to create distributed components from monolithic ones. Our proposal is based on a new adaptation technique allowing to reorganize the software component structure using code refactoring. In fact, as we explained, component deployment and execution are linked to its structure. So, we propose to use this approach in order to fragment existent components and generate new components which can be distributed on several hosts. This approach is implemented and a prototype has been developed using the Julia [5] software component framework which is the Java implementation of the Fractal component model [4]. Fractal and Julia are developed by the IN-RIA[3]. Fractal is a hierarchical component model quite close to that proposed by UML2 [6].

Our approach needs source code analysis and instrumentation. It does not consider run-time adaptation problems. However, it is generic enough to be applied to dynamic adaptation. Nevertheless, concerning this possibility, it is necessary to define, in addition to the presented process, mechanisms for the dynamicity management (e.g. disconnection, connection, interception of the invocations of services, service recovery, etc). Thus, this way constitutes one direction of our future work.

As we noted it before, the main application of our approach consist in realizing a flexible deployment of software components. A future work may consist in the deployment process automation according to the execution context.

References

1. H. Agrawal, R. Demillo, and E. Spafford: Debugging with dynamic slicing and backtracking. Software-Practice an Experience, 23(6): 589-616, 1993.
2. G. Bastide, A-D. Seriai, M. Oussalah: Adapting Software Components by Structure Fragmentation. The 21st Annual ACM Symposium on Applied Computing; Software Engineering: Applications, Practices, and Tools (SE), Dijon, France, April 2006.
3. J. Bosch: Superimposition: A Component Adaptation Technique. Information and Software Technology, 1999.
4. E. Bruneton, T. Coupaye, M. Leclercq, V. Quema, J.-B. Stefani: An Open Component Model and Its Support in Java. CBSE, 7-22, 2004.
5. E. Bruneton: Julia Tutorial. http://fractal.objectweb.org/tutorials/julia/
6. H.-E. Eriksson: UML 2 Toolkit, Wiley edition, ISBN: 0471463612, 2003.
7. B. Foote and W. F. Opdyke: Life Cycle and Refactoring Patterns that Support Evolution and Reuse. First Conference on Pattern Languages of Programs (PLOP '94), Monticello, Illinois, 1994.
8. M. Fowler, K. Beck, J. Brant, W. Opdyke, D. Roberts: Refactoring: Improving the Design of Existing Code. ISBN 0201485672, 1999.
9. K. B. Gallagher and J. R. Lyle: Using program slicing in software maintenance. IEEE Transactions on Software Engineering, 17(8):751-761, 1991.
10. G. T. Heineman and H. Ohlenbusch: An Evaluation of Component Adaptation Techniques. Technical Report WPI-CS-TR-98-20, Department of Computer Science, Worcester Polytechnic Institute, 1999.
11. R. Keller, U. Holzle: Binary Component Adaptation. ECOOP, 307-329, 1998.
12. A. Ketfi, N. Belkhatir, P.Y. Cunin: Automatic Adaptation of Component-based Software: Issues and Experiences. PDPTA'02, Las Vegas, Nevada, USA, 2002.
13. T. Mens, T. Tourwe: A Survey of Software Refactoring, IEEE Transactions on Software Engineering, Volume 30, Number 2, pp. 126-139, February 2004.
14. M. Weiser: Program Slicing. IEEE Trans. Software Eng. 10(4): 352-357, 1984.

---

[3] The French National Institute for Research in Computer Science and Control. http://www.inria.fr/

PAGE: A Distributed Infrastructure for Fostering RDF-Based Interoperability

Emanuele Della Valle, Andrea Turati, and Alessandro Ghioni

CEFRIEL - Politecnico of Milano, Via Fucini 2, 20133 Milano, Italy
dellavalle@cefriel.it, turati@cefriel.it, ghioni@cefriel.it

Abstract. This paper shows how to build a scalable, robust and efficient distributed Internet-scale RDF repository, that we name *PAGE* (**P**ut **A**nd **G**et **E**verywhere).

1 Motivation

In the recent years, the *RDF* (Resource Description Framework) *data model* is gaining momentum. Among other significant examples, take for istance the adoption of key players such as Adobe (i.e., the eXtensible Metadata Platform - XMP) and Oracle (i.e., the 10g version of the famous RDBMS promise to be the best RDF storage engine).

RDF enables the encoding of relational data over the Internet using *triples* usually denoted with (spo), where s is the subject, p is the predicate and o the object. Complex structures can be easily encoded in a set of RDF triples. But, what about managing them? Centralized solutions may help in the short term, but if RDF should become the basis of the Semantic Web, some sort of distribution must be take into account. What if we could *put and get* triples without bothering of the underlying infrastructure because such infrastructure is the whole Internet?

Such a distributed and decentralized RDF repository is not yet available, but the peer-to-peer community has been studying the "**turn on, put() and get() out**" paradigm using Distributed Hash Tables (DHTs) for almost a decade. In this paper we describe *PAGE* (**P**ut **A**nd **G**et **E**verywhere), an optimized peer-to-peer infrastructure for distributed RDF storing and retrieval: an original approach that comes out from the convergence between the current works on DHT in the peer-to-peer community and on optimized index structures for querying RDF in the Semantic Web community named YARS [1].

Our work aims at advancing the state-of-the-art in decentralized RDF repositories finding a convergence between peer-to-peer (i.e., DHT) and Semantic Web researches. In particular it belongs to the class of solutions which avoid flooding approach, previously investigated by RDFPeers [2] and GridVine [3].

2 State-of-the-Art

Optimized RDF Storing and Retrieval. In a single RDF statement (also called triple) (spc) the subject s can be either an URI reference or a blank node

F. Eliassen and A. Montresor (Eds.): DAIS 2006, LNCS 4025, pp. 347–353, 2006.

(that is an abstract entity), the predicate p is an URI reference and the object p can be an URI reference, a blank node or a literal (e.g., a string). In order to group triples, a *context* is often associated to each triple. A triple and it's context is named quad and it is denoted with (spoc), where c is the context.

In order to store and retrieve RDF triples, several storage systems have been developed. Many centralized RDF repositories have been implemented to support storing, indexing and querying RDF documents, such as RDFDB, Inkling, RDFStore, and Sesame. For this paper, we examine *YARS* [1], a recent solution that defines *an optimized index structure for fast retrieval of RDF* statements.

YARS index structure consists of two parts: the lexicon and the quad index. The former stores mappings from literals and URIs to internal object IDs (used for compactness), the latter stores the structure information (i.e. the quads).

Access patterns are strings that represents a set of RDF triples and are used as basic building blocks for more complex RDF query languages such as SPARQL. An access pattern is similar to a quad, in which at least one element is unspecified (and, for convention, is set to ?). So, for example, (s?oc) means that we are interested at all quads having relations between the subject s and the object o, in the context c (it's equivalent to say that we want to get all predicates that have been stated together with s, o and c).

All possible access patterns are 16, but YARS's authors suggest to combine them in six indexes (SPOC, CP, OCS, POC, CSP, OS) because a single index can be used to cover more than a type of query (see [1] for details). For example, the SPOC index is used to process (s???), but also (sp??) and (spo?). An index is a structure that stores objects in a way that allows fast retrieval: YARS uses B+-trees, because they support range queries.

Distributed Hash Tables. In DHTs each resource is associated with a *key* which can be produced by hashing a significant information (e.g. the name) related to the resource. Nodes have identifiers in the same space of the keys. Each node is responsible for storing a range of keys and corresponding resources. The DHT nodes maintain a routing table in which IDs of several other nodes are stored. When a node performs a get(key) request, the lookup message is routed through the overlay network to the node responsible for the key.

Several DHTs (e.g., CAN, Chord, Tapestry) have been designed with different functioning mechanisms, but everyone with the same main concepts: the keyspace partitioning and an overlay network. The former refers to the technique used to assign certain sets of keys to different nodes and the latter refers to the structure of links used by nodes to communicate via message exchanging.

Most DHTs assign a single key at each node, called its ID (identifier). Then, keys are assigned to nodes according to a particular function that gives a notion of the distance between two keys: a node with ID x is the root for all the keys for which x is the closest ID, measured according to a distance function.

Given a key k, it is necessary to send a message to the root of k in order to retrieve the corresponding value: at each step, the message is forwarded to the neighbour whose ID is closer to k, until there is no such neighbour, in which case we have arrived at the root node responsible for k. This process is called overlay routing and it can be done through the use of a routing table in every node. Indeed, each node maintains a set of links to other nodes (also called neighbours) such that for any key k, the node either is root for k or has a link to a node that is closer to k in terms of the keyspace distance. The more the number of hops in any route and the number of neighbours per node are low, the more efficient is routing. Among the various implementation available (see [4] for a comparison) we chose *Bamboo*, because it is suitable with the lookup expansion mechanism used in the retrieval process described in section 3.

3 Modifying DHT for Distributed RDF Storing and Retrieval

In order to design a distributed and decentralized system that allows efficient storage and retrieval of RDF statements, **we have created *PAGE*, a modified Bamboo DHT that implements YARS index structure.**
The rough idea is to store every quad in a YARS fashion in six indexes, using the **put** operation of key-value pairs available in DHTs, where values are quads and keys are special coding of the six IDs used in the six YARS indexes. This allows to exploit DHT routing method in order to implement a distributed version of B+-trees used in YARS.

Computing ID. Because we need a shared method for ID assigning, instead of using a centralized lexicon (like YARS), we followed DHT approach in using a hash function (indeed it can be used also in a distributed way with a statistical assurance to generate unique IDs).
The ID of a quad is built by concatenating four different parts: each part is the result of an hash function applied to the respective quad's element.
For example (see step 1 of figure 1), supposing that a server wants to put the quad "(m:Lennon m:sings m:Imagine m:70s)", the hashes of each quad parts could be: 1 for "m:Lennon", F for "m:sings", A for "m:Imagine" and 7 for "m:70s" (for readability, here we represent the 40 bytes long IDs with 5 digits).
Furthermore, in every ID it's necessary to encode the index that has been used to build the ID: to refer to SPOC index we use the digit 1, 4 for CP index, 6 for OCS index, 9 for POC index, C for CSP index and E for OS index.

Storing Process. As proposed in YARS, for efficient lookups, every quad has to be stored six times (once for each index) respecting the sort of its four components imposed by the type of index. For simplicity, the six storage messages are wrapped in a *PAGE* method named **put**.
Taking the previous example as a guide (see step 2 and 3 of figure 1), in order to store the quad "(1 F A 7)" in the six indexes, we have to store the following six IDs: "11FA7" for the SPOC index, "47F1A" for the CP index, "6A71F" for the OCS index, "9FA71" for the POC index, "C71FA" for the CSP index, and "EA1F7" for the OS index.

When an owner wants to make a quad public it calls the **put** operation that constructs six messages (each containing an ID of the quad) and dispatches them. Every message is forwarded toward the node with the most similar (numerically closer) ID to that contained in the message according to Bamboo standard behaviour: this node is the root of that quad. The root stores the quad and its ID and informs nearby nodes to store a copy of that information (replicas).

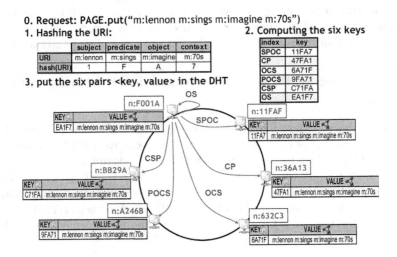

Fig. 1. Storing process

Retrieval Process. The *PAGE* get method wraps the query process: it takes an access pattern as input, computes the hashes, chooses the index, builds the access pattern ID and packages everything in a query message that is forwarded toward the corresponding root, which can answer with the asked quad.

Searching a single quad is not a very useful operation: if subject, predicate, object and context are already known, it means simply verify that that quad exists and it has been published. More interesting is asking quads of which some components are unknown (access pattern based query): (sp?c) finds all quads having specified subject, predicate and context, but having object unknown.

DHTs are designed mainly to perform efficient retrievals of individual values. The basic implementation of Bamboo does not manage queries about a range of values. Therefore, we have to modify a method that is able to perform single key lookups in order to build a method that allows lookups of a range of keys.

Queries have to be routed as messages, exactly as it happens for lookups of single quads, and thus we need to assign IDs to them.

At every possible query corresponds an access pattern. In order to assign an ID to a query it is sufficient to encode the corresponding access pattern by computing the hash of each its component (conventionally assigning a sequence of 0 to unspecified parts, pointed out with a ?) and then reorder them respecting the components' order imposed by the index that allows to answer to such query. Furthermore, a *"mask"* is associated to every query, likewise to what IP does in Internet where the netmasks are used for distinguishing some net addresses.

Since the zeros appear only at the end of every query ID, a mask is simply a flag that separates the known parts of the quad from those that we want to get (i.e. it points out the preceding position at that in which zeros begin). A mask is a number that specifies the position beyond which the quad parts is unspecified.

For instance (see figure 1), the access patter (m:Lennon m:sings ? ?), meaning all the songs performed by Lennon in any context, requires the SPOC index and it is converted to the ID 11F00/ 3. For this query, the mask is 3 and means that the first 3 digits of the ID are relevant (the index and the first two quad parts are specified), so only the last two elements of the quad are not specified (i.e., the object and the context). The mask, along with the index code, allows for realizing what type of query has to be processed. The first digit of the ID says what index we have to use, but this information is not sufficient to correctly process a query: it is necessary to know the exact point beyond which we want all values, i.e. the query pattern.

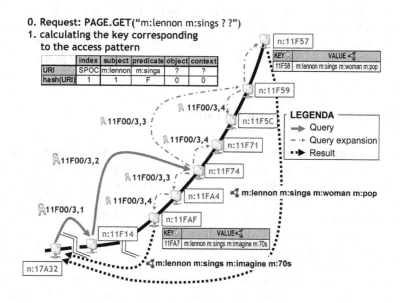

Fig. 2. Retrieval process

Along with the mask, another number is associated with the queries ID: *"hop"*, a sort of reverse time-to-live, equals to the number of digits of the query ID already considered during routing process. When a query is introduced in the network its ID is accompanied by a specific mask and a hop set to 0. While the message goes through the network, the hop increases by 1 at each crossed node.

The routing of query messages has to exactly begin equally to the routing of lookups: every single node forwards the message to its neighbours that possesses an ID that has a longer matching prefix with the query ID, until the final part of the query ID (beginning from the digit following that pointed out by the mask) is reached. At that point, in fact, the message has to be sent to all the nodes that share the same prefix with the query ID (obviously excluding the sequence of zeros), because we are interested to any value that quads state in that part. So, every node forwards the message to several nodes that are in its routing table, increasing the hop so that the next node will know at which nodes it has to forward the message (it is like if the matching prefix were every time longer).

For example, suppose that a node with ID 17A32 wants to perform the query 11F00/3,0: since it has the first digit in common with the query, it forwards the message 11F00/3,1 to a known node that has the first two digits in common with the query, whose ID is for instance 116D4. The node 116D4 forwards message 11F00/3,2 to the node having the same first three digits (e.g. 11F74).

Now, since the next digit to be matched is beyond the mask, the node 11F74 has to forward the message to all known nodes having the same prefix as query. Therefore, it sends the message 11F00/3,3 to all known nodes with ID in the range 11F00x-11FFx and the message 11F00/3,4 to all known nodes whose ID is in the range 11F70-11F7F: particularly, nodes 11F59 and 11FA4 receive the message 11F00/3,3 and proceed in the same way, while node 11F71 receives 11F00/3,4 and stop the propagation. Finally, all nodes involved in the lookup expansion send to the petitioner all quads that match the query prefix up to the mask.

4   Discussion and Conclusions

In this paper we have introduced *PAGE*, a distributed infrastructure that enables to *put* and *get* triples from everywhere, *simplifies the implementation.* PAGE *makes deploying* distributed Semantic Web applications *straight forward* because it avoids to implement from scratch all of the scalable routing, robustness, and management properties. Applications get all these properties at the cost of making available enough resources for processing the information it intends to exchange. Moreover, being PAGE self-organizing, each node is essentially independent from all other nodes and it only has to bother on making available enough resources to the infrastructure to make it grow incrementally. Therefore deploying an application just means either installing such application on pre-existing nodes, or adding nodes (with the application on top) to the infrastructure.

An advantage of our approach is the parallel execution of a query in the case of a lookup expansion: at the same time, several nodes retrieve a subset of query result. Because of results are returned when available, a clear drawback of PAGE is the impossibility of calculating the completeness of the result set: this aspect is a diffused problem of distributed systems that could be bypassed introducing a time threshold within which results are expected and beyond which results are rejected.

References

1. Harth, A., Decker, S.: Optimized Index Structures for Querying RDF from the Web. In: 3rd Latin American Web Congress, Buenos Aires - Argentina. (2005)
2. Cai, M., Frank, M.: RDFPeers: a scalable distributed RDF repository based on a structured peer-to-peer network. In: WWW '04, New York, NY, USA, ACM Press (2004) 650–657
3. Aberer, K., Cudré-Mauroux, P., Hauswirth, M., Pelt, T.V.: GridVine: Building Internet-Scale Semantic Overlay Networks. In: ISWC. (2004) 107–121
4. Li, J., Stribling, J., Morris, R., Kaashoek, M.F., Gil, T.M.: A performance vs. cost framework for evaluating DHT design tradeoffs under churn. In: Proceedings of the 24th Infocom, Miami, FL (2005)

Author Index

Almeida, João Paulo A.   213

Bakker, Arno   84
Bastide, Gautier   332
Berbers, Yolande   242
Bosch, Jan   1
Braun, Iris   181
Brzeziński, Jerzy   187

Cahill, Vinny   16
Chen, Huajun   128
Coulson, Geoff   199
Cunningham, Raymond   70

Danilecki, Arkadiusz   309
De Vlaminck, Karel   242
Della Valle, Emanuele   347
Domaschka, Jörg   256
Dowling, Jim   70

Eliassen, Frank   228

Floch, Jacqueline   64

Garruzzo, Salvatore   99
Ghioni, Alessandro   347
Gillen, Matthew   303

Hallsteinsen, Svein   64
Hamid, Brahim   289
Harrington, Anthony   16
Hauck, Franz J.   256
Holvoet, Tom   242
Hua, Lei   152
Hughes, Daniel   199

Iacob, Maria-Eugenia   213

Jonkers, Henk   213

Kapitza, Rüdiger   256
Karhinen, Anssi   1
Kobusińska, Anna   187
Kobusiński, Jacek   187
Kunze, Christian P.   32

Lamersdorf, Winfried   32
Loyall, Joseph   303
Lund, Ketil   228
Lundesgaard, Sten A.   228

Meier, René   16, 70
Merle, Philippe   272
Mosbah, Mohamed   289

Niu, Chunlei   152

O'Brien, James   48
Ogston, Elth   84
Oussalah, Mourad   332

Porter, Barry   199
Puder, Arno   138

Quartel, Dick   213

Reiser, Hans P.   256
Rosaci, Domenico   99
Rouvoy, Romain   272
Rubel, Paul   303

Sacha, Jan   70
Schaefer, Jan   169
Schantz, Richard   303
Schill, Alexander   181
Senivongse, Twittie   113
Seriai, Abdelhak   332
Serrano-Alvarado, Patricia   272
Shapiro, Marc   48
Spillner, Josef   181
Stav, Erlend   64
Suwannopas, Piya   113
Szychowiak, Michał   309

Tanter, Éric   316
Termin, Thomas   16
Tian, Wenya   128
Toledo, Rodolfo   316
Turati, Andrea   347

van Gurp, Jilles   1
van Steen, Maarten   84

Wei, Jun   152
Wils, Andrew   242

Zaplata, Sonja   32
Zheng, Haoran   152

Lecture Notes in Computer Science

For information about Vols. 1–3925

please contact your bookseller or Springer

Vol. 4044: P. Abrahamsson, M. Marchesi, G. Succi (Eds.), Extreme Programming and Agile Processes in Software Engineering. XII, 230 pages. 2006.

Vol. 4041: S.-W. Cheng, C.K. Poon (Eds.), Algorithmic Applications in Management. XI, 395 pages. 2006.

Vol. 4039: M. Morisio (Ed.), Reuse of Off-the-Shelf Components. XIII, 444 pages. 2006.

Vol. 4038: P. Ciancarini, H. Wiklicky (Eds.), Coordination Models and Languages. VIII, 299 pages. 2006.

Vol. 4037: R. Gorrieri, H. Wehrheim (Eds.), Formal Methods for Open Object-Based Distributed Systems. XVII, 474 pages. 2006.

Vol. 4034: J. Münch, M. Vierimaa (Eds.), Product-Focused Software Process Improvement. XVII, 474 pages. 2006.

Vol. 4027: H.L. Larsen, G. Pasi, D. Ortiz-Arroyo, T. Andreasen, H. Christiansen (Eds.), Flexible Query Answering Systems. XVIII, 714 pages. 2006. (Sublibrary LNAI).

Vol. 4025: F. Eliassen, A. Montresor (Eds.), Distributed Applications and Interoperable Systems. XI, 355 pages. 2006.

Vol. 4024: S. Donatelli, P. S. Thiagarajan (Eds.), Petri Nets and Other Models of Concurrency - ICATPN 2006. XI, 441 pages. 2006.

Vol. 4021: E. André, L. Dybkjær, W. Minker, H. Neumann, M. Weber (Eds.), Perception and Interactive Technologies. XI, 217 pages. 2006. (Sublibrary LNAI).

Vol. 4011: Y. Sure, J. Domingue (Eds.), The Semantic Web: Research and Applications. XIX, 726 pages. 2006.

Vol. 4010: S. Dunne, B. Stoddart (Eds.), Unifying Theories of Programming. VIII, 257 pages. 2006.

Vol. 4007: C. Àlvarez, M. Serna (Eds.), Experimental Algorithms. XI, 329 pages. 2006.

Vol. 4006: L.M. Pinho, M. González Harbour (Eds.), Reliable Software Technologies – Ada-Europe 2006. XII, 241 pages. 2006.

Vol. 4004: S. Vaudenay (Ed.), Advances in Cryptology - EUROCRYPT 2006. XIV, 613 pages. 2006.

Vol. 4003: Y. Koucheryavy, J. Harju, V.B. Iversen (Eds.), Next Generation Teletraffic and Wired/Wireless Advanced Networking. XVI, 582 pages. 2006.

Vol. 4001: E. Dubois, K. Pohl (Eds.), Advanced Information Systems Engineering. XVI, 560 pages. 2006.

Vol. 3999: C. Kop, G. Fliedl, H.C. Mayr, E. Métais (Eds.), Natural Language Processing and Information Systems. XIII, 227 pages. 2006.

Vol. 3998: T. Calamoneri, I. Finocchi, G.F. Italiano (Eds.), Algorithms and Complexity. XII, 394 pages. 2006.

Vol. 3997: W. Grieskamp, C. Weise (Eds.), Formal Approaches to Software Testing. XII, 219 pages. 2006.

Vol. 3996: A. Keller, J.-P. Martin-Flatin (Eds.), Self-Managed Networks, Systems, and Services. X, 185 pages. 2006.

Vol. 3995: G. Müller (Ed.), Emerging Trends in Information and Communication Security. XX, 524 pages. 2006.

Vol. 3994: V.N. Alexandrov, G.D. van Albada, P.M.A. Sloot, J. Dongarra (Eds.), Computational Science – ICCS 2006, Part IV. XXXV, 1096 pages. 2006.

Vol. 3993: V.N. Alexandrov, G.D. van Albada, P.M.A. Sloot, J. Dongarra (Eds.), Computational Science – ICCS 2006, Part III. XXXVI, 1136 pages. 2006.

Vol. 3992: V.N. Alexandrov, G.D. van Albada, P.M.A. Sloot, J. Dongarra (Eds.), Computational Science – ICCS 2006, Part II. XXXV, 1122 pages. 2006.

Vol. 3991: V.N. Alexandrov, G.D. van Albada, P.M.A. Sloot, J. Dongarra (Eds.), Computational Science – ICCS 2006, Part I. LXXXI, 1096 pages. 2006.

Vol. 3990: J. C. Beck, B.M. Smith (Eds.), Integration of AI and OR Techniques in Constraint Programming for Combinatorial Optimization Problems. X, 301 pages. 2006.

Vol. 3989: J. Zhou, M. Yung, F. Bao, Applied Cryptography and Network Security. XIV, 488 pages. 2006.

Vol. 3987: M. Hazas, J. Krumm, T. Strang (Eds.), Location- and Context-Awareness. X, 289 pages. 2006.

Vol. 3986: K. Stølen, W.H. Winsborough, F. Martinelli, F. Massacci (Eds.), Trust Management. XIV, 474 pages. 2006.

Vol. 3984: M. Gavrilova, O. Gervasi, V. Kumar, C.J. K. Tan, D. Taniar, A. Laganà, Y. Mun, H. Choo (Eds.), Computational Science and Its Applications - ICCSA 2006, Part V. XXV, 1045 pages. 2006.

Vol. 3983: M. Gavrilova, O. Gervasi, V. Kumar, C.J. K. Tan, D. Taniar, A. Laganà, Y. Mun, H. Choo (Eds.), Computational Science and Its Applications - ICCSA 2006, Part IV. XXVI, 1191 pages. 2006.

Vol. 3982: M. Gavrilova, O. Gervasi, V. Kumar, C.J. K. Tan, D. Taniar, A. Laganà, Y. Mun, H. Choo (Eds.), Computational Science and Its Applications - ICCSA 2006, Part III. XXV, 1243 pages. 2006.

Vol. 3981: M. Gavrilova, O. Gervasi, V. Kumar, C.J. K. Tan, D. Taniar, A. Laganà, Y. Mun, H. Choo (Eds.), Computational Science and Its Applications - ICCSA 2006, Part II. XXVI, 1255 pages. 2006.

Vol. 3980: M. Gavrilova, O. Gervasi, V. Kumar, C.J. K. Tan, D. Taniar, A. Laganà, Y. Mun, H. Choo (Eds.), Computational Science and Its Applications - ICCSA 2006, Part I. LXXV, 1199 pages. 2006.

Vol. 3979: T.S. Huang, N. Sebe, M.S. Lew, V. Pavlović, M. Kölsch, A. Galata, B. Kisačanin (Eds.), Computer Vision in Human-Computer Interaction. XII, 121 pages. 2006.

Vol. 3978: B. Hnich, M. Carlsson, F. Fages, F. Rossi (Eds.), Recent Advances in Constraints. VIII, 179 pages. 2006. (Sublibrary LNAI).

Vol. 3976: F. Boavida, T. Plagemann, B. Stiller, C. Westphal, E. Monteiro (Eds.), Networking 2006. Networking Technologies, Services, and Protocols; Performance of Computer and Communication Networks; Mobile and Wireless Communications Systems. XXVI, 1276 pages. 2006.

Vol. 3975: S. Mehrotra, D.D. Zeng, H. Chen, B.M. Thuraisingham, F.-Y. Wang (Eds.), Intelligence and Security Informatics. XXII, 772 pages. 2006.

Vol. 3973: J. Wang, Z. Yi, J.M. Zurada, B.-L. Lu, H. Yin (Eds.), Advances in Neural Networks - ISNN 2006, Part III. XXIX, 1402 pages. 2006.

Vol. 3972: J. Wang, Z. Yi, J.M. Zurada, B.-L. Lu, H. Yin (Eds.), Advances in Neural Networks - ISNN 2006, Part II. XXVII, 1444 pages. 2006.

Vol. 3971: J. Wang, Z. Yi, J.M. Zurada, B.-L. Lu, H. Yin (Eds.), Advances in Neural Networks - ISNN 2006, Part I. LXVII, 1442 pages. 2006.

Vol. 3970: T. Braun, G. Carle, S. Fahmy, Y. Koucheryavy (Eds.), Wired/Wireless Internet Communications. XIV, 350 pages. 2006.

Vol. 3968: K.P. Fishkin, B. Schiele, P. Nixon, A. Quigley (Eds.), Pervasive Computing. XV, 402 pages. 2006.

Vol. 3967: D. Grigoriev, J. Harrison, E.A. Hirsch (Eds.), Computer Science – Theory and Applications. XVI, 684 pages. 2006.

Vol. 3966: Q. Wang, D. Pfahl, D.M. Raffo, P. Wernick (Eds.), Software Process Change. XIV, 356 pages. 2006.

Vol. 3965: M. Bernardo, A. Cimatti (Eds.), Formal Methods for Hardware Verification. VII, 243 pages. 2006.

Vol. 3964: M. Ü. Uyar, A.Y. Duale, M.A. Fecko (Eds.), Testing of Communicating Systems. XI, 373 pages. 2006.

Vol. 3963: O. Dikenelli, M.-P. Gleizes, A. Ricci (Eds.), Engineering Societies in the Agents World VI. X, 303 pages. 2006. (Sublibrary LNAI).

Vol. 3962: W. IJsselsteijn, Y. de Kort, C. Midden, B. Eggen, E. van den Hoven (Eds.), Persuasive Technology. XII, 216 pages. 2006.

Vol. 3960: R. Vieira, P. Quaresma, M.d.G.V. Nunes, N.J. Mamede, C. Oliveira, M.C. Dias (Eds.), Computational Processing of the Portuguese Language. XII, 274 pages. 2006. (Sublibrary LNAI).

Vol. 3959: J.-Y. Cai, S. B. Cooper, A. Li (Eds.), Theory and Applications of Models of Computation. XV, 794 pages. 2006.

Vol. 3958: M. Yung, Y. Dodis, A. Kiayias, T. Malkin (Eds.), Public Key Cryptography - PKC 2006. XIV, 543 pages. 2006.

Vol. 3956: G. Barthe, B. Grégoire, M. Huisman, J.-L. Lanet (Eds.), Construction and Analysis of Safe, Secure, and Interoperable Smart Devices. IX, 175 pages. 2006.

Vol. 3955: G. Antoniou, G. Potamias, C. Spyropoulos, D. Plexousakis (Eds.), Advances in Artificial Intelligence. XVII, 611 pages. 2006. (Sublibrary LNAI).

Vol. 3954: A. Leonardis, H. Bischof, A. Pinz (Eds.), Computer Vision – ECCV 2006, Part IV. XVII, 613 pages. 2006.

Vol. 3953: A. Leonardis, H. Bischof, A. Pinz (Eds.), Computer Vision – ECCV 2006, Part III. XVII, 649 pages. 2006.

Vol. 3952: A. Leonardis, H. Bischof, A. Pinz (Eds.), Computer Vision – ECCV 2006, Part II. XVII, 661 pages. 2006.

Vol. 3951: A. Leonardis, H. Bischof, A. Pinz (Eds.), Computer Vision – ECCV 2006, Part I. XXXV, 639 pages. 2006.

Vol. 3950: J.P. Müller, F. Zambonelli (Eds.), Agent-Oriented Software Engineering VI. XVI, 249 pages. 2006.

Vol. 3948: H.I Christensen, H.-H. Nagel (Eds.), Cognitive Vision Systems. VIII, 367 pages. 2006.

Vol. 3947: Y.-C. Chung, J.E. Moreira (Eds.), Advances in Grid and Pervasive Computing. XXI, 667 pages. 2006.

Vol. 3946: T.R. Roth-Berghofer, S. Schulz, D.B. Leake (Eds.), Modeling and Retrieval of Context. XI, 149 pages. 2006. (Sublibrary LNAI).

Vol. 3945: M. Hagiya, P. Wadler (Eds.), Functional and Logic Programming. X, 295 pages. 2006.

Vol. 3944: J. Quiñonero-Candela, I. Dagan, B. Magnini, F. d'Alché-Buc (Eds.), Machine Learning Challenges. XIII, 462 pages. 2006. (Sublibrary LNAI).

Vol. 3943: N. Guelfi, A. Savidis (Eds.), Rapid Integration of Software Engineering Techniques. X, 289 pages. 2006.

Vol. 3942: Z. Pan, R. Aylett, H. Diener, X. Jin, S. Göbel, L. Li (Eds.), Technologies for E-Learning and Digital Entertainment. XXV, 1396 pages. 2006.

Vol. 3941: S.W. Gilroy, M.D. Harrison (Eds.), Interactive Systems. XI, 267 pages. 2006.

Vol. 3940: C. Saunders, M. Grobelnik, S. Gunn, J. Shawe-Taylor (Eds.), Subspace, Latent Structure and Feature Selection. X, 209 pages. 2006.

Vol. 3939: C. Priami, L. Cardelli, S. Emmott (Eds.), Transactions on Computational Systems Biology IV. VII, 141 pages. 2006. (Sublibrary LNBI).

Vol. 3936: M. Lalmas, A. MacFarlane, S. Rüger, A. Tombros, T. Tsikrika, A. Yavlinsky (Eds.), Advances in Information Retrieval. XIX, 584 pages. 2006.

Vol. 3935: D. Won, S. Kim (Eds.), Information Security and Cryptology - ICISC 2005. XIV, 458 pages. 2006.

Vol. 3934: J.A. Clark, R.F. Paige, F.A. C. Polack, P.J. Brooke (Eds.), Security in Pervasive Computing. X, 243 pages. 2006.

Vol. 3933: F. Bonchi, J.-F. Boulicaut (Eds.), Knowledge Discovery in Inductive Databases. VIII, 251 pages. 2006.

Vol. 3931: B. Apolloni, M. Marinaro, G. Nicosia, R. Tagliaferri (Eds.), Neural Nets. XIII, 370 pages. 2006.

Vol. 3930: D.S. Yeung, Z.-Q. Liu, X.-Z. Wang, H. Yan (Eds.), Advances in Machine Learning and Cybernetics. XXI, 1110 pages. 2006. (Sublibrary LNAI).

Vol. 3929: W. MacCaull, M. Winter, I. Düntsch (Eds.), Relational Methods in Computer Science. VIII, 263 pages. 2006.

Vol. 3928: J. Domingo-Ferrer, J. Posegga, D. Schreckling (Eds.), Smart Card Research and Advanced Applications. XI, 359 pages. 2006.

Vol. 3927: J. Hespanha, A. Tiwari (Eds.), Hybrid Systems: Computation and Control. XII, 584 pages. 2006.